AN ECOLOGY
OF WORLD LITERATURE

FROM ANTIQUITY
TO THE PRESENT DAY

ALEXANDER BEECROFT

VERSO

London • New York

First published by Verso 2015
© Alexander Beecroft 2015

1 3 5 7 9 10 8 6 4 2

Verso
UK: 6 Meard Street, London W1F 0EG
US: 20 Jay Street, Suite 1010, Brooklyn, NY 11201
www.versobooks.com

Verso is the imprint of New Left Books

ISBN-13: 978-1-78168-573-0 (PB)
ISBN-13: 978-1-78168-572-3 (HC)
eISBN-13: 978-1-78168-574-7 (US)
eISBN-13: 978-1-78168-729-1 (UK)

British Library Cataloguing in Publication Data
A catalogue record for this book is available from the British Library

Library of Congress Cataloging-in-Publication Data

Beecroft, Alexander, 1973– author.
An ecology of world literature : from antiquity to the present day / Alexander Beecroft.
pages cm
Includes index.
ISBN 978-1-78168-573-0 (pbk.) — ISBN 978-1-78168-572-3 (hardback)
1. Literature. I. Title.
√PN45.E34 2015
809—dc23
2014034308

Typeset in Minion by Hewer Text UK Ltd, Edinburgh, Scotland
Printed in the US by Maple Press

Contents

Acknowledgements

I began work on this project during my time in the Department of Comparative Literature at Yale University, and without the advice and encouragement of many people there, this book would never have been written, certainly not in anything like its current form. Katie Trumpener and Richard Maxwell generously opened their home to a small group who met regularly for a semester to discuss world literature as both a theoretical and a pedagogical project. All of us who attended (and so many more) remember fondly Richard's passion for, and courage in, exploring and discussing new texts and literary traditions, and I hope my own work on the subject continues that passion and courage in some way. Bernard Bate introduced me to Tamil poetry and to the work of Sheldon Pollock, mind-opening experiences both. Kathryn Slanski, Eckart Frahm, Beatrice Gruendler, Moira Fradinger, and Ed Kamens endured my occasional pestering and requests for bibliography; all errors in these regards are, needless to say, my own. David Quint, Dudley Andrew, Haun Saussy, Pericles Lewis, Christopher Hill, Jing Tsu, Corinne Pache, Anne Dunlop, Kate Holland, and so many others, offered collegiality, advice, support, and friendship. Barry McCrea has had faith in this project from the beginning, has read and offered invaluable comments on portions of this manuscript, and has borne witness to the development of my thinking on the questions it addresses, in locations from the cocktail lounges of New Haven to the cafés of Venice.

When the time came to seek a new academic home, the Department of Languages, Literatures and Cultures at the University of South Carolina greeted me with kindness, generosity, and warmth. Paul Allen Miller has been a wise and insightful chair, colleague and friend. I have learned from the work of Michael Gibbs Hill on Lin Shu and Republican China, from Jeanne Garane on postcolonial French literature, from Stephen McCormick on medieval Lombard epic, and, more broadly, from Guo Jie, Krista van Fliet-Hang, Stephen Sheehi, Hunter Gardner, Jill Frank, Heike Sefrin-Weis, Catherine Castner, Yvonne Ivory, Andrew Rajca, Isis Sadek, Danny Jenkins,

Kunio Hara, Brian Glavey, Catherine Keyser, and all of my colleagues, whose friendship I also cherish.

Work on this book was greatly facilitated by the award of a Charles A. Ryskamp Research Fellowship in the Humanities from the American Council of Learned Societies during the 2011–12 academic year, during which time a majority of the manuscript was written. Thanks are also due to the University of South Carolina for its generosity and flexibility in facilitating that leave so early during my time here. A visiting fellowship at Yale for that year allowed me the use of the Yale University Library system, invaluable for the purposes of a project such as this. Thanks are also due to the inter-library loan staff at the University of South Carolina Libraries, on whom this project made numerous and wide-ranging demands. Thanks are also due to Audrea Lim and Sebastian Budgen, and the rest of the staff at Verso Books, for their interest in the project and for their work on it.

Portions of this work have been presented to audiences at the University of Michigan, Pennsylvania State, the University of Notre Dame, and the University of Minnesota; in Salzburg, London, Santiago de Compostela, Heidelberg, Munich, Rome, Beijing, and Shanghai; as well as to annual conferences of the American Comparative Literature Association in Long Beach, Vancouver, Providence, and Toronto. I am grateful for the advice, encouragement, and commentary I have received in those contexts from (among so many others) Andrea Bachner, Shadi Bartsch, Adam Bohnet, Erica Brindley, Marcello Carastro, Jack Chen, Tamara Chin, Theo D'Haen, David Damrosch, Wiebke Denecke, Marcel Detienne, César Domínguez, Jonathan Eburne, Jacob Edmond, Daniel Fried, Avishek Ganguly, Gao Fengfeng, Rivi Handler-Spitz, Eric Hayot, Margaret Higonnet, Christian Jacob, Alexander Key, Liu Jinyu, Rama Mantena, Kathryn Morgan, Carla Nappi, Thomas Nolden, Christopher Nugent, David Porter, Lisa Raphals, Ronit Ricci, Bruce Robbins, Shuang Shen, Richard So, Darryl Sterk, Karen Thornber, Jing Tsu, Wen Jin, Zhang Hua, Zhang Longxi, Zhang Wei, and Zhou Yiqun.

Finally, but most importantly, thanks are due to my family, particularly to my parents, Bill and Joyce Beecroft, for their love and support over the years. My partner, David Greven, has been at my side during the years of transition that were also the years in which this book was written; as always, it is his love, patience, and wise counsel that makes my work possible.

Introduction

This book has its origins in a confluence of interests, derived alike from my prior scholarship and from pedagogical imperatives. I began my scholarly career as a student of the literatures of ancient Greece and early China, fascinated by each tradition individually and drawn to the institutional discipline of comparative literature as the only venue (if in some ways a reluctant one) for pursuing such divergent interests. The desire to find something useful to say about these two literatures in conjunction with each other that did not depend on claims of contact, and, in particular, to do so in a way that might speak to comparatists as well as to specialists in each language individually, led me to consider the phenomenon of authorship in both traditions, and particularly how stories about the lives of authors were used in each context to negotiate the transition from a predominantly oral transmission to transmission through writing. As I was studying, and writing about, that process,[1] I became especially interested in a similarity between the early Greek and Chinese contexts that I had not noticed, or paid enough attention to, earlier—in both cases, the historical record shows that literary texts (oral or otherwise), and other cultural artifacts, circulated across political boundaries so that the world of a common Greek (Panhellenic)[2] or Chinese culture was larger by far than that of any polity then in existence, providing some measure of cultural solidarity to a politically fragmented world.

---

1   Alexander Beecroft, *Authorship and Cultural Identity in Early Greece and China: Patterns of Literary Circulation*, Cambridge: Cambridge University Press, 2010.

2   My thinking on the Panhellenic owes a great debt to the work of Gregory Nagy and particularly to Nagy, *The Best of the Achaeans: Concepts of the Hero in Archaic Greek Poetry*, revised, Baltimore: The Johns Hopkins University Press, 1998; Nagy, *Pindar's Homer: The Lyric Possession of An Epic Past*, Baltimore: The Johns Hopkins University Press, 1994.

At the same time, I was involved in teaching a world literature course and in thinking about how to adapt and revise that course to better suit the needs of the undergraduate major of which it formed a part. As my then colleagues and I explored this question, we read together the burgeoning literature on world literature, notably the works of David Damrosch,[3] Franco Moretti,[4] and Pascale Casanova.[5] All three produced what seemed to me very valuable insights into how literature circulates across the large spaces of our contemporary world, but the discussions of Moretti and Casanova both focused almost exclusively on the literature emerging from the modern West and from the non-West's reaction to Western modernity, and it was difficult to use their theories to understand the ways in which texts that were pre-modern or non-Western (or both) were circulated and understood. Damrosch does have a great deal to say about such texts but avowedly and deliberately from the perspective of how the modern West understands and makes use of them. The ideas of all three were provocative and stimulating, but I was left searching for a theoretical model that could make sense of things like the relationship between political fragmentation and cultural unity I had found in early Greece and China and that would be useful for constructing an undergraduate world literature course not taking as its premise the value we, as modern readers, add to the texts we read.

In the context of that reading on world literature, I was also introduced to the work of the Sanskritist Sheldon Pollock.[6] Pollock's recent work has focused on two phenomena of interest to me: the sudden appearance, in the early centuries AD, of literary texts written in Sanskrit in regions from modern Afghanistan to Java, which he believes cannot be explained by the means obvious to moderns, such as conquest, trade, or colonization, but resulted rather from the charismatic prestige of the language itself (a phenomenon he refers to as "the Sanskrit cosmopolis"); and, about a millennium later, the equally sudden emergence of literature written in vernacular languages in South India and in Southeast Asia and, later, in the

---

3   David Damrosch, *What Is World Literature?*, illustrated edition, Princeton, NJ: Princeton University Press, 2003.

4   See especially Franco Moretti, "Conjectures on World Literature," *New Left Review* 1, 2000: 54–68.

5   Pascale Casanova, *La republique mondiale des lettres*, Paris: Editions du Seuil, 1999.

6   See now especially Sheldon Pollock, *The Language of the Gods in the World of Men: Sanskrit, Culture, and Power in Premodern India*, Berkeley: University of California Press, 2009, although that was not available to me when I began this work.

Sanskrit-derived vernaculars of North India (a phenomenon he calls the "vernacular millennium").

In reading Pollock, as well as Damrosch, Casanova, and Moretti, and in continuing to think about my own work, I began to think that each of us was in fact talking about different instantiations of the same question, which might, most simply, be put as "the interaction of literature with its environment." The circulation of Homeric epic between city-states in classical Greece; the use of Sanskrit to compose inscriptional poetry in Java and its later replacement with poetry in Javanese; the competition between national literatures for recognition in Paris that Pascale Casanova described in *The World Republic of Letters*—all of these, it seems to me, are not so much competing models for understanding how literature circulates, but rather different concrete answers, emerging in specific contexts, to the same set of problems about the interactions between literatures and their environments. With a bit of elaboration, I developed a scheme of six patterns for this interaction: the epichoric (or local), panchoric (a generic term I derived from Panhellenic), cosmopolitan, vernacular (drawing both from Pollock), national (where I was inspired to an extent by Casanova), and global.[7] In the simplest terms, this book represents the elaboration of that model under the label *An Ecology of World Literature*, and in the remainder of this introduction I hope to explain this project more fully by means of a series of questions. I begin by discussing an interlocking set of questions (What is a language? What is literature? and What is a literature?) before moving on to consider what I mean by ecology and why I use the term, a discussion that itself divides into several parts. I finish this introduction by revisiting the six ecological patterns I listed earlier, describing them in some detail and setting out thereby the structure for the six chapters of this book.

What Is a Language?

Since literature (whatever we might decide it to be) is certainly made out of language, and since the ability to understand the language in which a text is composed is the single most essential determinant of whether or not one will have access to that text, it is necessary to begin our search for an understanding of what literature is by beginning with the question of what constitutes a language. On an intuitive level, this first question may not

---

7   Alexander Beecroft, "World Literature Without a Hyphen: Towards a Typology of Literary Systems," *New Left Review* 54, 2008: 87–100.

seem to require any very detailed answer; speakers of English, in particular, understand their language as having fairly discrete and unproblematic boundaries. The differences between English and the other Germanic languages, such as Dutch, Norwegian, Swedish, Danish, and German itself, are considerable enough to present little ground for argument—despite what are, to linguists, obvious shared historical origins, each of these other languages is sufficiently different from English as to be mutually incomprehensible, while the fact that the homeland of English is physically separated from those of the other Germanic languages by the English Channel and the North Sea means that there are no dialects intermediate between English and, say, Dutch or Norwegian. There are some questions concerning internal boundaries within the family of English, so that, for example, Scots (and its close relative, Ulster Scots)[8] are frequently seen by their own speakers as distinct languages, rather than as dialects of English, while the creole Englishes of, for example, Jamaica and Nigeria are also sometimes seen as distinct languages. Since these boundary questions have little saliency for English speakers within England or the United States (and thus for the major arbiters of the language and culture), they intrude comparatively little on the minds of most speakers in those regions, leaving English, in the minds of its speakers, a relatively homogeneous language with quite distinct borders with other related languages.

In this as in so many other things, however, English speakers (and especially those not from Scotland, Northern Ireland, the Caribbean, or Africa) may run the risk of assimilating the rest of the world to their own experience and assuming that all languages are as clearly defined as English. This is, however, manifestly not the case. Even within the small family of the Germanic languages, for example, far more complicated questions exist concerning the boundaries of languages. Standard Dutch, for example, differs less in many respects from Standard German than a number of regional dialects of German do from each other, so that an educated Dutchman and German might be able to decipher each other's languages more readily than speakers of the local dialects of Zurich and of Hanover. At the same time, the question of whether Dutch and Flemish, or Dutch and Afrikaans, constitute different languages is far from unambiguous.

The Romance languages present an even more complex picture. On the

---

8   On Ulster Scots in particular, see D. H. Gabriel, *The Development of Vernacular Literatures: Case Studies in Old Irish, Ulster-Scots and Afrikaans*, Ph.D. dissertation, University of California, Los Angeles, 2006.

surface, French, Spanish, Italian, and Portuguese are each major and distinct languages, spoken by tens or even hundreds of millions, and each possesses a centuries-old literary tradition. Beneath that surface, however, the traditional everyday spoken languages of France, Italy, Spain, and Portugal are part of what linguists would call a "dialect continuum," a range of dialects shifting imperceptibly from village to village and town to town and more drastically from region to region. Within this continuum it is difficult to draw firm boundaries of mutual intelligibility, and to the extent that they exist such boundaries do not correspond to national boundaries; the spoken dialects of much of northern Italy, for example, have in some respects more in common with certain of the dialects of France than with those of Tuscany and points south. All of these dialects derive to some extent from Latin, though many details of when and how they diverged remain controversial. Likewise, the spoken dialects of the Arab world; of North India, Pakistan, and Bangladesh; and of China bear complex familial relationships to each other across large areas, derived in each case from common ancestors (classical Arabic, Sanskrit, and classical Chinese, respectively, or at least from the spoken equivalents to these highly literary and somewhat artificial languages), though as with the Romance languages many of these spoken varieties are today converging on single literary standards, thanks largely to mass education, film, and television. These Arabic, Indic, and Sinitic languages, like the Romance languages of Europe, vary community by community and can be consolidated to some extent in larger regional groupings, but can neither be assimilated into one homogeneous and mutually intelligible spoken language nor even into a small handful of languages divided according to strict, consistent, and unambiguous criteria. The case of many other parts of the world, from the Bantu languages of much of Africa to the languages of New Guinea, is still more complicated, especially where literary standard forms are lacking, and where scholarly efforts in linguistics have not been as extensive.

The question, then, of what constitutes a language is not an easy one to answer. To return to the Romance languages of Western Europe, it is clear enough that the standard forms of French, Italian, Spanish, and Portuguese constitute languages, each used in writing and in elite oral communication for centuries, and each today defined and maintained through a range of state institutions, from academies of language to public schools. But what of the dialect continuum? Do we (as some nationalists of the nineteenth century would have liked) subsume all the regional dialects within the nation-state of France or Spain or Italy into a single language, forcing the understanding of these spoken forms as dialects of the national language even where historical linguistics suggests a closer affinity to another national language or a history distinct from that of any national language? Do we (as regionalists in Spain have successfully argued and as their counterparts in France and Italy also argue) decide instead that the dialects of recognized regional levels of government constitute languages in their own right, again assimilating potentially quite divergent local dialects to a uniform standard of Catalan, Occitan, Neapolitan, or Venetian? Do we allow for these regional languages to break down still further into local varieties, proper to specific towns or groups of towns? And do we attempt to draw the boundaries between regional languages based on linguistic grounds (with the realization that linguists themselves dispute these matters) or according to regional or local political borders (recognizing that this might be an artificial imposition on lived linguistic experience)? None of these solutions is entirely satisfactory.

In practice, of course, the tendency until very recently has been to decide, in the words of a hoary cliché in the field, that "a language is a dialect with an army and a navy"; in other words, that the boundaries between languages should match those between nation-states. Dutch, then, is a language where Low German is not, because the Netherlands is a sovereign nation and "Low Germany" is not. Italian is a language because Italy is a nation, but Venetian, Lombard, Neapolitan, and Sicilian are not because Venice, Lombardy, Naples, and Sicily are no longer sovereign states. To some extent (and this trend is increasing, as I discuss in more detail in the final chapter), we should acknowledge the corollary that "a language is a dialect with a regional assembly," as Catalan, Valencian, Galician, and so on have gained official recognition as languages in Spain (and as, in India, status as an official language tends to go hand-in-hand with the establishment of a new state).

I would like to propose, however, an alternative, if equally simplistic, slogan, "a language is a dialect with a literature," as potentially a more useful way of thinking about these questions. The question of what exactly literature is is itself rather complicated, and I will return to that question in a later section of this introduction. For the moment, what I wish to emphasize is that the notion of "literariness," however manifested, necessarily involves a certain level of self-awareness concerning the linguistic form taken by a given text. For a text to be recognized within a given community as "literature," it usually must conform to some set of conventions regarding diction and syntax and in the process it will help to consecrate those conventions as culturally prestigious and desirable. I return to this process in Chapter 4, in particular, in my discussion of vernacular languages and literatures, a situation in which these processes are especially prominent, though they operate in other contexts as well. In writing (in Latin) the *De vulgari eloquentia*, for example, Dante was making an explicit and self-conscious argument for the legitimacy of the vernacular vis-à-vis classical Latin; in his vernacular writings, such as the *Commedia Divina*, he (as is well known) helped to establish certain vocabulary and certain grammatical structures as legitimate vehicles for cultural expression; to the extent that he was successful in so doing, his vernacular successors have adhered to the conventions he established (and have established some of their own), gradually building a sense of what is, or is not, acceptable usage in a literary text self-representing as written in "Italian" (even though that name was not used for the language until the early sixteenth century). Likewise, English speakers' understanding of what constitutes good written English has been shaped over the centuries by the works of Chaucer, Shakespeare, Milton, and so on, and lexical innovations and grammatical simplifications alike have gained legitimacy through their use in imaginative literature or in formal nonfiction prose.

Literature, especially of the written kind, is of course not the only means by which the notion of a language can emerge. A particularly significant alternative pattern is the gradual standardization of a lingua franca used by people of different regions to communicate with each other orally; thus, modern Standard Mandarin (which is, as we shall see in later chapters, in large part a self-consciously created language), developed to a great extent out of the so-called *guanhua*, or "official talk" used by government officials from different regions to converse with each other in Beijing, and some have argued (controversially) that Québec grew to speak a form of Standard French earlier than metropolitan France itself, thanks to a *choc des patois*, an interaction between the different regional languages spoken by settlers of New France leading to a standardized form used for mutual convenience.[9] It is also true that speakers of a local dialect, even one proper to a specific village, will generally have an intuitive sense of what is "correct" or "normal" usage within that dialect, whether or not there exists a literary or

---

9 Philippe Barbaud, *Le choc des patois en Nouvelle-France: Essai sur l'histoire de la francisation au Canada*, Québec: University Québec Les Presses, 1984. For the opposing view, see, e.g., Henri Witmann, "Le français de Paris dans le français des Amériques," Proceedings of the International Congress of Linguists 16, 1997, and note that Witmann's views similarly involve the emergence of a patois among speakers of different French dialects but in France rather than in Québec.

verbal-art tradition consecrating that set of forms. Nonetheless, the existence of a body of texts (oral or written) that legitimate certain linguistic forms at the expense of others does a great deal to establish that set of forms as constituting a "language" rather than a "dialect." This can be true, I would argue, independently of the medium in which those texts circulate, whether through oral storytelling and song, through manuscript or print culture, or through television, radio, film, and the internet. This is not to minimize the very real differences among these media, which I discuss to some extent in relevant chapters, but rather to emphasize that all of these media have the capacity to foster a given set of linguistic conventions, promoting the self-awareness among the community of users of that set of conventions to the point where it makes sense to describe those conventions as a language.

In this sense, then, a language is less a group of dialects, demarcated by a more-or-less arbitrary boundary based on criteria of historical development or mutual intelligibility than it is a standardized, refined, and developed collection of usages circulating between, around, or above those dialects. In this context, linguists speak of the difference between *Abstand* and *Ausbau* languages; that is, between languages understood as differing greatly enough from their neighbors as to be distinct (as I began by suggesting was the case with English) and languages constituted as such through their more or less self-conscious development as distinct linguistic media through their use in (among other things) literature and education.[10] Since an Ausbau language, almost by definition, does not quite correspond (at least at first) to anybody's native language, some process of education in the language and its norms is essential to its propagation and stability, whether in the form of modern public schooling, the training of educated elites in pre-modern states, or the training in the songs and stories of a traditional small-scale society. Although each of these processes of education is quite different, they share alike a need for standardized texts that can act as exemplars of prestige linguistic usage—for texts, in other words, that could be considered "literary."

What Is Literature?

What constitutes the literary is, of course, a fraught question both cross-culturally and, in many cases, within cultures. To the extent that we are unable

---

10 Heinz Kloss, "'Abstand Languages' and 'Ausbau Languages,'" *Anthropological Linguistics* 9 (7), 1967: 29–41.

to agree on a definition of "literature" that will operate across cultures, the project of this book will be rendered all but impossible. I identify two inter-related sets of problems surrounding my use of the term "literature," one of which (the question of what sorts of genres or varieties of texts count as literature) I address in this section; the other (which concerns whether literature extends throughout history or is a process with a clear begin-ning), I discuss in the section that follows.

Any definition of literature necessarily presents boundary questions. Do only fiction, poetry, and drama count as "literature," or is there room for nonfictional texts (in prose or verse) as well? Can philosophical, historical, scientific, and technical texts qualify as literary, or do texts need to be self-consciously belletristic, and is this distinction equally meaningful in all cultural contexts? What about texts viewed as sacred and/or divinely inspired? In practice, I find this first problem does not present insuperable obstacles to cross-cultural study of literary ecologies for two reasons. In the first place, concerns about the translatability of the concept of literature rest, I would suggest, on two false assumptions: that words for "literature" in major pre-modern literary languages differ incommensurably in mean-ing, and, still more significantly, that the terms in question have stable and uncontested meanings within their own linguistic contexts. The evidence for both claims is rather weaker than one might think. I discuss the histor-ical evolution of the English term "literature" and that of its equivalent in modern Chinese, wenxue 文學, in further detail in Chapter 5 because the debates about the meaning of both terms are a productive way of thinking about cultural exchange. In essence, however, both "literature" and wenxue evolve over time (the latter, certainly, under the pressure of the former, though not exclusively for that reason), moving, as for example Trevor Ross has argued in the English case, from describing the totality of texts that a well-educated member of the elite might read or choose to read and thus including such things as history, philosophy, and scientific writings, to a more specific emphasis on what we might call "imaginative literature"—the genres of fiction, poetry, and drama, which we associate today with the notion of literature.[11] Similar developments took place in Chinese (and in Japanese), where wenxue, which traditionally could (but did not always) include history and philosophy, came during the nineteenth century to

---

11   Trevor Ross, *The Making of the English Literary Canon From the Middle Ages to the Late Eighteenth Century*, Montreal: McGill-Queen's University Press, 1998, 293–301.

align itself as a translation of the European notion of literature. In a related vein, Sheldon Pollock discusses the Sanskrit conception of *kāvya*, which he glosses as texts that are "workly," or *wirklich*, in the Heideggerian sense of being texts where formal questions and traditions of interpretation are indispensable to understanding the meaning of the text. Pollock notes that *kāvya* in this sense is distinct from *śāstra*, texts that are expository or scientific in nature, and notes that the European notion of literature or literariness is thus close enough to the traditional meaning of *kāvya* to allow the interchanging of the terms in speaking about pre-modern South Asian texts.[12] Modern Standard Arabic uses the term *adab* as a gloss for the Western "literature"; as with wenxue in Chinese, scholars of the subject note both that the varieties of texts included in adab differ from those of its Western equivalents (the inclusion of "the repertoire of belletristic texts needed for polite conversation"; the exclusion of religious texts), and that usage of the term in pre-modern texts varies and indeed sometimes seems quite close to the modern, Western "literature."[13] Literature, wenxue (and its Japanese cognate, *bungaku*), adab, and kāvya, then, while not identical, do all share certain important family resemblances, including most importantly something of a tension in their definitions between "imaginative literature" and "the sum of all texts an educated person should know." As such, it does not seem to me (any more than it does to Pollock) like the differences in meaning among these terms prevents our talking about them in parallel with each other.

The second reason why the differences between these terms (such as they are) do not present an insurmountable obstacle to comparative work is that these differences themselves not only can be a genuine object of comparative study but form an integral part of the study of literary ecology that I undertake in this book. Certainly, each of the cultures that I discuss in any depth in the following pages understands its notion of literature as some kind of marked category of linguistic utterance, distinct from the unmarked use of language as an everyday part of human life. Where to draw this boundary will be of considerable interest to us as this study progresses, especially in the later chapters. In particular, the notion of literariness and its limits is crucial to the chapter on vernacular literatures,

12   Pollock, *The Language of the Gods*, 3–5.

13   See, e.g., Geert Jan Van Gelder, "The Classical Arabic Canon of Polite (and Impolite) Literature," in *Cultural Repertoires : Structure, Function, and Dynamics*, edited by G. J. Dorleijn and H. L. J. Vanstiphout, 2003, Peeters, 45–58, 46.

since it is clear that many languages are first standardized or committed to writing for use in administrative documents, religious sermons, dedicatory inscriptions, and the like, in many (though by no means all) of which cases language may be serving an extraliterary purpose. As I show in the vernacular chapter, the use of a language for literary purposes marks a decided shift from these nonliterary uses, making a very different claim on behalf of the language in question—usually, that it is a legitimate alternative to another, more cosmopolitan language, for cultural purposes. The transition from "documentary" to "workly" roles for a given language alters the literary ecology; as such, this transition is a legitimate object of study for literary ecology. Far from impeding the study of literary ecology, questions concerning what counts as literary, and when and how, are central concerns to the field.

Literature, Orality, Textuality

There is another problem surrounding the meaning of "literature," which is the relationship between the medium in which texts are composed (orality or writing) and their status as literature. As a student of the school of oral-traditional poetics nurtured over the generations at Harvard (Milman Parry, Albert B. Lord, Gregory Nagy), my training and inclinations urge me to insist that oral texts, be they proverbs or Homeric epic, should be considered as belonging to the category of "literature." There exist, however, powerful arguments to the contrary, developed explicitly by Sheldon Pollock and relied upon implicitly by Pascale Casanova. While Pollock takes pains to insist that texts produced without writing can constitute "something reasonable people would call literature," he also insists that the use of writing marks a decisive moment in the history of literature's becoming. For Pollock, the social, political, and epistemological privileges associated with writing, at least in pre-modern South Asia, confer both on those who write and on the texts they produce a kind of authority not available to the author who speaks his texts; further, he argues, it is writing that produces in texts a self-awareness of their status *as* literature, as "an artifact to be decoded and as a pretext for deciphering."[14] Finally, he argues, pre-modern theorists of kāvya themselves viewed writing as indispensable to their understanding of the term itself.

In thinking through these phenomena, Pollock coins a term, *literarization*,

---

14 Pollock, *The Language of the Gods*, 4.

which he uses to designate the emergence of a given language into the realm of literature and literariness as understood in a given cultural context (in his case, obviously, the Sanskritic world of pre-modern South or Southeast Asia). Literarization is for Pollock related to, yet distinct from, *literization*, the process by which a language is committed to writing; for a language to be literarized, it must first be literized, but (as I suggested earlier) literizing does not automatically entail literarizing, which includes other processes, such as the standardization of orthography and diction, the fixing of grammatical rules, the establishment of generic conventions, and the accumulation of literary prestige through the emergence of a literary tradition. By a curious coincidence, noted as such by Pollock, his word "literarization" was, nearly simultaneously, developed also by Pascale Casanova in her 1999 *La république mondiale des lettres*, speaking of the development of the French language in the seventeenth century:

> What is involved, rather, is a unique process of the establishment of theoretical, logical, aesthetical and rhetorical resources, through which would be constructed strictly literary value (a kind of symbolic "surplus value") – the *literariness* of the French language, that is, the transformation of the "langue françoyse" into a literary language. This mechanism, which operates simultaneously and inseparably across both the language and the development of literary forms, allows for the language itself to become autonomous, and gradually makes of it a literary and aesthetic raw material. The collective construction of the French language as a literary language is a kind of aestheticisation, that is, of gradual *literarisation*, which accounts for how French was able to become, somewhat later, *the* language of literature.[15]

Elsewhere, Casanova emphasizes the importance (for languages late to the game of literature) of translation into more powerful target-languages as a

---

15   Il s'agit plutôt d'un processus unique de constitution de ressources théoriques, logiques, esthétiques, rhétoriques à travers lequel va se fabriquer la valeur proprement littéraire (sorte de « plus-value » symbolique), la *littérarité* de la langue française, c'est-à-dire la transformation de la « langue françoyse » en langue littéraire. Ce mécanisme, qui s'opère à la fois et inséparablement à travers la langue et l'élaboration de formes littéraires, permet l'autonomisation de la langue elle-même et en fait peu à peu un matériau littéraire et esthétique. La construction collective du français comme langue littéraire est une sorte d'esthétisation, c'est-à-dire de littérarisation progressive, ce qui explique que le français ait pu devenir un peu plus tard la langue de la littérature. (Casanova, *La republique mondiale des lettres*, 95–6.)

mechanism for literarization.[16] This is, in no small part, because her definition of "literature" situates literature's origin with Joachim du Bellay's 1549
La Deffence, et Illustration de la Langue Françoyse, which acts as what I will
later call a "vernacular manifesto" for the use of the French language for
literary purposes.[17] For Casanova, this represents the first moment in which
a literature is self-consciously developed for a nation, which will be for her
the necessary precondition for that national literature's efforts to transcend
the nation-state, and to enter (as its founder) the "world republic of letters."
Casanova's republic, then, is singular, having been founded in a single place
and time, and other literatures (such as those of Asia) can only enter into
literature per se with the post-1945 era of decolonization.[18]

I discuss many of the questions this definition raises in the vernacular,
national, and global chapters that form the second half of this book but
begin that discussion here by noting that Casanova's definition also deliberately excludes from "literature" a great many European texts generally
described as such, from the literature of the Greek and Roman traditions,
to the religious texts of the Middle Ages, and even Dante, who might seem
to many to be an early pioneer of literature even on Casanova's definition.[19]
Even in the sense evoked by Pollock, who looks to the emergence of South
Asian vernaculars in the eighth century AD, rather than to sixteenth-
century France, for the origins of literature per se, Sanskrit epic, and
therefore also Homeric epic, among many other things, do not qualify as
literature, since their composition may have predated literization, and
certainly predated literarization.

The definitions used by Casanova and by Pollock thus exclude significant quantities of material that I believe need to be considered in a work
such as mine, if for no other reason than that the texts excluded from literature by Casanova and Pollock clearly circulate within the literary ecologies
they define and exert considerable influence. At the same time, the (different) concepts that Casanova and Pollock identify as literature seem, to me,
clearly to represent meaningful ideas very much in need of terminology to
describe them, and I would be reluctant to discuss their concepts under
other names.

This leaves me with three different working definitions of literature: my

---

16   Ibid., 192.
17   Ibid., 69–72.
18   Ibid., 24.
19   Ibid., 83.

own (which includes, at least in theory, all self-consciously aesthetic use of language); Pollock's (which requires the use of writing and a series of relationships between author, text, and tradition that writing for him implies); and Casanova's (in which literature must be in a particular kind of relationship to the nation). In many cases (as, for example, with all written texts composed in what I identify as national and global literary ecologies), these definitions coincide. Anything included in either Casanova's definition or Pollock's will be found in mine, and anything found in Casanova's definition will be found in Pollock's. There are, therefore, many situations in which I find it easy to use the term literature without qualification and others in which a reference to Pollock or Casanova is sufficient to illuminate what is meant. There are, however, still other situations (particularly in the first two chapters) in which I discuss texts that I am quite comfortable referring to as "literary" (Homeric epic, for example, with the understanding that oral composition or circulation is no impediment to literariness in the sense I mean) but for which Pollock and/or Casanova would resist the term. My use of the term "literature" (or occasionally "verbal art"), then, subsumes these other definitions of the literary within a broader category, just as I hope to show that the systems of literary circulation described by these authors are themselves examples of a larger range of possible systems.

What Is a Literature?

Alongside the question of "what is literature?" lies another, less-discussed question, though one that deserves, I believe, more thought and one that is central to this study: "What is a literature?" In our contemporary world, where, as Pascale Casanova reminds us, we think regularly about literature in national terms, phrases such as "French literature," "English literature," "American literature," "Latin American literature," "Ancient Greek literature," "Postcolonial literature," "African-American literature," and so on are a regular element of how we think about texts and their relationships, and yet we give little thought to the question of whether or not these terms are equivalent or of how to understand the relationships among them. Although we speak more generally about "national literatures" as a label for the set of terms suggested by the above list, it is clear that nation is not always, nor even necessarily that often, the determining criterion for bounding a literature. Does "French literature" include all literature composed in French or only that produced in the Republic of France, or that produced by its citizens? Does "English literature" begin with Beowulf, though that text is unintelligible to speakers of modern English without specialized training and though it was lost for centuries and thus had no influence over the development of the English literary tradition from the High Middle Ages through the nineteenth century? If English literature does not begin with Beowulf, where does it begin? How do we know when a text written in English in the Thirteen Colonies is a (peripheral and provincial) adjunct to British literature, and when does that text become instead part of American literature? Why do we (those of us in North America, at any rate) frequently talk about "Latin American literature," as if Latin America had a (single) national tradition, when the texts of writers as diverse as Gabriel García Márquez, Isabel Allende, and Mario Vargas Llosa are often so specifically narrating their nations, not a continental region? Why do we do the same with "Postcolonial literature" in English? Does it make sense to link the English- and French-language literatures of Canada under a single rubric, suggesting a stronger connection between them than either has with its peers in its own language, when questions of literary influence would likely point the other way? What of literatures by non-linguistic minorities, like African-Americans? Does talking about African-American literature as if it were wholly separable from American literature strengthen a sense of solidarity or ghettoize minority voices, hindering them from reaching the mainstream? Are these answers the same both inside and outside the African-American community, and do the answers remain constant over time?[20]

These questions are each discussed with some regularity within a localized context (and I address some of them myself in this book), but rarely, if ever, are these kinds of questions juxtaposed. This is unfortunate because this question of how we determine what is or is not a literature is extremely important to literary studies not merely because so much of the institutional study of literature (academic departments, subfields, journals, and so on) is built around the notion that the world of verbal art can be subdivided into discrete categories we can call "literatures," but also because without *some* such set of divisions the already unmanageably large bodies of material in many literatures would become truly overwhelming. Further, the methodological and ideological quandaries so many of the questions in the above paragraph pose might be rendered more soluble if we were able to begin from

---

20   For the argument that African-American literature, as such, is a product of the Jim Crow era, see Kenneth W. Warren, *What Was African American Literature?*, Cambridge, MA: Harvard University Press, 2011.

some kind of a priori notion of what a literature is, and, further still, such an a priori definition would provide the basis for a potentially fruitful comparative discussion. A quick review of those questions shows that the answers authors themselves might give will often differ from the answers we would find satisfactory. To give just two examples, the composers and redactors of *Beowulf*, though some of them may have been motivated by political impulses, were clearly not anticipating the emergence of the modern-day United Kingdom, and were not self-consciously founding a national literature for that nation; likewise, the views of African-American authors as to whether or not they were founding a "national literature" may or may not have influenced their readers' understanding of the role of their work.

It is, rather, in the world of audiences or readers that the notion of a literature really emerges. Literatures, in the sense in which I use the term, are techniques or practices of reading texts, and specifically of linking texts together, through a series of relationships that usually begins with language and/or the polity, but which also include questions of genre and influence, among other criteria. As such, it is important to underline that any given text may be found in more than one literature, as different modes of reading that text may contextualize it very differently. Literatures can emerge in which texts of verbal art circulate only orally, as for example Homeric epic (and the lyric traditions with which epic develops) not only develops a common language in which literature can be composed and consolidates a repertoire of stories suitable for literary representation but also helps to develop a self-conscious sense of "Greeks" as those who listen to, understand, and appreciate Homeric epic. To that extent, my use of the notion of a literature in this book resists the understandings of literature as a whole promulgated by Pollock and by Casanova. That said, because the concept of a literature is so dependent on the practices of audiences and critics, the use of writing (and the production of para-literary texts, such as commentary and criticism) helps to establish larger-scale and more enduring literatures. Readers and audiences construct literatures by making connections among texts, but authors themselves (who are of course a privileged class of readers of literary texts) frequently self-consciously found or develop literatures, with varying degrees of explicitness. In founding a literature, readers and writers are of course interacting with existing literary texts and traditions, and literatures take on meaningful form only when there are texts excluded from them. Excessively local and particular traditions, for example, get excluded from the tradition of "Greek literature," as that emerges, and Latin texts get excluded from the vernacular literature of England. Works composed in marginal dialects get excluded from the national literatures of Germany or Italy, and texts by colonial administrators get excluded from the national literature of a postcolonial nation. The texts excluded can be excluded either because they are deemed unworthy of the tradition (as with my first and third examples), or because they may be attached to a kind of social, cultural or political prestige that would obscure the literature in question (as in the second and fourth examples). In either case, texts are in competition with one another, and so are literatures.

Why Ecology?

In making this claim, I am of course saying nothing new; that texts and literatures are in competition with one another for the scarce attention of readers is a familiar point. Since economics is devoted to the study of how decisions are made about the allocation of scarce resources, it is no surprise that economic metaphors are frequently used to describe this process. To turn, again, to Pascale Casanova (who I believe is here, as elsewhere, articulating explicitly a series of ideas implicit but unexpressed in a great deal of other thinking and thus worth exploring in some detail):

> We can describe the competition in which writers are engaged as a collection of exchanges where the stakes are the specific value that has currency in global literary space, the common good sought and accepted everywhere: that which [Paul Valéry] calls "cultural or civilizational capital" and which is also literary in nature. Valéry believed possible the analysis of one specific value which had currency only in the "great market of human affairs," measurable according to the customs proper to the cultural world. This value lacks common measure with "the economic economy," but its recognition is the sure index of a space (never named as such), of an intellectual universe where these specific exchanges take place.[21]

---

21   On peut décrire la competition dans laquelle sont engagés les écrivains comme un ensemble d'échanges dont l'enjeu est la valeur spécifique qui a cours dans l'espace littéraire mondial, le bien commun revendiqué et accepté par tous: ce qu'il appelle le « capital *Culture* ou *Civilization* » et qui est aussi bien littéraire. Valéry croit possible l'analyse d'une valeur spécifique qui n'aurait cours que dans ce « grand marché des affaires humaines », évaluable selon des normes propres à l'univers culturel, sans commune mesure avec « l'économie économique », mais dont la reconnaissance serait l'indice certain de l'existence d'une espace, jamais nommé comme tel, univers intellectuel où s'organisent des échanges spécifiques. (Casanova, *La republique mondiale des lettres*, 26–7.)

Tellingly, for both Valéry and Casanova, this literary economy relates to "the economic economy" through relations of analogy rather than through metonymy; literary capital is *like* financial capital but can in no way be exchanged for it. This use of economics as a controlling metaphor has, of course, many precedents in recent scholarship in the humanities and in critical theory, from Pierre Bourdieu's notion of cultural capital to the use of the economy as a model for understanding the operation of desire, familiar now from countless works of literary-theoretical scholarship. The metaphor clearly has considerable explanatory value and articulates nicely a particular critical notion of modernity as the ever-advancing march of capitalist logic into domains previously thought exempt from its sway. That said, I have chosen in this book to advance instead a different controlling metaphor, that of ecology. It should be noted that these metaphors, economics and ecology, share a great deal, from their etymological derivation from the Greek (*oiko-nomos* vs. *oiko-logos*), to their shared interest in the invisible processes that regulate and manage scarcity. My choice of ecology here begins with the observation that, where economics tends to simplify our understanding of complex systems in order to make them easier to understand, ecology is more comfortable accepting that the complexity may be inherent to the system. The wisdom and utility of economic theory, in fact, comes from its insight that all of the various inputs into the economic system—land, labor, capital—can be made equivalent to each other through expressing the value of each in terms of money. If gold, land, wheat, factories, machinery, advertising space on Facebook, and my desire to have a four-day workweek can each be assigned a cash value, then it becomes easy to compare the role each of these things might play in the economy as a whole and to make decisions accordingly.

If, however, we are dealing with a system in which the various inputs are not in fact equivalent to each other, or if we wish to keep the significance of those inputs distinct, ecology may provide a more interesting and useful model. Ecologists examine the interactions between the different forms of life that exist in a particular region, as well as the interactions of those living things with their non-living environment. Particularly useful, for my metaphorical purposes, is that ecology understands, accepts, and insists on, the distinct and mutually interactive nature of these various inputs, so that changes in the external environment (more or less rain than usual, habitat destruction) can have complex and shifting impacts on the various species found in a given context.

As the previous sections of this introduction have already suggested, I believe that it is impossible to understand any given literature qua literature solely through an analysis of the texts read through it. Rather, any given literature must, I believe, be understood as being in an ecological relationship to other phenomena—political, economic, sociocultural, religious—as well as to the other languages and literatures with which it is in contact. As an example, if we are to think about, say, Canadian literature in English, and how and why texts come to be read as part of this literature, we must understand that that literature is shaped by numerous forces, both literary and extraliterary. English-Canadian authors read other texts, within and beyond their own tradition, and are influenced by them, and understanding these processes will be crucial to understanding English-Canadian literature. But we must also consider environmental forces operating on that literature—the role that political, cultural, and educational institutions play in creating a demand for a literature to correspond to their own position, the economic forces that dictate the relative marketability of novels with explicitly Canadian themes, the desire of individual Canadians to read books about their nation. We must also consider how readers situate English-Canadian texts vis-à-vis competing English-language literatures coming from the United States and the United Kingdom, and even the extent to which Canadian literatures in English and in French interact with each other, or fail to do so. Likewise, an attempt to understand the literature of early China will require us to investigate not only the texts themselves, but the roles those texts played in the complex political and cultural arena of the time, where regional states' leaders shared kinship ties and a common ritual culture but competed for hegemony with several states less completely integrated into a common cultural sphere.[22] As I explore in some detail below, I believe that ecology, rather than economics, provides the better model for understanding these complex interactions.

One of the consequences of adopting this ecological metaphor, rather than an economic one, is that we can see more clearly that both texts and literatures thrive in a wide variety of ways, rather than there being the single adaptive strategy that Casanova, for example, finds. For her, the only way a literature can thrive is by building recognition in key centers such as Paris, London, or New York; only with that recognition achieved can authors working in that literature compete for individual recognition in the World

---

22 I touch on some of these issues in the next three chapters; for a fuller discussion, see the final three chapters of Beecroft, *Authorship and Cultural Identity*.

Republic of Letters. Literary recognition is of course a scarce resource, and as such gains for one author, text, or literature must be balanced by losses for others. But if we use an ecological lens to understand this process of survival and recognition, we can see that different literatures over time have thrived in different ways. Oral transmission and circulation has allowed for verbal art to thrive for centuries, or even longer, in small-scale societies, and indeed strong associations between such texts and ritual activities may, in a small-scale context, prove a more effective means of survival and recognition than written transmission. Such an orally based strategy, however, would have been less effective in a larger-scale context, such as the world of the Roman or Han empires, where even the recitation of works of literature at the court (a major literary activity in both cultures) was ultimately less successful than the writing of texts and the production of manuscripts. In some contexts, it has made sense for authors to produce texts in so-called *cosmopolitan* languages, reaching large audiences thinly spread over space and time; at other moments, vernacular languages (which can penetrate a given region more deeply, but whose endurance is endangered more rapidly with increased distance and the passage of time) have seemed the wiser choice. Even national literatures of the modern era can make the choice between gaining recognition in Paris or London (perhaps at the expense of being meaningful to audiences at home) and speaking exclusively to local audiences at the expense of wider recognition. Individual authors, of course, face similar choices, always subject to the constraints imposed by local conditions, both literary and extraliterary (it is easier, for example, for an author writing in Spanish to gain recognition in Paris than for one writing in Korean, since there are more translators able to work from Spanish, more members of the Parisian intellectual elite themselves able to read Spanish, more presses willing to build on the success of past Spanish-language authors, but also more of a perception of affinity between Parisian and Spanish-language cultures). Authors, texts, and literatures, I would argue, respond to the scarcity of recognition not as economic beings but as actors in an ecological context, searching for the niche in which they are most at home.

This book is, therefore, not ecocriticism in the conventional sense,[23] and my use of the term "ecology" has more in common with linguistic

---

23   Timothy Clark, *The Cambridge Introduction to Literature and the Environment*, Cambridge: Cambridge University Press, 2011.

ecology[24] and media ecology,[25] which likewise examine the relationships between their objects of study and their (human) environments, than it does with, say, political ecology,[26] which lies at the intersection of the political world and the natural environment. I do not seek to discuss how literary texts represent or shape the natural environment, although I certainly see such projects as crucial and timely interventions in both our cultural and environmental lives. Further, while environmental constraints can certainly influence what I am calling literary ecology, (as when, say, past climate change has produced civilizational decline, necessarily reshaping the literary landscape in the process) that is not a phenomenon I will dwell on here. I do make use at various points of key ecological concepts, ranging from the discussion of the biome as a model for the comparative study of human cultures immediately below, to my borrowings from population genetics in the final chapter, in my discussion of the role that diversity might play in keeping a literary culture viable. It is my hope that my more abstract uses of ecological concepts and themes in this book augments, rather than detracts from, discussion of ecology per se in literary contexts, just as the use of language like "the economy of desire" in literary-theoretical contexts can awaken an interest in more profound interactions between economics and literature or the use of a phrase like "epistemological violence" can remind us of the ever present dangers of physical violence (though of course in both these cases, too, there is the danger that the metaphor might instead detract from the real-world questions it indexes).

---

24   See, e.g., Einar Haugen, "The Ecology of Language," in *Ecolinguistics Reader: Language, Ecology and Environment*, edited by Peter Mühlhäusler, New York: Continuum International Publishing Group, 2001, 57–66.

25   Neil Postman, "The Reformed English Curriculum," in *High School 1980: The Shape of the Future in American Secondary Education*, edited by A. C. Eurich, Pitman Publishing Corp., 1970.

26   Significant introductions to this field include: Roderick P. Neumann, *Making Political Ecology*, Human Geography in the Making, London: Hodder Arnold, 2005; Paul Robbins, *Political Ecology: A Critical Introduction*, Critical Introductions to Geography, Malden, MA: Blackwell Publishing, 2004; Neumann, "Political Ecology: Theorizing Sale," *Progress in Human Geography* 33 (3), 2009: 398–406 offers a useful critical review.

WHY A BIOMES APPROACH?

Although my appropriation of ecology as a metaphor for the systems of literary circulation I study does not altogether depend on a rigorous adherence to the categories or methods of that scientific discipline, I do find some of its concepts useful in understanding the project represented by this book. In particular, I find useful the distinction made in classifying ecological contexts between *biomes* and *ecozones*.[27] In terrestrial ecology, the *ecozones* are the eight large-scale geographic regions into which the earth's land surface are divided—roughly speaking, North America, South America, northern Eurasia, Sub-Saharan Africa, South/ Southeast Asia, Australia, Polynesia, and Antarctica. These large regions, long separated from each other by oceans, deserts, and mountains, have evolved quite distinct genetic, taxonomic, and historical profiles. Overlapping this classification are the series of biomes, a collection of fourteen types of environments, sharing conditions of climate, landscape, and major plant types, including such environments as deserts, tropical rainforests, tundra, boreal forests, Mediterranean climates, and so on. Each ecozone contains samples of a variety of these fourteen biomes, and regions of a particular biome the world over tend to share similar kinds of animal and plant life, which has evolved over time (with the particular genetic heritage of that ecozone) in response to the particular ecological constraints of the biome.

As an example, there are five regions of the world which share what the World Wildlife Federation calls a "Mediterranean" climate and ecology— the Mediterranean basin itself, California, parts of Southern and Western Australia, parts of South Africa, and parts of Chile. Each of these regions can be characterized by warm, dry summers, and cooler but generally mild and rainier winters, though of course there is considerable variation within each region. The long, hot, dry summers characteristic of the Mediterranean biome have led in each case to the prevalence of so-called sclerophyll vegetation—plants with small, dark, waxy leaves designed to conserve moisture. The specific kinds of sclerophyll plants found in each Mediterranean region differ, however, thanks to the very different ecological histories of the larger ecozones in which they are found, ranging from the oaks of Italy to the

---

27   David M. Olson, Eric Dinerstein, Eric D. Wikramanayake, Neil D. Burgess, George V. N. Powell, Emma C. Underwood, Jennifer A. D'amico, et al., "Terrestrial Ecoregions of the World: A New Map of Life on Earth," *BioScience* 51 (11), 2001: 933.

eucalyptus of Australia. A biome, then, represents a shared set of challenges and constraints to life in a given region, with distinct and characteristic types of adaptive features found in plants and animals that may not be genetically related to each other. The territory found in a given biome in each ecozone is then subdivided into a number of *ecoregions* (over 800 terrestrial ecoregions worldwide, according to the standard used by the WWF), each of which differs to some degree from its neighbors as a result of the specific combinations of plant and animal life found there. The temperate deciduous forests of the US East Coast, for example, are divided in this scheme into two parts (with the dividing line just north of Baltimore), with the (traditionally) oak and chestnut forests of the Northeastern Coastal Forests ecoregion giving way to the oak, hickory, and pine forests of the Southeastern Mixed Forests to the south.

I have discussed the classification of ecoregions at some length because I believe this discussion, and particularly the notion of the biome, has considerable relevance for the study and classification of human cultures. The boundaries between cultures represent just as complex a question as that of those between languages (and indeed the two categories often overlap), but broadly speaking most of those who classify cultures have been happy to identify relatively small groups of people situated in space and time as a "culture," reserving terms like "civilization" or "culture region" for larger-scale assemblages of cultures. The construction of these larger cultural areas presents certain unavoidable methodological problems. Like the languages I discussed earlier, cultures often blend gradually one into the other, with the inhabitants of each town or village sharing some customs with their neighbors, and innovating some of their own. As a result, it is difficult enough to draw anything like a strict border around a culture; a region of literary or verbal art circulation would provide one means of doing so, but (as we shall see many times over the course of this book) it is quite possible for a given region to be within the region of circulation for more than one literary tradition.

The difficulties multiply when we seek to aggregate local cultures into larger units, since even if we have managed to define individual cultures, their complex interrelationships and participations in multiple larger-scale networks will make defining the boundaries of the aggregate that much more difficult. One of the most famous efforts to divide the world's cultures (or at least those deemed sufficiently advanced) into "civilizations" is that of the midcentury British historian Arnold Toynbee, who, by the time his project was completed, had identified no fewer than forty-three civilizations in world history, though not all were present in his model at each stage.[28]

Numerous localized and empirical objections could be raised to Toynbee's scheme—why, for example, is the Greek world divided into three distinct civilizations (Cretan, Hellenic, and Byzantine), among the thirteen full-fledged civilizations he retains throughout the history of his own project, while China is represented as a single continuous civilization from the beginning of its history? Why are Chibchan and Araucanian cultures described as distinct satellites of "Peruvian civilization," while all of Southeast Asia is classified as a single satellite of Indian civilization? How, for that matter, can the category of "arrested civilization" be made to fit such diverse cultural formations as the Ottoman and the Polynesian, the Spartan and the Eskimo? Such concrete queries could, of course, be multiplied almost indefinitely. This is not, I would suggest, because there is something particularly ineffective about the specific scheme Toynbee developed over decades of research nor yet because he failed to develop a sufficiently coherent definition of what a civilization is, even though that is an obvious methodological problem. Rather, I would argue, the concrete problems of Toynbee's list of civilizations, and its tendency to break down the closer one looks at it, is a necessary consequence of the inherently interlinked and continuous nature of human societies around the inhabited world and the difficulties incumbent on the effort to break up this continuity into discrete spatiotemporal units. A thousand concrete improvements could be suggested to Toynbee's scheme, but none of these possible improvements would, I contend, be able to address these fundamental methodological impossibilities. At the same time, as a comparatist with an interest in studying literatures (specifically Greek and Chinese) whose relationships are based on something other than contiguity, I admire the early attempt at a global synthesis that someone like Toynbee represents, and I believe strongly that the attempt to think through comparisons on a global scale is more than worth the effort.

Ecology, I argue, provides a useful paradigm here; to begin with, the cultural notion of the "civilization" is analogous in many respects to the

---

28   Arnold Joseph Toynbee, *A Study of History*, 12th ed. (1961) London; New York: Oxford University Press, 1935. For a critical, but equally positivistic account, see Roger W. Wescott, "The Enumeration of Civilizations," *History and Theory* 9 (1), 1970: 59–85.

ecozone. Sometimes, ecozones have very coherent boundaries, as when the flora and fauna of the Americas differ from that of Eurasia, or where the Sahara or the Himalayas present so forbidding a barrier to many species as to constitute a fairly impermeable boundary. At other times, as in southern China where the Palearctic and Indo-Malayan ecozones meet, the borders are better understood as zones of transition. This notion, that borders can be zones of transition rather than fixed lines on a map, is itself illuminating for the project of enumerating human civilizations—certainly history has provided many examples of regions better understood as transitional between civilizations, or as participating in multiple civilizations, than as firmly in one or another of them.

But there is, I believe, something much more useful that ecology can contribute to this problem. As I suggested earlier, I think the notion of the biome—a set of typological conditions of climate and terrain found in different locations around the world and generating similar kinds of adaptations in plant and animal species—suggests a possible new approach to the comparative study of the literatures of the world. Rather than make, or in addition to making, the civilization our object of study (or its literary analogue, the region within which texts of a given language circulate), we might find it productive to think in terms of literary biomes as well; that is, in terms of particular patterns of ecological constraints operating on the circulation of literary texts in a variety of different historical contexts. In other words, rather than limit our study to specific systems within which literature circulates (Early Modern Europe, say, or East Asia, or the contemporary Anglosphere), we might want to think about how literature circulates, what sorts of constraints operate on that circulation, and how particular literary communities respond to those constraints. If patterns of temperature and precipitation, relief, the avail-ability of freshwater, and the quality of soil are among the most important determinants of ecological biomes, the most significant determinants of a literary biome might be:

The linguistic situation: How widely spoken and/or read is the language of a particular text? Is that language used by a tiny elite across a wide range of times and places, or is it the general mother tongue of a specific region? What sort of literary history does that language have, and what sorts of linguistic and literary resources (from dictionaries and grammars to genres and venues for recognition) exist? Moreover, how many other languages exist as viable media for literary expression for that author or community, and what sort of relationship obtains between those languages? Is the decision to compose work in that language a foregone conclusion for a given author or a choice made among two or more options, each, potentially, with different audiences and opportunities?

The political world: In the modern and Western world, but pretty much *only* there, as I demonstrate throughout this book, there exists a presumption that languages are properties of nation-states and that the entire human world can be (or at least should be) subdivided into nation-states. If this is not the case for the world of a given author or text, then what sort of political context is operative, whether tribal community, city-state, world-empire, or something else? How do the limits of polities correspond to the limits of linguistic circulation? Is one language shared by many polities, or does one polity possess many languages (or both)? Does a particular literary language provide a vehicle for intra-polity cultural relations, and does that language have a privileged relationship to one or more of those polities? How does the state intervene in cultural affairs, and does the state take an interest in the language or languages used for literary production?

Economics: What sort of economic relations link cities and polities to larger networks? What sort of relationship do those networks have to the structure of polities, and is there an economic system of core and periphery in place? To what extent is culture, and specifically literature, seen as an economic act, and to what extent is literature implicated instead in political, religious, and other symbolic networks?

Religion: If religion is a coherent and autonomous sphere of activity in this context (which is not necessarily the case), to what extent does it link the polity and the community to larger networks and/or define the limits of the polity? Is a given language (or languages) privileged within the literary ecology because of its association with sacred texts, and is that language still usable for other purposes? Does religion divide what might otherwise be a unified linguistic and cultural community?

Cultural politics: Is there a strong sense that literature should be an elite activity, a folk art, a mass-produced commodity? If the production of literature is itself a prestige activity in any way, to what extent are there gradations of prestige? Who assigns authors and texts to different levels of prestige and on what basis? Is valued literary production focused on one location (court, capital city, commercial center) or distributed more widely across a variety of centers? Is literary prestige and/or the evaluation of literary texts associated with particular institutions, such as academies or universities? How stable is this arrangement?

Technologies of distribution: Is verbal art produced and consumed orally only, or does writing play a role? Is writing in fact the dominant, or only, means by which prestige texts can be circulated? If both oral and written circulation are found, what are the respective valences of each, and what are the relationships between the two? Are theater, or other performing arts, important to verbal art? Does printing and the mass production of texts play a role, or more recent technologies, from radio and film through television to the internet and beyond? Which of these media are recognized as verbal art, and with what levels of prestige (and how does that prestige compare with economic recognition?

Six Literary Ecologies

This book cannot discuss all of these questions for all possible cultures over time, and of course the many possible answers to these questions could be combined (and, more importantly, *have* been combined) in a myriad ways. But just as the concept of the ecological biome seeks to generalize and to create a set of comparable circumstances in which species adapt in fairly predictable ways, so, too, I think the circulations of literatures have operated in similar enough ways that a relatively small set of biomes can offer considerable explanatory power. In what follows, and in the rest of the book, I work with a set of six literary ecologies, which I have discussed briefly elsewhere[29] and used in my earlier work.[30] I do not claim to have exhausted the range of possibilities; this set of six ecologies is empirically derived rather than theoretically complete. I also draw here on the understanding, inherent in ecology from its beginnings, that life on earth varies continuously rather than being divided into discrete and stable blocks. In a foundational and still-cited 1935 article, the biologist A. G. Tansley observed that the ecological boundaries we draw are frequently (though not always) "mental isolates,"

---

29   Beecroft, "World Literature Without a Hyphen."

30   Beecroft, *Authorship and Cultural Identity*; Beecroft, "When Cosmopolitanisms Intersect: An Early Chinese Buddhist Apologetic and World Literature," *Comparative Literature Studies* 47 (3), 2010: 266–89.

that is, intellectual constructions designed to make scientific study possible and not unambiguous features of the natural landscape.[31] Since they deal with human culture rather than the natural environment, my six literary ecologies are a fortiori just such "mental isolates," with all the usefulness and all the problems that such concepts necessarily entail. I would suggest, however, that the fact that my ecologies cut across traditional cultural boundaries and juxtapose unrelated cultures in deliberately artificial ways might be helpful as an antidote to civilizational thinking, which all too often forgets that civilizations are always, in the end, mental isolates as well, and that human cultural experience knows no firm or enduring borders.

I am certain that many specialists in many areas will challenge my association of particular cultural contexts with specific ecologies; since I do not see the purpose of this book as being to definitively categorize the world's literary ecologies but rather to provide a basis for further discussion, I do not believe that these concerns ultimately affect the value of this project. Indeed, I will view it as a measure of the success of this project if it invites further discussion and debate whether on the level of disputing the association of a given context with a particular ecology, the reduction of or addition to my list of ecologies, or indeed to disputes on the level of premise about the comparability of different cultural contexts. The goal of this book is to facilitate the comparative study of the interactions between literatures and their environments; to the extent that I have helped to further that discussion (even if it is only to conclude that the project is, in whole or in part, impossible), I will be happy.

EMIC AND ETIC: A SHORT INTERLUDE

At this point, it seems appropriate to dwell for a moment on one possible critique of this project, namely that the ecologies I am discussing are artificial constructions of my own (even if derived in each case from specialist scholarship in a relevant field) and do not reflect concerns indigenous to the cultures I discuss. The nature of this critique can be summed up in the sense that my conceptual framework is etic rather than emic, to borrow the terminology made popular by the linguist Kenneth Pike.[32] In the

---

31　A. G. Tansley, "The Use and Abuse of Vegetational Concepts and Terms," *Ecology* 16 (3), 1935: 284–307, 300n4.

32　Kenneth L. Pike, *Language in Relation to a Unified Theory of the Structure of Human Behavior,* 2nd rev. ed. Janua linguarum 24, The Hague: Mouton, 1967.

Pike-inspired use of the terms, which have considerable currency in the social sciences but which are less common in literary study,[33] "emic" concepts are those indigenous to a particular culture, while "etic" concepts are those introduced to the study of that culture by an outside observer. The terms derive from "phonemics," the study of the minimal linguistically meaningful units of sound in a language, and "phonetics," which studies instead the minimal units of sound in all languages, from a physiological and acoustic perspective. As an example, from a phonetic perspective, the sounds represented by the letter "p" in the English words *pit, spit* and *tip* are distinct, since the p in *pit* is aspirated slightly, while that in *spit* is not, and that in *tip* has no audible release. From a phonemic perspective, however, all three are identical because English speakers perceive them to be a single sound and because there are no cases in which the phonetic distinctions among these three sounds is used by the language to convey meaning (in the way, for example, that the difference between the initial consonants of *pet* and *bet* is productive in meaning for English speakers, since it is the only way to distinguish between these two words with different meanings).

It is true that, in general, the ecologies I describe in this book are etic concepts in this sense, although it should be noted, as I discuss in the relevant chapters, that "epichoric," "Panhellenic," and "cosmopolitan" are all emic terms to some extent within the Greek language and that the words "vernacular," "national," and "global" are also emic in certain contexts and to varying degrees. None of these terms (with the exception of the last two) are emic in Chinese, for example, or indeed in any of the other cultures I discuss, so I can reasonably be charged with imposing terminology borrowed either from the Ancient Greek[34] context or from modern

---

33   For a rare exception in the world of comparative literature, see Eugene Chen Eoyang, *The Transparent Eye: Reflections on Translation, Chinese Literature, and Comparative Poetics*, Honolulu: University of Hawaii Press, 1993, 62.

34   Throughout, I use "Ancient Greek" and "Classical Chinese" (or occasionaly the emic term *wenyan*) as if they are the proper names of specific languages, despite an obvious awareness that each term refers to a disparate collection of regionally, chronologically, and sociolinguistically variant forms, assembled variously in different surviving texts. The systems of literary circulation built around each make use of a assortment of linguistic registers, commented on in the text where appropriate. *Mutatis mutandis*, the same could be said about many of the "languages" I discuss. Similarly, I use the expressions "Archaic/Classical/Hellenistic Greece" and "Early China" at times as if they refer to coherent civilizational entities, in full awareness of the complexity of such a claim.

scholarship on radically distinct cultural contexts, rather than searching for whatever emic terminology in those contexts might identify the phenomena I discuss. Moreover, even within the Ancient Greek context, it can reasonably be argued that I (following the work of Gregory Nagy and others) am not so much using emic terminology as borrowing indigenous words to express etic concepts, since our modern scholarly discussion, say, of epichoric versus Panhellenic modes of reading of ancient Greek texts clearly depends on so many other concepts derived from the modern world and not strictly from an indigenous Greek context.

These concerns are certainly legitimate, and the reader of this book is well advised to bear in mind at any moment that I am imposing an artificially constructed conceptual framework on my unsuspecting source materials. As a scholar trained in the methodologies of (Western) Classics and Early China studies, both of which disciplines (like, I would suggest, all disciplines built around a specific linguistic or cultural object of study) lay considerable emphasis on an emic understanding of the culture under study, I take these concerns very seriously, and, elsewhere in my work, I attempt to (re?)construct parts of the emic frameworks of the cultures I study. It is as a practitioner of a third discipline—comparative literature—that I must come to the defense of the etic, for it is etic concepts that make that discipline possible. By definition, the comparative study of literature in different languages, coming from different cultures, must take place in some sort of critical language, and that language must be etic to at least one of the cultures under study, if it is not etic to both, or all, of them. In fact, those in search of a methodological description of comparative literature or of a ready means of drawing a distinction between that discipline and the study of the so-called national literatures, (an obviously problematic category which I discuss further in Chapter 5), could do much worse than to say that national-literature disciplines and departments study literature from an emic perspective, while comparative literature does so from an etic perspective.

In ascribing to comparative literature an etic perspective, I am not claiming to privilege the etic over the emic, let alone to give legitimacy to the etic alone. Nor do I mean to suggest that an etic perspective is somehow an objective or neutral one; necessarily all critical perspectives, whether etic or emic, are embedded in the cultural and ideological situation of their authors, and all necessarily result in (at best) a distortion of what they study, if not (at worst) the construction of the very object they hope to examine. This is, however, as true of modern scholars adopting an emic methodology as those using an etic one, since to use the emic as a critical methodology as an outside observer (or even as an "inside" observer speaking to a scholarly, therefore always-already partly "outside," audience) is already to begin the transformation of emic to etic. Moreover, as we have seen in the discussion of the translatability of "literature" as a term, one of the dangers of a scholarly methodology that overemphasizes the emic is that it runs the risk of reifying as meaningful and structuring indigenous concepts or terms whose meanings were or are in fact contested within the culture itself.

Given that both emic and etic frameworks alike can thus represent artificial impositions on the texts that are the objects of our study, there are certain advantages to the use of an etic framework. On one level, I would argue, the use of an etic framework has the advantage of highlighting the very artificiality of the concepts we use to study texts from other times and places. Unless we are extremely careful in our use of emic concepts, we always risk naturalizing our use of those contexts that are usually decidedly etic disciplinary contexts. The composers of Homeric epic had no notion of being studied by specialists in "Classics"; nor, for that matter, did Melville know that his work would be an object of study for "American Literature" (at least not as that field is now constructed), nor yet Goethe as an object for "German Studies." Even to the extent that authors self-consciously reflect on their position within a literature or a tradition (as Melville and Goethe surely did), their understanding of what that "literature" or "tradition" really is necessarily differs from ours. Valuable as the emic work we all do as "national-literature" specialists is, I believe that at least the occasional glance at an etic perspective can serve as a useful corrective for our natural tendency to equate our use of emic concepts with their use in their original context.

Most importantly, as I have already suggested, such a framework makes possible comparison across cultures and therefore also conversation across disciplines. Even as this book offers a framework through which the comparative study of literary ecologies might proceed, its greater commitment is to the creation of a common ground on which questions of comparison and comparability can be asked. I would be delighted, for example, to hear from Hispanists who object that contemporary Latin American literature is neither "national" nor "global" in my sense, or from Arabists who dispute my claim that Arabic literature remains in some sense "cosmopolitan," or from Egyptologists who might rightly point out that my scheme provides no obvious place for the literature they study. But beyond such terminological disputes, I also welcome debate that challenges my thesis that these literatures, as objects in their own right, are comparable on ecological grounds, whether by insisting on the *sui generis* nature of some particular literary tradition, by constructing an alternative framework based on concepts emic to a literature or through some other means. Such challenges will not invalidate this project, I contend, but rather demonstrate its worth, which lies very much, I believe, in its establishment of a basis for discussion.

I have elsewhere criticized Franco Moretti's model of world literature as one itself based on a core-periphery model of economic activity, with scholars of national literatures operating as the extractors of raw material on the periphery, while scholars of world literature perform the value-added labor of synthesis and analysis in the core.[35] I am aware that the mission I here propose for my own work risks reinscribing the very division of labor I criticize in Moretti's model. This is a danger I take seriously, and it is one that I hope to have resisted, at least to some extent, in the writing of this book. Most of all, I believe that I can function best as a theorist of world literature to the extent that I speak as a scholar of specific literatures, which is why where possible I offer examples from the literatures that I study (Greek, Latin, classical Chinese) or at least from modern Chinese or from the modern European languages in which I can read the original, with varying degrees of fluency and sophistication. As such, I also believe strongly that a critique of my approach undertaken from the perspective of any particular language or literature is also, inherently, a theoretical and/or methodological intervention in the field of world literature. This project is also by nature collaborative, at least in the sense that reading books from fellow scholars in other fields, and drawing inspiration from them, can be considered a collaborative project (and I believe it can); one of the most fervent hopes I have for this project is that it will encourage more such reading across disciplines, so that specialists in Old English might find theoretical insights in the work of specialists on early South Asian vernaculars, or scholars of nationalism in the literatures of Eastern Europe or Latin America might find insight in the work of specialists on the national literatures of Canada or of early twentieth-century China. I hope also to provoke other, more rigorous and extensive forms of collaboration, but simply to read each other's books would be a good start. My greatest hope for this book is that it will begin to provide scholars of different literatures with a common language with which to talk about a shared set of issues; the

---

35   Beecroft, "World Literature Without a Hyphen," 90–1.

richness of the discussions that could happen in that language are the greatest reward I can imagine.

Herewith, I introduce the six ecologies that form the core of this book. Each is the subject of its own chapter, which conveniently allows this concluding section of my introduction to serve as a summary of the book's chapters. I offer here a brief outline of each ecology, together with a mention of some of the key tropes found in texts that participate in that ecology, and which facilitate readings informed by that ecology. Since each of these ecologies are, in Benedict Anderson's happy phrase, "imagined communities," there is always a dimension of constructedness, or of the unthought, about each ecology, and I attempt to sketch these, too, here. More details, obviously, follow in each chapter. These ecologies are presented in the order in which I can identify their historical emergence, although I stress that my model is not an evolutionary one. I do not see any sense of historical inevitability to this list of ecologies, any more than deserts necessarily evolve into rain forests, and where appropriate in the text I note cases where a particular language or ecological context evolves against the order below (as when, for example, Latin moves from being a vernacular language to being a cosmopolitan one).

1. **Epichoric**, or local, literary ecologies are the limit case of literary circulation, where verbal art (frequently, though not necessarily, oral) may be transmitted over long periods of time but does not leave the small-scale local community (be it a Greek *polis*, a Chinese city-state of the Warring States era, or a tribal community among the aboriginal populations of the Americas and the Pacific). Epichoric readings of texts frequently emphasize the emplacement of those texts—the ways in which those texts both embody and construct a sense of place for the community in question, marking boundaries and imbuing mountains, rivers, trees, and other natural and artificial features with meaning. Since we as modern Westerners do not live in such a society, we by definition cannot read epichoric texts purely from "inside" their cultures, and so any text that may have begun as "local" must circulate in some other form for us to have access to it. As a limit case, the ideal epichoric culture would have no contact with any other culture, but since we know of no culture so isolated, epichoric readings of texts necessarily involve some kind of "forgetting" of broader cultural connections.

2. **Panchoric** ecologies are those that form in regions with small-scale polities but where literary and other cultural artifacts circulate more

broadly through a space that is self-aware of itself as some kind of cultural unity and that define themselves by the exclusion of other polities that do not share that culture. The paradigmatic example of this ecology is the Panhellenic culture of archaic and classical Greece (and my coinage, "panchoric," is a generalization of the more familiar Panhellenic), though I have attempted to show, here and elsewhere, that the Chinese world of the same era is comparably constituted, and there are a limited number of other possible cases around the world. Key tropes of the panchoric ecology are catalogues, anthologies, and genealogies—devices that bring into the structure of the text itself an understanding of literature and culture as the sum of a series of epichoric parts. Frequently, however, the elements of these catalogues, anthologies, and genealogies seem to have been constructed artificially to present the appearance of a "sum of parts." Panchoric cultures, in other words, are frequently more unified than they pretend to be and represent themselves as assemblages of traditions precisely in order to eliminate the space for whatever might be more genuinely local.

3. **Cosmopolitan** ecologies are found wherever a single literary language is used over a large territorial range and through a long period of time. Such languages frequently emerge as the result of a great world-empire (those of Alexander the Great, of the Guptas in India, the Han in China, or the Islamic Caliphate, for example), but the languages and literary cultures they spawn (almost necessarily written) long outlast those more transient political formations. Cosmopolitan literatures, especially those which evolved out of panchoric or vernacular languages (as many did), frequently indulge in the trope of universalizing imagery or themes from that earlier tradition, reworking what was once a more local tradition so that it can better serve a larger world. Cosmopolitan literatures, almost by definition, represent themselves as universal, and yet their very reach often brings them in touch with rival cosmopolitanisms. They also tend to represent themselves as universally accessible, with recognition within the tradition open to almost anyone who can learn the (often difficult and somewhat artificial) language, and yet cosmopolitan ecologies frequently conceal considerable inequalities of circulation, with cultural peripheries marginalized by the core.

4. **Vernacular** ecologies emerge (as Pollock describes) out of cosmopolitan ones when sufficient cultural resources accumulate behind some version of a locally spoken language to allow for its use for literary purposes. Vernaculars are often developed in the context of new political formations,

though their uses frequently spread beyond the borders of those polities, and their emergence is frequently accompanied either by translations of canonical works from cosmopolitan languages or by texts I call "vernacular manifestoes." Since many vernaculars emerge out of a dialect continuum (as, for example, Italian, French, and Spanish all do), they are often themselves somewhat abstract languages, generalized from a point on that continuum, rather than simply reflecting the speech habits of any one community (though they may represent themselves as so doing). Vernacular literatures exist in competition with one or more cosmopolitan languages (since they emerged in the context of one), as well as with each other.

5. The **national** literary ecology emerges out of the vernacular literary ecology of Europe, together with the emergence of nationalism per se, gaining considerable momentum in the aftermath of the French Revolution, Napoleonic Wars, and independence movements of the settler colonies in the Americas and continuing to grow throughout the nineteenth and twentieth centuries. This ecology spreads gradually around the world, as a direct consequence of European imperial expansion during this period, and corresponds very much with the ecological situation of literature as described by Moretti and Casanova, among others. Just as this period marks the first era in human history in which it is believed that the entire inhabited world should be under the rule of a single kind of polity (the nation-state), so too does this mark the first time a single literary ecology spreads worldwide (as opposed to cosmopolitan ecologies, which think of themselves as universal but spread instead only over a particular region). A key trope of the national literature is that of literary history, which emerges in Europe at this time and seeks to establish a progressive narrative for national literary history, beginning with rustic or folk foundational texts, and progressively shedding cosmopolitan elements, now represented as old-fashioned. Another trope of the ecology is that of the "Quarrel of the Ancients and the Moderns," a period, in other words, when the cosmopolitan language is supplanted completely, so that national literatures compete with each other just as nation-states do, freed (at least in principle) from non-national actors. Since the notion of the nation-state rests on the claim (only loosely connected with reality) that each nation speaks a single language, and is represented by a single polity, the national-literature ecology does the same. The national-literature ecology thus tends to forget works whose origins belie this congruence between nation and language, as well as works written in the cosmopolitan language after the

emergence of the vernacular and works that do not suit the narrative of national history.

6. Global literary ecology, my sixth and final category, represents another limit case—the literary circulation that truly knows no borders. As major languages (most obviously, of course, English) escape the bonds of the nation-state, and texts begin to circulate more rapidly around the planet, we may be moving in the direction of just such a borderless world (though linguistic competency will always create barriers of its own). The fantasy of a world without borders conceals within itself another fantasy, namely that borderlessness might create equal access to the literary world for all, regardless of political status or the position of one's native language within the global linguistic ecology. I identify as a key trope of this emergent ecology something that I call the "plot of globalization," the use of multi-strand narration to convey on a formal level our interconnected and polycentric world.

CHAPTER 1

Epichoric Literature

When imagining how a work of verbal art circulates, it is helpful to consider the limit case in which that work does not circulate at all. At its most extreme version, this limit case would probably correspond to the situation in which an author composed a work in his or her own head but never made it available to anyone else, through either written or oral circulation. Such an extreme case will be of little interest to us here; a tree falling in a silent forest may well make a sound, but a poem or story neither written nor spoken can scarcely be said to be a work of art at all in any meaningful sense. The limit case for literary circulation will, therefore, have to happen on something of a larger scale.

My conception of the epichoric is designed explicitly to provide that limit case. As I define it, epichoric literary ecologies are those that take place within a single, small-scale, political and/or cultural context. Verbal art within such a context may be transmitted continuously over a long period of time but in one place, rather than circulating more broadly, and it would disappear were the political and cultural substrate that nourished it to disintegrate. Moreover, for an epichoric ecology to be genuinely epichoric, it would have to exist in isolation from larger cultural formations, interacting economically and politically, perhaps, with other epichoric cultures in its region but remaining culturally distinct and not participating in the evolution of different, and translocal, cultural formations.

What do I mean by a "single, small-scale, political and/or cultural context"? Necessarily, this formulation will have to cover a variety of very distinct cultural systems. On the one hand, the smaller cultural units out of which panchoric cultures emerge (like Panhellenic Greek culture or Panhuaxia culture in China), would certainly qualify as epichoric, and indeed I borrow the term from Gregory Nagy's use of it in the context of the lyric poetry proper to the Greek polis,[1] though as we shall see it is difficult

---

1 See, for example, the discussion at Gregory Nagy, *Pindar's Homer: The Lyric Possession of an Epic Past*, Baltimore: The Johns Hopkins University Press, 1994, 66–7.

to identify specific texts that can or must be understood as epichoric in either the Greek or the Chinese case. On the other hand, small-scale tribal societies around the world, whether among the native peoples of the New World or anywhere the reach of the state and that, accordingly, of state culture have been minimal, are also always potentially epichoric as cultural ecologies, though we will need to be sensitive in each case to the possibility that seemingly local cultural practices are actually part of a panchoric system or relate in some other way to a larger cultural network.

In a certain sense, the ideal notional epichoric culture would be that of the "uncontacted tribe," the small-scale (most such peoples known to us likely number fewer than three hundred individuals) communities still found in the Amazon, on New Guinea, and in highland and island regions elsewhere in the world. One of the best known of these uncontacted tribes, the Sentinelese, provide a useful case in point.[2] Located on North Sentinel Island in the Andaman and Nicobar Islands, about 1,300 kilometers south of Calcutta, the Sentinelese are thought to have inhabited their island for as long as 60,000 years, representing perhaps part of the earliest modern human migrations from Africa to Asia.[3] The relationship between the Sentinelese language and the other languages of the Andaman Islands remains obscure due to a lack of available evidence.[4] Although often referred to as a "Stone Age" tribe, the Sentinelese in fact make use of tools made of metal cargo from ships wrecked on their shores; still, their technology and way of life seem likely to have changed little over time. As the great tsunami of December 26, 2004, struck the region, there were concerns the Sentinelese might have been exterminated, or severely weakened, by the event. According to a February 12, 2006, report in the *Guardian*, in the minutes prior to the tsunami's arrival, the Sentinelese performed what appear to have been propitiatory rites, scattering pig and turtle skulls, casting stones into the ocean, and gathering various objects, including what seem to have been amulets made of the bones of ancestors. Another report (cited in the *New York Times* on April 12, 2012) suggested, in what seems to be a telling gesture, that rescue helicopters arriving later were greeted by a

---

2   For a journalistic account of the situation of the Sentinelese, see Adam Goodheart, "The Last Island of the Savages," *American Scholar* 69 (4), 2000: 13.

3   Phillip M. Endicott, Thomas P. Gilbert, Chris Stringer, Carles Lalueza-Fox, Eske Willerslev, Anders J. Hansen, and Alan Cooper, "The Genetic Origins of the Andaman Islanders," *The American Journal of Human Genetics* 72 (1), 2003: 178–84.

4   Anvita Abbi, "Is Great Andamanese genealogically and typologically distinct from Onge and Jarawa?" *Language Sciences* 31 (6), 2009: 791–812.

single Sentinelese man firing arrows. According to Survival International, an advocacy group, the Sentinelese may represent the most completely isolated tribal community left in our world today.[5]

The Sentinelese thus provide something of a useful case in point for thinking about the epichoric. The seemingly ritualized activities observed prior to the arrival of the tsunami in 2004 suggest the presence of a sophisticated set of cultural and religious practices, and I take it as axiomatic that verbal art is likely to form a part of any human culture. What, however, could we possibly say about the verbal art of the Sentinelese, when their very language is all but unknown to us? Indeed, European or American scholarship likely has a secure grasp on the verbal art of only a tiny fraction of the seven thousand languages still spoken today; a community need not experience the isolation of the Sentinelese for its culture to fail to enter global circulation. Yet even the Sentinelese have not been cut off quite completely from the rest of the world; awareness on the part of Westerners that there was a human population on North Sentinel goes back at least to the voyage of an East India Company survey vessel in 1771. In 1867, 106 passengers and crew on the Indian merchant vessel the *Nineveh* were stranded on North Sentinel and fended off an attack by Sentinelese warriors (described as naked and with noses painted red) until being rescued by the Royal Navy a few days later. After an escaped convict was killed by the Sentinelese in 1896, the tribe seems largely to have been ignored until the arrival of a National Geographic crew in 1974. The former King Leopold III of Belgium came close enough to the island to be threatened with a bow and arrow the following year; this visit was followed at regular intervals thereafter by visits from Indian anthropologists bearing gifts.[6] As of 2014, permanent contact and exchange have never been established but to the extent that the Sentinelese are nonetheless established in the Western (and Indian) imaginaries as an idealized case of the uncontacted tribe, some construction of "the Sentinelese" has in fact circulated beyond their own island, and it seems hard to imagine that Sentinelese culture itself has been unchanged by the past century or more of intermittent contact.

A more thorough understanding of the global phenomenon of the uncontacted tribe suggests that in fact many such lost tribes (especially in the Amazon) have "lost" themselves, deliberately exiling themselves beyond the pale of the influence of globalized modernity in order to protect their

---

5   "The most isolated tribe in the world?" at survivalinternational.org.
6   Goodheart, "The Last Island of the Savages."

well-being, while those in New Guinea, for example, have frequently partic-ipated willingly in their own representation as "lost tribes," as part of rational strategies to obtain trade goods and health care, among other things, from the state.[7] Moreover, especially in the case of New Guinea, it is known that, while many of these "lost tribes" may have been unknown to Europeans (although inconsistent government records may be responsible for some tribes being "found" and then "lost" again) they were in regular contact with neighboring tribes, practicing trade and intermarrying with them; those neighboring tribes, of course, had opportunities to profit from being intermediaries between the state and global capitalism, on the one hand, and their "hillbilly" neighbors on the other.[8] Similar phenomena have been described in the upland areas of Southeast Asia, where Willem van Schendel (who labels the region "Zomia") and James C. Scott, among others, have suggested that hill tribes have consistently sought to escape the control of agrarian states based in the river valleys of the region.[9] Those most critical of Scott's work, in particular the scholar of peasant studies Tom Brass, have suggested that hill peoples most often are forced out of valley locations rather than deliberately seeking to elude the arm of the state.[10] For our purposes, however, these two phenomena (not necessarily mutually exclusive) amount to the same thing: Isolated hill tribes in Southeast Asia, as in New Guinea, are not isolated because they have not yet come into contact with more settled sociopolitical and economic structures, ranging from the traditional Burmese monarchy to the modern nation-state of Papua New Guinea to the power of multinational mining conglomerates. Rather, each of these authors suggest, isolation in remote regions is the direct consequence of interaction with those more settled structures, whether because more remote communi-ties wish to retain their autonomy or because they are unable to benefit from the interaction. Isolation is a by-product of interaction, not the failure of its conditions of possibility. When globalization or the reach of the state spread still further and encompass groups that have hitherto remained on the

---

7   Stuart Kirsch, "Lost Tribes: Indigenous People and the Social Imaginary," *Anthropological Quarterly* 70 (2), 1997: 58–67.

8   I borrow the term 'hillbilly' here from ibid., 63.

9   Willem van Schendel, "Geographies of Knowing, Geographies of Ignorance: Jumping Scale in Southeast Asia," *Environment and Planning D: Society and Space* 20 (6), 2002: 647–68; James C. Scott, *The Art of Not Being Governed: An Anarchist History of Upland Southeast Asia*, New Haven, CT: Yale University Press, 2010.

10   Tom Brass, "Scott's 'Zomia,' or a Populist Post-Modern History of Nowhere," *Journal of Contemporary Asia* 42 (1), 2012: 123–33.

margins of those forces, modern observers tend to construct those groups as lost or uncontacted tribes, allowing those groups to perform a certain kind of symbolic labor within national and/or global cultural networks. Lost tribes provide the raw material of primitivism, which, through its exclusion, allows emergent nation-states such as Papua New Guinea to align themselves with modernity while facilitating the Western desire to see such regions as "primitive." As Kirsch and others have observed, anthropologists, relief workers, missionaries and other "first contacters" perform what we might call the value-added labor of this production of primitive isolation, processing for external audiences the community they encounter, and generating what Kirsch notes is a fairly consistent basket of cultural phenomena: an unknown language, near-nudity, ignorance of agriculture, limited use of tools and a lack of awareness of the outside world.[11] At times, some or all of these traits (and most especially the latter) seem the product of deliberate self-representation or of exploitation of others rather than the simple presentation of unambiguous anthropological data.[12]

If even the most isolated of communities known to us today nonetheless seem consistently to have been in contact with their neighbors, to have become isolated as the consequence of processes of interaction, and to collaborate in their eventual representation as "lost tribes," then a fortiori the examples of Archaic Greece and Early China will not constitute realms of the epichoric pure and simple. I have discussed the constructed nature of the epichoric in the Greek and Chinese contexts in some detail elsewhere[13] and offer only a glancing view at these questions here through brief case studies in early Chinese poetry and in the ancient Greek use of the adjective *epichôrios* itself. In the context of these larger-scale cultures, the epichoric plays a structural role somewhat analogous to that played by "the country" in Raymond Williams's famous reading of the role of city and country in British literature—the role, in other words, as an Other, imagined as lacking both genuine regional specificity and change over time, in terms of which the dominant culture understands itself.[14] Although this structural

---

11   Kirsch, "Lost Tribes," 61.

12   See the discussion, with bibliography, of the controversy surrounding the discovery of the so-called Tasaday people of the Philppines in 1971, at ibid., 60–1.

13   Alexander Beecroft, "'This is not a true story': Stesichorus's Palinode and the Revenge of the Epichoric," *Transactions of the American Philological Association* 136 (1), 2006: 47–70; Beecroft, *Authorship and Cultural Identity*.

14   Raymond Williams, *The Country and the City*, Oxford: Oxford University Press, 1975, 10.

role is similar, the valuation applied is rather different; as we shall see in this chapter and in the one that follows, the Greek and Chinese contexts tend to represent the local as in some way inferior and less reliable than the dominant panchoric narratives and evince little of the nostalgia that Williams finds so ubiquitous in representations of "the country."

My Chinese case study is drawn from what is known as the second oldest poetic anthology in the Chinese tradition, the *Chu Ci* 楚辭, or *Songs of Chu*. The textual history of this anthology is complicated and will warrant further attention later. The anthology took its current form under the hand of its compiler, Wang Yi 王逸 (d. AD 158), while the oldest poems in the anthology were attributed to an official of Chu named Qu Yuan 屈原, who was supposed to have lived around 343–277 BC. The title of the *Songs of Chu* points to the origins of the poetic traditions it includes in the southern state of Chu, located along and south of the middle Yangtze valley (in modern Hubei and Hunan provinces) in what was at the time the southern periphery of the Chinese-speaking or Huaxia world. From a modern perspective it is difficult to know how sinicized Chu was at this time; recent archaeological work suggests that Huaxia culture spread gradually southward up the valleys of the tributaries of the Yangtze from the eighth through the third centuries, while the hills to each side were occupied by non-Huaxia peoples[15] whose languages may have been related to the modern Thai and Hmong languages.[16] Situated as it was on the fringes of the Huaxia world, Chu thus formed something of a test case of the limits of Chineseness and the beginnings of Otherness, with a secular trend over this time period towards recognition as part of the core of the Chinese cultural world, a recognition certainly fostered by Chu's military successes against the other states of the Warring States era and its status as one of the last states destroyed by the western state of Qin as it formed the First Chinese empire in the late third century BC. The poetry of this anthology differs in certain formal respects from the poetry found in the *Canon of Songs*, most notably in its use of a five-syllable line (where the *Songs* favors four-syllable lines), frequently punctuated by the onomatopoeic syllable *xi* 兮 between the third and fourth syllables of the line. The language of these poems is however largely the same as that of the *Canon of*

---

15   Lothar Von Falkenhausen, *Chinese Society in the Age of Confucius* (Monumenta Archaeologica), Los Angeles: Cotsen Institute of Archaeology Press, 2006, 285–6.

16   Randy J. LaPolla, "Language Contact and Language Change in the History of the Sinitic Languages," *Procedia - Social and Behavioral Sciences* 2 (5), 2010: 6858–68, 6862.

Songs apart from the greater prevalence of plant-names from the subtropical region where Chu was found.

The lush vegetation described in these poems combines with aspects of their content to create a general atmosphere of sensual and sensory excess. Many of the poems, including the poem I discuss here, describe what appear to be sexual relations between a male or female human officiant and a god or goddess (or, just as often, hope for such relations, followed by their failure). The *Nine Songs*, a collection of eleven songs within the *Chu Ci* and probably one of its earliest compositional layers, seems to use performative language to reenact these quasi-shamanic activities in a ritual or court entertainment context; inscriptional evidence confirms that several of the deities mentioned in these poems were actually known in Chu.[17] Another early poem in the collection, the *Li Sao*, makes use of this imagery to narrate the story of Qu Yuan, who has been maligned at court, and engages in a shamanic procession across the heavens before ultimately drowning himself in the Miluo River, a secondary tributary of the Yangtze. The *Li Sao* itself is rather vague on the question of just how Qu Yuan had been maligned; later tradition has it that, as chief minister of Chu, Qu Yuan had urged his ruler to resist the state of Qin, the western regional state that would later conquer the whole of China and (briefly) establish itself as China's First Empire. Since Chu's failure to stand up to Qin had disastrous results (and since Qin's rapid disintegration and replacement by the Han Dynasty contributed to its historiographic reputation as a brutal and repressive regime), Qu Yuan's alleged policy position led to his appropriation by the later Confucian tradition as an ideal of the worthy but unrecognized minister.

The poem I discuss here represents in particular an attempted encounter with a goddess known as *Xiang Jun*, or "The Lady of the Xiang River," sharing her name with the major river of Hunan province, which flows northward into Hubei, where it forms the vast Dongting Lake before joining the Yangtze:

The Lady of the Xiang

The lady does not go, still she lingers; for whom does she tarry on the
    midstream isle?

---

17   Li Ling, and Donald Harper, "An Archaeological Study of Taiyi (Grand One) Worship," *Early Medieval China* 1995 (1), 1995: 1–39, 22.

Lovely in her distant gaze, her mouth smiles; I swiftly board my cassia boat.

Bidding Yuan and Xiang Rivers be waveless; causing the Great River to flow in peace.

I gaze to the lady, who has not arrived; blowing on my panpipes, ah, for whom I yearn!

I yoke flying dragons, and head north; leading my path to Lake Dongting.

Sail of hanging moss, lotus screens; with iris for oars and orchid flags.

Gazing on the north banks of the Cen, its farther shores; across the Great River I cast my soul.

I cast my soul, but it reaches her not; the lovely and gentle woman sighs for me.

My tears flow freely, dripping down; sorrowfully, I think on her and am grieved.

With cassia paddles and orchid oars; I cut through the ice and break the snow.

As if gathering hanging moss in midstream; plucking lotuses on treetops.

Hearts that disagree weary the matchmaker; love that is not strong is lightly broken.

Stone shallows with swift currents; dragons fly with flapping wings.

The bond was not true, resentment lingers; breaking her vow, she said she had no leisure.

Dawn gallops on the river plain; slowed in evenings by the northern isles.

Birds roosted on the rooftop, waters circled beneath the hall.

I threw my broken ring into the river; leaving my pendants on the Li's shores.

I gathered lavender on the fragrant isles; to give to she who is below.

This moment may not come again; let us roam now at our ease.[18]

---

18   湘君
君不行兮夷猶，蹇誰留兮中洲？美要眇兮宜修，沛吾乘兮桂舟。
令沅湘兮無波，使江水兮安流！望夫君兮未來，吹參差兮誰思！
駕飛龍兮北征，遭吾道兮洞庭。薜荔柏兮蕙綢，蓀橈兮蘭旌。
望涔陽兮極浦，橫大江兮揚靈。揚靈兮未極，女嬋媛兮為余太息。
橫流涕兮潺湲，隱思君兮悱惻。桂櫂兮蘭枻，斲冰兮積雪。
采薜荔兮水中，搴芙蓉兮木末。心不同兮媒勞，恩不甚兮輕絕。
石瀨兮淺淺，飛龍兮翩翩。交不忠兮怨長，期不信兮告余以不閒。
鼂騁騖兮江臯，夕弭節兮北渚。鳥次兮屋上，水周兮堂下。
捐余玦兮江中，遺余佩兮醴浦。采芳洲兮杜若，將以遺兮下女。
旹不可兮再得，聊逍遙兮容與。

At least on the surface, this poem seems to narrate a (not entirely successful) erotic union between a goddess and her mortal ministrant, a union that
involves magical journeys, both on flying dragons and on boats made of
flowers, across the landscape of Chu, through a series of places both familiar to the audience and emplaced by the poem itself. The plants and flowers
with which the poem and its objects are adorned include, as do many of the
poems in the *Chu Ci*, plants native to southern China, which would be
exotic to the more northerly world of the *Canon of Songs*. The goddess, one
of a pair of goddesses of the Xiang, is herself interestingly poised between
epichoric and Panhuaxia; river goddesses are quintessentially local, and yet
at some point (and we cannot date this point) these two came to be associated with the most central myths of Huaxia culture. Understood as the
daughters of the mythical sage-emperor Yao 堯, who was traditionally
dated to the twenty-fourth–twenty-third centuries BC but is clearly a
projection of much later Huaxia charter-myths, they are said to have
married Yao's successor, Shun 舜. After a lengthy rule, Shun is said to have
abdicated and made a journey around his realm; dying on this journey near
a river (said by some to be the Xiang), his wives rushed to his side and,
overwhelmed with grief, drowned themselves in the river.

A key polarity in the interpretation of this poem, then, will be the
extent to which the Ladies of the Xiang are understood as local river
goddesses and the extent to which they are instead seen as deified daughters of Yao, and thus key figures in Panhuaxia myth. Tempting as it would
be to align the former reading with local practice in Chu and the latter
with the Han court of a few centuries later, where the poems came to be
collected as an anthology, we in fact know very little of the origin of these
poems. They are first connected to the story of Qu Yuan by the imperial
librarian and mythographer Liu Xiang 劉向 (79–8 BC), a key figure in the
redacting and interpretation of many ancient texts. There is good reason
to think they may date in their present form to the Chu court of the 240s–
220s BC,[19] although the matter is beyond proof, and we certainly have no
way of discovering much about how the poems would have been used in
that context. Further complicating matters, we have no way of knowing
the extent to which these poems reflect ritual practice as opposed to literary or courtly refinement of religious ritual, in which case Panhuaxia

---

19   David Hawkes, trans., *The Songs of the South: An Ancient Chinese Anthology
of Poems by Qu Yuan and Other Poets*, Harmondsworth, Middlesex, England:
Penguin Books, 1985, 98.

cultural narratives (such as those about Yao and Shun) might have assumed a larger role in how the poems were understood. What is epichoric about these songs, in other words, might represent a wide range of cultural sophistication, of levels of textualization, and of allegorization; as always, we should avoid too easy an association of the local with the naïve, the primitive, the oral.

Conversely, we should also be reluctant to associate the panchoric or the cosmopolitan with textuality and with subtle and didactic political allegory. We know that the early Han court extensively employed shamanic rituals, notably those from Chu, as the great historian Sima Qian informs us. The founder of the Han, Liu Bang (r. 202–195 BC), was in fact a peasant from Chu by birth; his great-grandson, Emperor Wu (r. 141–87 BC), the erstwhile patron of the historian Sima Qian, was known to have had shamans from Chu and from other states at his court and worshipped (among others) many of the gods of the *Nine Songs*, including the Great Unity (*taiyi*) and the Ladies of the Xiang. The court of Emperor Wu is traditionally thought of as the locus of the emergence of "orthodox" Confucian scholarship, which has tended towards imagining the performance of the *Nine Songs* at Wu's court in political terms. If the poems are associated with Qu Yuan, then of course it would be easy enough to read the erotic failures of the *Nine Songs* as allegories of Qu Yuan's failure to persuade the king (represented here by the goddesses of the Xiang River) of the need to repel Qin (recall that the Han Dynasty was of Chu origin and that, as Qin's successor to imperial power, any cultural artifact expressing hostility to Qin was always welcome at the Han court). Such, indeed, is the reading taken by the compiler of the *Chu Ci* anthology and its first commentator, Wang Yi (second century AD), by much of the later scholarly tradition in China and even by some today in the West.[20] Such readers draw further inspiration from the connection between the Ladies of the Xiang and the sage-emperors Yao and Shun; Shun originally served as Yao's minister (so the story goes), and one of the most important indexes of Yao's wisdom was his decision to make Shun, rather than his own son, his heir.

And yet we should be cautious about projecting this sort of reading backward from Wang Yi's position in the second century AD. Recent scholarship in China, Japan, and the West is increasingly skeptical of the notion that orthodox Confucian commentaries of Wang Yi's sort in fact reflect

---

20   Geoffrey R. Waters, *Three Elegies of Ch'u: An Introduction to the Traditional Interpretation of the Ch'u Tz'u*, Madison: University of Wisconsin Press, 1985.

ideas current in the era of Emperor Wu of the Han, back in the second century BC, preferring instead to see the emergence of this particular agenda in the Eastern Han (i.e., in Wang Yi's own time and the time of some of his predecessors, such as Liu Xiang).[21] Certainly, the prevalence of actual shamanic worship at Emperor Wu's court should make us skeptical of claims that shamanic poetry would have been read there as pure allegory. That would, of course, lead us back to a surface reading of the *Lady of the Xiang* for Emperor Wu's time and thus all the more for an earlier audience in Chu itself. Still, the allegorical reading has had an enormous influence within the Chinese tradition, and there is of course no reason why these poems might not have worked both as shamanic ritual and as political allegory, for different audiences or for different parts of the same audiences. We can't really know anything about how the poem was "read" (or heard) in its original context—were these poems a simple celebration of local religious traditions, much later appropriated by rigid Confucian systematizers at the later Han court? Or were those later readers in fact drawing on a legitimate aspect of the local use of these texts? Were the Ladies of the Xiang, as represented in these poems, epichoric nature goddesses, or did they already represent an attempt to integrate local traditions into a Panhuaxia narrative? These are questions without answers, but even this brief examination of the problems of interpretation with these poems should, I hope, serve as a cautionary reminder of the dangers of assuming too much when we start reading locally and start thinking about what happens when a text moves from a local context to a broader context.

Turning to the Greek context, I now examine the term I use for my local ecology, the "epichoric." The term has a long history of use in ancient Greek, beginning at least as early as Pindar, who employs it a dozen or more times in extant poems and fragments. Literally, *epikhôrios* is an adjective meaning "in or of the country" and derives from the closely related nouns *khôra* (f) and *khôros* (m). Both convey a similar range of meanings, from "partially occupied space," to "land," "estate," "countryside," "country town," and so on. *Khôra* was distinguished by the Stoics and others from *topos*, a word indicating something more like the modern notion of "place," of space, that

21   Baoxuan Wang, *Gu Jin Jian Zong: Liang Han Jing Xue*, Chu ban, Zhonghua wen hua bao ku 9, Taibei Shi: Wan juan lou tu shu you xian gong si, 90; Shigemasa Fukui, *Kandai Jukyō no shiteki kenkyū : Jukyō no kangakuka o meguru teisetsu no saikentō*, Tōkyō: Kyūko Shoin, 2005; John Lagerwey and Marc Kalinowski, *Early Chinese Religion: Shang through Han* (1250 BC–220 AD), Leiden, Netherlands: Brill, 2009.

is, imbued with meaning and made concrete and specific. The distinction between *khôra* and topos, of great interest to both Heidegger and Derrida, need not concern us unduly here except to suggest, perhaps, that the "epichoric," as that which pertains to *khôra*, therefore does not refer simply to territory as concrete and emplaced. Rather, it seems to refer to the *capacity* of territory to be emplaced, even as the specifics of that emplacement may remain vague and unspecified.

Thus, when Pindar speaks of the epichoric, it is frequently in the context of a generic "local-ness," rather than of a concrete and specific sense of place. Pindar's epichoric, then, is seen from the outside, generally contrasted with the Panhellenic in one guise or another. For example,

> The maidens saw you winning many times, Telesicrates, in the seasonal rites of Pallas, and in the Olympics, and in the contests of deep-breasted Earth, and in all the *ephikhôrios* contests, and silently prayed, each of them, that you would be her husband or her son. (Pindar, *Pyth.* 9.97–103)[22]

The finer points of this passage remain obscure; epigraphic evidence, for example, suggests that Telesicrates cannot have won a victory at the Olympics,[23] and the location of the games to Mother Earth remains uncertain. The general import of the passage, however, is clear: Telesicrates is to be honored for his success at a series of Panhellenic athletic contests, which are named, and also for victory in local contests within his own community of Cyrene (modern Benghazi, in Libya), which are unnamed and only localized to Cyrene by inference from the fact that the poem itself confirms that polis as Telesicrates' birthplace. The fact that the Panhellenic games are named, and the local ones are not, reinforces the generic quality of the local, here as often in Pindar. This is not to suggest that the epichoric in this ode is wholly devoid of content; far from it. Indeed, Pindar devotes a considerable section of the poem to recounting the myth of the foundation of Cyrene. Rather, I am suggesting that it is part of the function of the epichoric to operate as a foil to a larger-scale system when such a system refers to it. Where the epichoric exists as an alternative mode of reading to

---

22   πλεῖστα νικάσαντά σε καὶ τελεταῖς / ὡρίαις ἐν Παλλάδος εἶδον ἄφωνοί θ' ὡς ἕκασται φίλτατον παρθενικαὶ πόσιν ἢ / υἱὸν εὔχοντ', ὦ Τελεσίκρατες, ἔμμεν, / ἐν Ὀλυμπίοισί τε καὶ βαθυκόλπου / Γᾶς ἀέθλοις ἔν τε καὶ πᾶσιν / ἐπιχωρίοις.

23   Thomas Francis Scanlon, *Eros and Greek Athletics*, New York: Oxford University Press, 2002.

a larger-scale ecology, that larger ecology tends to strip it of its specific content (which would in any event generally be unintelligible to the larger audience), allowing it to operate as an empty signifier of locality, understood principally as an alternative to the larger system, rather than as generative of meaning on its own.

This understanding of the epichoric as inherently in opposition to a larger-scale system (in the ancient Greek case, the Panhellenic) persists in modern scholarship. The term "epichoric" seems first to have been used in discussions of local alphabets, described as epichoric in contrast with the alphabet that would eventually become standard in the Greek world; in the case of Greek scripts, it should be noted, the canonical understanding is that the alphabet was originally borrowed from the Phoenicians, then underwent local variations, before eventually merging back into the Panhellenic form of the alphabet.[24] From consideration of scripts, the term "epichoric" has been transferred to discussions of history (following the ancient practice of referring to polis-based historians as *hoi ephikhôrioi*)[25] and (most importantly for our purposes) to myth. Crucial here to an understanding of the epichoric as a modality in Greek myth, ritual and literature has been the work of Gregory Nagy. Perhaps most important for our purposes in Nagy's work on the epichoric is that he does not identify the epichoric with the polis per se:

> In these patterns of differentiation, it is clear that the concept of *local* in the opposition of *local* and *Panhellenic* is not to be equated with the concept of the polis itself. The polis is local only insofar as it absorbs the endoskeletal aspects of the tribe; but it is also Panhellenic in that it promotes the exoskeletal aspects. The ideology of the polis is not exclusively local, or epichoric: it is simultaneously Panhellenic. Thus whenever the chorus, as representative of the polis, speaks about things epichoric, it does so with a Panhellenic point of view.[26]

For Nagy, then, the polis is less the locus of epichoric cultural production than the matrix through which the epichoric and the Panhellenic are integrated. The epichoric is to be understood as both a product of smaller

---

24   See, e.g., R. Carpenter, "The Antiquity of the Greek Alphabet," *American Journal of Archaeology* 37 (1), 1933: 8; R. M. Cook and A. G. Woodhead, "The Diffusion of the Greek Alphabet," *American Journal of Archaeology*: 175–8, 1959.

25   T. J. Figueira, *Excursions in Epichoric History: Aiginetan Essays*, Rowman & Littlefield Pub Incorporated, 1993.

26   Nagy, *Pindar's Homer*, 145.

geographic scale (local communities within the polis) and also, perhaps, of a chronologically prior era. The lyric poets so often associated with the polis, such as Solon in Athens, Alcman in Sparta, Sappho and Alcaeus on Lesbos, or Theognis in Megara (and a fortiori poets who themselves circulated between poleis, such as Pindar and Bacchylides), are for Nagy figures whose works mediate between local tradition and Panhellenic tradition and who, moreover, do so through a Panhellenic lens. Important here is the fact that most Archaic Greek lyric is composed in a dialect determined not by the polis in which it first circulated but by the genre in which it was composed,[27] even as much of the poetry composed for inscriptional purposes was composed in local dialects or in a hybrid of local dialect and the artificial language of Panhellenic epic.[28] In a pattern we shall see repeated many times in this chapter, the epichoric as we have access to it is always already mediated through something else, even when it takes on something more than a generic quality.

The Epichoric and the Oral

Part of our construction of the local as primitive is a strong association between local culture and orality. This is not without foundation. Understood as a technology, writing involves considerable sunk costs (the labor required to develop a written language as well as that required to master reading and writing it) as well as potentially high variable costs (especially in the pre-modern world, where both the materials used to reproduce written texts and the labor required for that reproduction were generally quite costly). As such, the advantages conferred by the written circulation of verbal art (such as greater textual consistency and durability), argue for an economy of scale, in which the sunk costs can be spread over as wide a population as possible in both spatial and temporal terms. Oral transmission has high sunk costs of its own (in particular, the extensive training needed to perform many forms of oral verbal art) but has the

27   Stephen Colvin, "The Greek Koine and the Logic of a Standard Language," in *Standard Languages and Language Standards: Greek, Past and Present*, edited by Alexandra Georgakopoulou and M. S. Silk, Farnham, Surrey, England: Ashgate Publishing, Ltd., 2009, 35.

28   Catherine Trümpy, "Observations on the dedicatory and sepulchral epigrams, and their early history," in *Archaic and Classical Greek Epigram*, edited by Manuel Baumbach, Andrej Petrovic, and Ivana Petrovic, Cambridge: Cambridge University Press, 2011, 167–80.

potential to be enjoyed readily by any individual who knows the language in question. Both the question of training performers and that of audience familiarity with a language reinforce the advantages of a local audience for oral production. In a society without the printing press (or cheap paper), the optimal strategies for the survival of verbal art would thus probably be to transmit orally anything primarily local in audience (and thus exceptionally expensive to transmit in writing), saving written transmission only for those works able to circulate on a larger scale, as can be the case with panchoric, cosmopolitan, and vernacular circulations. This is not to say that writing cannot be a part of epichoric traditions, especially when those are expressed in a linguistic form close to that used in writing on a larger scale and especially for practical purposes, such as the transcription of laws, for which the permanence of writing might be thought to have special value.[29] There is further evidence from the very early beginnings of dedicatory and sepulchral epigrams, in the eighth century BC, which already from the earliest examples we know bear the traces of participation in a Panhellenic tradition.[30] Writing is thus not wholly alien to the Archaic Greek epichoric culture of verbal art, even if many significant genres (especially epic and lyric) were produced and circulated orally.

THE EPICHORIC AS LIMIT CASE AND AS MODE OF READING

If no man is an island, it is all the more true (as we have seen) that no culture is an island. Indeed, it might be argued that the very notion of a "culture" implies some form of boundedness and thus some interaction with an Other that is somehow outside that particular culture. No culture that we know about has existed purely in isolation from other cultures and has developed its own traditions of verbal art without at least some influence from the mythemes, plots, diction and poetics of their neighbors. Moreover, if such a culture were actually to exist, or to have once existed (the Sentinelese would be an obvious candidate here), then nonmembers of that culture could only come to know something about that verbal art once the isolation of that culture had been ruptured—and, as I have suggested with reference to the Sentinelese, it is difficult to imagine how such a

---

29   See, e.g., the discussion on the use of writing for archaic Greek laws at Rosalind Thomas, *Literacy and Orality in Ancient Greece*, Cambridge: Cambridge University Press, 1992, 71.

30   Trümpy, "Observations on the dedicatory and sepulchral epigrams."

moment of rupture could fail to find expression in cultural products such as verbal art, if only perhaps through the disappearance of older forms no longer relevant to a radically changed world.[31]

In addition, prior to the twentieth century, when audio and video recording led to a substantial transformation of the possibilities for circulation for nonliterate works of verbal art, the broader circulation of epichoric culture was likely to require the use of writing, whether through the development of a method for writing a previously unwritten language or through the medium of translation into another, already written, language. Both of these options involve considerable challenges. Examples of translation in the pre-modern world are relatively rare, especially from a less central source language to a more central target language[32] and especially when the source language does not itself have a written literature. As for the development of writing for a previously unwritten language, this typically takes place in reaction to an existing use of writing in a cosmopolitan or other large-scale language, leading to what I would describe as a vernacular, rather than an epichoric, literature, and in any event the very decision to commit verbal art in a given language to writing almost certainly implies significant shifts in how that verbal art is produced and consumed. Even if we assume that a "true" epichoric exists, therefore, we (necessarily outsiders as individuals reading and writing in the English language in the twenty-first century) can have no access to that epichoric culture without both the culture itself, and its products, being transformed in the process.

That being so, to the extent that the epichoric *as such* exists, it exists as a mode of reading adopted in more complex literary ecologies. The Sentinelese critic of her own verbal art culture will not interpret that culture as "local," a conception that inherently requires something larger to which the local can be compared; only an audience already engaged in that larger cultural context can return to the local and interpret it as such. The question, then, turns to what work is performed within a complex literary ecology by reading locally. As I have argued elsewhere[33] and will argue in more detail in the following chapter, there is a real sense in which the epichoric, even in its

---

31   Elvira Pulitano, *Toward a Native American Critical Theory*, Lincoln: University of Nebraska Press, 2003, 59–100 for a discussion of the controversial theoretical implications of this phenomenon within Native American studies.

32   I discuss a significant exception at the beginning of Chapter 4, Ch'oe Haenggwi's translation into classical Chinese of the monk Kyunyŏ's Korean-language poetry.

33   Beecroft, *Authorship and Cultural Identity*, 161–3.

eponymous context in Archaic Greece, exists principally as the generic product of a panchoric system. Audiences for lyric poetry may choose to experience a given work either as epichoric, taking the poem as an emplaced form of knowledge, or as Panhellenic, integrating it within the mythical and cultural system of the Greek world. A specific local audience may be able to emplace the poem with considerable precision, if it makes concrete reference to places or myths of a profoundly local nature. Other audiences, removed from earlier sites of composition or performance, may nonetheless consume the same poem as generically "local," as possessing the property of locality without being localized (or perhaps even localizable) to a specific place.

An integral part of our understanding of the notion of the local in verbal art is a sense of emplacement, of a verbal art that links its creators to the landscape in which they dwell. Texts circulating in larger and more complex ways, of course, are also frequently emplaced: Virgil's *Aeneid*, for instance, takes great pains to map the journeys of its hero within the confines of the Mediterranean world as it was known. Aeneas's entry to the underworld is not, as with Odysseus, at some unknown location at the ends of the earth but at Cumae, near Naples in southern Italy. Likewise, when Aeneas strolls around the village ruled by the Arcadian king Evander, his steps take him through what will become the Roman Forum and the various hills of the city. Still later, Balzac and Dickens will take their readers on painstakingly accurate journeys around Paris and London, as Salman Rushdie will take his readers around the Bombay of his childhood.

When we read verbal art as epichoric, however, we tend to have a rather different kind of literary emplacement in mind. We expect epichoric verbal art not merely to enumerate the spaces through which its creators and audience move but to constitute them as place and further to construct the defining sense of place for their communities. Exemplary in this regard would be the *kungax* tradition of the Wet'suwet'en people of northern British Columbia in Canada.[34] Kungax, or "own song," as it is glossed by anthropologist Antonia Curtze Mills, is derived from the Wet'suwet'en word *kun*, meaning both "song" and "spirit power." The term kungax, then,

---

34   For an overview of Wet'suwet'en culture, see both Richard Daly, *Our Box Was Full: An Ethnography for the Delgamuukw Plaintiffs*, Vancouver: University of British Columbia Press, 2005; Antonia Curtze Mills, *Eagle Down is Our Law: Witsuwit'en Law, Feasts, and Land Claims*, Vancouver: University of British Columbia Press, 1994.

refers to the complex of song, oral narrative, inherited personal crests, associated with particular clans within the Wet'suwet'en people.[35] This complex of traditional cultural materials then indicates both the origins and genealogy of the clan, and, through that historical narrative, traces the territories associated with the clan.[36] While Wet'suwet'en kungax represents the nation as indigenous to its current territories, many of the feast names and crests are imported from neighboring communities, such as those of the Gitksan, the Carrier, and the Nisga'a. As Mills reports:

> Such crests were, and are, enacted in the feasts without it being necessary to recite a kungax which explained their origin. This is because the acting out is, in itself, a kungax in the Witsuwit'en language and tradition. What the adaawa are for the Gitksan, the songs are for the Witsuwit'en. As the Witsuwit'en follow the trails to their territories, so they seek to capture the songs that go with their titles to these territories – they erupt in song from their deepest visionary travels to the spirit territories of the animals, the salmon, and the sky. The power of hereditary titles and crests is continually renewed for the Witsuwit'en by the highly personal and individual experience of being captured by song.[37]

Although Mills is here speaking about one very specific indigenous culture in Canada, the homology she describes between song, people, and place, is paradigmatic of the epichoric notion of emplacement. Examples can be found in abundance within the anthropological literature, such as Deborah Bird Rose's discussion of *kuning*, or Dreaming, which links the paternal ancestors of an individual to totemic animals and to specific territory, or Country, among the Yarralin people of the Northern Territory of Australia.[38] What makes the Wet'suwet'en (and their neighbors the Gitksan) unique in this respect is that these epichoric narratives of emplacement are among the first to achieve a formal recognition in a European-derived legal system, thanks to the landmark Supreme Court of Canada ruling in *Delgamuukw v. British Columbia* (1997). This case, alongside the earlier *R. v. Van Der Peet* (1996), which concerned the fishing rights of the Stó:lō nation of the Fraser valley in southern British Columbia, established under Canadian law that

---

35   Mills, *Eagle Down is Our Law*, 121.
36   Ibid., 75ff.
37   Ibid., 127.
38   Deborah Bird Rose, *Dingo Makes Us Human: Life and Land in an Australian Aboriginal Culture*, Cambridge; New York: Cambridge University Press, 2000, 85–7.

the oral traditions of First Nations could be treated as evidence, even if they did not meet the standards of evidence in other kinds of cases. As the court said in *R. v. Van Der Peet*:

> A court should approach the rules of evidence, and interpret the evidence that exists, conscious of the special nature of aboriginal claims, and of the evidentiary difficulties in proving a right which originates in times where there were no written records of the practices, customs and traditions and customs engaged in. The courts must not undervalue the evidence presented by aboriginal claimants simply because that evidence does not conform precisely with the evidentiary standards applied in other contexts.[39]

In their ruling in *Delgamuukw v. British Columbia*, the Supreme Court of Canada went further, censuring the trial judge in the original case (a land claims suit brought by Delgamuukw, the head of one of the Gitksan houses, and by all the Gitksan and Wet'suwet'en houses generally) for not having accepted the *kungax* of the Wet'suwet'en and the *adaawa* of the Gitksan as evidence of aboriginal title.[40] As such, the verbal art of these two nations (and potentially that of many others) gained a new role as it were, becoming a viable basis for claims to territory under Canadian law. The epichoric could now be re-performed in a new context, where new audiences would give it new meanings.

In advocating for the status of these traditions as indicative of land title, Antonia Curtze Mills drew an explicit parallel between the kungax of the Wet'suwet'en and Homeric epic, suggesting that just as the *Iliad* had inspired Heinrich Schliemann's excavations at Troy and Mycenae, and had, in the process, been shown to contain some kernel of historical truth; so, too, should the kungax be seen as a legitimate source of historical tradition, accurately preserving genealogical and historical information in the midst of other content that modern Europe-oriented readers would consider mythological.[41] This comparison is a telling one, not only for the fact that the ancient Greek past is here identified as a source of legitimation for a modern Canadian audience, but also for the implicit parallel Mills draws

---

39   *R. v. Van der Peet* [1996] 2 S.C.R. 507
40   *Delgamuukw v. British Columbia* [1997] 3 S.C.R. 1010
41   Mills, *Eagle Down is Our Law*, 74–5. I leave to the side here the thorny question of the relationship of the archaeological record at Troy to the narrative of Homeric epic.

between the culture of Archaic Greece and that of the Wet'suwet'en. Despite obvious differences, the parallels between the two are indeed instructive; both are cultural contexts in which nonliterate people were able to organize historical, territorial, and genealogical knowledge through a system of orally performed verbal art that linked an assemblage of communities. As with Archaic Greece, we can see with the Wet'suwet'en that it is impossible to speak of epichoric narratives in isolation from each other; just as the epichoric myths and rituals of a specific Greek polis are always-already integrated in some way into a Panhellenic system of such myths and rituals, so too are the Wet'suwet'en linked to the neighboring Gitksan, Carrier, Nisga'a, and others (all of whom speak essentially unrelated languages) through the borrowings of feast-names and the interlacing of narratives. Even before the reimagining of kungax as legal evidence in Canadian courts of law, the tradition was always inherently trans- and inter-cultural, mapping and narrating relations between distinct peoples.

Epichoric, "Folk Society," and Gemeinschaft

In thus expanding my use of the epichoric ecology beyond the world of archaic and classical Greece (and equivalent periods in China), I am at once inspired by, and draw caution from, a series of related concepts in the social sciences, most notably Ferdinand Tönnies's notion of *Gemeinschaft* (or community) as opposed to *Gesellschaft* (or civil society), and Robert Redfield's notion of "folk society." Tönnies's distinction between Gemeinschaft and Gesellschaft, dating originally from the late nineteenth century, continues to have a considerable influence on our unthinking assumptions about the differences between small-scale and large-scale societies, even as generations of sociologists and anthropologists have called into question the usefulness of the model and even though Tönnies himself (like Redfield after him) saw his opposition as between normal types rather than actually existing communities. For Tönnies, the idealized Gemeinschaft is a small-scale society whose structure is modeled on that of the family, mapped onto the community as a whole through structures such as the clan or tribe. Gemeinschaft implies both a measure of economic self-sufficiency and a high level of fellow-feeling, together with a stable and homogeneous culture.[42] All of this is, of course, contrasted with its other,

---

42   Ferdinand Tönnies, *Community and Civil Society*, Cambridge Texts in the History of Political Thought, Cambridge: Cambridge University Press, 2001, 22–51.

modern civil society or Gesellschaft, which emphasizes the essential autonomy of individuals and subgroups, bound together not by kinship-like ties of loyalty and shared values but through legal and contractual obligations. In all of this, there is, of course, more than a whiff of nostalgia for Gemeinschaft (whether or not it exists, or has ever existed, in its pure form), as the simpler, more natural, and therefore more enduring, model for social relations.[43] Tönnies's discussion of the culture of Gemeinschaft societies itself bears a family resemblance to the assumptions we tend to bring to discussions of the epichoric:

> Whatever its empirical origins, its existence must be viewed as a totality, together with the individual associations and families that belong to it and are dependent on it. With its language, its customs, its beliefs, as well as its land, buildings and treasures, it forms a permanent entity that outlives the changes of many generations. Due partly to its own resources, partly to the inheritance and education of its citizens, it goes on reproducing basically the same character and mental outlook. If it can secure its food and raw materials from its own possessions and those of its citizens, or by regular supplies from the surrounding area, it can then devote all its energies to the higher activities of brain and hand, giving *harmonious* form to things and making them generally pleasing to everyone's mind and senses, which is the very essence of *art* . . .
>
> Strict attention is given to pleasing combinations of speech, movements and actions, to everything that contains rhythm and harmony and suits the peaceful mood of those attending the ceremony, as though they had created it themselves. All that is jarring, lacking in restraint, or contrary to tradition is abhorred and rejected.[44]

The culture of Gemeinschaft, then, is stable and self-reproducing, harmonious and pleasing. It instinctively rejects anything contrary to tradition, and therefore by implication outside influences. It shapes, and is shaped by, the daily lives of the people; one might go so far as to suggest that the art of

---

43   J. Christopher Brown and Mark Purcell, "There's Nothing Inherent about Scale: Political Ecology, the Local Trap, and the Politics of Development in the Brazilian Amazon," *Geoforum* 36 (5), 2005: 607–24, 608 describe a comparable phenomenon in political ecology, a "'local trap' that leads researchers to assume that the key to environmental sustainability, social justice, and democracy (commonly desired outcomes among political ecologists) is devolution of power to local-scale actors and organizations."

44   Tönnies, *Community and Civil Society*, 48–9.

Gemeinschaft is inseparable from daily life, forming with it a seamless and organic whole.

Likewise, the American anthropologist Robert Redfield understood human culture in terms of a related binary of ideal types, folk culture and urban culture. Redfield's discussion of folk culture contains a number of tropes key to our understanding of the epichoric:

> This society is, as Sumner put it, composed of "small groups scattered over a territory." The population of any one group is homogeneous in that in race and custom any individual is much like any other. The group is isolated from others. The technology is simple. The community approaches economic self-sufficiency. The division of labor is simple; activities appropriate to the sexes are sharply distinguished, but activities carried on by any one member of a sex-and-age group are much the same as those carried on by others of that group. There is little or no use of writing, or if writing is used it is a mere adjunct to oral tradition and, like the latter, serves to conserve the local heritage. The habits of members of the society tend to correspond with customs. The society is relatively integrated in that the component groups are closely interdependent and the ways of life are correspondingly interrelated and consistent with one another. Change in the society is slow. The prevailing forms of control are informal and traditional, and control to the members of the society appears in large degree spontaneous. The intimate and primary institutions, such as the family and the local group, play relatively large parts in that organization of the groups and institutions which make up the society. Many objects, conceptions, and forms of control partake of those qualities of unquestionable power and prestige which we denote as "sacred."[45]

Particularly significant here for our purposes are the alignment of a series of terms in an imagined binary: local (vs. large-scale); traditional (vs. innovative); oral (vs. written); sacred (vs. secular); homogeneous (vs. heterogeneous). For Redfield, of course, each of these terms finds its opposite in urban culture (and, again, both folk and urban culture are for Redfield ideal types rather than Procrustean beds on which living cultures are stretched or chopped). Quick reflection will show that our contemporary and unthinking understanding of what I am calling epichoric culture inherits a great deal from Redfield and from Tönnies. There is much of value in both Gemeinschaft and in folk culture as theoretical constructions with which to measure the

---

45   Robert Redfield, "The Folk Society and Culture," *American Journal of Sociology* 45 (5), 1940: 731–42, 737.

world, especially if we accept that these terms are in many ways vehicles for imposing (and thus testing the limits of) our preconceptions about the world of human culture outside the modern West.

And yet we must be cautious in assuming a too-easy equivalence among these terms. Even the brief discussion of Archaic Greece earlier should serve as a cautionary tale. There is no doubt that most (or all) of the life and meaning of verbal art in an Archaic Greek polis took place in oral performance, not in writing and reading, but as the discussion of epichoric alphabets reminds us, we also know that writing formed a part of epichoric culture from a very early stage. Likewise, while our fantasies of the epichoric tend to assume the chronological priority of the epichoric over the panchoric or other larger-scale formation, the history of the Greek alphabet likewise shows that sometimes cultural formations begin on a large scale and are then subjected to adaptive variation on the local level. What is definitely true for Greek scripts may also be true for Greek myth, as Christiane Sourvinou-Inwood and others have argued. Given that the earliest literary evidence we have for Greek myth is already enmeshed within a series of Panhellenic narratives, we cannot assume that the origins of Greek myth are entirely epichoric, and that the Panhellenic represents merely a weaving-together of prior epichoric materials. More likely, even in the earliest cultural phases of which we have awareness, there is a process of mutual exchange between larger-scale and smaller-scale circulations of myths, themes, figures, and texts. As a consequence, where we know of alternative versions of mythic narratives (as in the case, discussed by Andrew Alwine, of the version of the Cyclops tale in the *Odyssey* where Odysseus abducts the Cyclops's daughter), we should not rush to assume that what we are encountering is an epichoric tradition suppressed by the Panhellenic; we might, instead, have a rival Panhellenic tradition, rooted to no particular place, ultimately deleted from Panhellenic epic narrative for reasons other than its epichoric specificity.[46] The purely epichoric Greek culture, uncontaminated by Panhellenizing influences, may need to join the uncontacted tribe, the folk culture, and Gemeinschaft on the heap of zero-grade models of culture that are more useful as intellectualized abstractions about the limits of cultural simplification than as concrete models for understanding actual cultural contexts.

It is, then, precisely as a "zero-grade" form of literary circulation that I

---

46   A. T. Alwine, "The Non-Homeric Cyclops in the Homeric Odyssey," *Greek, Roman, and Byzantine Studies* 49 (3), 2009: 323–33.

find the epichoric ecology most useful. I borrow the term (used also by Roland Barthes in the title of his *Le degré zéro de l'écriture*), from Indo-European linguistics, and the famous (in that context, at least) phenomenon of *ablaut*, in which a given root is inflected in three different forms, into each of which is inserted a characteristic vowel: an e-grade (where the vowel of the root is "e"), an o-grade, and a zero-grade, in which no vowel is added at all. Many strong verbs in English exhibit this phenomenon among their principal parts, as with *sing* (which is how the e-grade evolved over time); *sang* (o-grade); *sung* (zero-grade). The zero-grade thus represents something of a limit case, a basic form without further additions or complications, which can be opposed not merely to a single more complex form but to a range of complex forms. Where, therefore, Tönnies and Redfield and I all construct some kind of model of local culture as an extreme and limit case, Tönnies and Redfield explicitly imagine their ideal or normal types of culture as the limit case of a polarity (Gemeinschaft vs. Gesellschaft; folk culture vs. urban culture), where I understand the epichoric literary ecology as a zero-grade, not merely in opposition to the notion of literary circulation but rather as one possibility in a series of models of literary circulation—the model in which there is no circulation at all. As with global literary ecology (which I turn to in the final chapter), I believe the epichoric does not really correspond to any culture of verbal art of which I am aware. Rather, it represents the hypothetical possibility of such a culture existing in a vacuum, all but impossible both in theory and in practice and yet useful as a way of understanding how certain kinds of texts have been experienced in practice.

The epichoric, then, provides the first, and clearest, demonstration of why my literary ecologies are primarily models of how texts are consumed, rather than of how they are produced. If (as this chapter explores, however briefly) Archaic Greek lyric, the Chinese *Songs of Chu*, and even the kungax tradition of the Wet'suwet'en nation of British Columbia cannot be understood as produced within a simply epichoric context, there are practices of reading that make this possible. If a poem of Alcman, celebrating the martial prowess of Spartan soldiers or the beauty of young Spartan women, is performed in the context of a regularly recurring Spartan ritual, that poem acquires much of its meaning through the details of that performance and through the interactions of performers, audience, and place; in that sense, the text is interpreted as a work of epichoric literary culture. If that same poem is performed at a symposium, in Sparta or elsewhere, alongside songs by Alcaeus, Solon, Theognis, or others, it may instead be understood as a work of Panhellenic culture, part of a system of lyric poems sung and appreciated wherever Greek is known, and perhaps stripped for that purpose of its more specifically Spartan emplacement. Read by a scholar of Hellenistic Alexandria in the third century BC (or, differently, by a scholar in the United States in the twenty-first century AD), it can function in either way, as an embodiment of Spartan or of Panhellenic cultural values, as a text deeply emplaced in its local environment or as a text read and appreciated across the Hellenic world. It seems likely, as Nagy would argue, that archaic lyric was produced in a cultural context in which both the epichoric and the Panhellenic were resonant. Its various audiences and readers will have understood it in either, or both, ways as well, depending on the cultural context in which they received it and depending also on the filiations they establish for it, whether with other texts and cultural artifacts from Sparta or with other poems of its kind from across the Greek world. Even in the very different cultural context of the Wet'suwet'en, it is clear that a given text or cultural artifact can be understood in both an epichoric sense (as recounting the origins and emplacement of a clan) and in a larger-scale sense (as representing the relationships between the Wet'suwet'en and their neighbors). As we turn to the next chapter, these somewhat larger-scale circulations and practices of reading will be our focus.

2

Panchoric Literature

In the second month of the year, [the ruler] would go on a royal inspection tour in the east, reaching as far as Mount Tai. He burned brushwood [in sacrifice] and gazed toward and sacrificed to the mountains and streams. He gave audience to the gathered lords, and, asking after the centenarians, visited them. He commanded the Grand Official to present poems, so that he might see the customs of the people. He commanded that the market present merchants, so that he might see what the people liked and disliked. (*Record of Rites*, "The Royal Regulations.")[1]

[Homer] went around the cities singing his poems. Later Peisistratus gathered them up, as the following epigram makes clear:

> Thrice tyrant, and as often banished,
> The Erecthean people thrice again brought back;
> Peisistratus, mighty in counsel, who assembled
> Homer, sung before in scattered form.
> He was our golden citizen,
> If ever the Athenians did found Smyrna.
> (*Lives of Homer*, 4.8–16)[2]

These two passages narrate in compressed form key myths about the assembly of panchoric texts out of local materials in early Greece and China.[3] The Chinese citation is from a text called the *Record of Rites* (*Li Ji*, 禮記),

---

1　歲二月，東巡守至于岱宗，柴而望祀山川；觀諸侯；問百年者就見之。命大師陳詩以觀民風，命市納賈以觀民之所好惡. 禮記. 王制 (p. 226)

2　περιιὼν δὲ τὰς πόλεις ἧδε τὰ ποιήματα. ὕστερον δὲ Πεισίστρατος αὐτὰ συνήγαγεν, ὡς τὸ ἐπίγραμμα τοῦτο δηλοῖ•

τρίς με τυραννήσαντα τοσαυτάκις ἐξεδίωξε /δῆμος Ἐρεχθῆος καὶ τρὶς ἐπηγάγετο, / τὸν μέγαν ἐν βουλαῖς Πεισίστρατον ὃς τὸν Ὅμηρον / ἤθροισα σποράδην τὸ πρὶν ἀειδόμενον / ἡμέτερος γὰρ κεῖνος ὁ χρύσεος ἦν πολιήτης / εἴπερ Ἀθηναῖοι Σμύρναν ἐπῳκίσαμεν.

3　For further discussion of these two passages, see Alexander Beecroft, *Authorship and Cultural Identity in Early Greece and China: Patterns of Literary Circulation*, Cambridge: Cambridge University Press, 2010.

which claims to be a compendium of ritual practices edited by Confucius; it purports to describe the annual ritual activities of the early kings of the Western Zhou Dynasty (eleventh–eighth centuries BC), which would include sacrifices to local deities, as well as investigations of the practices of local merchants. In addition, as this passage relates, the king was said to ask officials to collect poems sung by the local populace in order to gauge their mood; texts related in the tradition tell us that this process involved not merely the content of the songs but also their music, since happy people sing harmonious songs, and unhappy people disharmonious songs. Further, it is suggested that the songs collected in this way were themselves eventually edited by Confucius, who chose among the three thousand songs available to him the three hundred he thought most suitable; the collection he is said to have edited is that known to later eras as the *Canon of Songs*, or *Shi Jing* (詩經).

The Greek text, taken from one of the *Lives of Homer*, tells us an analogous tale about the recension of Greek epic under the Athenian tyrant Peisistratus (ruled 546–527 BC). According to fuller versions of this narrative, Homer travelled from town to town, singing part of the *Iliad* here, a section of the *Odyssey* there (or, in some more text-based versions, writing a book here and a book there). These fragments of heroic epic remained in isolation for centuries, until the benevolent interest of Peisistratus, who gathered the scattered remains of epic and assembled them in the correct order to produce the poems we know today, in a narrative likely connected with the Panathenaic festival, an annual event established by Peisistratus at which Homeric epic was recited and which represents one of the earliest moments at which we have clear evidence that our poems existed in something like their final form.

These two stories clearly have a great deal in common; royal heroes who create, for *raisons d'état*, a coherent whole out of an inchoate mass of folk poetry. Both stories, too, clearly act as allegories for, or literalizations of, some sort of imagined historical process by which local traditions were gradually assimilated to an emergent Panhellenic (or, in the Chinese case, what I would call Panhuaxia) culture. Both, too, are later fabrications; we cannot be certain that the *Li Ji* passage dates from even the Western Han (206 BC–8 AD), nor do we have any text dating to before the fourth century BC in which any of the songs in the *Canon of Songs* are associated with specific localities. It is highly unlikely that any ruler of the Western Zhou ever collected folk poetry in the manner suggested here (and the rulers of this period likely had little more than a ritual or symbolic primacy over other rulers), and there is not, in fact, any evidence that Confucius played any role in editing the *Canon of Songs*.[4] Likewise, the life of Homer from which this anecdote is drawn is found in an eleventh century AD manuscript of the *Iliad*, although it is clearly earlier in date and makes use of still earlier material of unknown provenance. A variant informs us that the epigram is written on a statue of Peisistratus in Athens, although we have no independent corroboration for the existence of the statue or the epigram. The anecdote may well reflect an ancient tradition, but we cannot say how ancient, still less identify its origins.

The piety of these later fictions of compilation is matched by the artlessness they assume on the part of the compiler, who has little more to do than to stitch together the fragments he gathers with a good eye for the narrative sequence (in the case of Peisistratus) and for the appropriateness of his selections (in the case of Confucius). The wholes that these men create are essentially equal to the sums of their parts. The actual historical processes at work were no doubt rather different. The songs of the *Canon of Songs* may not so much have been drawn from regional states as assigned to them at a later date after several centuries of independent circulation, and Homeric epic may not have been compiled out of shorter units of narrative so much as out of competing versions of the same longer narrative, and in each case, as I will argue, the act of compilation creates a whole that is not only greater than the sum of its parts but in fact a radically distinct entity. Panchoric culture, in other words, may present itself as the artless compilation of epichoric materials, but in practice it creates entirely new cultural artifacts that frequently all but obliterate the traces of what went before. What gets understood as "local" in the presence of a panchoric culture is often a fiction of the local, a generic element in a set rather than a genuinely autonomous tradition. As we shall see in the final chapter, this bears some similarity to what some scholars identify as the generic use of "local color" in the contemporary global novel, providing a pleasing ambience for a plot that could take place anywhere.[5]

Furthermore, recent scholarship has challenged easy traditional assumptions about the emergence of both "Greek" and "Chinese" (both

---

4   For example, the historical text the *Zuozhuan*, thought to date to the late fourth century BC, and in any event describing events after the death of Confucius, cites songs inside and outside our *Canon of Songs* using the same language, implying that it makes no distinction between them.

5   Vittorio Coletti, *Romanzo mondo. La letteratura nel villaggio globale*, Bologna: Il Mulino, 2011.

terms are anachronisms here) identity in the first half of the first millennium BC. The Ruist, or Confucian, narrative, which became orthodox in later imperial China, assumed that the prehistoric and protohistoric Xia and Shang Dynasties succeeded each other (and were followed by the Zhou) in orderly fashion as universal rulers and that the political disunity of the latter half of the Zhou Dynasty (the so-called Spring and Autumn [776–475 BC] and Warring States [475–256 BC] eras) was the exception rather than the rule during ancient times. While twentieth-century and contemporary archaeology has done much to confirm the historical record of the Shang and Zhou in terms of the succession of rulers, it has also demonstrated very clearly a lack of central control prior to the beginning of the Qin Dynasty in 256 BC, and it has even been suggested that the Xia, Shang, and Zhou, rather than being successive dynasties, were in fact different ethno-political communities who were in succession the most powerful of the regional states but who coexisted over a long period of time.[6] While considerable archaeological evidence attests to the familial links among the regional rulers of the Spring and Autumn Era and for very similar assemblages of ritual vessels (suggesting similar ritual practices, at least at elite levels), evidence for the emergence of a shared cultural identity is much more problematic. Certainly, by the Warring States era, there is strong evidence for an elite culture that crossed political boundaries and for a sense of ethnic identity as *Huaxia* 華夏, a term that gradually came to encompass most of the Yellow River basin and points south and east.[7] Since, however, as we saw in the previous chapter, most of our textual evidence comes from the latter part of this period and mostly reflects what I call "Panhuaxia" values, it is difficult to be certain at which point this sense of Huaxia cultural identity began to permeate more broadly. Those later texts project their Panhuaxia vision onto earlier periods, although tracing how they do so is complicated by two factors: that the texts themselves are aggregates accumulated over time and that they are constructing the very

---

6   Kwang-Chih Chang, "China on the Eve of the Historical Period," in *The Cambridge History of Ancient China: From the Origins of Civilization to 221 B.C.*, edited by Michael Loewe and Edward L. Shaughnessy, Cambridge: Cambridge University Press, 1999, 37–73.

7   See, e.g., Ming-ke Wang, "Western Zhou Remembering and Forgetting," *Journal of East Asian Archaeology* 1 (1–4), 1999: 231–50; Chun-shu Chang, *The Rise of the Chinese Empire: Nation, State, and Imperialism in Early China, ca. 1600 B.C.– A.D. 8*, Ann Arbor: University of Michigan Press, 2007.

vision of the "local" they claim to represent.[8] The Panhuaxia emerges gradually over time, coexists with other kinds of identity (regional and non-Chinese-speaking), and is most clearly understood as constructed by and for literary texts.

We may see something similar in the emergence of so-called Panhellenic identity in Greece. The term Panhellenic itself is first found at *Iliad* 2.530 in the so-called *Catalogue of the Ships*, where its use is geographically restricted, and the terms Achaean, Danaan, and Argive are used to describe the totality of the allies of Agamemnon. The earliest use of the term for something like the territory and population of the Greek world occurs in Hesiod, *Works and Days* 528, where the sun is said to shine in winter on darker men (i.e., on Africa) and not on the Panhellenes. In like manner, we find the poet Archilochus describing the colony of Thasos, founded by his homeland of Paros, as receiving the "cries of the *Panhellênoi*" (Πανελλήνων ὀϊζύς, fr. 120.1), a term that again seems to imply a broad geographic reach, though (as with Hesiod) not necessarily any very strong sense of cultural identity. Only with Pindar's *Paean* 6.62, commissioned by Delphi which speaks of sacrifices for "glorious Panhellas" (ἀγλαᾶς ὑπὲρ Πανελλάδος), do we encounter a version of the word "Panhellenic" that seems clearly to indicate something like a self-aware community of cultural practice.

Jonathan Hall and others have traced the expansion of the term Panhellenes, and Hellas itself (perhaps derived from Panhellene), from its original application to the Spercheios Valley of Thessaly in North-Central Greece to cover the larger community of speakers of Greek dialects and have linked this expansion to the increasing circle of *poleis* bound into the Amphictyony, the league that assumed significant responsibilities over the sacred area of Delphi, and to the increasing number of cities from which Olympic victors were drawn, over the course of the Archaic period and into the fifth century BC.[9] Panhellenism proper, in the sense of an ideology of shared identity explicitly opposed to non-Greek Others and making a claim surpassing that to the polis is a phenomenon that may have begun in the mid-fifth century in Athens in the aftermath of the Persian wars but that

---

8 See my *Authorship and Cultural Identity in Early Greece and China* for a fuller account of these phenomena. On the retrospective construction of the local, see also Chapter 1.

9 Jonathan M. Hall, *Hellenicity: Between Ethnicity and Culture*, Chicago: University of Chicago Press, 2002, 134ff.

reached its fullest flowering only with rhetoricians, such as Isocrates, active in the fourth century BC.[10]

Over the course of the Archaic and Classical periods, then, Hall and many others would argue that any notion of a Panhellenic "identity" is extremely problematic. Some, notably Michael Scott, have gone so far as to reject the use of the term altogether.[11] Clearly, there are things that the "Greeks," or at least shifting and expanding groups of them, share in this period—notably ritual connections through Delphi, Olympia, and a few other centers and a shared body of mythical narrative, parts of which take form in Homeric epic—but there are multiple other levels on which identity seems to operate. To take one example, a resident of Hyria, the first community mentioned in the *Catalogue of Ships* in the *Iliad*, may, in late Archaic or Classical times, have thought of himself or herself as a citizen of the polis of Hyria;[12] as a member of the ethnos of the Boeotians; as an Aeolian (a broader dialectal community also potentially referred to as an ethnos); and as a Hellene. Each of the larger identities is in some sense built out of the smaller ones—someone is a Boeotian because they live in a Boeotian polis, Aeolian because Boeotia is an Aeolic-speaking region, Hellenic because of membership in polis and ethnos. As Jonathan Hall has argued, this "aggregative" function essentially defines Hellenic identity, at least until the Persian Wars,[13] and in some senses afterwards, such that Hellenism is defined by membership in smaller units, rather than in opposition to other "ethnic" identities, be they Persian, Egyptian, Scythian, or anything else. An analogy to this Hellenic sense of nested identities might be sought in the modern world; in the way, for instance, that someone might identify as at once from the city of San Antonio, as a Texan, and an American, or for that matter a Pisan, Tuscan, Italian, and European. There

---

10   Ibid., 205–20.

11   Michael Scott, *Delphi and Olympia: The Spatial Politics of Panhellenism in the Archaic and Classical Periods*, Cambridge: Cambridge University Press, 2010, 272. While I accept Scott's argument that the term "Panhellenic" is made to cover far too many kinds of dissimilar practices and identities, especially in the archaeological context and that its continued usefulness should be questioned, I would like to suggest that the term has more value when it comes to literary texts such as Homeric epic, and particularly to readings of such texts.

12   Although the actual status of Hyria as a polis is uncertain. See Mogens Herman Hansen, and Thomas Heine Nielsen, *An Inventory of Archaic and Classical Poleis: An Investigation Conducted by The Copenhagen Polis Centre for the Danish National Research Foundation*, New York: Oxford University Press, 2005, 434.

13   Hall, *Hellenicity*, 164.

are, I would argue, significant differences. In the modern cases, the small-scale and large-scale identities can move more independently of each other; but more significantly, there is more variation in our times in the degree of affiliation at different scales. It is, today, not terribly difficult to imagine someone who feels a strong sense of loyalty to the nation-state, but little or no affiliation with smaller-scale units, something that would have been impossible in ancient Greece. Certainly, it would be inconceivable in our time to insist that loyalty to the city was constitutive of loyalty to a national or ethnic identity, yet in the Hellenic world such was very much the case— it was not possible to identify as Hellenic if one did not first identify with a polis and/or ethnos, and it was that more local identity, not the Panhellenic, that was fundamental.

As in Spring and Autumn and Warring-States China, then, evidence for panchoric identity is clearest in products of elite culture, notably in literary texts. Moreover, as I will argue, panchoric identity can express itself as much in modes of reading those texts as in the texts themselves. Some texts, such as Homeric epic, and the Chinese *Canon of Songs* when viewed as a collection, function as panchoric texts par excellence, as texts, in other words, that exist with the explicit aim of asserting a common identity across a politically fragmented world. Other texts, such as Pindaric epinician poetry and the poems of the *Canon of Songs*, when read individually, can function on both levels. A Pindaric victory ode is written for a specific local context (the victory at a Panhellenic athletic contest of a particular individual from a particular polis) and will have had an audience for whom that epichoric dimension was paramount, and likewise it is plausible (though far from certain) that at least some of the songs of the *Canon of Songs* may also have begun in a specific local context. At the same time, the fact that the Pindaric ode is performed in reaction to a Panhellenic event and that the poems themselves certainly soon circulated in other contexts, points to its inherently Panhellenic nature. In like manner, the fact that the earliest textual citations of songs from the *Canon of Songs* are found in a historical text (the *Zuozhuan*) in which they are frequently used in interstate negotiations between states other than that with which the poem is associated in the *Canon*, reminds us that the difference between an epichoric song and a Panhuaxia one lies entirely in the reading of it. As this chapter will argue, key panchoric texts like Homeric epic and the *Canon of Songs* aim not only to construct a panchoric culture but also to consolidate panchoric readings of the literary tradition as a whole through the use of key devices, such as genealogies, catalogues, and the anthology structure, as well as through the consolidation of a shared literary language, one which is in some measure removed from local particularities. On the surface, these devices work to assemble a shared culture out of parts gathered from epichoric traditions, but I will argue that the work they do is more complex; in addition to fitting local traditions together, these panchoric devices aim at obliterating the genuinely local and at replacing it with a panchoric consistency, where the local is replaced by the pseudo-local.

In thinking about panchoric literary practices, it is helpful to turn to the archaeological record, and particularly to the buildings and dedications set up in the great Panhellenic sanctuaries at Delphi and Olympia. As Michael Scott has recently argued, these two sites express Hellenic identities in quite different ways. The sanctuary at Delphi, which is located on a steep hillside and was only weakly influenced by the local polis of Delphi, permitted a wide variety of styles and media for the monuments and dedications set up by other city-states (such as the monumental sphinx erected by the island of Naxos around 570 BC),[14] many of which reflected aspects of local identity. In contrast, the larger site of Olympia, located on level ground, was more tightly controlled by its governing polis (usually Elis), which reserved for itself the privilege of erecting locally distinctive monuments and tended to restrict other city-states to stereotyped dedications, such as the ubiquitous military commemorative statues of Zeus found near the Bouleuterion of Olympia by the early fifth century.[15] Scott himself argues that these and other differences across time, space, and context cast doubt on the very notion of the Panhellenic as a distinctive cultural formation. Since, as with the other ecologies under discussion, I identify Panhellenism as a mode of reading texts, rather than necessarily a mode of production, I would argue that the concept of Panhellenic readings of texts remains useful, especially in the sense of a reading that operates against a backdrop of assumed cultural unity rather than insisting on the reality of that unity. Further, I would like to draw from Scott's analysis two distinct modes of Panhellenism, which we might call Delphic and Olympic: the former (which is the kind envisioned by the narrative of the Peisistratean recension) understanding Panhellenism as an aggregate of local traditions and practices and the latter as a distinctive homogenizing practice that transforms real difference into imagined unity. As I will argue in the remainder of the chapter, while panchoric reading practices can be and frequently are Delphic in this sense

---

14   Scott, *Delphi and Olympia*, 46.
15   Ibid., 173–5.

(as seen in the anecdotes that open the chapter), key panchoric texts, like Homeric epic and the *Canon of Songs* as a whole, are decidedly Olympian, using charter-myths and devices such as genealogies, catalogues, and the anthology structure as means of constructing narratives capable of obviating local tradition.

Importantly, I am not here claiming a chronological priority for either the local or the panchoric; indeed, the notion of the primordially local is (as we saw in the first chapter) as much a by-product of modern thinking as it is of panchoric rhetoric. Since the local can only circulate *as local* if it is incorporated into some larger ecology, we can in fact say that the epichoric and the panchoric are mutually constitutive. A panchoric reading presumes a selection from among epichoric alternatives, and an epichoric reading presumes the existence of a larger panchoric backdrop because without this context the epichoric would instead be interpreted, within its limited context, as universal. This mutual constitution of the epichoric and the panchoric is a reminder that, as we shall see throughout this book, literary ecologies are best seen as complementary rather than as succeeding one another in a preordained chronological sequence. Temporal change is as much a part of literary ecology as it is of the natural world, but, as with the natural world, the evolution of a literary ecology does not follow an entirely predictable path. In what follows, I examine some of these key panchoric devices (with examples drawn from the traditions I know best: Greece and China), and demonstrate the ways in which those devices construct distinctive cultural artifacts, even as they claim merely to aggregate existing elements.

CHARTER-MYTHS AND KEY PANCHORIC TEXTS

The Panhellenic and the Panhuaxia worlds are alike defined by charter myths, which in turn underlie the key literary works of each ecology: the Trojan War in the case of the former and the Zhou conquest of the Shang Dynasty for the latter. The ecological challenges each charter-myth faces are, as we shall see, rather different. The Trojan War is one of several possible Panhellenic mythical nodes, and it must in some sense compete for ecological space with the others in order to thrive. The Zhou conquest of the Shang, in contrast, is unrivalled as a touchstone of Panhuaxia sentiment (in part because most of the regional states were ruled by families derived from the Zhou ruling clan) but can convey very different values depending on how it is represented, becoming either an account of glorious triumph and savage revenge or of mercy in victory; while the latter eventually became the orthodox interpretation, the former is likely nearer the truth.

The centrality of the *Iliad* and the *Odyssey* to the Greek literary and cultural tradition is a familiar phenomenon; less frequently considered is the question of why this should be so. Certainly, the story of the Trojan War is a striking example of a Panhellenic myth, bringing together heroes from across the Greek world, but it is far from the only such myth. Martin West has suggested that there are in fact four major Panhellenic mythical narratives, each embedded within a regional cluster of myths:[16]

1. The story of Jason and the Argonauts, part of a cycle of myths tied to the royal family of the city of Iolkos, in Thessaly, in the north-central region of modern Greece,

2. The story of the Calydonian boar hunt, which is linked to other myths involving Aetolia, Elis, and Pylos, all on the western edges of modern Greece,

3. The so-called Theban cycle, focused on Oedipus and the quarrel between his sons, known as the Seven Against Thebes, and the next-generation replay of this conflict, whose combatants are known as the *Epigonoi*, or offspring,

4. The Trojan cycle, relating events beginning with the abduction of Helen, the buildup to the war, the war itself, and then the homecomings of the various heroes.

Each of these cycles, in other words, was a potential candidate for the role of key Panhellenic integrating narrative and charter myth. What factors, then, led the Trojan cycle to take on this role? Further to this point, why, given the choice of the Trojan cycle, did the *Iliad* and the *Odyssey* become the chief representatives of that cycle, despite the fact that their narratives each cover so little of the combined mythic territory of the cycle—about

---

16   Martin L. West, *The Hesiodic Catalogue of Women: Its Nature, Structure, and Origins*, Oxford; New York; Clarendon; Oxford University Press, 1985, 137. The issue here is less with the precise arrangement of the mythical material, which is open to multiple interpretations, but rather with the more general evidence for multiple strands of Panhellenic myth.

seven weeks in the tenth year of the war in the case of the *Iliad*, the home-coming of one hero alone, Odysseus, in the case of the Odyssey? To be sure, and as I will demonstrate further later, each of our Homeric epics finds ways to incorporate mention of other events from the Trojan cycle and, for that matter, finds ways to allude to the other mythic cycles as well. The fact remains that the core of the Panhellenic tradition as it evolves rests around a strikingly small percentage of the available material. Nor was this choice constant throughout Greek history; the other poems in the Trojan cycle remained in some form of circulation throughout the classical period and beyond.[17] Visual representations of myth, ranging from vases to the sculptural friezes adorning temples, show a strikingly catholic taste in Panhellenic myth; as Jonathan Burgess has shown, while representations of the Trojan War generally are quite common in Archaic times, there is little evidence for representations of specifically Iliadic scenes until the late seventh century or even afterwards.[18] Likewise, the tragedians represent a wide variety of mythical narratives in their plays, drawn from each of these four cycles and beyond, but comparatively few of their plays draw directly on the plots of the *Iliad* and *Odyssey*.

Why the Trojan War (and then the *Iliad* and the *Odyssey*) were eventually to assume such prominence is, of course, a question on which we can only speculate. Each of the four great complexes of myth—the Argonauts, the Calydonian Boar Hunt, and the Theban and Trojan cycles—brings together a large number of heroes from across the Greek world; each, in fact, draws on a number of the same heroes, or at least their fathers or sons or brothers. Each cluster of myths thus provides a mechanism for linking local heroes together into a larger narrative structure. The Trojan War does, however, arguably possess certain advantages over its rival mythic traditions as a paramount Panhellenic narrative. Unlike the Calydonian boar hunt, it involves a large-scale, long-term event. The same could be said for the story of the Argonauts (traditionally understood as the first journey by ship, or at least the first journey by ship into the Black Sea),[19] and for the Theban cycle, both of which might easily be imagined to have significant cultural and geopolitical consequences as well.

---

17   Jonathan S. Burgess, *The Tradition of the Trojan War in Homer and the Epic Cycle*, Baltimore: The Johns Hopkins University Press, 2003, 44–6.

18   Ibid., 89.

19   Steven Jackson, "Argo: The First Ship?" *Rheinisches Museum für Philologie* 140, 1997: 249–57.

I would suggest, however, that the Trojan War has one particular advantage over the voyage of the *Argo* and the Theban cycle as a vehicle for Panhellenic ambitions, which is its geographic location. For the Theban cycle to have emerged as the preeminent Panhellenic charter-myth would have invested a politically significant city—Thebes—with a symbolic importance perhaps beyond endurance for Thebes' rivals. As one of the leading centers of Archaic and Classical Greece, Thebes simply had too much to gain from being at the heart of the mythic tradition, with, I suspect, long-term consequences for the Panhellenic significance of that tradition. The voyage of the *Argo*, by contrast, was perhaps set too far beyond the limits of the Greek world. Iolcos itself, home to Jason, is in Thessaly, in the north of the Hellenic world (though, to be sure, comparatively close to those first "Hellenes," located in the Spercheios valley not far to the south), while Colchis, home to the Golden Fleece and to Medea, roughly corresponds to the modern-day Black Sea coast of Georgia, on the edges of the known world. Troy, by contrast, seems ideally suited for a role as the seat of Panhellenic myth. Largely unoccupied between around 1100 BC (the fall of Troy VII, sometimes associated with the Trojan War of myth) and around 750 BC (when Troy VIII was re-founded) and never a particularly important polis thereafter, Troy's possession of mythic centrality posed no immediate threat to the prestige of other, more powerful, cities.[20] At the same time, the site of Troy, on the Dardanelles straits between Europe and Asia, overlooking the entrance to the Black Sea, remained strategically significant and arguably much more visible to the larger Greek world than, say, Colchis. Neither too prominent nor too remote, Troy (and thus the Trojan War) possessed exactly the qualities one might wish for in the locus of a panchoric charter-myth. But why, given the choice of the Trojan War as charter-myth, do the *Iliad* and the *Odyssey* in particular become the masterworks of Panhellenic literature, given that the episodes they narrate comprise a rather small part of the whole story? Why do the other poems of the Epic Cycle not assume greater prominence? As we know it, largely from a summary composed by an otherwise unknown man named Proclus, this Cycle would have consisted of the following works:[21]

---

20   Elsewhere, I argue similarly about the association of Homer's birth with Smyrna, a city largely deserted between its sack by the Lydians in 545 BC and its later rebuilding after the death of Alexander the Great. See Beecroft, *Authorship and Cultural Identity*, 74–5.

21   On the cycle generally, a good introduction is Burgess, *The Tradition of the Trojan War*.

1. The *Cypria*, an account of the causes of the Trojan War and of the conflict down to the action of the *Iliad*,

2. The *Iliad* itself,

3. The *Aethiopis*, which describes the combats between Achilles and Penthesilea (the Amazon queen) and Achilles and Memnon (the Ethiopian son of the dawn goddess), along with the death of Achilles at the hands of Paris,

4. The *Little Iliad*, which describes the contest between Ajax and Odysseus for Achilles' armor after his death and the construction of the Trojan Horse,

5. The *Sack of Troy* (*Iliou persis*), whose title is self-explanatory,

6. The *Nostoi*, which describes the homecomings (*nostoi*) of the Greek heroes generally,

7. The *Odyssey*, which describes the last of the *nostoi*, that of Odysseus, and

8. The *Telegony*, which continues the action of the *Odyssey*, down to the accidental death of Odysseus at the hands of Telegonus, his son by Circe.

As a whole, then, the epic cycle presented at least a notionally complete version of the mythical events surrounding the Trojan War, from its earliest causes through to the deaths of the last of its heroes (and thus, in the tradition, of heroes per se).[22] The works so named very likely began as at least somewhat autonomous poetic traditions, gradually (by the classical era) fashioned together to form a complete and largely non-redundant narration of the myths associated with the Trojan War.[23] While the poems of the Epic Cycle may have survived to at least some extent into the second century A D, or even later, long before then they had been marginalized by the *Iliad* and the *Odyssey*.[24] Arguments as to why this happened have, since at least

---

22   José M. González, "The Catalogue of Women and the End of the Heroic Age (Hesiod fr. 204.94–103 M-W)," *Transactions of the American Philological Association* 140 (2), 2010: 375–422.

23   Burgess, *The Tradition of the Trojan War*, 13.

24   Ingrid Holmberg, "The Creation of the Ancient Greek Epic Cycle," *Oral Tradition* 13 (2), 1998: 456–78.

Aristotle, frequently been based on claims about literary merit;[25] certainly, this may well have played some role in the increased salience of our two Homeric epics over and against the rest of the tradition, but the very non-survival of the rest of the Epic Cycle makes it difficult for us to assess what its literary merits would seem like to us and still less how the ancients would have perceived these works.

Other arguments have been based on the relative Panhellenism of the various epics and have argued, using an evolutionary approach, that those texts most likely to survive were those that appealed most successfully to the largest share of the Greek world. It is worth noting that, for this argument to succeed, it is not necessary to make any very large claims about the relative importance of a putative Panhellenic identity compared with more local sources of identity. What is at stake here is not the question of how the ancient Greeks thought about their identities, individually or collectively, nor even the nature of the imagined community for whom poets composed their work. Rather, it is a question of which works happened to thrive in wider circulation and which did not. All other things being equal, those texts that happened (for whatever reason) to appeal to the largest number of people and cities were more likely to survive to be circulated further in the future, while those with more limited appeal (whether because they were too "local" or for any other reason), were less likely to receive such wide circulation and were therefore, I would argue, more likely to be lost in the long run. Further, we can imagine something like this Darwinian model at work on the level of the content of the individual poetic work as well, especially in the context of an ongoing oral tradition; those innovations in plot that elicit greater support are more likely to become accepted as canonical elements of the text, while those that are less popular with audiences are less likely to survive.[26]

In the Chinese tradition the charter-myth equivalent to the Trojan War is the Zhou Dynasty's conquest of its predecessor, the Shang, an event with fewer rivals than its Hellenic analogue. Traditionally dated to the late twelfth century BC (and thus, by a pleasing coincidence, roughly contemporary with the traditional dates for the Trojan War), the conquest of the Shang by the Zhou represented, to the orthodox Ruist (i.e., Confucian) tradition beginning in the Han Dynasty, a paradigm for the righteous

---

25   On the emergence of more negative views on the Cycle, see Ross Scaife, "The 'Kypria' and Its Early Reception," *Classical Antiquity* 14 (1), 1995: 164–92.

26   Gregory Nagy, *Pindar's Homer: The Lyric Possession of an Epic Past*, Baltimore: The Johns Hopkins University Press, 1994, 70–1.

overthrow of a corrupt regime by a worthier individual or clan and was thus conveniently resuscitated at moments of dynastic transition, such as the usurpation of the Western Han Dynasty by Wang Mang (ruled 9–23 AD) and the restoration of the Eastern Han at the end of the Wang Mang interregnum.[27] In this version of the narrative, the final Shang king, Zhouxin, is represented as depraved, cowardly, and corrupt, notorious for (among other things) constructing a lake of wine large enough for small boats to sail in. In the orthodox historiography, the Zhou leader, posthumously King Wu of Zhou, is by contrast a paragon of virtue and restraint who succeeds in defeating the Shang with a minimum of violence and a maximum of popular support.

What is likely the earliest account of the Zhou conquest of the Shang, the *Great Capture* (世俘) chapter of the *Remnants of Zhou Documents* (逸周書), describes the conquest as violent and vengeful; only the much later (but soon orthodox) account inserted into the *Canon of Documents* makes the claim that King Wu of Zhou was merciful in victory. This claim, however, is central to the Ruist understanding of the entire early Chinese tradition, including the orthodox interpretations of the *Canon of Songs*, which view much of the collection as directly or indirectly praising King Wu; his father, King Wen; and the other leading figures of the early years of Zhou rule.[28] It may be, in fact, that those of the *Songs* that made it into the *Canon of Songs* were selected to at least some extent for their usefulness as a medium for interstate relations or for their narration of the foundational events of the Zhou Dynasty (something that is very explicit in the latter two sections of the collection, the *Greater Court Songs* and the *Temple Hymns*, even as it is at most a tenuous dimension of many of the poems in the earlier sections, the *Airs of the States* and the *Lesser Court Songs*). While the narrative of Confucius's editing of the *Canon* with which this section began is unlikely to contain any truth, we know that there were many other songs, treated as equivalent to the *Songs* in early texts but not included in our edition of the *Canon of Songs,* and while we cannot be certain of the motives of the

27   Michael Nylan, "Classics without canonization: learning and authority in Qin and Han," in *Early Chinese Religion*, edited by Lagerwey and Kalinowski, Leiden, Netherlands: Brill Publishers, 2009, 721–76.

28   For more on these issues, see Beecroft, *Authorship and Cultural Identity*. See also Alexander Beecroft, "Authorship in the Canon of Songs (Shi Jing)," in *That Wonderful Composite Called Author: Authorship in East Asian Literatures from the Beginnings to the Seventeenth Century*, edited by Christian Schwermann and Raji C. Steineck (Leiden, Netherlands: Brill Academic Publishers, 2014).

compilers of our anthology (since we do not know who they were), it seems likely that the suitability of songs to interpretation in a broader cultural context would have been a factor encouraging inclusion. Where the *Iliad* and *Odyssey* had to compete for panchoric space among a variety of mythical alternatives, the conquest of the Shang Dynasty remained largely unchallenged within this niche but had to adapt its tone to suit its new literary and cultural environment.

Here, again, it is important to remember that panchorism (like my other ecologies) is something that emerges primarily in the act of reading and/or interpreting a text. The *Iliad* and *Odyssey* themselves, like the poems of the *Canon of Songs*, likely began their evolution in an era long before anything recognizable as a widespread sense of panchoric identity existed in their respective contexts. As we have already seen, the ethnonyms Hellene and Huaxia both gradually expanded from relatively small geographic regions to cover larger and larger groups of people, and to encompass quite new models of cultural relations in the process. The texts in question likely evolved considerably in this period as well, adapting to changing audiences and circumstances and gradually winning out over their rivals. Certainly, it seems clear that it was in the fifth century BC, and no earlier, that the *Iliad* and *Odyssey* took on their unassailed Panhellenic role; the *Canon of Songs* as we know it probably took shape in the fourth century. Alternative readings remained available; certainly readers in both traditions could respond to these texts with local pride where appropriate, and, as we shall see in the next chapter, cosmopolitan readings began to emerge even as panchoric readings were consolidating.

Genealogies

Similarly, the key panchoric device of the genealogy evolved gradually, and particular readings could evolve independently of the core material. Both the Greek and Chinese mythico-historical traditions provide at some point for ultimate ancestors for their peoples: Hellas for the Greeks[29]; the Yellow Emperor (*huangdi*, 黄帝) for the Chinese.[30] In each case, the mythical figure

---

29   Key discussions here are R. L. Fowler, "Genealogical Thinking, Hesiod's Catalogue, and the Creation of the Hellenes," Proceedings of the Cambridge Philological Society (44), n.d.: 1–19; Hall, *Hellenicity* 2002.

30   Here the English-language bibliography is less extensive, but see the contrasting discussions in Michael J. Puett, *The Ambivalence of Creation: Debates Concerning Innovation and Artifice in Early China*, Stanford, CA: Stanford

in question is the head of an extensive and complex genealogy, linking together the various foundational figures of tribal and local identities in Greece and of royal and noble clans in China. These genealogies function on one level as a rhetorical and figurative legitimation of their respective peoples and are in a sense the panchoric figures par excellence, and yet, as with our charter myths, we know that the history of the evolution of these genealogies is rather complex.

The historical development of the role of the Yellow Emperor is somewhat unclear. According to the historian Sima Qian's "Monograph on the *Feng* and *Shan* Sacrifices," the state of Qin had established an altar to the Yellow Emperor on Mount Wu, near the capital region of Xianyang, in the fifth century BC.[31] In the archaeological record, the earliest attestation of his name is on a bronze vessel dedicated by Duke Wei of Qi (r. 356–320 BC), whose grandfather, Tian He, had overthrown the previous royal house in Qi in 386;[32] this and a few textual sources suggest that by this time the Yellow Emperor was at least a known figure across the Huaxia world (Qi being very far to the east of Qin), though in what role we cannot be certain. By the time of third-century texts such as the *Shangjunshu* 商君書, the canonical text of the Legalist political philosophy associated with Qin, we see the Yellow Emperor represented as a culture-hero of the state but not yet as an ancestor figure. This development seems to be tied to the reign of the Emperor Wu of the Han Dynasty (r. 141–87 BC), who consolidated the power of the central state after the rise of regional states under his predecessors. In so doing, he seems to have used the Yellow Emperor as part of his propaganda; Sima Qian, his subject, reports that the Emperor Wu made a pilgrimage to the tomb of the Yellow Emperor, and later Sima Qian identifies the Yellow Emperor as the common ancestor of the aristocratic clans.

Since we have relatively little evidence from before 400 BC, it is difficult to trace the early history of the Yellow Emperor as a mythical or divine figure with much confidence. The evidence we do have does, however, arrange

---

University Press, 2001; Mark Edward Lewis, *Sanctioned Violence in Early China*, New York: SUNY Press, 1990.

31   Lewis, *Sanctioned Violence in Early China* 1990, 180. While Lewis is right to point out that the evidence of this passage argues against the idea that the Tian clan invented the Yellow Emperor in the mid-fourth century, the possibility certainly remains that this is the point at which the figure was adapted for a more general use as an ancestor-figure across the Huaxia world.

32   For a discussion of these points, see Puett, *The Ambivalence of Creation* 2001, 112–13.

itself into a very tempting narrative, whereby a figure of local cult in Qin gets borrowed for cultic and political purposes in other parts of China before becoming first a culture hero and finally an ancestor figure. If this narrative is accurate (a problematic assertion, to be sure), where if anywhere along the way do we find the panchoric? Not, obviously, while the Yellow Emperor is still a local god in the state of Qin, but when he is deployed for local political purposes in Qi? When Qin writers use him as a paradigm for the kind of imperial rule they wish to establish across the Huaxia world? When the mid-Western Han decides it needs a common ancestor? The first and last of these represent different kinds of panchoric readings—the first a model in which local traditions circulate between localities for local purposes while remaining distinctive (a variant, perhaps, of my "Delphic panchorism"), the last an Olympic panchorism that attempts to impose a uniform structure on local traditions from above. The Legalist deployment of the figure of the Yellow Emperor, by contrast, models one of the tropes of cosmopolitanism that I will develop in the next chapter, the universalization of panchoric traditions. Episodes such as these remind us not to force the evidence to fit a preexisting (and externally imposed) set of options. Here, part of the difficulty lies, I think, in a different terminological imposition—that of the word "empire," with its modern Anglo-French colonial associations, on early China. The Western Han was at once a cosmopolitan and universalist empire, projecting its cultural products as universally applicable and a panchoric political assemblage, struggling to construct a culture that could bind together the still-disparate Huaxia regions under its sway.

Similar complexities hold true when we look at the Greek equivalent, the Hellenic Genealogy. In its fullest form, this genealogy encompasses all Greek-speaking peoples, deriving them from Hellen, the son of Deucalion and Pyrrha, the lone survivors of the Greek flood myth. Through his sons Aeolus and Dorus, he is the ancestor of the Aeolian and Dorian Greeks; through his son Xouthos, he is also the grandfather of Ion and Achaeus, the ancestors of the Ionian and Achaean Greeks.[33] The various descendants of these four are the eponymous founders of the various cities and regions of the Greek world; together, then, Hellenic identity is collectively expressed through a shared descent from Hellen—on the level of the community, if not explicitly on the level of the individual. No more elegant or concrete demonstration of Panhellenic identity could be imagined.

---

33   For an excellent introduction to this genealogy and its history, see Hall, *Hellenicity* 2002, 56–89.

And yet the reality is much more complicated than that. To begin with, this genealogy is not featured in Homeric epic, and even the ethnonyms on which it is based—Hellene, Dorian, Ionian, Aeolian, Achaean—are only rarely encountered there as such. The Hellenes are for Homer a minor people governed by Achilles; for the larger community of those who attack Troy, Homer uses the words Achaean, Argive, and Danaan—words not used in that sense in later writers. The ethnic names Achaean, Dorian, Ionian, and Aeolian are similarly either not encountered at all in Homer, encountered only exceptionally, or (as with Achaean) used in a different sense. These eponymous heroes of ethnicities, regions, and cities are also relatively rarely encountered in extant literature (Euripides' *Ion* being a notable exception), and do not seem to have been exceptionally important figures of local cult. The Panhellenism of epic and the Panhellenism of the Hellenic genealogy exist almost in isolation from each other.

Where we *do* significantly encounter the Hellenic genealogy is in the poem known as the *Catalogue of Women*, attributed to Hesiod in ancient times. Later lost as a complete work, enough fragments of the *Catalogue of Women* survive (more than a thousand lines are now known) to give a good sense of its contents.[34] This poem, thought perhaps to date in its current form from the sixth century BC, traces the lines of descent from Deucalion and Pyrrha as well as the mythical lines not assimilated to the Hellenic genealogy, identifying and integrating the whole of the heroic tradition thereby; it is a major source for later mythographers, and for Ovid's *Metamorphoses*, and through Ovid for much of what we think of today as "Greek Mythology." The *Catalogue of Women* can be interpreted as beginning where Hesiod's *Theogony* (which recounts the creation of the world and the genealogies of the gods) leaves off and concludes with a listing of the suitors of Helen of Troy; as such, it provides a key link in what becomes with its help an unbroken chain of narration between the creation of the universe and the end of the race of heroes after the *nostoi* from the Trojan War. Collectively, therefore, the Homeric and Hesiodic epic tradition provides a totalizing account of the shared deep past of the Hellenic world, an account that could thereafter be contested but never ignored.

---

34   For a recent edition, see Martina Hirschberger, *Gynaikōn katalogos und Megalai ēhoiai: ein Kommentar zu den Fragmenten zweier hesiodeischer Epen*, München: Saur, 2004. Richard L. Hunter, ed., *The Hesiodic Catalogue of Women: Constructions and Reconstructions*, Cambridge: Cambridge University Press, 2005, and; West, *The Hesiodic Catalogue of Women* 1985 both contain important discussions of this crucial text.

The Hellenic genealogy thus plays a greater role in the Greek tradition than genealogies of the Yellow Emperor do in the Chinese tradition. And yet it is also true that it is not the *Catalogue of Women* (which, in spite of its title, is more about male heroes than about the women who bore them and contains much mythic material beyond the mere enunciation of genealogies) but Homeric epic that plays the more pivotal role in the development of Panhellenic reading and thinking. I have already suggested why this might be so, in connection with other rival charter-myths; just as the Trojan tale, by its nature, was better able to gather local elements into a new structure than were other mythical narratives, so, too, it was superior to genealogical epic in this respect. Genealogy can provide an articulating structure for local traditions (a role it plays in many traditional cultures besides Greece),[35] but in the end a genealogy is only as meaningful as its constituent elements (the people it links). Narrative heroic epic was more effective at integrating the local into something larger and new; I now turn to a discussion of some of the devices it used to do so.

Catalogues and Anthologies

The devices of catalogues and anthologies—specifically, the *Catalogue of the Ships* in the *Iliad* and the section of the *Canon of Songs* titled the *Guofeng* 國風, or *Airs of the States*—seem at first to provide the most vivid representation of what I have called above a Delphic panchorism, that is, of the self-image of a culture seen as the sum of its parts. Both of these texts produce the effect of geographically comprehensive listings of the constituent polities forming the larger cultural order: the cities and kingdoms of the Hellenic world and the regional states of the Western Zhou and Spring and Autumn eras. And yet in both cases the geography is glaringly flawed; important places are omitted, comparatively minor places are given strange prominence, the same territories are identified by more than one name, and polities that did not exist contemporaneously are anachronistically brought together. I would argue that this is a feature, not a flaw, of the panchoric system, that the system benefits from this very geographic imprecision in that it puts the device to work in the service of an "Olympian" panchorism, one where the component parts are rendered uniform by a centralizing authority. Devices like catalogues and anthologies literalize

---

35   Fowler, "Genealogical Thinking, Hesiod's Catalogue, and the Creation of the Hellenes."

and literarize this notion of culture by aggregation, but completeness and accuracy are clearly not essential to the effectiveness of the system. Indeed, I will go so far as to argue that both the Greek and Chinese panchoric ecologies thrived in full awareness of, and in part *because* of, this imprecise aggregation, which allowed the whole to represent itself as greater than the sum of its parts by making the listing of those parts always somewhat arbitrary and incomplete.

A case in point is the *Catalogue of Ships* in book two of the *Iliad*, a listing (with occasional geographic detail and mythological ornament) of twenty-nine lands (and many of the cities located within them) that have sent their troops to the fight at Troy, naming also the forty-six heroes leading the soldiers of those lands and enumerating how many of the 1,186 ships deployed they commanded. The total passage, 266 lines in length, tends to have a somewhat soporific effect on modern readers of the *Iliad*, unused to such catalogues and unfamiliar with many of the locations and heroes mentioned.

To an ancient Greek audience, of course, this material was of much greater potential interest, potentially linking the audience member's own community to the great Panhellenic charter-myth of the Trojan War, and we know that the *Catalogue* was frequently cited in ancient times. That said, there are many mysteries concerning the *Catalogue*, beginning with the fact that it is present in the *Iliad* at all, given that that poem opens nine years into the conduct of the war, an unlikely moment in many ways to enumerate the troops fighting, though if, as I suggested earlier, the *Iliad* evolved in such a way as gradually to supplant the other parts of the epic cycle, then the presence of the *Catalogue* in the poem may make more sense. Further, there is one special reason why the *Catalogue* may be appropriate here and not earlier, a reason I have not seen discussed. Close attention to the forty-six heroes named in the *Catalogue* reveals a striking fact. Of those heroes, six are relatively minor figures whose fates are either not mentioned in extant sources or are the subject of conflicting information. Twenty are definitively claimed to have survived their *nostos*, or homecoming, while four died during that *nostos*. Of the fifteen who die during the Trojan War itself, fully eleven die during the action of the *Iliad*—and the deaths of three of the remaining four *must* remain outside the action of the *Iliad* as we know it: Protesilaus, the first Greek to land at Troy and thus the first to die, Achilles, whose death is foreshadowed but not narrated in the *Iliad*, and Ajax, whose suicide is a reaction to his loss to Odysseus in the contest for Achilles' armor after the latter's death; only the death of Machaon, one of

Asclepius's twin sons, is said to occur in a later part of the action of the Trojan War in a way that does not seem essential to the plot of our poem. If (as the poem itself makes explicit) the purpose of the *Iliad* is to magnify the greatness of Achilles as a warrior by representing the desperation of the Greeks in his absence, then the *Catalogue's* reminder that nearly one in four of the Greek leaders die during Achilles' absence from the battle surely reinforces that purpose and provides a meaning for the *Catalogue* in this particular context.

There are a number of geographic and chronological difficulties with the *Catalogue*, which I will only briefly indicate here. Many of the places mentioned in the *Catalogue* (not merely the minor cities mentioned but even some of the regional kingdoms) are obscure in the extreme, and there is little to no evidence for their existence in Mycenean or Archaic times; others seem to have existed *only* in the earliest of times and to have disappeared by the Classical era. Conversely, some quite important and long-established cities, such as Megara, are omitted altogether, as are almost all of the Aegean islands. The kingdoms of several of the important heroes, including those of Agamemnon, Ajax, Diomedes, Odysseus, and Achilles are strangely configured in the *Catalogue*.[36] Political arguments have been adduced to account for these discrepancies,[37] but the very abundance of geographic problems with the *Catalogue* suggests also the argument that inconsistency might have had the positive value of rendering the text relatively ineffectual as a tool for local propaganda of this kind.

One of the aspects of the *Catalogue* that is most often adduced as evidence that it is poorly adapted to its role in the *Iliad* is the frequent disproportion between the interest taken in a particular hero or kingdom by the *Catalogue* and his or its significance to the larger narrative. Certainly, the *Catalogue* lavishes minor attention on certain figures while dismissing in very brief terms much more significant figures. At the same time,

---

36   A still useful summary of the geographic complexities of the *Catalogue* is T. W. Allen, *The Homeric Catalogue of Ships*, Oxford: Oxford University Press, 1921, which offers the interpretation, contested by many, that Pelasgian Argos is a synonym for Thessaly. Peter Loptson, "Pelasgikon Argos in the Catalogue of Ships (681)," *Mnemosyne* 34 (1/2), Fourth Series, 1981: 136–8.

37   See, e.g., Margalit Finkelberg, "Ajax's Entry in the Hesiodic Catalogue of Women," *The Classical Quarterly* 38 (1), New Series, 1988: 31–41 for the possible interests that Athens, Argos, and Corinth might have had in representing Agamemnon's kingdom in the way Homer does.

however, a closer examination of many of these detailed descriptions of minor figures reveals more significance than might be apparent on a casual reading. As an example, the first sixteen lines of the *Catalogue* are devoted to Boeotia and its leaders, five grandsons of the little-known Itonus. Of these five, three (Arcesilaus, Prothoenor, and Clonius) are mentioned only once more in the *Iliad*—at their deaths; one (Peneleus), is also killed during the action of the poem but is additionally mentioned three other times (once when exhorted by Poseidon and twice when he kills Trojan heroes); the only one to survive the poem (Leitus), is mentioned three times (once to be exhorted by Poseidon in the same passage as his brother, once when he kills a Trojan, and once when wounded in the wrist by Hector). At first glance, these figures seem like nothing more than the archaic equivalent of cannon fodder, faceless figures remembered only because they are among the thousands who die at Troy.

A closer examination, however, illuminates something about the *Catalogue's* role as a work of Panhellenic synthesis. These "Boeotian Five" heroes are part of the Hellenic genealogy as are certain other obscure figures in the *Catalogue*, like the leaders from Arcadia and Phocis. There are also some indications that the Boeotian Five may have been the object of hero-cult in Boeotia itself (see, e.g., Pausanias 9.39.3 on the tomb of Leitus). Further, the decision to emphasize the Boeotian Five seems deliberately to exclude Thersander, the son of Polyneices, and heir to the Theban throne in the Theban cycle of myth. According to the *Cypria*, indeed, Thersander was the original leader of the Boeotian troops at Troy, but died at the hands of Herakles' son Tlepolemus, during the Greek siege of Mysia, mistaken for Troy during an early phase of the war. The *Iliad* ignores Thersander's role, part, I would suggest, of a general downplaying of the Theban cycle in the Homeric epic, a phenomenon seen also at Iliad 4.370-410, when Agamemnon refers to the Theban war as part of an exhortation to Diomedes, in language which seems to diminish the earlier conflict by comparison with that at Troy.

The choice of the "Boeotian Five" as leaders of the Boeotian contingent in the *Catalogue of Ships*, then, represents not merely a pedantic listing of invented names, nor does it simply reflect a kind of Delphic Panhellenism, assembling a collection of heroes rich in local tradition to create a whole greater than the sum of its parts. While these five heroes do seem to have been a part of Boeotian epichoric tradition and were likely the object of hero-cult, their selection also has the effect of sidelining figures from another mythic tradition centered in Boeotia, one with its own Panhellenic circulation: the Theban Cycle.[38] As such, and in line with the discussion earlier in the chapter, I would argue that the *Catalogue*'s choice of the Boeotian Five as the leaders of their contingent, rather than Thersander, is less a question of choosing the local over the Panhellenic than of deciding what sort of local can be represented in a Panhellenic context, with the selected option chosen because it was more Olympic than Delphic.

The device of the anthology works very similarly, as I will show with an example from China. The first section of the *Canon of Songs*, the Chinese collection of ancient poetry traditionally attributed to Confucius, is the *Airs of the States*, a collection of some 160 relatively short poems, many of which are dominated by imagery of the natural and agricultural world, and frequently interpreted in modern times as popular in origin. The *Airs of the States* is divided in the orthodox Mao-school edition (of the last few centuries BC) into fifteen sections based on a notional geography of the states into which China was divided during the Spring and Autumn period, which covered the early part of the second half of the Zhou Dynasty (771–476 BC) and was named after an annalistic history also said to be edited by Confucius. As I have already noted in *Authorship and Cultural Identity*, this geography is notional rather than real; there is no historical moment at which all fifteen states represented in the collection existed simultaneously, some states overlap in geography, and some may never have existed at all:[39] The *Airs of Qin*, the *Airs of Zheng*, and the *Airs of the Royal Domain* (Wang), for example, were associated with the late Western Zhou and early Spring and Autumn Period. Bin, however, is a polity always associated with the pre-dynastic stage of the Zhou, while the *Airs* of Zhounan, Shaonan, Bei, Yong, and Tang all seem to reflect, if anything, the political terminology of the early Western Zhou. There is thus no century, much less year, within which all the states represented in the *Airs of the States* might have coexisted.

As with the *Catalogue of Ships*, there are also strikingly wide disparities in power and significance among the states. The *Zuozhuan* tells us of twenty-six states established by Kings Wen and Wu and by the Duke of Zhou; of

---

38   Although "Boeotian" and "Theban" mythology often seem to exist in separate universes, so much so that a recent and very thoughtful study of Boeotian mythology and the construction of local identity does not once mention the Theban Cycle or its contents. See Stephanie L. Larson, *Tales of Epic Ancestry: Boiotian Collective Identity in the Late Archaic and Early Classical Periods*, Wiesbaden, Germany: Franz Steiner Verlag, 2007.

39   Beecroft, *Authorship and Cultural Identity*, 202–4.

these, only three (Wei, Cao and Jin) are directly represented in the *Airs of the States* (*Zuozhuan* Xi 24; p. 47). Of a fairly standard list of the fifteen major states of the Spring and Autumn era, ostensibly the time of composition of most of the *Songs*,[40] only seven (Qi, Jin, Qin, Cao, Zheng, Chen, Wei) are represented in the *Airs*. Three more (Chu 楚, Wu 吳, and Yue 越) are excluded as still on the southern borders of the ethnically Huaxia world before about the sixth century BC, after the presumed closing of the canon of the *Songs*,[41] while Lu and Yan, are represented through genealogical metonymy; Lu through its connections to the Duke of Zhou (and thus to the *Airs of Zhounan*) and Yan through its associations with the Duke of Shao (and thus to the *Airs of Shaonan*). Lu and Song are additionally represented in the *Hymns* section of the *Songs* through, respectively, the *Lu Hymns* and the *Shang Hymns* (since the state of Song was understood as ruled by the heirs of the Shang). The reasons for the exclusion of Cai 蔡 and Xu 許 are more obscure.

When looked at from a geographic perspective, the states represented do at least provide a fairly broad degree of coverage of the two capital regions and of points east and west along the major river valleys. Four of the states (Wei, Tang, Qin, and Bin) can be associated with the areas to the west of the old Western Zhou capitals near modern Xi'an, while two (Zhounan and Shaonan) have a connection to the region as well as to points east; to the extent that the *Airs of Qin* reflect the Spring and Autumn period, they, too, can be connected to the Western Zhou capital regions. No fewer than five (Bei, Yong, Wei, the Royal Domains, and Zheng) relate to the general area around Luoyang. Finally, four relate to areas east of Luoyang: Chen and Kuai to modern Henan; Qi and Cao to modern Shandong. Viewed within the sequence of our text, the move is broadly from core to periphery, with the Western Zhou capital region first, then the Luoyang region, then a move east to Qi, then west to the Qin and those associated with it, then the relatively minor states of Chen, Kuai, and Cao. The collection concludes with Bin, a move that brings us to the far west geographically but, temporally, back to origins. The collection's movement is thus both geographic and

---

40   Cho-yun Hsu, "The Spring and Autumn Period," *The Cambridge History of Ancient China: From the Origins of Civilization to 221 BC*, edited by Michael Loewe and Edward L. Shaughnessy, Cambridge: Cambridge University Press, 1999, 545–86

41   For a discussion of the cultural integration of these states into the Huaxia sphere, see Lothar Von Falkenhausen, *Chinese Society in the Age of Confucius* (Monumenta Archaeologica), Los Angeles: Cotsen Institute of Archaeology Press, 2006, 262–83.

chronological, as David Schaberg has noticed.[42] Within the geographic structure of representing the music of different regional polities, we find encoded a narrative of the rise and fall of the Zhou Dynasty, with those states associated with the pre-dynastic and early Western Zhou understood as embodying the virtues of idealized rule and those associated with later times representing decadence and decline. With the exception of the final section, the *Airs of Bin*, which as noted returns us to origins, the general movement of the collection thus mirrors the general movement of Western Zhou history as understood by the Ruist tradition, from triumphant foundation to decadence. This structure of historical decline is then reproduced within each of the state collections, as read by the Mao preface.

But whose thinking does this arrangement reflect? We cannot be certain when exactly the division of the *Airs of the States* assumed its final form. The recovered *Confucius' Discussion of the Songs*, dating from the fourth century BC, identifies songs as coming from the *Airs of the States* but at no point identifies which state any given song comes from; the local, here as so many times, is generic rather than genuine. Likewise, and for the most part, citations of the *Airs of the States* in the historical text the *Zuozhuan* (also likely from the fourth century BC) make no mention of the association of particular poems with particular states; indeed, such citations frequently take place in a performance context of interstate negotiation in which fragments of the poem are deployed without regard for the sense of the poem as a whole, let alone any imagined originary compositional context. The Shuanggudui manuscript, excavated from a tomb sealed in 165 BC, does identify and (in some cases) discuss the divisions of the *Airs of the States* into essentially the same states as the Mao tradition, in spite of its very considerable manuscript variations from that tradition; we may, perhaps, thus assume that the collection had assumed something like its current organization by at least that date. While it is possible that the poems were already associated with specific states by the early fourth century, it is striking that almost no text that might date from that period identifies them in this way; it is as if the *Airs of the States* are generically regional (as opposed to Panhuaxia), without any specific regional associations. There is one final piece of relevant evidence, also found in the *Zuozhuan* in the entry for the year 543 BC when Prince Jizha of Wu, a powerful state in the Lower Yangtze (then the southern periphery of the Huaxia world) travels to the state of Lu and hears a complete

---

42   David Schaberg, *A Patterned Past: Form and Thought in Early Chinese Historiography*, Cambridge, MA: Harvard University Asian Center, 2001, 89.

performance of the *Songs*; as Jizha listens to the airs from each state, he offers sage comments on the moral qualities and political fate of that state. The Jizha anecdote is almost certainly not an authentic account of events but probably dates from the late fourth century BC; it offers a largely similar listing of the states in the collection, with, however, subtle differences, which I have argued reduce the significance of the state of Lu, of special significance to Ruists as Confucius's home, and elevate the state of Qin, loathed by Ruists as the origin of the harshly Legalist Qin Dynasty.[43]

With both the *Catalogue of Ships* and the *Airs of the States*, then, we can see that a text that appears on the surface to offer a Delphic panchorism, in which the best of the local traditions is combined into a notional whole, is in fact much more complicated. In neither case is there a possible historical moment in which all of the parts in question could have coexisted, nor is there any definition of the limits of the cultural world that would encompass all of the parts, and nothing further. These anachronisms and inconsistencies, I would argue, do their own work within the tradition, insisting on the panchoric culture as the sum of parts, while simultaneously reshaping those parts and detaching them from any specific local context. The question of the historical evolution of Homeric epic and of the *Canon of Songs* is complicated and controversial, and impossible to resolve with any certainty given the evidence available. It would therefore be a mistake to assume that the texts as we have them were necessarily arranged and edited with this objective in mind; rather, using my ecological model, I would suggest that the fact that the texts in question evolved in this particular way left them more susceptible to panchoric readings and thus more likely to thrive in a panchoric context. Just as excessive reliance on any one local context makes a text problematic from the perspective of panchoric appropriation, so, too, does too fastidious an attention to the membership and borders of the panchoric cultural world.

The Panchoric and Other Ecologies

From this examination of some of the specifics of the panchoric ecology, as observed in Archaic and Classical Greece and in pre-Qin China, I now move to a more general discussion of the ecology, including a brief discussion of other possible cases. As we have already seen in the previous chapter, the notion that the panchoric emerges out of the epichoric is to at

---

43   Beecroft, "Authorship in the Canon of Songs (Shi Jing)."

least some extent an illusion, a function of thinking of the ecology as a description of lived experience rather than a mode of reading. Lyric poets such as Pindar and Stesichorus make use of local traditions, but are themselves panchoric figures, and often the precise local referent of their work is obscure or even purely notional; likewise, in our earliest citations of the *Airs of the States* from the *Canon of Songs*, we hear of the poems as signifiers freely circulating among regional states; only slightly later do we encounter clear associations between particular poems and particular states. We saw further that the epichoric mode of reading has different valences when operating within the local community that claims affiliation with a work of verbal art (whether that community be an Archaic Greek polis or a First Nations community in Canada) and when operating elsewhere. Within the epichoric context itself, the epichoric mode of reading represents a textual device for constituting the community, whether by establishing the geographic space of that community, by establishing its origins, or by legitimating its practices and institutions. To some extent, these may be strategies aimed at contrasting with or complementing larger-scale narratives, but at the local level the positive and constitutive dimensions are crucial.

At the opposite extreme, when epichoric textual traditions circulate in modern or large-scale contexts, their local origins tend to imbue them with notions of chronological depth, closeness to nature (human or otherwise), traditional values, and all the other assumptions that tend to accompany the folkloric. As such, it is very clear that the local has escaped the bonds of mere locality, that localness as a value is no longer tied to the specific location of one's birth and life, but rather to the notion of the small-scale and traditional per se. Within a predominantly panchoric ecology, however, the epichoric and the panchoric are therefore (as we have seen with the Greek and Chinese cases) mutually constitutive. Since the panchoric is a specifically aggregative identity, it is clear that it is in some sense constituted by the epichoric, but at the same time the status of the epichoric *as such* (rather than as the unmarked product of a purely local culture somehow isolated from outside influences) depends on the larger context and the system of differences generated thereby. That larger context, to be clear, need not be panchoric; ecologies from the cosmopolitan Hellenistic world to the contemporary Americas integrate epichoric texts and readings into their own systems. The panchoric ecology is, however, uniquely dependent on the epichoric, a dependency that is at the same time that ecology's distinguishing feature.

The relationship between panchoric and cosmopolitan ecologies is complex and difficult to generalize, for reasons inlcuding the relative rarity of each ecology, the fact that many languages transition from the one to the other (with substantial periods of coexistence), and the enormous weight that several of these languages (including Greek, Latin, Sanskrit, Arabic, and Chinese) bear within the later literary history of large regions of the world. My first book discussed several symptomatic moments in the panchoric and cosmopolitan reading practices of Greece and China, and I return to some of these issues in the chapter on cosmopolitan ecologies that follows this one. There is, therefore, not always a hard and fast distinction to be made between the two ecologies, although the following features are, I argue, diagnostic.

First of all, and most significantly and straightforwardly, the linguistic situation in panchoric and cosmopolitan contexts is quite different. Where panchoric readings circulate within a space defined by a shared language (even if likely one subject to regional variations) and a divided political environment, cosmopolitan literary languages by definition circulate across boundaries of mutual intelligibility of spoken language. Building on Sheldon Pollock's observations about the "Sanskrit Cosmopolis," where polities from the Indus River to Java, speaking (and writing in) a multitude of languages from unrelated language families used Sanskrit to articulate and aestheticize the legitimacy of their power, I suggest that it is the use of a language for literary purposes by non-native speakers that confirms that language's cosmopolitan status. Greek, then, becomes fully cosmopolitan in the Hellenistic era, when polities from the Western Mediterranean to the Persian Gulf begin to use Greek language and culture as tokens of exchange of cultural capital. *Sensu stricto*, the Han era in China, when a transregional empire ruling over a diverse array of ethnolinguistic communities uniformly articulates its identity in a standard classical idiom, does not quite fit Pollock's understanding of the cosmopolitan; a status more clearly established when the literary language is used as a medium for inscriptions and other official texts in non-Han polities, beginning perhaps with the Paekche Dynasty in modern Korea in the 470s AD.[44] Likewise, by Pollock's own model (but in spite of Pollock's own claim), the circulation of Latin as a literary and bureaucratic language during the Roman empire does not fully qualify as cosmopolitan, a status more securely established after the fall of

---

44 Peter H. Lee, *A History of Korean Literature*, Cambridge: Cambridge University Press, 2003, 87.

the empire, when Latin continued as the major language for culture, learning, the legitimation of rule, and the relationship between states for over a millennium.[45]

Secondly, the aggregative nature of cultural identity in the panchoric context is much less salient in cosmopolitan eras. The example of the Greek language is instructive here; where panchoric texts like Homer and archaic lyric make use of artificial dialects or use non-local dialects as a programmatic index of genre (and thus require an awareness of a variety of local and translocal registers of the language, to the perpetual frustration of students of Greek to this day), the standard written Greek language in the Hellenistic era is the *koinê*—literally, the common speech, understood at the time as a merging of the major literary dialects but more clearly understood as a simplification and generalization from the Attic dialect, used in Athens, the culturally hegemonic center of the Greek world prior to the conquests of Alexander.[46] Cosmopolitan users and readers of a language can thus tend toward simplified and highly controlled versions of language, in order to maximize the language's capacity for circulation, even if (as I discuss in more detail in the next chapter), we might see the fondness of Hellenistic poets for obscure, archaic, and dialectal words as a reaction against the generalized nature of the koinê, a kind of anti-cosmopolitanism of the center, a phenomenon that has interesting implications for Global English in our time.

Thirdly, in Pollock's model, cosmopolitan literary languages like Sanskrit are used to articulate ideologies of rule that are universal in their claims, whether because they represent the ambitions of a world-empire or because the various polities making such claims do so in strongly parallel and analogical terms. The slippage here, between ideologies of universal rule and universal ideologies of rule, is an especially problematic aspect of Pollock's model of the cosmopolitan language; I have discussed the issue elsewhere,[47] and return to it in the chapter on cosmopolitan literatures below. In my previous work, I have also emphasized how elements of what

---

45   Ernst Robert Curtius, *European Literature and the Latin Middle Ages*, Princeton, NJ, Princeton University Press, 1991, 28–9.

46   See Stephen Colvin, "The Greek Koine and the Logic of a Standard Language," in *Standard Languages and Language Standards: Greek, Past and Present*, edited by Alexandra Georgakopoulou and M. S. Silk, Farnham, Surrey, England: Ashgate Publishing, Ltd., 2009.

47   Alexander Beecroft, "The Sanskrit Ecumene: Review of Pollock, Sheldon. The Language of the Gods in the World of Men: Sanskrit, Culture, and Power in Premodern India," *New Left Review* 72, 2011: 153–60.

I would see as cosmopolitan thinking in this sense can be found as early as Herodotus in Greece and sections of the *Zuozhuan* in China; it will thus be apparent that panchoric and cosmopolitan readings interact in both Greece and China (and elsewhere) for some time. However this issue is understood, any sort of reflection on political and/or cultural practices as extending beyond the immediate linguistic community of the author does seem to suggest a qualitative change. Where panchoric identities emerge out of the aggregation of local identities (which may be oppositional in relation to each other), cosmopolitan readings in particular frequently transcend oppositional differences between cultures.

Panchoric and vernacular ecologies share one crucial trait: both entail the emergence of a new medium of exchange, with a concomitant interest in both cases in establishing the linguistic and literary conventions of that medium. The movement in the two cases is, however, opposite; where panchoric readers seek to build texts and worlds out of smaller units, the work of vernacular readers and writers is culturally separatist, aiming to create a narrower, smaller-scale alternative to cosmopolitan literary traditions. Put another way, the ecological competition for each is different. Panchoric literatures endeavor to supplant epichoric traditions and use for the purpose devices such as genealogies, catalogues, and anthologies to embed epichoric traditions into a larger whole, possibly even with the aim of supplanting the epichoric or even rendering it unreadable. Vernaculars, by contrast, aim not to supplant the cosmopolitan outright in all its roles (since by definition no one vernacular is ever in a strong position to replace a cosmopolitan literature everywhere) but rather in specialized regional and/or generic contexts; as such, and as we shall see in more detail in the relevant chapter, they employ the particular devices of the vernacular manifesto and the translation of canonical cosmopolitan texts.

National and panchoric ecologies enjoy still more obvious similarities, in that each is built around the foundation of some kind of larger and more coherent community, be it political, cultural, or both (simultaneously or successively). The sorts of communities imagined in each case, however, differ in important ways. In the case of the national literary ecology, the notion of spatialized, one-on-one correspondence between a literary language and a polity is essential, although the existence of a literary tradition can act as a harbinger of the political (as, for example, in Italy), or the political achievement of the nation-state can induce a perceived need for a national literature (as in the Americas in the nineteenth century and postcolonial Africa and Asia in the twentieth). Further, the national-literature

ecology (uniquely among those studied in this book) entails a universalization of its principles, such that literatures can only enter the ecology on its
own terms, as national, in a manner analogous to the unique insistence in
post-Westphalian international relations that all actors be treated as ontolog-
ically equal nation-states, regardless of size and power. Regionalism and
other aggregative representations of identity can have their place within the
national-literature ecology, but the greater emphasis is on reducing the noise
of the particular to the signal of the national, and on opposing the national to
its rivals in other nations. A panchoric ecology, by contrast, can only accept
texts on the claim that they are, in some way, local or engaged with the local;
certain traditions or texts may receive greater prominence or circulation
because they are more successful at integrating local traditions with a minimum of disturbance, but the ecology remains a shared space for contention.

WHERE IS THE PANCHORIC?

I derive my (admittedly unlovely) term panchoric from the ancient Greek
notion of the Panhellenic, admirably described by Gregory Nagy and
others,[48] and there is no doubt that Archaic Greece provides the paradigm
of an emergent sense of cultural unity laid across a political world of small-
scale and competitive polities. As I have shown at some length in my first
book and discussed again in this chapter, early China, particularly in the
Eastern Zhou era (i.e., 770–221 BC) represents a very similar case, in which
lineage connection, as well as shared literary and ritual practices, linked an
ecumene of small-scale polities in an almost constant state of conflict.[49]
But are there other regions, other chronologies that can be illuminated
through this rubric? My answers here must necessarily be more speculative,
and it should be clear that the paradigm of the panchoric is not universally
applicable and most certainly does not reflect a stage of development
through which all civilizations must pass. Panchoric ecologies are unlikely
to thrive in regions where unrelated languages coexist side-by-side and
resist integration into a larger regional system. They are also unlikely to
exist in regions where literacy and literary culture are imported from
outside at a stage of small-scale development. The number of potential sites
for the panchoric ecology is therefore not unlimited, and I consider the

---

48   Gregory Nagy, *The Best of the Achaeans: Concepts of the Hero in Archaic
Greek Poetry*, revised, Baltimore: The Johns Hopkins University Press, 1998.
49   Beecroft, *Authorship and Cultural Identity*.

leading candidates in what follows below. My aim here is naturally not to pronounce dogmatically on fields outside my own expertise, but rather to start a dialogue on points of commonality and difference, where the latter will be much more illuminating than the former.

One literature that certainly shares features of the panchoric is the pre-Islamic poetic tradition. The legendary account of the first anthology of *qasida* poetry in Arabic, the *Mu'allaqat*, traces its origins to an annual fair held in pre-Islamic times near Mecca, where there was a competition among poets representing different Bedouin tribes, with the winning odes suspended from the Ka'ba; the surviving collection of seven to ten *qasida* odes being drawn from among these poems.[50] This account has been dismissed as a folk-etymologic narrativization of the title of the collection, which can be translated as "the suspended ones."[51] From a mythic perspective, however, this device of competition (which mirrors devices of poetic circulation found in Greece and China), certainly reads very naturally as a narrativization of the emergence of a panchoric reading practice for the pre-Islamic *qasida*, regardless of the truth-value of the story. Moreover, the poems themselves contain descriptions of caravan routes as well as mockery of other tribes, certainly lending themselves to both epichoric and panchoric reading practices.

South Asia prior to the cosmopolitan era represents another possible site for a panchoric ecology, although the evidence for the period is scanty and difficult to interpret. Certainly, Sheldon Pollock argues that Sanskrit, even in the era of composition of the *Mahābhārata* and *Ramayana*, is never a local language, based rather in the Brahminic community,[52] though not all Sanskritists would agree. As such, one could certainly argue that Sanskrit epic language functions in something of the same way as Homeric epic and archaic lyric, or the *Canon of Songs*, as a *Kunstsprache* and a repertory of narratives that provide a means of communication across a larger dialect region. Further, there are a number of ways in which the text of the Sanskrit epics establishes the geographic space within which its narratives take place

---

50   Michael Anthony Sells, and 'Alqamah ibn 'Abadah, *Desert Tracings: Six Classic Arabian Odes*, Middletown, CT: Wesleyan University Press, 1989, 3.

51   A. F. L. Beeston, T. M. Johnstone, R. B. Serjeant, and G. R. Smith, *Arabic Literature to the End of the Umayyad Period*, Cambridge: Cambridge University Press, 2010, 111–13.

52   Sheldon Pollock, *The Language of the Gods in the World of Men: Sanskrit, Culture, and Power in Premodern India*, Berkeley: University of California Press, 2009, 39–42.

(the *Āryavārta*), achieving some of the same effects, arguably, that I describe for the genealogies, anthologies, and catalogues of the Hellenic and Huaxia traditions. For example, when in book three of the *Mahābhārata* Yudhi hira is sent on a pilgrimage to the sacred fords,[53] J. A. B. van Buitenen, the noted translator of much of the epic, observes that "not many of the places . . . can be identified. The text itself describes a number of them as hard to find, and suggests that one should go there "mentally."[54]

Ancient Near Eastern literature, especially of the Sumerian period, offers several possibilities. Certainly, the Sumerian King-List provides a suggestive parallel to the mythical history of early China as discussed earlier: the millennia-long universal rule of early mythical kings gradually gives way to more plausible reign-lengths found in dynasties where supreme rule shifts from city to city over time, although it has been noted that the author of the King-List seems to have taken liberties with the sequence of his material, dividing into distinct chronological periods what seems to have been the continuous hegemony of one city.[55] Slightly later, and in another text more documentary than avowedly literary, we find the "Genealogy of Hammurabi," where many of the ancestors of the great Babylonian king of the eighteenth century BC share the names of Amorite tribes, possibly constructing some sort of ideological claim that the Babylonian monarchy symbolically represented the whole of which the tribes were parts.[56] As translated by Finkelstein, the text concludes as follows:

> The *palū* of the Amorites, the *palū* of the aneans, the *palū* of Gutium, (32) the *palū* not recorded on this tablet, (33) and the soldier(s) who fell while on perilous campaigns for their (lit: 'his') lord, (34) princes, (35) princesses, (3S38) all "persons" from East to West who have neither *palū* nor s., (39) come ye, eat this, (40) drink this, (41-43) (and) bless Ammisaduqa the son of Ammiditana, the king of Babylon.

---

53   For a discussion of these sacred fords, or tirthas, and the role of Sanskrit epic in the construction of sacred geography, see Diana L. Eck, "India's 'Tīrthas': 'Crossings' in Sacred Geography," *History of Religions* 20 (4), 1981: 323–44.

54   J. A. B. van Buitenen, *The Mahabharata, Volume 2: Book 2: The Book of Assembly; Book 3: The Book of the Forest*, Chicago: University of Chicago Press, 1981, 186–7.

55   See the discussion at J. J. Finkelstein, "The Genealogy of the Hammurapi Dynasty," *Journal of Cuneiform Studies* 20 (3/4), 1966: 95–118, 105.

56   Finkelstein, "The Genealogy of the Hammurapi Dynasty," 1966 has a further discussion of this text. Piotr Michalowski, "History as Charter Some Observations on the Sumerian King List," *Journal of the American Oriental Society* 103 (1), 1983: 237–48.

The *palū* of this text is the "turn" at rule of a particular dynasty or region; the "Genealogy of Hammurabi" thus concludes by tracing backwards in history a chain of hegemony over Western Semitic peoples into which Babylon can fit as the next link. Typically panchoric devices of the catalogue and the genealogy are obviously at work here, but note also that the earliest *palū* is that "not recorded on this tablet," that is, (for Finkelstein) a placeholder for past rulers unknown in the writer's time. Further, it is worth noting with Finkelstein that what is represented as a chronological sequence of West Semitic hegemonies conceals complex relationships with other centers of power in the region (such as the dynasty of Akkad, which significantly overlapped with the Gutians) and that the seamless whole of history that the document represents is as much a geographical-historical fabrication as the *Catalogue of Ships* or the *Airs of the States*.

In his comparative study of early state-formation, Norman Yoffee compares the early Mayan world to that of early Mesopotamia, as a region where a "common ideology . . . stretched over politically independent states . . . marked in material culture and literature and played out in economic and political interactions among the independent city-states."[57] Others have noted, for example, the presence of similarly formatted "Emblem Glyphs" in the archaeological remains of Mayan city-states, which indicated the names of local rulers and demarcated the territories they ruled.[58] The textual tradition, including the *Popol Vuh*, makes extensive use of the device of genealogy to link divine ancestors to leading families of the here-and-now.[59] All of these features are certainly suggestive of something like a panchoric ecology; as more epigraphical evidence becomes available and is studied, it will be interesting to think further on whether the Mayan world might be another instance of a panchoric environment; better understanding of the spoken language environment of the classical Mayan city-states would be of particular interest.

The Mayan case also acts as a reminder of the particular challenges of thinking comparatively about these panchoric contexts. In many cases, our

---

57 Norman Yoffee, 2005, *Myths of the Archaic State: Evolution of the Earliest Cities, States, and Civilizations,* Cambridge: Cambridge University Press, 44.

58 Nikolai Grube, "The City-States of the Maya," in *A Comparative Study of Thirty City-State Cultures: An Investigation*, edited by Mogens Herman Hansen and Københavns universitet, Polis centre, Copenhagen: Kgl. Danske Videnskabernes Selskab, 2000, 547–66.

59 Dennis Tedlock, *Popol Vuh: The Mayan Book of the Dawn of Life*, New York: Simon and Schuster, 1996, 194ff.

evidence for these cultures is spotty; moreover, the categories of evidence available in one case are often unavailable in another. Without extant literary texts, it is of course impossible to say much about a particular literary ecology, but discrepancies in the kinds of texts available (and in the prestige associated with different texts) can also make it difficult to draw general conclusions. My purpose in linking these cultures (pre-Islamic Arabic, Vedic Sanskrit, ancient Near Eastern, Mayan) to the panchoric ecology I have identified in early Greece and China is not to force each of these quite distinctive cultural worlds into an artificially homogeneous scheme. Rather, it is my intention to provide a basis for further discussion. Each of these contexts seems to involve a linguistic and literary world that is larger than the local horizons of the polity; a lively comparative discussion of the different textual and hermeneutic strategies employed in these contexts can only, I think, enrich the study of each.

Panchorism in Evolutionary Perspective

Empirically speaking, the panchoric ecologies I have enumerated seem all to have been comparatively unstable, always while active oscillating between the epichoric and the panchoric, and almost always evolving into something else in short order. Indeed, of the possible panchorisms I discuss, most—Archaic Greece, Eastern Zhou China, South Asia during the era of the epics, pre-Islamic Arabia, Babylonia—transformed into cosmopolitan ecologies relatively soon after establishing themselves as panchoric, often, in fact, exhibiting signs of incipient cosmopolitanism while the panchoric was still consolidating (as, I argued in my previous book, was the case with Greece and China). The only exceptions to this pattern of panchorism evolving relatively rapidly into cosmopolitanism would seem to be the Mesoamerican cases, where the evolution of the cultural ecology was utterly transformed by the crisis of conquest. The converse is also generally true; almost all the major cosmopolitan languages seem to have begun as panchoric languages. The exceptions, such as Latin, New Persian, and (perhaps) medieval and early modern French, seem mostly to have been secondary formations, vernaculars that eventually partly or completely supplanted the cosmopolitan languages against which they had originally competed.

Is there anything inherent to the panchoric ecology that would explain this phenomenon? In my view, there is. Panchorism as a process involves two phenomena: the construction of a space of shared culture out of a collection of related but distinct local cultures and the creation of new cultural objects (such as Homeric epic or the *Canon of Songs*) designed to speak across those local cultures and, in the process, homogenize them to some extent. Taken to their logical conclusions, each of these phenomena has its own effect. The construction of a shared cultural space, while it does not by any means require the creation of a common political regime, certainly facilitates that creation. Alexander the Great, Qin Shi Huangdi, Chandragupta Maurya,[60] Muhammad, Hammurabi—all certainly manipulated existing cultural artifacts as part of the process of consolidating their conquests, but to the extent that they could draw on an existing cultural repertoire to do so, the community their conquests forced lived more durably in the imagination. At the same time, the fact that panchoric cultural practices themselves had needed to assert themselves over and against a range of local alternatives may have made these cultures especially well suited to new cosmopolitan contexts where they still competed against the local, if now a local that no longer bore any necessary relationship to them. The process by which this took place forms the subject of the next chapter.

---

60 For a thoughtful discussion of the relationship between the text of the Mahabharata and what James L. Fitzgerald sees as a "crisis of dharma" roughly contemporaneous with the rule of Ashoka, Chandragupta Maurya's grandson, see Fitzgerald, *The Mahubhārata, Volume 7: Book 11: The Book of the Women Book 12: The Book of Peace*, Chicago: University of Chicago Press, 2004, 100–42.

CHAPTER 3

Cosmopolitan Literature

In the middle of the first century AD, a Pharisee from Asia Minor, Paul the Apostle, writes in koinê Greek to the emergent Christian community in Rome, citing passages from the *Psalms* and *Deuteronomy* to do so. About a century later, a Chinese intellectual, known to us as Master Mou, living in exile in what is now Hanoi during the collapse of the Han Dynasty, is said to write a *Treatise on Removing Doubts* (牟子理惑論), which uses quotations from the by-then canonical Confucian classics to advance the Buddhist cause. Both men, in other words, are circulating in complex cultural worlds. Paul (or Saul, to give him his pre conversion name) was by birth a Jew, a Pharisee of the Tribe of Benjamin, born in Tarsus in Asia Minor (near modern Adana and the Mediterranean coast of Turkey), though apparently raised in Jerusalem itself (*Acts* 26:4); while Hebrew still had liturgical functions within Judaism, and Aramaic was the spoken language of most Jews living in Judea, Paul/Saul was likely more comfortable in the koinê Greek in which he wrote his epistles. He was also a Roman citizen (*Acts* 16:37–8) and as such participated in multiple social, cultural, and political networks—Jewish, Christian, Hellenistic Greek, Roman. Master Mou (if he existed; there are reasons to doubt; see below) likewise inhabited multiple cultural worlds. A scholar-official trained in Ruist (i.e., Confucian) texts, Mou Rong was forced to flee the center during the Yellow Turban rebellion near the end of the Eastern Han Dynasty (184 AD) and is said to have ended up in Jiaozhou, then a peripheral province of the crumbling Han but today roughly northern Vietnam. Jiaozhou was, at the time, the leading Chinese port for trade with the West, and it may have been through maritime contacts here, rather than through more familiar terrestrial contacts along the Silk Road in the following centuries, that China first encountered Buddhism.[1]

---

1 Yong Wu, "Shilun 'Mouzi lihuolun' zhi zhenwei," *Zongjiaoxue yanjiu* 7 (2), 2007: 68–73; Dung Ngoc Duong, 2001, *Buddhist Discourse in Traditional Vietnam*, Boston: Boston University, 2007; Cuong Tu Nguyen, *Zen in Medieval Vietnam*, Honolulu: University of Hawaii Press, 1997.

According to the preface to the text, Jiaozhou was also home to many Daoist practitioners, differing in their religious and philosophical convictions from Master Mou's more orthodox Ruism but likewise refugees from the collapse of the Eastern Han. Master Mou, like most other Han Chinese of the pre-modern era, will likely have spoken a Sinitic language somewhat removed from the classical Chinese in which he wrote. The linguistic environment in Jiaozhou is somewhat more uncertain, but there is reason to think that the common language spoken there may have been the ancestor of what is now Vietnamese, though other languages, from other language families, may have been spoken as well.[2]

I have discussed Master Mou's text in more detail elsewhere and offer only a sample of my findings here.[3] Briefly, where other early Chinese Buddhist texts frequently make use of vernacular registers (used for the first time for literary purposes),[4] Master Mou's text is not only composed in the classical idiom, but also makes frequent use of allusions to major texts of the philosophical tradition, playfully quoting these texts against their own intentions as a rhetorical device to present Buddhist ideas in a favorable light. As a brief example, consider the following passage:

> Someone asked: "You use the classics and the *Commentaries* to explain Buddha's words. Your words are abundant and your meaning lucid, your prose vigorous and your speech beautiful. But it goes nowhere; these aren't the Buddha's truths, they're your debating points." Master Mou said: "They're not my debating points; it's just that I see broadly and <u>am not confused</u>." He was asked: "What is your technique for seeing broadly?" Master Mou said, "It comes from the Buddhist canons. At the time when I did not yet understand the Buddhist canons, my confusion was deeper than yours. Though I recited the Five Classics, I treated them as flowers, and did not attain their fruits. Once I observed the Buddhist canons, and perused the essentials of Laozi, I was <u>able to preserve a tranquil</u>

---

2   William Meacham, "Defining the Hundred Yue," *Bulletin of the Indo-Pacific Prehistory Association* 15, 1996: 93–100.

3   Alexander Beecroft, "When Cosmopolitanisms Intersect: An Early Chinese Buddhist Apologetic and World Literature," *Comparative Literature Studies* 47 (3), 2010.

4   Victor H. Mair, "Buddhism and the Rise of the Written Vernacular in East Asia: The Making of National Languages," *The Journal of Asian Studies* 53 (3), 1994: 707–15. As we shall see in the chapter on vernacular ecologies which follows, religious prosyelyetizing is frequently an impetus for the development of vernacular literature.

nature and gaze at the conduct of nonaction. When I turned to inspect worldly affairs, it was as if I looked down on the Heavenly Well Pass and stole a glance at mountainous ravines. I ascended <u>Mounts Song and Dai and saw hillocks and anthills</u>. The Five Classics are the Five Flavors; the Way of the Buddha is the Five Grains. After I heard the Way, it was as if the clouds parted and I saw the blazing sun, as if torches entered a gloomy room." (1:19b–20a)[5]

I have elsewhere discussed this passage in some detail; for my purposes here it is sufficient to note that the three underlined passages are, respectively, citations of Confucius, the *Zhuangzi* and the Mencius—three very different, yet each highly influential, philosophical texts from the Chinese tradition, each already several hundred years old by Master Mou's time. Most suggestively for my purposes, note the final underlined passage, which is a reference to a passage in the Mencius where it is claimed that Confucius exceeds ordinary men in the way that Mounts Song and Tai (both sacred in traditional Chinese practices) exceed anthills and hillocks. This trope, of taking a referent or figure from the epichoric or panchoric tradition and universalizing it, is one of the key organizing tropes of cosmopolitan discourse. In Mencius, Mounts Song and Tai are seen as vastly exceeding hillocks in height but nonetheless as real places, locatable within a map of the Chinese politico-cultural world. In Master Mou's text, by contrast, they have become pure allegory, representing not themselves but sheer vastness—and the tenor of the simile here is the Buddhist tradition, outside the world of traditional Chinese religion and representing itself both through this trope and everywhere as more completely universal.

As a follower of Jesus, Paul likewise universalizes tropes found in more local contexts. I am not a scholar of religion, but I would like to draw attention in passing to a brief moment of the sort I am describing in Paul's letter to the Romans. The epistle as a whole is concerned, in part, with the roles of both Jews and Gentiles as potential followers of Jesus and famously reduces the commandments to the proscription to love one's neighbors as one does oneself, for love is the completion of the law (πλήρωμα οὖν νόμου ἡ ἀγάπη, Romans 13:10). This is already interesting as a universalization of

---

5   問曰。 吾子以經傳理佛說。其辭富而義顯。其文熾而說美。 得無非其誠是子之辯也。牟子曰。非吾辯也。見博故 不惑耳問曰。見博其有術乎。牟子曰。由佛經也。吾未解佛經之時。惑甚於子。雖誦五經適以為華。未成實矣。既吾睹佛經之說。覽老子之要。守恬憺之性。觀無為之行。還視世事。猶臨天井而闚溪谷。 登嵩岱而見丘垤矣 。五經則五味。佛道則五穀矣。吾自聞道以來。如開雲見白日。矩火入冥室焉。

the more specific provisions of the ten commandments, but Paul goes further a little later in the epistle, arguing that Jesus appeared among the Jews not only to confirm the promises made to them earlier but also that the Gentiles might praise God. He cites from Deuteronomy to do so, specifically (of course) from the Hellenistic Greek translation of the Hebrew Bible, the Septuagint. The very fact that the sacred scriptures of an ethnically based religious group who did not proselytize were translated into Greek in the first place is, of course, an index of the spread and influence of the Greek language in the centuries immediately preceding Paul. But the passage itself has further interest. I cite only one line, from Romans 15:10: "and again it says, 'Rejoice, nations, with his people'" ("καὶ πάλιν λέγει 'Εὐφράνθητε, ἔθνη, μετὰ τοῦ λαοῦ αὐτοῦ.'"). In the context of Paul's argument, the "nations" (sometimes translated, as in the King James Version, as "ye Gentiles"), are the non-Jewish followers of the (Judaeo-) Christian God, rejoicing that that god has honored the Jews.

The relation to the source text in Deuteronomy (32:43) is complicated here. The Septuagint text for the passage is identical to that quoted by Paul, and the Masoretic text of the Hebrew Bible (that is, the text canonical in Judaism) contains a Hebrew original that, while somewhat convoluted, is consistent with the sense of its Greek translation.[6] In the context of the text of Deuteronomy, however, the sense is focused on divine revenge. I quote from Robert Alter's translation here:

> I will make My shafts drunk with blood,
> and My sword will eat up flesh,
> from the blood of the fallen and captive,
> from the flesh of the long-haired foe.
> Nations, O gladden his people,
> for His servants' blood will He avenge,
> and vengeance turn back on His foes,
> and purge His soil, His people.

While the passage is hardly flattering to God's own people, making clear that they require vengeance themselves, it is clear in context that the author of the passage in Deuteronomy does not imagine the "nations" (*goyim* in Hebrew) as rejoicing but rather that their own torments should be a delight

---

6   Robert Alter, *The Five Books of Moses: A Translation with Commentary*, New York: W. W. Norton & Company, 2008, 1046.

to the chosen people, who will see their enemies vanquished even as they suffer themselves. In a manner rather like Master Mou, then, Paul quotes his tradition against itself, in the service of rendering it in some way universal: where Master Mou used the tropes of Confucian rhetoric to establish Buddhism as greater than its rivals, here Paul uses rhetoric from the Hebrew Bible, which in context suggests that "the nations" will be punished, to suggest instead that (should they follow Jesus) they will join in the glories to come. The matter is still more complicated: the Dead Sea Scroll text from Qumran of the Deuteronomy passage reads quite differently. As Robert Alter translates verse 43 in the Qumran version, "Gladden, O heavens, His people, / and let all divine beings bow before Him. // For his sons' blood He will avenge / and vengeance turn back on His foes. // And His enemies He will requite /and purge His people's soil."[7] Alter suggests that this may be the earlier version; if he is correct, then the earlier passage will have been directed as much at rival deities as at rival nations, and our current text will have won out thanks to the support of the more rigorous monotheists of later eras. Monotheism will have gone hand in hand with a stronger sense of rivalry with other traditions and peoples, leading to the Masoretic and Septuagint text, which Paul then transforms to suit his own agenda.

Both Saul/Paul and Master Mou, then, participated in what the Sanskritist Sheldon Pollock would call a literary cosmopolis, a vast, transcultural, translingual, transpolitical space within which a single literary language predominates—Saul/Paul within a world of cosmopolitan Greek culture under Roman rule, Master Mou within a cosmopolitan order built on classical Chinese, in his era slowly being permeated by another cosmopolitan order built around Buddhism. Pollock develops his thinking around the case of Sanskrit in the first millennium AD. Pollock defines the Sanskrit cosmopolis (for him, paradigmatic of the cosmopolitan system as a whole) as a region, stretching from Afghanistan to Java, in which written Sanskrit literary texts are used for the aesthetic self-representation of political power, especially over the course of the first millennium AD. Much of the evidence Pollock uses comes from inscriptional evidence; in much of the Sanskrit cosmopolis during this period, what Pollock calls "documentary" inscriptions—those endowing land to a particular family, for instance—are frequently written in the vernacular, while Sanskrit is used for those inscriptions that are "workly," the term Pollock (drawing on Heidegger) uses for texts in literary language whose goal is aesthetic self-representation.

---

7   Ibid., 1043.

Crucially for Pollock, the choice to use Sanskrit for these purposes arises not as a result of conquest, colonization, trade, or religious proselytizing. Rather it is a consequence of the charismatic power of the Sanskrit language and of the cultural products written in it.

It is important to notice here that the claim is not that the Sanskrit cosmopolis is somehow divorced from the political, a free-floating cultural public sphere unconstrained by kingly or imperial ambitions. Far from it; as the previous paragraph makes clear, the clearest evidence for the emergence of the cosmopolis comes from inscriptions erected by rulers—a political use of culture if ever there was one. Rather, the interesting phenomenon here is that the relationship between culture and power is very different in the case of the Sanskrit cosmopolis from that encountered in the modern world. Why do Javanese, Khmer, and South Indian courts go to such trouble to master the difficult and alien language of Sanskrit in order to represent their power to themselves and to the world, even after they have the means of doing so in their own languages? Why, for that matter, do kings in what is now Afghanistan continue to build Greek-style theaters centuries after Alexander's conquests have come and gone? Why do successive ethnically Turkic dynasties in South Asia use Persian (native neither to themselves nor to their subjects) as their literary and administrative language? Why do Japanese rulers seeking to express their domination over the entire known world do so in terms obviously borrowed from Chinese (and thus from a people not subject to their power)? To imagine modern equivalents to these phenomena, it would be as if the British rulers of India in the nineteenth century had communicated with their colonial subjects in French, or as if American soldiers in the early twenty-first century in Iraq and Afghanistan had inspired the composition of poetry in Greek and Latin among the civilian officials they trained there.

I use these modern parallels advisedly. It is problematic to project modern notions of empire and imperialism onto regimes of the distant past, regimes as diverse as the conquest empires of Alexander and Genghis Khan, or the more settled and bureaucratic systems of Rome, the Islamic Caliphate, the Gupta Empire in India, and the Han and Tang Dynasties in China, which among them pursued radically different strategies for managing linguistic, cultural, and religious difference, not to mention holding radically different kinds of authority across the territories nominally or actually under their rule. That said, there is no question that all of these regimes exploited the populations subject to them, with varying degrees of efficiency and to varying extents, and that these regimes were built and maintained through a level of violence that we rightly condemn when we see it in our own time.

Violent and exploitative as they undeniably were, political systems in and around Pollock's cosmopolitan millennium (very roughly, the first millennium AD, though with earlier beginnings in some cases, and continuing later, even to the present, in others) frequently saw fit to promote their own power in languages that were neither their own nor native among their subjects. As such, these regimes represented a relationship between culture and power quite distinct from that of the modern nation-state (where language and polity at least notionally coincide), or even the European empires of the nineteenth and twentieth centuries, or the global capitalism of the twenty-first, in which military and economic power is used to project dominant culture into dominated areas but under which the dominant culture is generally that of a nation-state. To pursue the Sanskrit case very briefly, it is not that there were no transregional political formations within the Sanskrit cosmopolis; indeed, the Gupta Dynasty ruled in some fashion over much of modern South Asia during the fourth through sixth centuries AD, and Pollock acknowledges that it was under the Guptas that Sanskrit cosmopolitan style "crystallized."[8] Rather, the emergence of Sanskrit for the kinds of "workly" inscriptions (and of poetry) predates the Gupta period, long outlasts it, and circulates far more broadly than any notion of Gupta political power. Although in many of the regions of the cosmopolis writing and Sanskrit arrive simultaneously, and so systems for writing the vernacular emerge only out of the cosmopolitan practice, this is not the case in the northern Indian heartlands of Sanskrit themselves (where so-called daughter languages of Sanskrit, including the Prakrits and Pali, were already in regular use), and, as Pollock notes, those polities that did employ vernaculars long tended to use them for more mundane functions.

Pollock takes great pains to distinguish his notion of the Sanskrit cosmopolis from two potentially similar constructs, those of the nation-state and the "civilization."[9] That the Sanskrit cosmopolis is neither a nation-state nor even the precursor to one should be clear from the geographic and cultural breadth of the Sanskrit cosmopolis as Pollock

---

8   Sheldon Pollock, *The Language of the Gods in the World of Men: Sanskrit, Culture, and Power in Premodern India*, Berkeley: University of California Press, 2009, 139.

9   Ibid., 538.

describes it. The distinction between Pollock's cosmopolis and notions of the civilization requires, perhaps, more unpacking. It is important first of all to understand that Pollock is here referring to the notion of a civilization as a constant and unchanging perception of the world, of the kind adopted by, for example, by Samuel Huntington, and not (to take a different model) that of the "smallest intelligible unit of study," favored by Toynbee, and which I discuss at greater length in the introduction. To some extent, indeed, Pollock's cosmopolis overlaps with Toynbee's civilization as a unit of study (though in practice the cosmopolitan millennium Pollock identifies cuts across Toynbee's civilizational divide between "Indic" and "Hindu" civilizations).[10] Both categories, as I suggest in the introduction, fall victim to the same methodological flaw, which is that they of necessity impose chronological and geographic boundaries (however fluid) on phenomena qualitatively unsuited to them. As we shall see below, participating in more than one cosmopolis at a time is not only possible but perhaps even normal: India under the Mughals was fully part of both a Sanskrit and a Persian cosmopolis; Java, both a Sanskrit and an Arabic cosmopolis, without necessarily shifting from one to the other; many parts of the Middle East under Ottoman rule simultaneously inhabited the Arabic, Persian, and Turkish cosmopoleis. If Buddhism and Christianity can be said to constitute a different kind of cosmopolis, then even China and modern Europe have been bicosmopolitan, the former Buddhist and classical Chinese; the latter, Greco-Roman and Christian. Regions, and frequently individual authors, also participated in both panchoric and cosmopolitan, or both cosmopolitan and vernacular, ecologies, as we shall see in more detail in the chapter on vernacular ecologies. An ecological approach, which seeks typological similarities between different environments but does not need to draw strict boundaries between their geographically and chronologically bound expressions, may prove more methodologically fruitful here.

That said, the question remains of whether Pollock's notion of the literary cosmopolis is transferrable to other contexts. Pollock himself compares the Sanskrit cosmopolis to the world of Latin in the European West, arguing that the use of Latin as a language of culture and power is much more directly the result of conquest, exploitation, and the eradication of alternative languages, where Sanskrit seems to spread more peacefully. To varying degrees, this seems to be true of all of the languages that are suitable

10   Arnold J. Toynbee, *A Study of History, Vol. 1: Abridgement of Volumes I–VI*, Oxford: Oxford University Press, 1987.

candidates for cosmopolitan status. By its nature, the literary cosmopolis is destined to be a category with few members; only a small number of languages have ever had anything like the range of use over and beyond where they are natively spoken or spread solely by conquest or colonization. In the paragraphs that follow, I consider a small number of candidate cosmopolitan languages: Sumerian, Akkadian, Greek, Latin, Arabic, New Persian, and classical Chinese.

I believe that each of these languages bears enough ecological similarity to the patterns Pollock observes with Sanskrit to warrant consideration as a group, but several preliminary caveats are in order. First of all, if Pollock is correct that the Sanskrit cosmopolis was formed without significant assistance from conquest or colonization, it is the only such case I have uncovered. Each of the other candidate languages I discuss certainly spreads to at least some extent through these violent means; they earn their cosmopolitan status through the fact that their usage persists long after the empires that gave them rise had faded away or spread their influence in regions beyond their empire's farthest border. The literary status of Sumerian outlasts its population of native speakers, and Akkadian likewise remained (with Sumerian) the major literary language of the ancient Near East for nearly a millennium and a half after the fall of the Akkadian Empire around 2154 BC. Greek similarly maintained its status in the eastern Mediterranean long after the Roman conquests of the mid-second century BC and onwards, over the five hundred years or so before the division of the Roman Empire into Eastern and Western halves gave Greek again a firmer official footing in the East. Latin's status as the leading language of intellectual and cultural life in Western Europe continued after the fall of Rome in AD 476, arguably until the seventeenth century; during the so-called Dark Ages, peripheral regions, such as Ireland and the north of England, either never under Roman rule or far from its center, maintained the prestige of Latin. New Persian likewise was spread beyond the regions ruled by Persians, as when the Mughal emperors (originally speakers of Chagatay Turkish) spread the use of Persian as a literary language across India; New Persian's cosmopolitan status endured from its ninth-century origins through into the nineteenth century and encompassed regions, such as South Asia and the Ottoman Empire, not under the rule of native Persian speakers. Arabic (together with Islam) spread rapidly through the conquests of the early Islamic era, but, fourteen hundred years later, the language of Mohammed is still largely the literary language of a vast area. Classical Chinese spread throughout the territory of the modern People's Republic of China and beyond in central Asia and in Vietnam as a result of conquest, but its use in Korea and (especially) in Japan was far more the result of emulation than of force.

A workable definition of a cosmopolitan literature, then, will be one for which the cultural resources acquired by the language may have been accumulated in part as the result of conquest, trade, or colonization, but that persists in the absence of those factors. If we think of cosmopolitan literatures in this way, we see perhaps that the contrasts Pollock draws between Sanskrit and Latin as model cosmopolitan languages are less sharp than his argument suggests. In its earliest stages, as I have already suggested and will argue further in the next chapter, Latin was a paradigmatic vernacular language, beginning its literary career through the translation of cosmopolitan texts (just as Pollock finds the vernaculars of South and Southeast Asia to have done). At the height of Roman imperial power, from the second century BC through the fifth century AD, Latin indeed became the dominant language of the Western Mediterranean, but in the East, Greek endured, both as a language of political power and as a language of cultural prestige (in this role sometimes with Roman imperial patronage).[11] Latin spread at the point of a spear but was held back in the Greek East not by arms but by the charismatic force of the Greek language. Only after the fall of Rome and the emergence of vernacular polities in the early and high Middle Ages was the role of Latin clearly entrenched as cosmopolitan in Pollock's sense, serving as an essential medium for the aesthetic expression of rule by rival polities as the language of the church and as the language of written literature, culture, and education. To a significant extent, this cosmopolitan status was because of the role of the church as the predominant mechanism through which intellectual and cultural activity circulated in the period, but the status of Latin outlasted Catholic religious hegemony in Europe, and many Protestants, religious skeptics, and Jews relied on Latin as the most effective vehicle for their literary ambitions, secular as well as spiritual. As we shall see in the chapter on national literatures, intellectuals of the early modern period frequently found, in the Latinate "republic of letters," a space within which cultural production could, to at least some extent, escape the increasingly pervasive grasp of the emergent authoritarian state. The Latin cosmopolis, then, was neither as "demonic" as Pollock, with acknowledged polemical intent, suggests, even if

---

11   *Pace* Pollock, who seems to suggest that Latin was the only language used for literature and inscriptions in the Roman empire. Pollock, *The Language of the Gods*, 270.

it was not exactly "angelic"; it can be understood neither as simply a vehicle of imperialist hegemony nor as a space innocently free of political domination.[12] Rather, the Latin cosmopolis, like the other literary ecologies we have examined (and like all such ecologies, including the Sanskrit cosmopolis), featured a complex symbiosis between politics and culture, where the former frequently, but not always, drives the latter.

To explore the ecological situation of the literary cosmopolis further, the available evidence suggests three environments within which cosmopolitan literatures tended to flourish: panchoric environments, which for political or cultural reasons expanded to include large non-native-speaker communities; regions previously illiterate or with limited use of writing, which acquired literacy through contact with a cosmopolitan literary language; and regions where one cosmopolitan language was already in use and where a new cosmopolitan language either replaced or supplemented the first. Combinations of these scenarios are, of course, possible. Examples of the first model, as I argued in my previous book and as I will discuss in more detail later, include Greek and Chinese;[13] If Sheldon Pollock is right about Sanskrit as always-already a transregional sacred language never spoken as a mother tongue by any community, then it, too, might fit this paradigm.[14] Many of the regions into which these three languages expanded may fit the second model, as with Japan, Vietnam, and Korea from Chinese, and Java and the Khmer from Sanskrit. More complex is the third model, in which one cosmopolitan language supplants or supplements another; examples here may include Akkadian's coexistence with, then supplanting of, Sumerian in the ancient Near East (not to mention Akkadian's gradual replacement with Aramaic and/or Greek) as well as the emergence of New Persian as a cosmopolitan literary language alongside Arabic within the Muslim world beginning in the tenth century AD; the emergence of French as what Pollock would call a "cosmopolitan vernacular" in early modern Europe might provide a further example of this third model, which I will discuss further in the following chapter.

---

12   Ibid., 574; see the further discussion in Alexander Beecroft, "The Sanskrit Ecumene: Review of Pollock, Sheldon. The Language of the Gods in the World of Men: Sanskrit, Culture, and Power in Premodern India," *New Left Review* 72, 2011.

13   Alexander Beecroft, *Authorship and Cultural Identity in Early Greece and China: Patterns of Literary Circulation*, Cambridge: Cambridge University Press, 2010.

14   Pollock, *The Language of the Gods*, 262.

What all three models have in common is that in each case the region adopting a cosmopolitan literary language either lacks a strong written vernacular, or has a long history of diglossia (or rather digraphia) between cosmopolitan and vernacular literary languages. Since even today the range of spoken languages is much broader than the number of written languages, the choice of literary language in which to write has always been a trade-off between using a written language that circulates over a broad area but will as a result be harder for many people to learn, as it will deviate more from their spoken language, and using a written language that circulates over a narrower area but, because it more closely approximates the spoken language for more people, can be understood by a deeper cross-section of that regional population. In the pre-modern context, cosmopolitan languages represented the most extreme version of the first of these options; texts produced in these languages could be read across thousands of miles and often for thousands of years, although inequities in the systems of circulation, as we have seen, may have prevented this from happening in practice. The cost of so doing was always that the cosmopolitan literary language was remote from spoken language almost everywhere (and in many cases highly complex to learn) so that a relatively small percentage of the population in any given region would be able to read texts written in it. In modern times, this is of course an ecological disadvantage for a literature; however, in an era of generally low literacy and in a region where vernaculars generally were not used for literary purposes, cosmopolitan languages would in fact be the most ideally suited medium for ensuring the most successful transmission and circulation of literary texts. In an era of low literacy and high costs of textual production, breadth trumps depth.

Even when vernaculars emerged, of course, the accumulated cultural resources of the cosmopolitan literary language often remained impressive enough to ensure that the vernacular was long only a supplement to the cosmopolitan, not a replacement. Thus written literature in vernacular Latin begins in the third century BC with Livius Andronicus's *Odusia* (as we shall discuss further in Chapter 4), yet for centuries to come knowledge of cosmopolitan Greek remained an essential prerequisite of refinement and sophistication in the Roman world, and Roman writers continued to find Greek literature at least as influential as Latin until after Virgil. Moreover, in the eastern Mediterranean, Greek literature continued to be lively and productive throughout the era of Roman rule; while Latin was used for some administrative and epigraphical purposes, Greek writers of the period demonstrated little if any sense of Latin literature as holding a cultural prestige commensurate with its political position. The vernacular literatures of modern Europe likewise remained peripheral to Latin (now elevated to cosmopolitan status) until the seventeenth century; writing in classical Chinese long remained a strong alternative to vernacular Japanese in that nation; and the use of Sanskrit in the seventeenth century in India rivaled or surpassed that of the by then well-entrenched vernaculars for many purposes.[15] Even in the face of direct competition with vernacular literatures, then, cosmopolitan languages frequently remained vital. In part, this was because of continuing low levels of literacy and because of elite education systems, which, for the most part, continued to emphasize the learning of cosmopolitan literary languages into the early twentieth century, whether in university study at Heidelberg, Bologna, Oxford, or the Sorbonne, or in preparation for the civil service examinations in China. Beyond this, of course, vernacular languages (as we shall see in more detail in the next chapter) were frequently themselves quite far removed from the spoken languages of everyday people, as they are still today in many places, so that the relative advantage of ease of learning to be gained from using a vernacular rather than a cosmopolitan language was often smaller than a modern reader might suppose.

In what follows, I trace first the general outlines of the literary cosmopoleis I have identified—Akkadian/Sumerian, Greek, Latin, Arabic, Persian, and Classical Chinese[16]—in order to provide a general context for understanding the above observations. I then move on to consider a series of issues relevant to all cosmopolitan ecologies, with specific reference to a few in each case. The issues I explore are questions of literary circulation and polycentricity, the trope by which questions of literary style are projected onto the geography of the cosmopolis, and the use of explicitly cosmopolitan vocabulary and thinking within a cosmopolitan tradition, incipient or fully formed. Each of these issues illustrates something important about the structure and function of the literary cosmopolis, which can range from highly monocentric and hierarchical in circulation to highly polycentric and egalitarian in circulation and from highly self-conscious to rather more implicit in nature. These differences, as I suggest in the

---

15   Sheldon Pollock, "New Intellectuals in Seventeenth-Century India," *Indian Economic & Social History Review* 38 (1), 2001: 3–31.

16   I omit here a discussion of the Sansrkit cosmopolis, already much more ably documented in Pollock, *The Language of the Gods*.

conclusion, say something about the durability of each cosmopolis and about the changes it may have undergone over time.

CASE STUDIES IN THE LITERARY COSMOPOLIS

The earliest languages that could be described as cosmopolitan are Sumerian and Akkadian, both languages of the ancient Near East. These two languages, genetically unrelated to each other (Akkadian is a Semitic language; Sumerian has no certain linguistic relatives), successively emerged as literary and workly languages in Mesopotamia, though for long periods they performed this role jointly, even as neither was a major spoken language.[17] Writing itself was invented in southern Mesopotamia in the mid-fourth millennium BC; by around 2600 BC (about a thousand years later), we find the first literary texts, which archaeological evidence shows to have spread already beyond political boundaries and beyond Sumerian city-states to non-Sumerophone regions, such as Syria. Very shortly there-after (at least on the timescales of the ancient Near East), we find evidence for the use of other regional languages, Akkadian and Eblaite, for literary purposes. Though these uses seem indebted to prior developments in Sumerian, it should be noted that the latter language did not function at this time as a medium for interregional discourse.

The rise of the dynasty of Akkad around 2500 BC and its spread into Syria and Elam (i.e., what is now southern Iran) led to the spread of written Akkadian for administrative purposes across the empire—probably the first instance of the spread of a language as an instrument of empire, although Sumerian is thought to have remained the principal subject of education. When Akkad fell around 2100 BC, the king and lawgiver Ur-Namma established the so-called third dynasty of Ur, whose center was in the region formerly associated with Sumerian; although there is reason to believe Sumerian was no longer a spoken vernacular, it did become the major administrative and literary language of the empire. By the seven-teenth century BC, roughly a thousand years after the earliest uses of the language for literary purposes and two thousand years after it was first

---

17　This discussion of the history of Sumerian and Akkadian follows, as it greatly simplifies, Piotr Michalowski, "The Lives of the Sumerian Language," in *Margins of Writing, Origins of Culture*, edited by S. L. Sanders. Chicago: University Of Chicago Press, 2006. Michalowski notes that his own thinking on these issues derives in part from Pollock's work.

committed to writing, Sumerian was no longer used for accounting, having been replaced by Akkadian, though Sumerian was still what was taught in school. No longer the mother tongue of any population, Sumerian remained the basis of the education system and (along with other languages such as Akkadian and Elamite) was in daily use for ritual purposes, though increasingly Akkadian was used for all other purposes. The ensuing few centuries saw a further decline in the role of Sumerian; school texts in Sumerian were now bilingual in Akkadian or, on the periphery of the Akkadian world, in local vernaculars; nonetheless, Sumerian persisted as a scholarly and liturgical language into the first couple of centuries AD. By this time, Akkadian itself was no longer the everyday spoken vernacular of Mesopotamia (having been replaced in that role by Aramaic), though it too persisted as a literary language; consequently two "dead" languages coexisted as cosmopolitan literary languages, even as Aramaic and Greek began to be used for everyday purposes.[18] The exact date Sumerian ceased to be a spoken vernacular is strongly contested, and the question becomes as much a matter of terminology and theory as of evidence. Some have argued that Sumerian died out as a spoken language during the third dynasty of Ur (2100–2000 BC), precisely as it was being revived as a literary language;[19] others believe that the spoken language became extinct much earlier, during the social turmoil of the middle Uruk period (i.e., in the mid-fourth millennium BC, at the very time it was committed to writing); according to some, it was never really a spoken language. Others think it continued as a spoken language much later.[20] Whatever the case, it is clear that the lives of both Sumerian and Akkadian as written and cosmopolitan languages across broad swathes of territory not only long outlasted the states that propagated them but also likely operated quite independently of their lives as spoken vernaculars. If Sumerian and Akkadian were the first cosmopolitan languages, they exhibited the features of that ecology spectacularly.

I offer here only a brief introduction to the Greek cosmopolis, which features prominently in the later sections of this chapter and on which I have of course written before.[21] After the conquests of Alexander the Great, kingdoms ruled by his Macedonian compatriots controlled the entire former

---

18   Ibid., 172–3.
19   Ibid., 176.
20   C. Woods, "Bilingualism, Scribal Learning, and the Death of Sumerian," in *Margins of Writing, Origins of Culture*, edited by S. L. Sanders, Chicago: University of Chicago Press, 2006, 91–120.
21   Beecroft, *Authorship and Cultural Identity*.

Persian Empire, from Egypt to Bactria (modern Afghanistan), and the use of Greek as an official language spread across this vast region. The cultural role played by Greek in the Hellenistic era is highly complex, and it is necessary to examine several kinds of evidence. There is considerable evidence that the day-to-day use of Greek in many parts of the Hellenistic world, particularly Persia, was relatively limited and largely confined to Greek émigré communities.[22] We know of the building of theaters and other typically Greek structures as far afield as Bactria (modern Afghanistan) and also of the erection of "workly" inscriptions in Greek there—there are edicts of Asoka (304–232 BC) transcribed into Greek in Gandhara (near modern Peshawar in Pakistan); although again we should probably think of a narrow urban elite speaking Greek and of the use of Greek as a prestige literary vehicle rather than as a language of daily use by a large population.[23] Closer to the traditional centers of Greek culture, the inscriptional record shows that Greek became almost the exclusive language of inscriptions in Asia Minor after the conquests of Alexander, and most of the other languages of that region seem to have become extinct or extirpated during the Hellenistic era. Tellingly, in Asia Minor under Roman rule, Latin was used for a number of "workly" inscriptional purposes, but the use of Greek remained intact for most private purposes and remained, in many ways, the "language of power."[24] This fact is one of the most telling in support of the cosmopolitan status of Greek in Pollock's sense; the language may have entered the heart of Asia Minor only as the result of conquest, but it became the dominant regional language and remained dominant even in the face of a very similar politico-military incursion by the Romans less than two centuries later. Similarly, and in spite of Pollock's seeming claims to the contrary that "if one wrote literature at all in the Roman Empire, one wrote in Latin,"[25] Greek literature in fact thrived during the centuries of Roman rule.[26]

---

22   Giusto Traina, "Notes on Hellenism in the Iranian East (Classico-Oriental Notes, 6–8)," *Iran and the Caucasus* 9 (1), 2005: 1–14.

23   N. Kazansky and E. Kriuchkova, "Translating Buddhist Texts into Hellenistic Koine (Marginal Notes to the Greek Translation of Ashoka's Edicts)," *Manuscripta Orientalia* 12 (3), 2006: 15–21, has an extensive reading of the Greek texts here. See also Pollock, *The Language of the Gods*, 265.

24   Claude Brixhe, "Linguistic Diversity in Asia Minor during the Empire: Koine and Non-Greek Languages," in *A Companion to the Ancient Greek Language*, edited by Egbert Bakker, Malden, MA; Oxford: Wiley-Blackwell, 2010, 228–52, 248.

25   Pollock, *The Language of the Gods*, 270.

26   For a recent discussion of the Greek literature of this period, see Tim

This brings us to the Latin cosmopolis, which began rather differently. Whereas Classical Chinese and Greek emerged as cosmopolitan languages out of a panchoric past (and Sanskrit and even Arabic seem to have done the same), Latin began very much as a vernacular literature, formed around a local polity and very much in competition from the beginning with an existing cosmopolitan literature, Greek; only later, and after Rome's military might had passed its peak, did Latin take on a fully cosmopolitan role. I discuss the early Latin tradition in more detail in the following chapter; for the moment, I draw attention only to the fact that many of the earliest works of Latin literature—Livius Andronicus's *Odusia*, Ennius's *Annales*, the dramas of Naevius and Plautus—are either direct translations of works of Greek literature or else (as with some of Naevius's tragedies and with Ennius's epic) adaptations of existing Greek genres to themes from Roman history—very much, in other words, the kinds of works that Pollock finds at the origins of vernacular literatures in South and Southeast Asia.

As Pollock himself notes, the Latin language spread with conquest and quickly grew to supplant all other languages in the inscriptional record in the Western Mediterranean. Given that almost all of the spoken languages of the region today are either derived from Latin (as with the Romance languages) or descend from the vernaculars of peoples who arrived after the Romans (as with Arabic and the Germanic and Slavic languages), Latin seems to have supplanted the spoken languages of its Western Empire as well, with a few exceptions in more remote regions, such as the Celtic languages, Basque, and Berber. The latter of these was in fact used for some inscriptional purposes during the Roman era, while evidence from the jurist Ulpian (170–228) and the church father Irenaeus (died c. 202), bishop of Lugdunum, suggest that in the later second century AD, languages such as Punic, Syriac, and the Celtic languages of Gaul enjoyed at least limited use in legal matters and in sermons, while literature in Syriac began to emerge in the second and third centuries.[27] The picture is thus more complex than Pollock represents it, as non-Latin languages certainly persisted in many domains throughout the history of the Western Roman Empire (and, in fact, it is arguably the Germanic languages, rather than

---

Whitmarsh, *Greek Literature and the Roman Empire: The Politics of Imitation*, New York: Oxford University Press, 2004.

27   R. MacMullen, "Provincial Languages in the Roman Empire," *American Journal of Philology* 87 (1), 1966: 1.

Latin, that are responsible for the disappearance of many Celtic languages and the marginalization of those that remain). Still, it is clear that Latin remained the almost exclusive linguistic vehicle for workly and aesthetic expression in the Western Empire, at least until the emergence of vernacular languages during the Middle Ages, while in the East, Greek maintained its cosmopolitan function throughout this period.

While it is certainly true that Latin spread in this function as a result of Roman conquest, and the continued vitality of Latin literary culture during the middle ages had much to do with the support of both the Church and the state (beginning at least with Charlemagne's reforms), this later medieval and early modern phase of the history of Latin literature certainly resembles more closely the literary cosmopolis as modeled by Pollock. Relevant here are the notions of *translatio imperii* and *translatio studii*, or the "transfer of rule" and the "transfer of learning," by which medieval Europeans like Otto of Freising (1114–58) and Chretien of Troyes (fl. late twelfth century), [28] accounted for the historical shift of political power and (from their perspective) cultural knowledge, from the Greek world to Rome to northern Europe.[29] Connected to some extent to the Crusades, these notions of "translation" linked political and cultural authority, but they did so in a reproducible way, since the process of translation was always open to repetition and to multiple pathways of reception such that, for example, England, France, and the Holy Roman Empire could each consider themselves in some way the legitimate heir to Rome and to Roman learning. Only after the discovery of the Americas radically transformed the scale and scope of *imperium* for Europeans did this universalizing yet reproducible rhetoric lose its power.[30] This reproducibility of cultural and political legitimation is conceptually similar to the patterns observed by Pollock in the Sanskrit cosmopolis, by which emblems of royal authority, such as features of sacred geography, could be mapped onto new physical locations such that many kingdoms throughout South and Southeast Asia found themselves along Ganges rivers and

---

28   For a recent study of the issue, see Sharon Kinoshita, "The Poetics of Translation: French-Byzantine Relations in Chrétien de Troyess Cligés," *Exemplaria* 8 (2), 1996: 315–54

29   J. G. A. Pocock, "The Historiography of the Translatio Imperii," in *Barbarism and Religion, Vol. 3*, Cambridge: Cambridge University Press, 2003.

30   Donald R. Kelley, *Faces of History: Historical Inquiry from Herodotus to Herder*, New Haven, CT: Yale University Press, 1998, 158.

in the shadows of Mounts Meru.[31] As in the case of the Sanskrit cosmopolis, cultural and political power proceeded hand-in-hand in medieval Europe, but in both cases the culture in question was transregional in scope, deriving its own legitimacy as much from its long history and charismatic authority as from its association with contemporary political power. The notion that political power should seek legitimation chiefly in the vernacular language of its subjects would have to wait for the emergence of the nation-state.

Arabic, like Latin, becomes cosmopolitan through conquest and remains cosmopolitan (to this day) in no small part because of its association with Islam. In its origins, as I suggested in the previous chapter, however, it may have begun as something more like an epichoric/panchoric system, on the lines of Greek, Sanskrit, and Classical Chinese, during the pre-Islamic era, when the tradition of the *qasida*, or ode, circulated as a medium through which tribal relations could be understood. First emerging as a world-language in the seventh century as a result of the Islamic conquests and quickly spread by those conquests from Spain to Central Asia (and later further still, from Timbuktu to the Moluccas), Arabic poetry certainly always had a strong affiliation with court culture, originally at the Umayyad Caliphate, centered in Damascus. With the fall of the Umayyad Dynasty in 750, the flight of its remnants to Cordoba, and the subsequent move of the successor Abbasid court to Baghdad in 762, the Arab-Islamic cosmopolis gained new centers of cultural prestige and recognition. Over the next two centuries, as *de facto* Abbasid power waned and regional emirates emerged, still more centers of Arabic court culture became possible in Fez and Kairouan, in Cairo, in Shiraz, and elsewhere. Although Arabic literature went into something of a decline after the Mongol conquests of the thirteenth century (at least according to traditional literary-historical narratives) and found itself in competition both with Ottoman Turkish and with Persian, the literary language has of course persisted to this day and continues to function as a cosmopolitan medium and as a national one.

The history of Persian as a cosmopolitan literary language has complex origins. Zoroastrian and other texts have their origins in Old Persian traditions dating back well into the first millennium BC but were for the most part not written down until much later. The great Persian empire of the sixth and fifth centuries BC did use the Old Persian language in writing, notably in inscriptions, but for most purposes the empire made use at first

---

31   Pollock, *The Language of the Gods*, 246.

of Elamite (a language indigenous to the region of the capital, Susa) and then of Aramaic, which served as a cosmopolitan language of sorts in the Near East at the time. Thus, the great inscription erected at Behistun by the emperor Darius in the 480s BC was written in Old Persian, Elamite, and Babylonian (i.e., in a version of Akkadian). Old Persian was thus used within the Achaemenid Empire for the "workly" purposes described by Pollock, but less as a cosmopolitan language than as a vernacular, with Babylonian serving the cosmopolitan role. After the Greek conquest, as we have seen, the Greek language increasingly took on the roles previously occupied by Aramaic. Of the next dynasty to rule the region, the Parthians (247 BC–AD 224), few directly transmitted written records remain; literature appears mostly to have been oral in nature, although we know also that various regional Persian dialects were written using a modified version of the Aramaic script.[32] A much more significant body of literature exists in Middle Persian texts from the Sassanid era (224–651), and Middle Persian seems likewise to have been the major language of administration, though many other languages were spoken across the vast and diverse empire of the Sassanids. Although clearly a major language of culture and of power, the Middle Persian of the Sassanids is not truly a cosmopolitan language in Pollock's sense, tied as it was to the ethnicity of the ruling dynasty of this multiethnic empire and used, therefore, to aesthetically represent their power and theirs alone.

In a pattern that would seem odd, were it not now familiar from the traditions discussed earlier, the New Persian language seems to have become truly cosmopolitan only in an era when it was not tied directly to power. After the fall of the Sassanid Empire to Muslim conquerors in 651, Arabic became the official language of the territories formerly under Sassanian rule (and Arabic began its own cosmopolitan career). The Persian language was temporarily marginalized only to reappear as a major literary force a few centuries later.

When New Persian began this career, it did so on the eastern edges of the Persian world; the tradition reports the first poetry in New Persian as coming from Sistan and Heart, in what is now Afghanistan and the eastern regions of Iran, in the mid-ninth century.[33] Traditionally, therefore, the

32   Mary Boyce, "Parthian Writings and Literature," in *The Seleucid, Parthian and Sasanian Periods,* edited by Ehsan Yarshater, 3:1149–65. Vol. 3, The Cambridge History of Iran, Cambridge: Cambridge University Press, 1983.

33   G. Lazard, "The Rise of the New Persian Language," in *The Period from the*

New Persian language is seen as having emerged from the court cultures of the kingdoms of that region. It has recently been argued instead that New Persian evolved from a lingua franca amalgam of earlier Persian dialects used on the Silk Road, as attested in Manichaean manuscripts from Turfan, deep inside what is now Xinjiang province in China, dating to the late ninth/early tenth centuries.[34] This latter view, if correct, would provide an interesting parallel to Sanskrit as understood by Pollock as always already a transregional formation (and would contrast with Pollock's own thoughts on Persian, which he identifies as always, and in contrast to Sanskrit, retaining a sort of "tribal authenticity").[35]

As Pollock himself notes, perhaps the closest approximation to the Sanskrit paradigm of the literary cosmopolis is classical Chinese.[36] The literary language used in the ancient classics and Eastern Zhou (770–256 BC) philosophical texts became standardized (especially with respect to script) under the Qin (221–206 BC) and Han (206 BC–AD 220) Dynasties. Even under the Eastern Zhou, the language was used for cultural purposes at the courts of states that were not ethnically Huaxia, or what is today called Han Chinese; in particular, southern states, such as Chu and Wu, used the literary languages for interstate communication and (at least in the case of Chu) to create poetry, such as in the Chu Ci 楚辭, parts of which anthology date to the Warring States era. Although the actual ethnic composition of Chu was likely complex and certainly not homogeneously Huaxia; the use of classical Chinese as a literary language for ritual inscriptions and for the production of poetry in these contexts is thus ambiguously cosmopolitan in Pollock's sense.[37] Although both Wu and Chu were hegemons of the Huaxia world for periods of time, they used classical Chinese as their vehicle for literary expression, partly as a result of the political, economic, and military power of the ethnically Huaxia states prior to their own rise and also

---

Arab Invasion to the Saljuqs, edited by N. R. Frye, Cambridge: Cambridge University Press, 1975, 595.

34   Lars Johanson, Christiane Bulut, and Bo Utas, eds., "A Multiethnic Origin of New Persian?" in Turkic-Iranian Contact Areas: Historical and Linguistic Aspects, Wiesbaden: Harrassowitz, 2006, 241–51.

35   Pollock, The Language of the Gods, 254–5.

36   Ibid., 259.

37   Constance A. Cook, "The Ideology of the Chu Ruling Class: Ritual Rhetoric and Bronze Inscriptions," in Defining Chu: Image and Reality in Ancient China, Honolulu: University of Hawaii Press, 1999, 67–76.

perhaps as a consequence of clan and ethnic ties between elites in those states and the Zhou clans.

The Han Dynasty quickly expanded its sway over non-Huaxia territories, in the northeast onto the Korean peninsula and across modern Manchuria, bringing Huaxia rule for the first time to all of what is now southern China (and into northern Vietnam) and moving westward along the Silk Road. Since these expansions were the consequence of military and diplomatic campaigns, the expansion of the classical Chinese language into these regions does not fit the spirit of Pollock's Sanskrit cosmopolis. More aptly, the classical Chinese language began its use outside the territory of the Han for purposes similar to those identified by Pollock, with one of the earliest examples being the erection of steles in classical Chinese by the Paekche Dynasty on the Korean peninsula in the 470s AD.[38] Likewise, and even more impressively, by the eighth century, Japan (outside the range of Chinese military ambitions and of relatively minor diplomatic or commercial interest to the Chinese at the time) began to make use of classical Chinese for the writing of historical texts, official documents, and poetry in the classical Chinese style (although poetry was also written in Japanese, using Japanese verse forms). Likewise, the earliest writing in Vietnam was in classical Chinese, beginning in the first few centuries AD; the conquest of what is now northern Vietnam by the Han Dynasty was certainly a factor there, although the persistence of classical Chinese as the only literary language of Vietnam until the thirteenth century, in spite of the loss of Han Chinese political control centuries earlier and the development of the indigenous chữ Nôm writing system, is a testimony to the power of classical Chinese in something like the sense of Pollock's Sanskrit cosmopolis.[39] Further testimony to this power is found with the use of classical Chinese by many of the ethnic groupings of the northern steppe, whose political sphere of influence frequently included all or part of northern China, from the conquests of the Jin Dynasty by northern tribes in 316 AD through the Qing Dynasty (1644–1911), ethnically Manchu. The latter example is especially telling in some ways; a Manchu dynasty and aristocracy controlled China for nearly three hundred years, by the end of which time their own language was nearly extinct.

---

38   Peter H. Lee, *A History of Korean Literature*, Cambridge: Cambridge University Press, 2003, 87.

39   John DeFrancis, *Colonialism and Language Policy in Viet Nam*, The Hague: Mouton, 1977, 23.

Systems of Cosmopolitan Circulation

When discussing cosmopolitan literary traditions, it is important to be sensitive to the different dynamics at work regulating literary circulation in each context. Circulations are rarely even and generally reflect differentials of cultural power (linked or not to political or economic power). In what follows, I survey briefly what we know about the situation in the various cosmopolitan literary languages. This question of the circulation of texts in cosmopolitan languages beyond modern national borders has everywhere been much under-studied as an inadvertent consequence of the increasingly national orientation of literary scholarship in the nineteenth and twentieth centuries. Some cosmopolitan languages, notably Latin, found themselves stateless in this process; others, such as classical Chinese, found themselves marginalized within national literary histories that emphasized the vernacular tradition. Wherever nation-states emerged, their scholars tended to valorize texts in the national vernacular over those in a cosmopolitan language so that, for example, literature written in Chinese in Japan or in Persian in what is now Turkey or India found less space within emergent national accounts of literature, both in the nation that claimed the cosmopolitan language as its own and in the other nations that now privileged their vernacular literary histories. What follows is thus patchy and anecdotal, rather than comprehensive, but nonetheless allows us to make some observations about the different distributions of power and circulation across different cosmopolitan landscapes.

I begin with the case of the ecology built around classical Chinese, or *wenyan*, as a cosmopolitan language. As already discussed, wenyan was not only the exclusive literary language of the empires that reigned across modern China from the Han (220 BC–AD 206) to the Qing (1644–1911) and of the regional states that occupied the interregna between dynasties but also that of the various polities that existed in Korea, Japan, the Ryukyu islands to Japan's south, Vietnam, and the Mongolian and Manchurian steppe. Many of these regions, of course, also have early and lengthy vernacular literary traditions of their own, making terminology complex. "Japanese," "Korean," and "Vietnamese" literatures, as conventionally constructed today, do not necessarily include texts produced in wenyan; the terms used indigenously in these languages to refer to such texts, *kanbun, hanmun,* and *hán văn* (respectively, the Japanese, Korean, and Vietnamese pronunciations of the Chinese characters *hanwen* 漢文, meaning in context "literature in Han Chinese"; i.e., in wenyan), are unable to distinguish between texts written in wenyan in China itself and those produced in other countries. The convention in English is to refer to these literary traditions as Sino-Japanese, Sino-Korean, and Sino-Vietnamese,[40] although due caution must be taken to avoid assimilating and reifying what are in fact complex continua of texts, ranging from flawless wenyan that would have met with approval from the most demanding of Chinese critics, to strongly hybrid texts bearing significant markers of the substrate vernacular.[41] Wenyan poetry was produced in quantities in Japan, Korea, and Vietnam, and those regions continued throughout their pre-modern histories to consume newly produced wenyan poetry produced in China, although these nations were far from representing a unified market for such literary production. At the same time, the consumption of wenyan poetry from Japan, Korea, and Vietnam within China itself was all but nonexistent, as was the circulation of wenyan texts from one peripheral nation to another. There are exceptions, here and there; the Korean scholar Hong Taeyong (1731–83) is known, for example, to have maintained a correspondence with Chinese scholars after a diplomatic visit in 1765–6, while Pak Chega (1750–1805) not only corresponded with the Chinese scholar Li Tiaoyuan (1734–1803) in 1777 but as a result of that correspondence was able to get the latter to publish in China a collection of Sino-Korean poetry, *The Collection of the Small Bookcase*.[42] Vietnamese envoys likewise exchanged Sino-Vietnamese poetry with their Chinese counterparts.[43] In the eighth and ninth centuries, Buddhist writers from Japan and Korea were read in China, as well as in each other's regions, and in later times, Confucian scholars from both regions, notably the Korean Yi T'oegye (1501–70), likewise circulated more broadly.[44] Returning to the poetic tradition, poets from Korea, Japan, and the Ryukyu islands had their works included in wenyan collections compiled in China from the ninth-century Silla Dynasty poet Wang Koin, included in the *Complete Tang Poetry* 全唐

40   John Timothy Wixted, "Kanbun, Histories of Japanese Literature, and Japanologists," *Sino-Japanese Studies* 10 (2), 1998: 23–31.

41   Wiebke Denecke, "Chinese Antiquity and Court Spectacle in Early 'Kanshi,'" *Journal of Japanese Studies* 30 (1), 2004: 97–122.

42   JaHyun Kim Haboush, *Epistolary Korea: Letters in the Communicative Space of the Chosŏn, 1392–1910*, New York: Columbia University Press, 2009, 205–6.

43   Liam C. Kelley, *Beyond the Bronze Pillars: Envoy Poetry and the Sino-Vietnamese Relationship*, Ann Arbor, MI: Association for Asian Studies, 2005.

44   Peter Kornicki, "A Note on Sino-Japanese: A Question of Terminology," *Sino-Japanese Studies* 17 (0), 2010: 34–5.

詩 (compiled in 1705), through the various more contemporary poets from these regions included in the *Huangqing shi xuan* 皇清詩選, an anthology of Qing Dynasty poetry likewise compiled in the same year under the auspices of the Kangxi emperor.[45]

Further study of this under-explored field has the potential to reveal many more examples of authors from the wenyan periphery who gained acceptance in the core (i.e., in China itself), or whose works circulated along the periphery, and even the brief data cited above make clear that there were enough contacts among literati in the different wenyan-using nations, at least in the eighteenth century, to justify comparison, albeit a disadvantageous comparison, with the circulation of cosmopolitan texts in Latin among scholars and authors in early Modern Europe.[46] Nonetheless, it is clear that this wenyan cosmopolis has a clearly structured core (China itself) and periphery (the other nations of the cosmopolis), with the core of the core being the Chinese capital of the day and with very unequal flows of literature between core and periphery. Writers from the periphery may occasionally have achieved forms of recognition in the core, but achieving that recognition cannot have been a reliable goal, given the rarity with which it happened. Instead, most writers in Sino-Japanese, Sino-Korean, and Sino Vietnamese sought recognition within their own nations, among other writers in their tradition and in the vernacular, and, a fortiori, few writers from China itself were invested in their reception on the periphery.

The evidence available for literary circulation within the Sanskrit cosmopolis is still scantier, especially for the non-specialist. Pollock himself spends little time on the question. Certainly, many of the Sanskrit literary texts Pollock discusses from Southeast Asia are inscriptional in nature; the inscriptional format is by definition one that is not designed to facilitate circulation; although inscriptional texts can and do circulate in transcribed form or in oral performance, their physical situation is also constitutive of their meaning in significant ways, and so inscribed texts are unlikely to be texts written with the expectation of circulation or with breadth of circulation as a criterion of their success. Further, of course, the purpose of many of these inscriptions was to represent in a universally accessible form the royal authority of the inscriber; while this purpose was certainly reproducible across the cosmopolis, its content was not so welcome. The ruler of a

---

45 Ibid., 36.
46 Kornicki, "A Note on Sino-Japanese," makes the comparison explicit.

kingdom might have emulated his neighbor's expression of authority, but he would have been unlikely to circulate it. We do hear isolated cases of literary circulation; for example, Buddhist scholars from late Śrīvijaya (a Malay kingdom located on the island of Sumatra and active in the seventh–thirteenth centuries AD) are said to have attracted students from India itself, and their works were to have been translated into Tibetan.[47] It is striking that, as with wenyan, the instances of literary circulation in the Sanskrit cosmopolis that we know of seem to involve religious texts; it is unclear whether this means that it was easier for religious texts to circulate across the cosmopolis or between peripheries than it was for poetic texts to do so, or whether our awareness of such phenomena is merely an artifact of the transregional focus of Buddhology as a Western academic discipline. In any event, in the cases of both classical Chinese and Sanskrit, we are aware of a prodigious volume of verbal art produced across the cosmopolis and certainly of the profound influence works from the center had on the periphery; evidence for the literary influence of peripheral texts on the core or on other peripheries is much more fragmentary. Patterns of circulation within the cosmopolis, in other words, are likely to have been highly uneven.

The Arabic cosmopolis, which grew very rapidly in the second half of the first millennium AD and whose major centers were removed from the homelands of the language, has always been highly polycentric and has promoted a broad circulation across regions. Even within the heartlands of the Abbasids, centered around the great cities of Baghdad, Aleppo, and Damascus, a survey of a few of the major poets of the era demonstrates the polycentricity of the tradition. Abu Nuwas (756–814), one of the greatest poets of the tradition, had a Persian mother and was raised in Basra. Most of his literary career was spent at the Abbasid court in Baghdad, except for a brief period of exile in Egypt. Bashar bin Burd (714–84), also part Persian, moved from Basra to Baghdad. Abu l-'Atahiyya (828–748), was originally from the Iraqi desert but made his name in Baghdad. Al-Mutanabbi (915–65) was born in Kufah in Iraq but educated in Damascus; much of his poetry was written at the courts of the Hamanids in Aleppo and at the ethnically Ethiopian Ikhshidid court in Egypt. Abu Firas al-Hamdani (932–68) was one of the Hamanid rulers in Aleppo. Abul 'Ala Al-Ma'arri

---

47   Stuart Robson, "On Translating the Arjunawiwāha," *Bijdragen tot de Taal-, Land- en Volkenkunde* 157 (1), 2001: 35–50. Robson cites here J. A. Schoterman, *Indonesische sporen in Tibet: lazing,* Leiden, Netherlands: Brill, 1986.

(973–1058), born in Ma'arra in Syria, spent time at court in both Aleppo and Baghdad but returned to his hometown for much of his career. Abu Tammam (788–845), a noted poet and anthologist, was born in Syria but enjoyed patronage at various times in Egypt, Damascus, Baghdad, Mosul, Armenia, and Khorasan.[48] Al-Būsīrī (1211–94) was a Sufi poet, originally born in the Maghreb, mostly active in Egypt, but also living for significant periods of time in Jerusalem and Medina.[49] Abu-l-Faraj (897–967), poet and anthologist of pre-Islamic Arabic poetry, was born in Isfahan and raised in Baghdad; a descendant of the Umayyads, he remained in correspondence with their descendants in Cordoba, and his literary life was spent largely in Aleppo.[50] The great mystic poet Ibn al-Farid (1181–1235), from a Syrian family, was raised in Cairo and spent most of his career there, but also lived for fifteen years in Mecca. Ibn Duraid (837–934), born in Basra, fled to Oman and then to Persia, where he produced his greatest work, before finishing his career in Baghdad. Beyond these figures, there lie considerable literary traditions of the period centered in what is now Spain[51] and in Egypt,[52] to say nothing of the lesser-known traditions of the Yemen.[53] In the centuries after the final defeat of the remnant Abbasids by the Mongols in 1258, Arabic literature becomes still more cosmopolitan, with poets across the cosmopolis continuing to write poetry on the same universal themes (albeit work mostly now disparaged in the literary tradition).[54] In the Ottoman period, the tradition continues, although the Maghreb, less directly under Ottoman influence and thus less subject to the competitive pressures of Persian and Ottoman Turkish as literary languages,

---

48   Felix Klein-Franke, *The Ḥamāsa of Abū Tammām*, Leiden, Netherlands Brill Archive, 1972.

49   Salma Khadra Jawusi, "Arabic Poetry in the Post-Classical Age," in *Arabic Literature in the Post-Classical Period*, The Cambridge History of Arabic Literature, Cambridge: Cambridge University Press, 2006, 23–59, 46.

50   Hilary Kilpatrick, *Making the Great Book of Songs: Compilation and the Author's Craft in Abū L-Faraj Al-Iṣbahānī's Kitāb Al-aghānī*, New York: Psychology Press, 2003, 14–20.

51   María Rosa Menocal, Raymond P. Scheindlin, and Michael Sells, eds., *The Literature of Al-Andalus*, Cambridge: Cambridge University Press, 2006.

52   S. M. Ayyad, "Regional Literature: Egypt," in *Abbasid Belles-lettres*, edited by Julia Ashtiany, Cambridge: Cambridge University Press, 1990, 412–41.

53   A. El-Shami and R. B. Serjeant, "Regional Literature: the Yemen," in *Abbasid Belles-lettres*, edited by Julia Ashtiany, Cambridge: Cambridge University Press, 1990, 442–68.

54   Jawusi, "Arabic Poetry in the Post-Classical Age," 39.

may have generated a disproportionate number of well-known poets.[55] Beyond the regions traditionally thought of as Arabic (or even, sometimes, Muslim), the influence of the Arabic literary cosmopolis was deeply felt, as far afield as the Tamil lands and Java.[56]

The Hellenistic cultural world was also highly polycentric, with most of the major centers located outside what had been the Greek world prior to Alexander's conquests. The most obvious case in point was Alexandria, the Hellenistic capital of Egypt and home to the greatest library of the ancient Greek world, as well as to a great tradition of textual scholarship on Homer and other early texts and to a lively poetic culture (whose membership overlapped with that of the scholarly community) as well. But there were other centers; Pergamon likewise had a great library and its own coterie of scholars and poets, as did Antioch and the Macedonian capital of Pella.[57] The libraries themselves were often the product of royal acquisitions from the Greek mainland; thus, Alexandria claimed to derive the core of its collection from Aristotle's own library, including his own text of Homer;[58] while Pergamon claimed Euripides' text of Homer as one of its own treasures.[59] Scholars and poets likewise migrated from place to place, as attested in the names by which they are known to posterity: Ptolemy II of Egypt founded the Library of Alexandria on the advice of his first tutor, Philetas of Cos, and installed Zenodotus of Ephesus as the first head of the library; Zenodotus's successors included Aristophanes of Byzantium and Aristarchus of Samothrace, all of them influential editors of the text of Homer. The work of Callimachus of Cyrene, the Sicilian Greek Theocritus, and Apollonius of Rhodes added further to Alexandria's cultural glory. At Pergamon, the philosopher Crates of Mallos offered his own rival Homeric

---

55   Lutfi Muhammad al-Yousfi, "Poetic Creativity in the Sixteenth to Eighteenth Centuries," in *Arabic Literature in the Post-Classical Period*, edited by Roger Allen and S. D. Richards, Cambridge: Cambridge University Press, 2006, 63.

56   Ronit Ricci, *Islam Translated: Literature, Conversion, and the Arabic Cosmopolis of South and Southeast Asia*, Chicago: University Of Chicago Press, 2011.

57   Margalit Finkelberg, "Regional Texts and the Circulation of Books: The Case of Homer," *Greek, Roman, and Byzantine Studies* 46 (3), 2010: 231–48.

58   Gregory Nagy, *Poetry As Performance: Homer and Beyond*, Cambridge: Cambridge University Press, 1996, 203; For a critical perspective on this tradition, see Andrew Erskine, "Culture and Power in Ptolemaic Egypt: The Museum and Library of Alexandria," *Greece & Rome* 42 (1), 1995, Second Series: 38–48.

59   Gregory Nagy, *Homer's Text and Language*, Champaign: University of Illinois Press, 2004, 51n41.

text, while at Pella the poets Alexander Aetolus and Aratus added their own cultural capital.

Many of these scholar-poets were born in the Greek heartlands or in regions long since colonized by the Greeks, but each of them pursued their work in cities on the periphery of the older Greek world—and at the center of the new cosmopolitan world. There was a certain amount of exchange and circulation among these centers as well—Pergamon is said to have attempted to take Aristophanes of Byzantium from Alexandria, while Aratus moved from Pella to Antioch and then back.[60] Although Athens had been a major influence on the emergence of the koinê standard for Greek and had been enormously influential in the earlier codification of Homeric epic, that city is conspicuous for its comparative absence from these Hellenistic networks. In greatly expanding the horizons of the Hellenic world and in creating new centers of cultural prestige and recognition, Alexander and his successors had the perhaps inadvertent effect of making the original centers of the Greek world peripheral. Since these regional centers were only politically united by the Romans, and since the Romans, while valuing and even promoting Greek culture, did not impose a centralizing authority on it, the Greek cosmopolis remained strikingly polycentric. Although some emperors, notably Hadrian (r. 117–38 AD), actively promoted Greek culture as part of their political program, and although Rome quickly became a key source of patronage and therefore recognition for intellectuals writing in Greek, this polycentric nature of the Greek cosmopolis under Roman rule likewise kept Greek culture and Roman power in a relatively loose relationship, a situation that was only to change after the splitting of the Roman empire into Eastern and Western halves in the early fourth century, the consequent change to sole official status for Greek in the East, and the emergence of Constantinople as the final court of authority for Greek cultural matters as for political ones—the first era in which the Greek cultural world had had a single common cultural center. The role played by imperial Constantinople in the regulation and transmission of early Christian texts in Greek is well attested; Margalit Finkelberg has argued that the city may have played a similar role in producing and transmitting the text of Homeric epic known to us today.[61]

---

60 Finkelberg, "Regional Texts and the Circulation of Books," 2010, 237–8.
61 Margalit Finkelberg, "Ajax's Entry in the Hesiodic Catalogue of Women," *The Classical Quarterly* 38 (1), New Series, 1988: 243–5. For a discussion of the similar role played by the Eastern Han in the emergence of the "Confucian Classics" in

The emergence of the koinê standard for the Greek language is somewhat unclear, although most scholars agree with the ancient Greeks themselves, who saw koinê (literally, "common" Greek) as evolving from the Athenian dialect. The Athenian empire seems to have played a role in the emergence of this standard, as even in the fifth century BC inscriptional evidence shows that the Greek poleis with whom Athens negotiated treaties recorded their terms in the Attic dialect, even when they themselves spoke a quite divergent form of the language.[62] A further empire, that of Macedon, played an even greater role not only in ensuring that the Greek language spread across the eastern Mediterranean and Near East (and beyond) but in determining which form of the Greek language was to be spread. It is unclear what the native language of the Macedonians themselves was—it may have been, for example, a relatively remote dialect of Greek or a non-Greek language within the Indo-European family, related to some degree to the Greek dialects. Whatever the case, the evidence is fairly clear that early on the Macedonians adopted the Athenian dialect for political and diplomatic purposes;[63] this choice presumably depended on the previous Athenian decision to use their own dialect as a standard across their own empire and had significant implications for the emergence of the koinê across the territories conquered by Alexander.

The koinê was thus an imperial language on multiple levels, developed out of the standard dialect used in the Athenian empire and disseminated over much wider areas by the Macedonian empires. And yet, with the exception of the New Testament and, to a lesser extent, of historiographic writing, the koinê was not much used for literary purposes. Most prose authors of the Hellenistic and Imperial periods used some form of Attic or Atticising dialect (maintaining the prestige of that earlier cosmopolitan form). In the case of poetry, the Greeks already had, by this date, a long and complex history connecting dialect, genre, and author. As I noted in the previous chapter, the variety of Greek used in Homeric and Hesiodic epic is traditionally understood as a Kunstsprache, or "art language," never a spoken language anywhere and integrating forms from a variety of dialects. Epic, in other words, is Panhellenic on the level of linguistic register as

their canonical form and interpretation, see "Classics without Canonization," Nylan, 2009.

62   Emilio Crespo, "The Attitude of the Athenian State towards the Attic Dialect in the Classical Era," in *Indo-European Perspectives: Studies in Honour of Anna Morpurgo Davies*, Oxford: Oxford University Press, 2004, 109–18.

63   Claude Brixhe and A. Panayotou, "L'atticisation de la Macédoine: l'une des sources de la koiné," *Verbum* 11, 1988: 245–60.

much as on the levels of plot and circulation. Lyric genres developed along a different pattern, with specific genres associated with specific dialects, usually involving some measure of Doric dialect, regardless of the native dialects of the poets working in that genre.[64] A comparison may be made here with the use of the Prakrits, the languages descended from Sanskrit, within specific literary genres, rather than as markers of regional identity (though they do seem to have regional origins). A comparison may also be made with the tendencies to identify literary "styles" with regional names, which I discuss below for Sanskrit and New Persian, as well as for Greek.[65] Rather than work in the koinê, poets of the Hellenistic era (many of them also leading scholars of the earlier tradition) not only continue the Archaic and Classical tendency to deploy distinctive dialects for distinctive genres, but they in fact intensify this practice, regularly going out of their way to employ the most obscure, archaic, and difficult words in what has been seen as an overt reaction to the simplifying and standardizing tendencies of the koinê, perhaps seen as too much associated with the bureaucratic and the commercial to function as a poetic art-language.[66] I will tentatively suggest here a parallel from the early cosmopolitan period in China (beyond the *Mouzi*, which I discussed briefly at the beginning of this chapter), in the genre known as the *fu* 賦, generally translated as "rhyme-prose" or "rhapsody." This genre generally takes the form of an address to the emperor, counseling him on some issue (typically, whether or not to move the capital, or to urge economic restraint), but using elaborate and exotic language to do so. As Tamara Chin has argued,[67] this language represents a kind of

---

64   Michael Silk, "The Invention of Greek: Macedonians, Poets, and Others," in *Standard Languages and Language Standards : Greek, Past and Present*, Farnham; Burlington, VT: Ashgate Publishing, 2009, 3–32; Michael Silk, "The Language of Greek Lyric Poetry," in *A Companion to the Ancient Greek Language*, Hoboken, NJ: Wiley-Blackwell, 2010, 424–40.

65   Pollock, *The Language of the Gods*, 98.

66   Silk, "The Invention of Greek" 24; Geoffrey C. Horrocks, *Greek: A History of the Language and Its Speakers*, New York: John Wiley and Sons, 2010, 98–9. For an alternative view see C. J. Ruijgh, "Le dorien de Théocrite: dialecte cyrénien d'Alexandrie et d'Égypte," *Mnemosyne* 37 (2), 1984: 56–88, who argues that Theocritus's Doric is actually an urban dialect of Cyreneans living in Alexandria (i.e., basically Theocritus's own dialect). Whether nostalgically preserving his own dialect, or exploiting the resources of the history of the language, Theocritus is at any rate definitively not using the koinê.

67   Tamara T. Chin, *Savage Exchange: Historical Imaginations of Han Trade and Expansion*, East Asian Monographs, Harvard University Asia Center, 2014.

"lavish expenditure," stimulating the imagination as certain economic theorists of the era felt that lavish expenditure on goods stimulated the economy. There are arguably affinities as well to the conflicts in our own time between Global English as a simplified lingua franca for the globalized economic system and literary English (whether in its American or Anglo-postcolonial forms), as fully committed as ever to exuberance and variety in its diction. Contemporary English-language writers are perhaps not so different from Hellenisitc or Han Dynasty poets in their desire to exploit every register of their linguistic and literary heritage as a means of marking their language as proper to them, rather than merely universal.

In its turn, Latin was a thriving cosmopolitan literary language in Europe well into the seventeenth century, and for much of that time it remained the dominant literary language, a fact now largely obscured by the effects of national literary history, which privileges texts in national languages and their vernacular precursors at the expense of (among other things) the Latin tradition.[68] As a result of developments I discuss in the chapter on national literatures, this nationalization of European literary space had the consequence of both converting Latin and Greek literary studies into quasi-national fields of inquiry and of bounding those nations chronologically (as part of Europe's distant past), further marginalizing Neo-Latin literary studies even within the emergent discipline of Classics.[69] The volume of texts published in Latin before roughly 1800 is quite staggering, and bears repeating: until around 1575 in France (and later in Italy), a majority of books published were written in Latin; while this percentage dropped rapidly thereafter, for works of a scholarly or scientific nature, the numbers were higher, so that of the books published by Oxford's university press between 1690 and 1710, a majority were still in Latin.[70] Nor should we imagine that these were works of a purely antiquarian nature; as Hans Helander convincingly shows, many of the most "modern" developments of Early Modernity were transacted in Latin texts, from new, more rigorous forms of historical inquiry, to the scientific works of Newton and Bacon, to

---

68   For a discussion of the methodological challenges around the field of Neo-Latin studies (i.e., the study of Latin literature written after c. 1300), see Hans Helander, "Neo-Latin Studies: Significance and Prospects," *Symbolae Osloenses* 76 (1), 2001: 5–102.

69   Ingrid A. R. De Smet, "Not for Classicists? The State of Neo-Latin Studies," *The Journal of Roman Studies* 89, 1999: 205–9.

70   Waquet, Françoise, *Latin: Or, The Empire of a Sign: From the Sixteenth to the Twentieth Centuries*, London: Verso, 2003.

inflammatory political polemics.[71] Major works of the vernacular tradition, such as those of Descartes and Pascal, were translated into Latin and circulated widely in that form.[72] Nor was Neo-Latin exclusively a language of science and learning; Latin epic celebrated military and political heroes from Gustavus Adolphus of Sweden (1594–1632) to Elizabeth I of England and events from the Gunpowder Plot of 1605 to John III Sobieski's defeat of the Turks at the gates of Vienna in 1683, while lyric poets such as Sarbievius ("the Horace of Poland," 1595–1640) and John Milton expressed their divergent views on the Reformation in Latin verse.[73] The works of these writers circulated widely across the Latin cosmopolis, highly polycentric as a result of the political fragmentation of early modern Europe and the many centers of learning and of publishing that proliferated in the era. Earlier medieval Latin literature continued to be read as well, for all of the Renaissance disdain of medieval learning and culture,[74] generating a fairly continuous literary tradition in Latin over two millennia (with periods of greater and lesser richness), covering most of the European world at one time or another. The loss of continuity with this vast and complex tradition, multiply marginalized within the modern academy despite its once-hegemonic status in the heartlands of the West, is one of the regrettable consequences of the national-literature ecology, one which, as we shall see in Chapter 5, has been replicated to some extent elsewhere.

Most of the literary cosmopoleis I have discussed, then, feature relatively high degrees of polycentricity with relatively free circulation of texts among centers. Classical Chinese, in particular, was rather less polycentric (though certainly at least partly open to circulation) thanks to the continued patronage of a world-empire throughout its history and to the preponderance of Sinophones within that cosmopolis (although *within* China, literary production and circulation was quite complex and polycentric); other cosmopolitan ecologies were likewise more monocentric and less free in their literary circulation during periods of empire (as during the Roman Empire and the Umayyad Caliphate, for example). When a literary cosmopolis and a universal empire coincide, the former naturally becomes

---

71   Helander, "Neo-Latin Studies: Significance and Prospects," 2001.

72   Peter Burke and R. Po-chia Hsia, "Translations into Latin in Early Modern Europe," in *Cultural Translation in Early Modern Europe*, Cambridge: Cambridge University Press, 2007.

73   Helander, "Neo-Latin Studies: Significance and Prospects," 2001, 24–6.

74   Ernst Robert Curtius, *European Literature and the Latin Middle Ages*, Princeton, NJ: Princeton University Press, 1991, 28–9.

something of an instrument of the latter; it is only in other phases, wherein the language is the cultural vehicle of states that do not or cannot claim to rule the world, that more egalitarian forms of circulation emerge.

GEOGRAPHIES OF STYLE

An interesting index of the nature of literary circulation within the literary cosmopolis is the representation of literary style using the trope of geography. Just as we have seen that within a panchoric ecology the local can become little more than a device to mark the triumph of the translocal, so in many cosmopolitan literary ecologies the names of geographic regions are used as a means of identifying distinct literary styles. While these style designations may initially have derived from the actual practices of writers or groups of writers from a region, they function more as a cosmology of style, a mapping of literary difference onto broader thinking about a region. As an example, late nineteenth-century intellectuals divided the history of Persian literature into three stylistic periods identified through geographic referents: first, a "style of Khorasan" (*sabk-e-Khorâsâni*), that is, of the eastern regions of the Persophone world, prevalent in the mid-ninth through mid-eleventh centuries AD when the major centers of New Persian literature were the regional courts of what are now Afghanistan, eastern Iran, and the former Soviet Central Asian republics; these were regions, as we have noted, on the periphery but where weaker knowledge of Arabic may have promoted the use of Persian as a literary language. As the Saljuq Turks conquered most of the Persian world in the mid-eleventh century, the use of Persian for literary purposes spread further west, to the traditional Persian heartlands, and a second style, the "Iraqi style" (*sabk-e-Erâqi*), emerged. Finally, as the Mughal Dynasty (its rulers ethnically Turkic and Mongol) conquered India in the sixteenth century, a new style emerged in their courts, the so-called Indian style (*sabk-e-Hendi*).[75] Despite the geographic origins of these names, however, the styles so described were not limited to the regions indicated; rather, all three styles circulated in varying ways across the entire cosmopolis, even though the historical origins of each style can be found, to some extent, in that region. As further proof of the rootless nature of these regional stylistic categories, we find

---

75   J. T. P. de Bruijn, "Classical Persian Literature as a Tradition," in *General Introduction to Persian Literature: A History of Persian Literature*, edited by J. T. P. de Bruijn and Ehsan Yarshater, London: I. B. Tauris, 2008, 1–42.

alternative names for some of them: the *sabk-e-Khorâsâni* is also known as the *sabk-e-Torkestâni*, or "Turkestan Style," a designation loosely indicating the Turkic-speaking regions of Central Asia, overlapping with, yet not identical to, those areas known as Khorasan. Likewise, the *sabk-e-Hendi* is sometimes referred to today as the *sabk-e-Esfahâni*, after the city of Esfahan, capital of the Iranian Safavid Dynasty in the sixteenth century, in large part because of a contemporary reluctance to recognize stylistic features of Safavid poetry as originating in Mughal India despite evidence to the contrary.[76] The simultaneous use of Persian as a cosmopolitan literary language at three great imperial courts—the Ottoman court in Istanbul, the Safavid court in Esfahan, and the Mughal court in Delhi—necessarily complicates any model of core-periphery literary interactions; rather, a polycentric system, with perhaps uneven circulation among centers, seems the most useful model here. The identification of distinct, historically emergent styles with specific regions acts as a further index of circulation, reminding us that poets from one region were read in another.

The penchant for naming styles after geographic regions, while those styles were then used by writers across the cosmopolis, is a phenomenon also found in the case of Sanskrit. As Pollock demonstrates, with reference to the *Śṛṅgāraprakāśa* of Bhoja, an early eleventh-century AD king of Malwa in central India, Sanskrit poetics featured a quadripartite regionalization of literary style into the *Pāñcālu*, *Gauḍīya*, *Vaidarbha*, and *Lāṭīya* styles, representing, respectively, the western plains of the Ganges, west Bengal, eastern Maharashtra, and southern Gujarat (thus, roughly, northern, eastern, southern, and western), and differing from each other in phonology, syntax, lexicon and figuration.[77] It is worth noting that Bhoja's own kingdom of Malwa, located in what is now the western part of Madhya Pradesh, was at the center of the four cardinal directions represented by these styles (two of which, the *Gauḍīya* and *Vaidarbha*, are also found in earlier texts). Bhoja's stylistic inventory, then, may have political connotations, not because he has made the style of his own kingdom dominant in literary terms but because he has positioned the styles around his kingdom in such a way as to make of himself a kind of golden mean of them. Similar also is the distinction in Greco-Roman rhetorical theory between the more austere "Attic" and more florid "Asiatic" styles. To be sure, the origin of each is

---

76   Shamshur Rahman Faruqi, "A Stranger in the City: The Poetics of Sabk-e Hindi," *Annual of Urdu Studies* 19, 2004: 1–59.

77   Pollock, *The Language of the Gods*, 208–22.

traced to orators from those respective regions, but by the Roman era (and it is the Roman writers Cicero and Quintilian who provide our best sources for these terms), it is clear that both styles were understood as points on a continuum of options open to contemporary orators.

The generic quality of these regional attributes in New Persian, Sanskrit and Greco-Roman poetics, then, serves as an index of the cosmopolitan character of each of these literary ecologies. It also, of course, parallels the kinds of generic localism I find in the Greek and Chinese panchoric traditions and which I identified in the previous chapter as "Olympic" panchorisms, that is, as panchoric cultures that build a translocal culture not by assembling bits and pieces of local tradition but rather by transforming that local tradition into a new and unified tradition and then making room for the "local" within that tradition as a standardized component, stripped of local specificity. As I already suggested in my first book, this capacity to evacuate the local of its content and then represent the local through a new panchoric formation may have been the technique that made Greek and Chinese particularly effective languages at repeating that feat in a cosmopolitan context.

Self-Conscious Cosmopolitanism

In that previous book, I also argued for an understanding of literary cosmopolitanism that includes, at least in an incipient form, thinking that stretches the region of applicability to a culture's ideas to the world as a whole (or at least the world as it is known).[78] Since my interest in literary ecology focuses around these ecologies as practices of reading, I contend that such incipient thinking about the universality or otherwise of culture constitute a dimension of the cosmopolitan literary ecology, even before a given language actually circulates in that context. Such an elaboration of the notion of the literary cosmopolis, I argue, allows us to identify continuities in reading and thinking about literature and the world that transcend historical moments of conquest and exchange. In what follows, I trace this phenomenon in the Greek and Chinese contexts, as those most familiar to me; readers more knowledgeable about other cosmopolitan contexts may well find parallels in the traditions they know.

The term "cosmopolitan" is itself, of course, a Greek formation, whose first use is supposed to be that by the fourth-century BC philosopher

---

78   Beecroft, *Authorship and Cultural Identity*, 6.

Diogenes the Cynic, who is said to have responded to the question of where he was from (i.e., what his polis was) by proclaiming that he was a κοσμοπολίτης (Diogenes Laertius 6.63); that the city of his birth, and the community to which he owed his political allegiance, was the entire world. This notion of cosmopolitanism, which in a Cynic context may have been more a negative rejection of local allegiances than a positive declaration of responsibilities on a larger scale, will be developed more explicitly and rigorously by Stoic philosophy, in texts poorly transmitted but known to us from other sources. Cicero, for example, explains the Stoic notion of the cosmopolis as follows:

> For the world is as a common home for gods and men, or as a city for both of them; for they alone, since they employ reason, live according to justice and law.[79]

Expanding this rather concise description, the Stoics believed that any polis of their time, organized as it was by rather fallible humans, was not in fact governed by justice, law, and reason, and accordingly was not a true polis; the world as a whole, by contrast (and here we should remember that the Greek *kosmos* means not only "world" but also "order"), is under the authority of the gods and is thus just and rational and more truly deserves the status of polis than does any individual city-state. It is worth noting in passing that the cosmopolitanism thus imagined is in fact very deeply rooted in the thoroughly Greek notion of the polis, or city-state; as we have seen, the basic device of the cosmopolitan ecology is the universalizing of local culture. The cosmopolitan as such does not require the invention of new concepts of the political but rather their projection onto the largest possible scale.

Stoic philosophy will not emerge until the third century BC, by which time of course new political formations have in fact emerged—first the conquest empire of Alexander the Great, then its successor states, the Hellenistic kingdoms that ruled over the Eastern Mediterranean (and beyond, as far, at times, as Afghanistan) for the next three centuries. But we can find, I have argued, hints of an incipiently cosmopolitan worldview as early as Herodotus and Socrates. In Herodotus, for example, I have discussed a famous episode in the *Histories*, which claims to recount a visit

---

79   Est enim mundus quasi communis deorum atque hominum domus aut urbs utrorumque; soli enim ratione utentes iure ac lege vivunt (Cicero, *Nat D* 2.154).

by Herodotus's predecessor Hecataeus to Egypt.[80] Hecataeus's text, the
Genealogies, is said to have presented a history based on a rationalizing
of the genealogies in Greek mythology (which formed, of course, one of
the subjects of the previous chapter). Herodotus recounts (at 2.143) that
Hecataeus himself boasted to the priests at a temple of Amun in Egypt
to be the sixteenth-generation descendant of a god; the priests rebut his
claim by showing him a series of 345 statues representing the continuous generations of priests of the temple—all, according to them,
descended from other mortals, not from gods. Herodotus tells this
story, I argue, for several reasons: most straightforwardly, to demonstrate to his reader the great antiquity of Egypt but also as part of his
rhetorical campaign against Hecataeus. Beyond these objectives, the
passage amply demonstrates an awareness of one of the key conceptual
aspects of modern cosmopolitanism, the notion that people in different
places understand the same situation in different ways, a point
Herodotus makes explicit elsewhere (3.38).

Socrates' views lead less straightforwardly toward cosmopolitanism. For
example, while the kinds of reflection on ideal political arrangements found
in Plato's *Republic* have, at least implicitly, a universal applicability, within
the text of the *Republic* itself, Plato has Socrates suggest that Greeks and
non-Greeks should be treated differently. He argues that the people of his
imagined polis should behave with mercy towards their fellow Greeks
(5.469b–71b), not enslaving them, despoiling their corpses, or burning
their crops, even in victory (while such procedures are explicitly not prohib-
ited when at war with "barbarians"), and in the process has his interlocutors
agree that the polis he describes must necessarily be both Hellenic and phil-
hellenic. That notwithstanding, the polis Plato has Socrates construct, while
Greek in name and in many details (its gods, for example, remain Greek,
and the "noble lie" of the birth of the men of the polis from different metals
clearly owes much to Hesiod), is unlike any Greek polis yet known in many
of its social and cultural practices, from the sharing of women and children
in common to the promotion of the wisest and most thoroughly educated
to rule rather than the most nobly born. By imagining his polis as both
Greek and unlike any other known, Plato is in a sense imagining a new
formation altogether, one that, as (notionally) an ideal state, does not replicate the customs of his people but transforms them utterly. Further, Socrates'
concern with stripping away merely phenomenal differences to arrive at the

---

80   Beecroft, *Authorship and Cultural Identity*, 133–8.

universal, unchanging truths of the Forms is necessarily in tension with his Hellenocentrism expressed in the *Republic* and elsewhere.

In China, as I have argued, we find incipient cosmopolitan tendencies in portions of the Confucian *Analects* and of the historical text the *Zuozhuan*, in layers in both cases likely dating to the fourth century BC. An important index of that thinking is the appearance of the term *tianxia* 天下. Meaning literally "beneath the sky" or "[all] under heaven," the term performs much of the work of the term "empire" within European thinking about large-scale cosmopolitan political orders. Yuri Pines has traced the history of the term, which is poorly attested in the inscriptional record or in the textual tradition, to before the late Spring and Autumn era (i.e., roughly the sixth century BC). The earliest uses of the term emphasize tianxia as a region of shared moral and cultural values and thus refers mostly to the territory of the states accepting the rituals of the Zhou, for the most part, those that were ethnically Huaxia.[81] In the Warring States era (c. 475–221 BC), the Huaxia world changed in a number of ways: the authority of the Zhou royal court lost even the purely nominal and ritual role it had previously enjoyed; peripheral states, many of them incompletely assimilated to the Huaxia world, assumed a greater role in that world's politics; ritual practices diverged increasingly, but there was also an increasing sense of a shared textual culture.[82] During this era, the political dimensions of tianxia, as a territory ruled (or to be ruled) by a single power, began to emerge, as did a sense that this world might extend beyond the ethnically and culturally Huaxia populations of the so-called Central States, (*zhongguo*, 中國, the name later used as an autonym for "China"). The matter is not, however, a simple one; the Western state of Qin (which conquered tianxia in the mid-third century BC) was increasingly represented as outside tianxia,[83] while the erstwhile "barbarians" of the south and east, in the states of Chu, Wu, and Yue, were increasingly represented as inside tianxia. Where tianxia is described in terms suggesting the ideal of political unification of those states, it is always in the *Zuozhuan* the rulers of Chu who express such desires.[84] In later texts of the Warring States era

---

81   Yuri Pines, "Changing Views of Tianxia in Pre-Imperial Discourse," *Oriens Extremus* 43 (1–2), 2002: 101–16.

82   I discuss many of these phenomena in the previous chapter. For further discussion, see the Pines article cited in the above footnote, as well as chapters 5–7 of Beecroft, *Authorship and Cultural Identity*.

83   Pines, "Changing Views of Tianxia in Pre-Imperial Discourse," 2002, 112.

84   Yuri Pines, "Imagining the Empire? Concepts of 'Primeval Unity' in Pre-imperial Historiographic Tradition," in *Conceiving the Empire: China and*

(notably Mozi but also others), Pines finds increasing evidence for both the political dimension of tianxia as a concept and for at least a textual desire for the genuinely universal application of the concept. It is only when Qin succeeded in unifying the Huaxia world under its rule in 221 BC that we begin to see the term tianxia used to describe an (actual and ideal) cosmopolitan state of affairs in which everything under heaven, or at least everything under heaven visible from the Han court, was either under direct Han control or paid some sort of notional or real homage to the Han. The First Emperor of the Qin (*Qin Shi Huangdi* 秦始皇帝; r. 221–210 BC), in the workly inscriptions he erected, never mentions his former regional state of Qin but talks instead frequently of tianxia, saying that, for example, he has pacified it, united it, made it one family (平天下；闡并天下；壹家天下).[85] The territories over which Qin Shi Huangdi claimed to have achieved such successes included both Huaxia and non-Huaxia regions, reinforcing the sense that the term was increasingly an index of a claim to cosmopolitan rule, using, of course, the trope we have already discussed, by which cosmopolitan ecologies appropriate and universalize originally local or panchoric terms. Over the Han Dynasty and its successors, the list of territories submitting, notionally or in fact, to Chinese imperial authority expanded to include much of the known world; the claim that tianxia, in fact, equaled the entire world, was one that would only face significant challenge in Chinese thinking during the nineteenth century.

Just as the historical evolution of tianxia as a concept in China itself acts as something of an index of the emergence of cosmopolitan thinking out of an originally local, then panchoric, worldview, so too the appropriation of the concept in other East Asian cultures allows us to map the uneven terrain of the cosmopolis the term at once constructs and embodies. In Japan, long open to Chinese influence but geographically isolated enough never to have been under direct Chinese threat, the term, pronounced *tenka* in Japanese, had a long history, dating back at least to the early eighth century. The early historical text the *Chronicles of Japan* (*Nihon Shoki*, 日本書紀), compiled in AD 720, traces the history of Japan from its mythical origins to about twenty years prior to the present of its authors. Written in classical Chinese, its account of the origins of the world (i.e., of Japan) contain a

Rome Compared, edited by F. H. Mutschler and A. Mittag, Oxford: Oxford University Press, 2008, 74n18.

85   Pines, "Changing Views of Tianxia in Pre-Imperial Discourse," 2002, 116 with references.

mixture of traditional Japanese myth and imported Chinese cosmology. As part of the narrative, the sun goddess Amaterasu is born from the god Izanagi after he ritually cleanses himself from his journey to the underworld to recover his sister and wife goddess, Izanami:

> Then Izanagi and Izanami spoke together, saying "We have now given birth to the Great Land of Eight Islands [Japan], and to mountains, streams, grasses and trees. Why not create someone to rule over *tenka* [tianxia, 天下]. After this, they gave birth to the sun goddess, and named her Ōhirume-no-muchi [i.e., Amaterasu].[86]

The sun goddess is the notional ancestor of the Japanese imperial dynasty, which reigns to this day, while *tenka* remained in use as a term for the territory of Japan throughout pre-modern times. As late as the Edo period (1603–1868), the territory of the Japanese archipelago was conventionally referred to as tenka, with the term *koku* (i.e., *guo* 國; the same term used in Warring States China for the regional states) used principally to refer to regional feudal territories. Although the term *koku* was occasionally used in the eighteenth century to describe Japan in its diplomatic relations with Korea and China, it was only with the Meiji restoration in 1868, when Japan underwent a decisive transformation in the direction of the West, that Japan began to refer to itself principally by this term, appropriating what was once an epichoric term for the new status of the modern nation-state, and abandoning the notion that Japan was, like China, tenka, or "All Under Heaven."[87]

In the territory of what is now Korea, the term tianxia, or as it is pronounced in Korean *cheonha* 천하, was used somewhat less frequently than in Japan, in part, perhaps, because the various kingdoms that ruled Korea over its history were always much more vulnerable to Chinese attack than Japan could be and, as a result, all the more aware that their rule was meaningfully non-universal. Still, we find its use from the earliest stages of Korean history; one of the earliest inscriptions in classical Chinese found in Korea uses the expression tianxia. The tomb is that specifically of Modoru, an aristocrat and local administrator of the reign of the King Jangsu (r. 413–91) of the Goguryeo Dynasty, which ruled much of what is now northern Korea and eastern Manchuria during the third through seventh

---

86   既而伊奘諾尊・伊奘冉尊、共議曰、吾已生大八洲國及山川草木。何不生天下之主者歟。於是、共生日神。號大日孁貴。(日本書紀。卷第一神代　上)

87   R. P. Toby, "Rescuing the Nation from History: The State of the State in Early Modern Japan," *Monumenta Nipponica* 56 (2), 2001: 197.

centuries AD. The inscription praises the king, saying, "All the world [天下] and four regions knew of the sageliness of this kingdom and this village."[88]

This praise of Jangsu, then, describes him in terms very specifically derived from the kinds of universalist claims first made by the Qin and Han Dynasties; in so doing, he may have been aided to some extent by the fact that the Chinese heartlands were in disarray during this period. In the early fifth century, the Jin Dynasty, which was the ethnically Huaxia successor state to the Han (and its immediate successor, the Wei), was confined to southern China, with its capital in the lower Yangtze. Northern China was under the rule of what are referred to as the "Sixteen Kingdoms," a shifting series of mostly non-Huaxia states. In the years prior to Jangsu's erection of the stele to his father in 414, the ethnically Qiang Later Qin Dynasty was in a hegemonic position in northern China, but from around 408 onwards, a series of military defeats and internecine conflicts within the royal family greatly weakened the Later Qin, which did not long outlast the death of the dynasty's second ruler, Emperor Wenhuan, in 416. Wenhuan himself only sporadically used the title *huangdi* 皇帝, the term invented by the First Emperor of the Qin[89] and conventionally translated as "emperor"; the ruler of the Later Qin preferred for the most part to refer to himself as a "heavenly king," *tianwang* 天王, a term roughly parallel to the "Great King, "*tai wang* 太王 title used by Jangsu of Goguryeo to describe his father. Certainly, the early fourth century was a time in which the rulers of what is now China were hardly in a position to enforce their own monopoly on cosmopolitan terminology, something they may have done to some extent in later periods in Korean history.

As these two examples make clear, one of the features of cosmopolitan rhetoric is that it is very easily appropriated by new regimes and spreads readily from one state to another. Even terms whose internal logic makes

---

88   天下四」方知此國郡最聖▨▨▨」治此郡之嗣. National Research Institute of Cultural Heritage. http://gsm.nricp.go.kr/_third/user/search/KBD007.jsp?ksmno=3085, accessed April 17, 2012. For a discussion of this and other inscriptions, see Tae-don Noh, "The Worldview of the Goguryeo People as Presented in Fifth-Century Stone Monument Inscriptions," *Seoul Journal of Korean Studies* 17, n.d.: 1–43; Hung-gyu Kim, "Defenders and Conquerors: The Rhetoric of Royal Power in Korean Inscriptions from the Fifth to Seventh Centuries," *Cross-currents: East Asian History and Culture Review* (2), 2012: 1–41.

89   Note that the "Later Qin" (AD 384–417) has nothing other than its name in common with the Qin dynasty established by the First Emperor in 221 BC.

them inherently universal, like tianxia, are terms that can be borrowed from one polity to another and even, potentially, used by more than one state at a time. There is, however, a particular consequence to such cosmopolitan terminology, which is that in its very universality and erasure of local distinctions it renders difficult the possibility of converting the cosmopolitan identity to a national one. For many modern nations whose traditional rulers had made cosmopolitan claims, of course, this presented only a minor challenge; nations like Korea, Japan, and Vietnam, for example, were able to use their already existing vernacular language and literature as one basis for a modern national identity (and Japan and Korea in particular, being comparatively ethnically homogeneous, lent themselves unusually well in certain ways to the model of the modern nation-state). Arabic-speaking regions made the opposite choice, to preserve a unified written language, based on the cosmopolitan language, valuing transnational solidarity over particularist nationalism; I discuss this choice briefly in the national literatures chapter.

The Fates of Literary Cosmopoleis

This distinction between the fates of the Chinese and Arabic cosmopoleis illustrates some of the possible transitions made over time by cosmopolitan literary ecologies. Arabic, perhaps uniquely, remains extant as a literary cosmopolis today, with native speakers of dozens of Arabic dialects across many nations, from Mauritania to Oman, using Modern Standard Arabic (itself relatively little changed from the classical language) as their medium of literary expression and the language playing a significant auxiliary role across the larger Islamic world, from West Africa to Indonesia and beyond. Other cosmopoleis of the past simply shifted their cosmopolitan language of choice. The region around the modern city of Baghdad, for example, has used, in succession, Sumerian, Akkadian, Aramaic, Greek, Arabic, Persian, and Arabic again as its chief vehicles for literary expression; none of these languages (with the exception of Akkadian) originate in the region, but the local populations over time adapted to different (and frequently overlapping) cosmopolitan idioms. Some regions have been part of more than one cosmopolis at a time, as in the case of much of South Asia, where, in the centuries prior to British colonization, both Persian and Sanskrit served cosmopolitan functions, linking different individuals in the region to distinct, if sometimes overlapping, large-scale networks, while some vernacular languages, including Urdu, various dialects of what would become Hindi, and Marathi, served transregional functions alongside the larger cosmopolitan languages.

In the case of China, as I showed briefly earlier, the cosmopolitan register of the language gave way to a vernacular register, understood now as a "national" language, with the consequent construction of a vernacular literary history along European lines, as I will show in the chapter on national literatures. Across Eurasia and Africa, it was the advent of European colonialism that dealt the harshest blows to many cosmopolitan languages, whether in the South Asian development of Hindi and Urdu as "national" languages for India and Pakistan, with dozens of other languages acting as national at regional levels, or in the emergence of "national" languages as the sole media of literary expression in southeast Asia. With the arguable exception of Arabic, no cosmopolitan language has survived the transition to the model of the nation-state unscathed; the particular kind of elite universalism fostered by these languages having seemed unsuited to the modern era of competition among nations.

Many cosmopolitan languages, however, (and most notably Latin and Sanskrit) began their declines long before modernity, nationalism, and colonialism. Instead, they were supplanted by regional vernacular language sat first only as supplements to the cosmopolitan, often directed towards particular functions, but gradually, in each case, taking over more and more of the functions of the cosmopolitan language, until eventually they had replaced it altogether. Lost in the process, of course, was the immense geographic and chronological breadth of audience opened up by cosmopolitan languages, as well as the capacity to make one's claims about the political world on a notionally universal stage; what was gained will be the subject of the next chapter.

CHAPTER 4

Vernacular Literature

At some time not long before 967 AD, a Buddhist monk named Kyunyŏ 均 如 of the Kingdom of Koryo, which then comprised much of the Korean peninsula, composed a series of vernacular-language poems on Buddhist doctrinal themes. This was not in itself an unprecedented activity—the historical record contains evidence that vernacular poetry had been composed for several centuries by this time, nor was Kyunyŏ the first to write Buddhist vernacular poetry in what is now Korea. What is more remarkable is that one of his contemporaries, the scholar and diplomat Ch'oe Haenggwi 崔行歸, chose to translate those poems into classical Chinese, still the dominant language for intellectual and literary discourse on the Korean peninsula, and the only linguistic choice available to an author in Koryo who wished his work to be read beyond the peninsula's boundaries. Ch'oe composed a preface to his translation of Kyunyŏ's poems, itself necessarily written in classical Chinese, in which he advocates for their merit, and explains his decision to translate them:[1]

> But these *shi* poems (by other Korean poets) used Chinese (Tang) words, polished like jade into five words or seven characters. The (Korean) songs were drawn up in our rustic speech, fashioned into three phrases and six names.[2] In terms of their sound, they are as far apart as Orion and Antares, easily distinguished in the Western and Eastern skies. According to their principles of construction, they are

---

1 然而詩搆唐辭. 磨琢於五言七字. 歌排鄉語. 切磋於三句六名. 論聲則隔 若參商. 東西易辨. 據理則敵如矛楯. 強弱難分. 雖云對衙詞鋒. 足認同歸義海. 各得其所. 于何不臧. 而所恨者. 我邦之才子名公. 解吟唐什. 彼土之鴻儒碩德. 莫解鄉謠. 矧復唐文. 如帝網交羅. 我邦易讀. 鄉扎似梵書連布. 彼土難諳. 使梁 宋珠璣. 數托東流之水. 秦韓錦繡. 希隨西傳之星. 其在局通. 亦堪嗟痛. 庸詎 非魯文宣. 欲居於此地. 未至鰲頭. 薛翰林. 強變於斯文. 煩成鼠尾之所致者歟. Translation adapted from Adrian Buzo and Tony Prince, *Kyunyo-jon : The Life, Times and Songs of a Tenth-Century Korean Monk*, Broadway, Australia: Wild Peony PTY, 1993, 52–55.

2 A famously difficult phrase; see the discussion at ibid., 53n164.

as opposed as spear and shield. Although they seem to vaunt themselves as sharply distinct, yet it is clear that they will return to the same ocean of righteousness, and each will find its place. How could this not be a good thing?

And yet it is a pity that our country's men of talent and renowned officials can understand and recite Chinese (Tang) poetry, but of the venerable scholars who have mastered virtue in that land, none can understand our rustic chants. This is because Chinese characters (Tang *wen*) spread out like Indra's net,[3] and the people of our country can read them easily. Our *hyangchal* writing is connected tightly like Sanskrit writing, and the people of that land (China) sound it out with difficulty. This is why the rough and smooth pearls of Liang and Song (i.e., Chinese literature) often catch an eastward-flowing stream, but the brocades and embroideries of Qin and Han (i.e., Korean literature) rarely follow a westward-turning star. This hindrance to communication makes one deeply sigh and ache. Did not the Exalted King of Culture of Lu (i.e., Confucius) wish to dwell in this land (Korea), though he did not ascend the sea-turtle's head (to do so)? Did not Sŏl Hanrim energetically transform education, with the only result a rat's tail prolixity?

Ch'oe's chief theme here is the one-way nature of literary circulation in his era; texts in classical Chinese (wenyan), part of a network of texts reflecting each other like Indra's net, cross political boundaries and circulate everywhere, while Korean-language texts, in this era awkwardly transcribed using Chinese characters, are caught up in a narrower network and do not travel (though at the same time they do resemble Sanskrit, which as the source of Buddhism acts as a kind of counter-cosmopolis to wenyan). The pearls of Chinese literature can be sold in Korea, but the brocades of Korean-language literature cannot be sold in China. Koryo can compete with metropolitan China in terms of its Confucian virtue and has long been able to do so (hence Confucius's alleged desire to dwell in Korea), but the word of that achievement, conveyed as it often is in the "rat's tail prolixity" of Sŏl Hanrim's awkward system of transcription in which Chinese characters were used to transcribe Korean words, go nowhere.

The monk Kyunyŏ offers something of a paradigm for the early use of a vernacular language (in Sheldon Pollock's sense)[4] for literary purposes.

---

3   A jeweled net said to hang over the palace of the (Hindu) god Indra, in which each jewel reflects all the other jewels.

4   Sheldon Pollock, "India in the Vernacular Millennium: Literary Culture and Polity, 1000–1500," in *Public Spheres and Collective Identities*, edited by Shmuel

Pollock understands the process of vernacularization as "the historical process of choosing to create a written literature, along with its complement, a political discourse, in local languages according to models supplied by a superordinate, usually cosmopolitan, literary culture."[5] As such, foundational vernacular authors, such as Kyunyŏ, are usually more than fluent readers and writers of the cosmopolitan language from which they draw their models. Kyunyŏ, in addition to having an extensive knowledge of the Chinese tradition, has access through it to a vast corpus of Indic Buddhist texts, including in particular the *Bhadracarīpraṇidhāna*, on which his vernacular poems are dependent for their content.[6] He is thus very far from anything like a "folk" poet, composing indigenous verbal art in a cultural vacuum, which I argue in this chapter and the next represents rather more the later nationalist fantasy of the emergence of the vernacular rather than observed practice. Kyunyŏ uses the vernacular to discuss religious doctrine, suggesting affinities with theories by which religious proselytization provides the justification for the vernacular. At the same time, and as this very text notes, the *hyangchal* system of transcription, in which Chinese characters were used phonetically to represent Korean-language syllables, was far from a transparent medium for expressing the vernacular language. Indeed, so opaque was this medium that knowledge of hyangchal was all but lost for centuries and recovered to a significant extent in the 1920s because of Ch'oe Haenggwi's translations of Kyunyŏ's poems into Chinese, which offered a sort of bilingual "Rosetta stone" permitting the decoding of the Korean-language originals.[7] Kyunyŏ's Korean-language poems would thus have been little easier to read than poems in classical Chinese; only with the development of the Hangul alphabet in the mid-fifteenth century would vernacular literacy begin to offer genuine advantages of ease of learning over wenyan. Moreover, as Ch'oe Haenggwi's preface laments, the use of the Korean language guarantees that only Koreans will read a given text.

The choice to write in a vernacular language (and it is always a choice, given the availability of the cosmopolitan language) is thus, especially at first, not simply a question of ease of use or the ability to communicate

Noah Eisenstadt, Wolfgang Schluchter, and Björn Wittrock, Transaction Publishers, 2001, 41–74.

5   Sheldon Pollock, *The Language of the Gods in the World of Men: Sanskrit, Culture, and Power in Premodern India*, Berkeley: University of California Press, 2009, 23

6   Buzo and Prince, *Kyunyo-jon* 1993, 75–88.

7   Buzo and Prince, *Kyunyo-jon*, 2. Note that the recovered ability to interpret the Korean-language text here is itself very much a product of a nationalist era.

more effectively with a population unfamiliar with the prevailing cosmopolitan language. Rather, as Pollock emphasizes, this choice is an aesthetic choice, with the potential for political overtones, where authors writing in the vernacular construct a narrower audience for their work and, through that construction of an audience, construct some sort of cultural community.

Cosmopolitan languages, as we have seen, are almost by definition few in number, while the number of panchoric languages is likewise not very large. Vernaculars, like national languages, are considerably more numerous, but where the construction of national languages and literatures developed first in one localized region (Western Europe) and spread outward from there, vernacularization began independently in a number of different regions, in several different historical waves, beginning with the emergence of ancient Near Eastern vernaculars about three thousand years ago, followed by the emergence of a series of vernaculars in Europe and the Mediterranean between the third century BC and the fourth century AD, and then by Pollock's "vernacular millennium" beginning around the eighth century AD. As a result of this series of multiple and independent emergences, it is particularly difficult to reduce the story of vernacularization to a single narrative. In what follows, instead, I examine multiple dimensions of vernacularization in sequence, looking for commonalities within and beyond regions. First, I distinguish between vernacularization and similar-seeming processes—the use of local languages for chancery or proselytizing purposes, and oral-traditional culture—in order better to understand the limits of vernacularization. Then, I examine two key tropes of vernacularization: the vernacular manifesto and emulation of the cosmopolitan literary tradition, briefly examining some key case studies of each. I then explore a series of vernacularizations, beginning in the ancient Near East and moving through early Medieval Europe, which I believe complicate the picture offered by Pollock, before closing with a consideration of the two great cosmopolitan regions that did not undergo vernacularization in the usual way: the Arabic world and China proper.

Literization and Literarization: The Limits of the Vernacular

Cosmopolitan literary ecologies, designed as they are to function across great distances and for speakers of many languages, are also able to endure for very long periods of time; thus, each of the cosmopolitan languages we discussed in the previous chapter endured in that role for a millennium and several for much more, often in the total absence of native speakers (at certain periods Sumerian and Akkadian, Latin, Sanskrit) or in the virtual impossibility of their serving as everyday spoken languages (classical Chinese). At least one literary cosmopolis, that based on Arabic, remains alive today and shows little signs of changing in the near future. Of all the literary formations we have studied, in fact, the cosmopolitan seems to have the greatest potential for long-term stability.

And yet, in most cases, we also know that cosmopolitan literary ecologies do not remain stagnant but grow and change and adapt. Sometimes, as in the case of Akkadian supplementing Sumerian, or Persian supplementing Arabic, one cosmopolitan language gives way to, or accommodates, another. Sometimes, as in the case of classical Chinese within China itself, a cosmopolitan language remains dominant until its encounter with European modernity and the national literature ecology. More often, however, when cosmopolitan ecologies evolve they generate vernaculars. These literary languages emerge in symbiosis with existing cosmopolitan languages, serving distinct functions. Casual habit associates vernaculars with the spoken language of everyday people, with the establishment of local kingdoms rather than universal empires, and with new religious movements (particularly the three great proselytizing religions, Buddhism, Christianity, and Islam). In truth, each of these can be a factor in the emergence of vernacular literatures, though it is not clear that any or all of these factors need to be in place.

Indeed, the available evidence resists any easy assertions about the conditions of emergence of literary vernaculars. They are, indeed, usually much closer to daily spoken language than are cosmopolitan languages, and they most often emerge first in regions where the cosmopolitan language is especially far removed from spoken language (as with Old Irish and Anglo-Saxon in the Latin cosmopolis, with Japanese in the classical Chinese cosmopolis, or with Javanese, Khmer, Kannada, and Tamil in the Sanskrit cosmopolis), emerging only later, if at all, in linguistic heartlands (France, Italy, Spain; China proper; the North Indian Gangetic plain, respectively) where the cosmopolitan language is much closer to spoken dialects. That said, early vernaculars often contain heavy admixtures of their cosmopolitan parent language (especially in the South and East Asian cases) and/or represent artificial standardizations at points along a complex dialect continuum (as with the Romance and Indic languages in particular) such that the differential ease with which the cosmopolitan and the vernacular may be learned is not as great for as many people as might be imagined.

The effects of religion and of the political order on the vernacular is likewise complex and requires us to pay attention to an important distinction Sheldon Pollock draws between the literization of a language and its literarization.[8] In this context, the literization of a language is the development of a system by which that language may be set to writing, for any purpose; as such, it includes such phenomena as the development of an alphabet or other writing system, developed indigenously or adapted from abroad, the development of at least some minimal standards of orthography, and the dissemination of these systems across a body of people sufficient to justify the innovation. Literarization, on the other hand, refers to the development of the aesthetic resources of a given language so that it will be a suitable vehicle for verbal art of a written kind. The processes inherent to literarization will include such phenomena as the compiling of dictionaries (and particularly of bilingual dictionaries with the cosmopolitan language or with other prestige vernaculars), the editing of grammars, and the development of a rich and supple lexicon, able to express complex ideas with subtlety and frequently borrowing considerably for that purpose from cosmopolitan languages. Only languages that have undergone both literization and literarization, I will argue, emerge as true vernaculars.

In the sense meant here, a traditional and oral folk culture, operant in some peripheral or marginal region of a cosmopolitan ecology or circulating amongst the lower social orders in the ecology's heartlands, will not qualify as a vernacular literature. Such cultures of verbal art are, presumably, ubiquitous in the historical record. Gauls, no doubt, had songs and stories they told in their own languages, before and during the era of Roman rule; hill peoples of southwest China could (and did, and still do), perform and transmit their own transitions in the context of Chinese imperial rule, under which the Chinese language held a monopoly on the technology of writing. For that matter, the songs sung by the urban proletariats of Rome and Chang'an, performed in variants of the standard language, must have echoed around the residences of the great and officially sanctioned poets of each regime, leaving only the occasional trace for posterity through accidental survival or literati appropriation. The fact that such works, numerous though they must have been, were not written down, not only ensured their eventual

---

8   Pollock, "India in the Vernacular Millennium," 41–74; Casanova, Pascale, *La republique mondiale des lettres*, Paris: Editions du Seuil, 1999, 188–93, independently coins the term, as Pollock will observe in later work.

demise as the cultural configurations that gave them birth themselves shifted to new forms. Just as significantly for our purposes, since cosmopolitan literatures are by definition transmitted through writing, a verbal art communicated orally marks itself thereby as interested in a different kind of circulation altogether, one not directly in competition with the cosmopolitan.

Oral works can circulate for long periods of time and over fairly broad geographic regions, as the cases of Homeric epic and of the South Slavic tradition attest. That circulation is not, however, unlimited; changes in dialect, for example, bind oral traditions both geographically and chronologically, even if, as in the case of Homeric Greek, very real efforts at standardization across dialects have taken place in a panchoric context. Moreover, the audiences for oral and written verbal art, especially in pre-modern times, are radically different. Oral art has the potential for a very deep penetration of a geographically and chronologically limited region. Written verbal art may not penetrate so deeply into a community, thanks both to low levels of literacy and to the high costs of the reproduction of written text prior to commercial printing, but it can circulate much more broadly through a transregional elite and, within that elite, across long periods of time, as we have seen in the cosmopolitan chapter. To perform a poem or song orally, then, is not to place it in competition with a written cosmopolitan tradition, and the various local oral cultures of pre-modern cosmopolitan ecologies are better understood, perhaps, as forms of epichoric, or panchoric, circulation. While such literatures could and did find themselves transposed into writing on occasion, it was that transposition, and not the original composition of a work, that marked the entry into the vernacular order. Moreover, from a purely pragmatic perspective, if such oral verbal art was *not* committed to writing, then we are unlikely to know anything of it today (as with my notional Gaulish folk poetry), and as such, it will not function as part of any literary ecology for us. Without literization, then, there can be no vernacular.

And yet, while literization may be a necessary condition for vernacularization, it is far from sufficient in the absence of literarization. Languages are frequently first written down to fulfill functions other than the literary and, notably, for political and religious reasons; the former because polities wish to monitor more effectively the populace they administer (and to maintain the laws they use for that administration with more consistency), the latter because a religion will penetrate more deeply into a population the more that population has access to verbal art espousing the religion in appropriate terms, such that writing at once broadens access to religious knowledge, and regulates its production and circulation more effectively. As such, scriptures and homilies and handbooks of spiritual or ethical practice are frequently among the first literary, or quasi-literary, texts to be committed to writing in a newly literized language.

Many languages are first committed to writing as what Thomas Kamusella calls "chancery languages," languages used by imperial or at least transregional polities for the recording of official documents (tax records, testimony in criminal proceedings, deeds of property) in regions under their rule, where the cosmopolitan or transregional language preferred by the state is inadequately known by local officials or by the local elites they managed.[9] Kamusella argues that many of the languages of Central and Eastern Europe first entered into writing in this way— German, Bohemian/Czech, Polish, Magyar, Ruthenian, and others. While use as a chancery language does imply some level of standardization and refinement to the level necessary to discuss complex legal and financial matters, it does not automatically entail the use of that language for literary purposes; indeed, that use can easily lag behind chancery uses by several centuries, as Kamusella's Central and Eastern European cases generally do.

Nor does the use of a language in writing as a vehicle for proselytization automatically confer vernacular status upon it; such literizations of language, usually for the translations of scripture, do, as with chancery languages, standardize previously complex dialectal continua and enrich local languages with sophisticated technical vocabularies, key elements of literarization. At the same time, they are frequently driven by outside agendas, even by outside individuals, and need not spark the development of an indigenous literary tradition beyond the work of scripture. Scriptural translations, whether Luther's translation of the Bible into German or translations of the Therevada Buddhist canon from Pali into Burmese, can, and frequently do, provide a foundation on which a vernacular literature is built, but examples also abound, particularly in Christian missionary work from Fujian to Nigeria to the Amazon, where the development of a written form of a spoken language for the purposes of scriptural translation does not lead to the production of any significant body of other material in that written language. Literization for scriptural purposes is not automatically

---

9   Tomasz Kamusella, *The Politics of Language and Nationalism in Modern Central Europe*, Basingstoke: Palgrave Macmillan, 2009.

equivalent to literarization, though it can provide a basis on which that literarization takes place.

The point is that a real vernacular literature represents a decision to transmit in writing a literary tradition in a new language, constructed for that purpose and intended in some way to compete with, complement, or otherwise coexist with a cosmopolitan literary language. Vernaculars, in the definition I am using, exist in symbiosis with one or more cosmopolitan literary languages and potentially with other vernaculars as well. As we shall see in more detail later in this chapter, they frequently announce this symbiosis in some explicit form, whether through a vernacular manifesto or through emulation of major works of the cosmopolitan canon (or both). Vernacular ecologies always, then, exhibit some level of diglossia, or rather digraphia, with the choice to write in the vernacular (or in *a* vernacular, since the choice of vernaculars in such a system is itself often complex) always also a choice *not* to write in the cosmopolitan idiom. That choice can be motivated by questions of audience or of genre and can take place in the contexts of radically different configurations of political and cultural power with respect to the available languages. The choice to write in a particular vernacular can even be motivated, among other things, by the native language of the author or his or her desire to write in alignment with a particular political regime or to espouse a particular set of religious views, but it rarely, if ever, reduces simply to those factors.

This fact is why a vernacular language is also never created with the explicit and simple aim of providing the basis for a national movement. Many of the languages of Eastern Europe, for example, fall into this category, in which the modern written form of the language is largely, or even entirely, the product of the nineteenth century and the ripple effect of nationalisms beginning in France and then in Germany. Languages such as Estonian; Latvian and Lithuanian; and Belarussian and Ukrainian; exist as we know them as products of just such nationalist movements, despite the use of versions of these languages as chancery languages and/or as vehicles for Christian (and frequently specifically Protestant) proselytizing for as many as four or five hundred years prior to the nationalist moment. The first text composed in Lithuanian that we know of, for example, was a catechism published in a low-country dialect in Königsberg in 1547, and from the 1620s onward, fragments of Lithuanian language survive in court transcripts. For centuries prior to that, Lithuanian had been the home language of the Jagiellonian Dynasty, which ruled Poland and Lithuania from the late fourteenth through the late sixteenth centuries, although for administrative purposes the Jagiellonians used Latin, Polish, and Ruthenian, while German was also prevalent in urban areas. Folk literature of various kinds must have existed in dialects that could be recognized as related to modern Lithuanian, but it was only in the 1880s that the literary form of the language was standardized, at a point on the dialect continuum deliberately chosen to be relatively distant from Latvian, with an orthography derived from Czech (rather than an earlier, Polish-inspired orthography, rejected in the nationalist era because of tension with Poland).[10] Only at this point did it become possible to publish work in any significant quantity in Lithuanian, although here again the very nature of Lithuanian as a nationalist project ran up against equally nationalist but more powerful antagonists in German and Russian/Soviet imperial rule. As such, Lithuanian as a literary language was always engaged in a kind of ecological competition with larger regional national languages, such as German and Russian (and, of course, with still more powerful national literary languages, such as English and French), but not significantly in competition with Latin, since by the time Lithuanian emerged as a genuinely viable literary option, Latin had ceased to be a major structuring feature of the literary ecology of Europe.

Not all spoken languages are equally available for use as literary vernaculars; some are spoken by too few people, and differ too much from their neighbors, to make easy reading for enough people to justify their use. In linguistic terminology, these languages differ from their neighbors through Abstand; that is, differences of mutual unintelligibility marking clear linguistic borders, as between Spanish and Basque, or French and German.[11] Usable literary vernaculars will need to be close enough to the spoken language of a large enough number of people to generate viable audiences for such work; as such, they are well suited to regions of dialect continuum, such as the Germanic and Romance languages of Europe or the Indic and Dravidian languages of South Asia. These dialect continua bring their own problems, of course; when the spoken language of each village varies slightly, the differences across larger regions does become unmanageable; moreover, the question of where and how along that continuum a written literary standard should emerge becomes a complex matter of cultural politics. This question forms, in fact, a central concern of one of the key manifestoes of vernacularization in the European

---

10   Ibid., 180–91.
11   Heinz Kloss, "'Abstand Languages' and 'Ausbau Languages,'" *Anthropological Linguistics* 9 (7), 1967.

tradition, Dante's *De vulgari eloquentia*, and I will return to it in my discussion of that text. However this question is resolved, resolved it must be, and a literary language emerging from a dialect continuum will need to choose a point or region on that continuum and then develop it through processes linguists describe as Ausbau, or building-up. Vocabulary must be managed by selecting from the range of available possibilities; syntactical structures must be regularized (often through assimilation to the syntax of the cosmopolitan language); frequently, though not always, grammars and dictionaries are compiled.[12]

LANGUAGE NAMES

Even the naming of a vernacular language is an act of significance and an act that betrays the difference between vernaculars and national languages. Because modern national languages are understood as in some way the embodiment of a nation-state and of a people, the names of national languages tend quite straightforwardly to derive from the names of the nation they embody, or at least the nation where they originate. Thus, the French speak French in France; Finns speak Finnish in Finland; Americans, the English of their English forebears in England.

Pre-modern European vernaculars were, however, much more complexly territorialized, if at all. While their early use was frequently correlated with courtly or monastic centers, the relationship between the two was frequently complex, as was the relationship between either language or polity on the one hand and any notion of a "people" on the other. Thomas Kamusella notes several examples of the ways in which regional identity was often constructed in pre-modern Europe. Orthodox believers located within the territory of the Grand Duchy of Lithuania, and those in the Kingdom of Poland (polities combined through dynastic union for much of the middle ages), initially identified the languages they spoke as "Ruthenian," but came over time to identify the Lithuanian–Polish border as a boundary between "White Russia" and "Little Russia," or between Belarusians and Ukrainians. While this border continued to have political significance under the jurisdiction of states centered elsewhere, it only became the basis for a boundary between a Belarusian and a Ukrainian

---

12   Casanova, *La republique mondiale des lettres* 1999, 108 claims, I think wrongly, that the failure of English to develop rigorous linguistic norms prior to the eighteenth century hindered the autonomy of literature in England.

state (and only briefly then) in the immediate aftermath of the First World War, and more enduringly in 1991. Likewise, the people now known as the nation-state of Slovenia began as Slavic migrants to the Alpine region and fell, for complex historical reasons, under the territory of the Duchy of Bavaria and thus of the Carolingian empire. Ecclesiastical boundaries between dioceses tended thereafter to reinforce a sense of difference between Slovenes and their fellow Catholic South Slavs, the Croats, but the term "Slovenian" did not emerge until the late eighteenth century; it is etymologically almost identical to the words "Slav" and "Slovak," such that the words for Slovene, Slovak, and Slav in today's Slovenian and Slovak are almost indistinguishable. Prior to this somewhat arbitrary naming, inhabitants of the general region tended to identify themselves through sub-regional toponyms, such as Carinthia, Carniola, or Styria, regardless of whether they spoke a Germanic or a Slavic dialect.[13]

In a somewhat analogous manner, the historian of late imperial China Pamela Crossley has shown, for example, that the Qing Dynasty (1644–1911) carefully constructed a new sense of identity for both its own Manchu ethnicity and for the Mongols.[14] For example, "Mongol" identity under Genghis Khan had been largely a question of personal loyalty, with many Mongolian-speaking groups excluded from such identity as not sworn to loyalty and other, Turkic, groups identified as "Mongolian" because they were loyal. After the fall of the Mongol Yuan Dynasty in China in 1368, the groups identified as "Mongol" became still more diverse, including a wide range of linguistic communities, from Jurchen to Kirghiz, as well as multiple religious and political affiliations, even among the leaders of the groups called "Mongol" by the Ming court. Finally, as the "Manchu" (itself a problematic identity) Qing Dynasty took power, they sought legitimacy in part through an affiliation with the cult of Genghis Khan and thus co-opted Mongol elites into their political structure. Over time, the Qing court in Beijing sponsored the production of literature in Mongolian and mandated literacy in Mongolian for the groups they had labeled as "Mongol" (whether or not that was the native language of the individuals in those groups),

---

13   Kamusella, *The Politics of Language and Nationalism*, 288–300.

14   For the Manchus, see Pamela Kyle Crossley, *A Translucent Mirror: History and Identity in Qing Imperial Ideology*, Berkeley: University of California Press, 2002, 281–336; For the Mongols, see Crossley, "Making Mongols," in *Empire at the Margins: Culture, Ethnicity, and Frontier in Early Modern China*, edited by Pamela Kyle Crossley, Helen F. Siu, and Donald S. Sutton, Berkeley: University of California Press, 2006, 58–82.

helping in the process to construct a new, linguistically based Mongolian identity that would later serve both as a basis for the nationalism of the modern state of Mongolia and for the acceptance by other Mongols of citizenship within an officially multiethnic People's Republic of China.

In this sort of context, in which shifting political and religious borders overlay complex dialect continua and in which cultural formations could be as much the product of imperial strategy as of indigenous self-identification, it is hardly surprising that it was not always easy to define language names unambiguously. As a result, a great many vernacular languages either have multiple names or no name at all or very generic names. We shall see below how Ramon Vidal refers to the language his text describes as "Limousin," although his own home is far from Limoges and although many other writers of the time refer instead to the language of the troubadours as the language of Provence. Dante, likewise, speaks of the "language of *si*" and of a vulgar Latin but never of Italian per se. The first known use of the term *linguaggio italiano* is in an undated letter of Leonardo da Vinci, to Leo X, probably written between 1513 and 1516, though Dante himself does speak of the "volgare *italico*" (*Convivio*, I-vi-8),[15] using a related glottonym that is clearly not, however, the origin of the modern name. This relatively late naming of Italian as such contrasts with the significantly earlier dates at which other Romance language names are attested; for example, *franceis* is found as early as 1100, *castellana* and *espannol* in 1254 and 1284 respectively, and even *portugues* by 1437.[16] Although these other languages first received names earlier, in part because each was more clearly associated with a single polity than was Italian, it is nonetheless striking that the language names long post-date the first written texts known in each language: for French, the Oaths of Strasbourg (842); for Spanish, the *Glosas Emilianenses* (c. 1000); for Portuguese, texts from the late ninth century AD. In contrast to the "national languages," which emerge as literary standards in the nineteenth and twentieth centuries and were developed specifically for the use of an actual or emergent nation-state, the Romance languages first emerged for pragmatic reasons and for significant early periods operated without fixed names. Poets themselves frequently described

---

15   Muljacic Zarko, "Perché i glotonimi 'linguaggio italiano', 'lingua italiana' (e sim.) appaiono per indicare 'oggetti' reali e non soltanto auspicati molto più tardi di altri termini analoghi che si riferiscono a varie lingue gallo ibero-romanze?" *Cuadernos de filología italiana* (4), 1997: 254.

16   Ibid., 257.

vernacular language as "Latin," *lati*, a term used, indeed for the singing of birds, as well as for Latin itself;[17] when the need arose to discuss Latin, however, both Dante and Ramon Vidal prefer the term *gramatica*. From a comparative perspective, similar kinds of terminological ambiguities can be found in South Asia: the Dravidian language now known as Malayalam, spoken in the southwestern Indian state of Kerala, was not normally given that name until the colonial era; the term Malayalam emerged first in the sixteenth century for the region of south India west of the Western Ghat mountains and for a script that is neither the one now used for Malayalam nor its ancestor. Down to the colonial period, the term Tami, or just *bhāṣā* ("language"), was more commonly used for the continuum of Dravidian dialects used for literary purposes in the territory of modern Kerala.[18]

This vagueness of linguistic terminology was inevitable, I would argue, in an ecological context in which it was impossible to draw one-to-one relationships between languages, peoples, and polities. That Italy was politically fragmented in Dante's time and that it was also a battleground for the competing interests is a fairly familiar story; that the territory of modern France took some time to coalesce into its current form may bear repeating. The province of Limousin was at the time an English possession (though one contested heavily in the Hundred Years' War), and it would not be officially annexed to the French kingdom until 1607; likewise, the County of Provence, with fluctuating borders, joined the Kingdom of France only in 1481, and only as an inheritance. The regions of southern France, of Italy, and of those parts of Spain no longer under Muslim rule, thus comprised a complex political terrain, and one in which the future emergence of France, Spain, and Italy as we know them would have been unimaginable. The territory of Kerala, likewise, was subsumed under a wide variety of local and transregional polities throughout much of its history. Small wonder, then, that the languages used by poets from these regions had inconsistent names even in theoretical treatises, let alone in the work of poets.

---

17   For the suggestion that "lati" in this context means specifically a language difficult for the speaker to understand, see Simon Gaunt, "Sexual Difference and the Metaphor of Language in a Troubadour Poem," *The Modern Language Review* 83 (2), 1988: 309–10.

18   Rich Freeman, "Genre and Society: The Literary Culture of Premodern Kerala," in *Literary Cultures in History : Reconstructions from South Asia*, edited by Sheldon I. Pollock, Berkeley: University of California Press, 2003, 441.

VERNACULAR MANIFESTO AND COSMOPOLITAN EMULATION

Once a vernacular has been literized and literarized—that is, made available for written literary production—it remains actually to produce literature, and particularly works of literature that will make the case for the vernacular as a literary language. This case can be made either directly, through the publication of literary manifestoes of one kind or another, or indirectly, through the composition of works of literature designed to emulate works in the cosmopolitan tradition. In the case of European and South and Southeast Asian languages, this often involves the composition of vernacular translations of cosmopolitan epic; in the case of Japanese, the gesture of emulation is rather one of the anthologization of poetry, with the *Man'yōshū* (759) compiling earlier poetry in a form designed to rival the Chinese *Shi Jing* and other poetic anthologies. I now consider these two phenomena, the vernacular manifesto and the emulation of the cosmopolitan tradition.

For most modern and Western readers, Dante's *De vulgari eloquentia*, likely composed between 1302 and 1305 but left incomplete by its author and unknown for two centuries following his death, likely constitutes the most familiar example of what I am characterizing as the "vernacular manifesto." Dante is not, in fact, the first European, even in modern times, to compose such a manifesto, a distinction that belongs to the Catalan Ramón Vidal, whose *Razós de trobar* (c. 1210), advocates for and seeks to define the terms of the language we call either Provencal or Occitan, which he himself characterizes as "Lemosin," or of the region of Limoges, in southwest France. I return to Vidal's manifesto below, and for the moment note only that it appears likely that Dante was familiar with the work and/or with its verse translation into Italian by the troubadour Terramagnino of Pisa in the late twelfth century.[19] While not the first modern European vernacular manifesto, then, Dante's *De vulgari eloquentia*, though incomplete, is nonetheless much more sophisticated and detailed in its argumentation and deserves a more detailed scrutiny. In what follows, I discuss a few passages that I consider to be critical to the work as a whole:

> XIX So now we can say that this vernacular, which has been shown to be illustrious, cardinal, aulic, and curial, is the vernacular that is called Italian [*vulgare latium*]. For, just as one vernacular can be identified as belonging to Cremona, so can another that belongs to Lombardy; and just as one can be identified that

---

19   Already recognized by, e.g., A. Ewert, "Dante's Theory of Language," *The Modern Language Review* 35 (3), 1940: 355–66.

belongs to Lombardy, so can another that belongs to the whole left-hand side of Italy [*totius sinistre Ytalie*]; and just as all these can be identified in this way, so can that which belongs to Italy as a whole [*totius Ytalie*]. And just as the first is called Cremonese, the second Lombard, and the third half-Italian [*semilatium*], so this last, which belongs to all Italy [*totius Ytalie*], is called the Italian vernacular [*latium vulgare*]. This is the language used by the illustrious authors who have written vernacular poetry in Italy [*qui lingua vulgari poetati sunt in Ytalia*], whether they came from Sicily, Apulia, Tuscany Romagna, Lombardy, or either of the Marches. And since my intention, as I promised at the beginning of this work, is to teach a theory of the effective use of the vernacular [*de vulgari eloquentia*], I have begun with this form of it, as being the most excellent; and I shall go on, in the following books, to discuss the following questions: whom I think worthy of using this language, for what purpose, in what manner, where, when, and what audience they should address. Having clarified all this, I shall attempt to throw some light on the question of the less important vernaculars, descending step by step until I reach the language that belongs to a single family.[20]

One of the first points to observe is that Dante nowhere identifies the vernacular language he defends as "Italian." He does use *Ytalia* to describe a geographic region corresponding fairly closely to both the Roman understanding of Italy and to the modern nation-state and refers at times to the *Ytalii* as the inhabitants of that territory. It is therefore all the more striking

---

20   XIX 1. Hoc autem vulgare quod illustre, cardinale, aulicum et curiale ostensum est, dicimus esse illud quod vulgare latium appellatur. Nam sicut quoddam vulgare est invenire quod proprium est Cremone, sic quoddam est invenire quod proprium est Lombardie; et sicut est invenire aliquod quod sit proprium Lombardie, [sic] est invenire aliquod quod sit totius sinistre Ytalie proprium; et sicut omnia hec est invenire, sic et illud quod totius Ytalie est. Et sicut illud cremonense ac illud lombardum et tertium semilatium dicitur, sic istud, quod totius Ytalie est, latium vulgare vocatur. Hoc enim usi sunt doctores illustres qui lingua vulgari poetati sunt in Ytalia, ut Siculi, Apuli, Tusci, Romandioli, Lombardi et utriusque Marchie viri.

2. Et quia intentio nostra, ut polliciti sumus in principio huius operis, est doctrinam de vulgari eloquentia tradere, ab ipso tanquam ab excellentissimo incipientes, quos putamus ipso dignos uti, et propter quid, et quomodo, nec non ubi, et quando, et ad quos ipsum dirigendum sit, in inmediatis libris tractabimus.

3. Quibus illuminatis, inferiora vulgaria illuminare curabimus, gradatim descendentes ad illud quod unius solius familie proprium est.

Dante, *Dante: De vulgari eloquentia*, Translated by Steven Botterill, Cambridge: Cambridge University Press, 2005, 45.

that the term he uses for the generalized vernacular common to that population is consistently *Latium vulgare*, or "vulgar/popular Latin." The choice of this term is, I would argue, significant. Dante divides the linguistic geography of the world into a Greek part, a northern European part, corresponding roughly to the Germanic and Slavic languages (where, according to Dante, the word for "yes" is *io*), and a third part, corresponding in essence to the Romance languages, which is itself divided into three, based on the different words for "yes" used there:

> All the rest of Europe that was not dominated by these two vernaculars was held by a third, although nowadays this itself seems to be divided in three: for some now say oc, some oïl, and some sì, when they answer in the affirmative; and these are the Hispanic, the French, and the Italians [*Latini*]. Yet the sign that the vernaculars of these three peoples derive from one and the same language is plainly apparent: for they can be seen to use the same words to signify many things, such as "God," "heaven," "love," "sea," "earth," "is," "lives," "dies," "loves," and almost all others.[21]

Dante's linguistic geography conforms in part to our own, with two interesting exceptions. The less immediately relevant exception is that the language of "oc" for him is not simply what we would call the language of "Languedoc" (i.e., Provencal/Occitan), but in fact the language of Spain, understood, presumably, as including what is now southern France (but which was not, of course, under the territorial administration of the French monarchy in Dante's time). More immediately striking is that Dante here identifies the people of "si" not as "Ytali" (a term, remember, that he does use elsewhere), but as "Latini," or Latins. That Dante is positioning Italy as the direct heir of Rome is made explicit shortly thereafter, as he seeks to identify which of the three parts of what he sees as a common language is best suited to literature:

> and second, because they seem to be in the closest contact with the gramatica which is shared by all—and this, to those who consider the matter rationally, will appear a very weighty argument.[22]

---

21   Totum vero quod in Europa restat ab istis, tertium tenuit ydioma, licet nunc tripharium videatur: nam alii *oc*, alii *oïl*, alii *si* affirmando locuntur, ut puta Yspani, Franci et Latini. Signum autem quod ab uno eodemque ydiomate istarum trium gentium progrediantur vulgaria, in promptu est, quia multa per eadem vocabula nominare videntur, ut Deum, celum, amorem, mare, terram, est, vivit, moritur, amat, alia fere omnia. 1.VIII.6 (trans. Botterill).

22   secundo quia magis videntur inniti gramatice que comunis est, quod

I return below to the earlier part of Dante's distinctions between the three varieties of this language, which relates to questions of genre. Here, I wish to observe that Dante makes explicit the claim that "Italian" (which he calls "vulgar Latin") is closer to "Latin" (which he calls "gramatica") than are either of the other Romance dialects. Nor is it accidental that Dante uses the term gramatica to describe Latin. In part, this is because he is already using the terms "Latin," "Latins," and "Latium" to refer to the language, people, and territory of Italy, and so he needs to avoid ambiguity by using another term for Latin itself. Beyond this, however, the term gramatica itself has significant connotations and does not simply substitute for "Latin." As Dante introduces the term at 1.1.3, gramatica is a secondary language, possessed by the Romans but also by the Greeks and by some, but not all, other peoples.

Dante thus understands human language as divided into two *locutiones*, namely gramatica and the vulgare. Both are, he claims, in some sense the same the world over, though *diversas prolationes et vocabula sit divisa* ("the vernacular [is] divided into different pronunciations and [uses] different names"), a somewhat remarkable claim that is more intelligible in the immediate context of Dante's world, where most of the linguistic variety he would have encountered would have differed chiefly in these respects from his own speech. Because, for Dante, all peoples have a vulgare but not all have gramatica, the former is more honorable, *nobilior*; a term whose use as a descriptor borders so close on the oxymoronic as to insist on the polemical nature of Dante's claim here. At the same time, gramatica has advantages of its own, as a fixed and unchanging standard:

> This is where the inventors of the art of grammar began, for this gramatica is nothing other than a certain unchanging speech, the same across different times and places.[23]

Although the details of Dante's theory of language (or, perhaps better, the theory of language that can be inferred from his somewhat scattered observations) remain obscure and contested, I would argue that gramatica here functions as a sort of template-language for local vernaculars, a kind of

---

rationabiliter inspicientibus videtur gravissimum argumentum. 1.X.4.

23   Hinc moti sunt inventores gramatice facultatis: que quidem gramatica nichil aliud est quam quedam inalterabilis locutionis ydemptitas diversibus temporibus atque locis. 1.IX.11.

unchanging deep structure, of which vernacular speech and writing is a temporally and spatially bound external manifestation. Thus, in exalting the vulgare as nobilior, Dante also maintains a privileged position for gramatica as the paradigm for each version of the vulgare, and as a stable means of communication across time and place:

> [Gramatica's inventers] designed it thus, lest, through changes of speech due to the judgment of individuals, we should either be unable, or only imperfectly able, to gain access to the authorities and deeds of the ancients, or from those who have, as a result of difference in location, become different from us.[24]

If gramatica is constant over time and place, then, the *vulgus* is not—it is a locally bound form of speech, which, as Dante notes, can vary from street to street within a city, as well as between cities or regions, and which, not being codified as gramatica, is also subject to change over time. This almost infinite linguistic variety is not suitable for literary purposes. What is needed here is a vernacular common to all cities, which seems to belong to none (*omnis Latie civitatis est et nullius esse videtur*); a vernacular language that operates in much the same way as gramatica does (and which Dante thinks it will resemble in formal terms as well). Dante thus famously calls for a *vulgare illustre* that is *cardinale, aulicum et curiale* (1.XVI.6). Each of these four adjectives requires some unpacking, even for Dante himself, as their uses here are far from intuitive. Dante glosses *illustre* as *illuminans et illuminatum prefulgens*, that is, as giving off light or reflecting the light given off by other things; Dante further explains that language that is *illustre* is sublime in power and in learning, *sublimatum est magistratu et potestate*. This vulgare must also be *cardinale*, an adjective conventionally glossed as "pertaining to a hinge; principal, chief." Dante uses the vehicle of this adjectival metaphor quite seriously, making the argument that the vulgare illustre should be the hinge on which the other vernaculars depend, a language that avoids the excessive movements of more peripheral forms of speech but whose shifts are indexical for the shifts of all the others. The adjectives *aulicum* and *curiale* suggest that this vernacular should pertain to both the royal court and to the law-courts. Dante here engages in

---

24 Adinvenerunt ergo illam ne, propter variationem sermonis arbitrio singularium fluitantis, vel nullo modo vel saltim imperfecte antiquorum actingeremus autoritates et gesta, sive illorum quos a nobis locorum diversitas facit esse diversos. 1.IX.1.

productive slippage between two senses in which these adjectives could be meant: either metaphorically, that the vulgare illustre acts as a (royal/legal) court at which other linguistic forms are judged; or literally, as the language actually used in the courts both royal and legal. Italy in Dante's time famously lacks the former, and also, therefore, a systematic version of the latter; Dante's double usage of the adjectives *aulicum* and *illustre* explicitly suggests that the vulgare illustre can be both a substitute for and a precursor of these institutions for which Dante longs so profoundly, in the *De vulgari eloquentia* and elsewhere.

In the remainder of the text as we have it, Dante begins his quest for the precise location of his vulgare illustre, though he seems not to have completed the text according to its original plan, and as a result we are left with no clear sense of where to find this elusive "panther," as Dante terms the vulgare illustre at I.XVI.1. He does, of course, offer several hints: just as he suggests that the closeness of the "language of *sì*" to gramatica is a mark in the former's favor, so, too, his cautious, backhanded praise for both the dialect of Bologna (I.XV.5) and for at least certain individual writers from Florence and environs (I.XIII.3) (even as he rejects their dialects as suitable in themselves for service as the vulgare illustre) suggests that key models for this elusive linguistic standard are to be found in this general region, more than in any other. Nonetheless, as suggested earlier, the key to Dante's notion of the vulgare illustre is that it be a form recognizably related to the spoken dialects of each Italian city yet proper to none on its own. That the actual form of that vernacular as it historically emerges, beginning a few years after the *De vulgari eloquentia* with Dante's own *Commedia divina*, is in fact heavily indebted to the specific language of Florence, indicates of course a certain disingenuousness on the part of Dante, who on some level is seeking to enshrine his own native dialect through a form of "bad universalism."[25] At the same time, Dante's notion of the vulgare illustre as some kind of abstraction or generalization of the dialect continuum fits rather well with the empirical reality not only of literary vernaculars in the

---

25   A term I borrow from, e.g., feminist and postcolonialist discourses, where in which it acts as a shorthand for the ideological use of universalism by hegemonic groups as a means of projecting their own identities and experiences onto those in a marginalized position. See, e.g. Fredric Jameson, "Symptoms of Theory or Symptoms for Theory?," *Critical Inquiry* 30 (2), 2004: 403–8, 405. Dante here performs, I argue, a similar move, by claiming to select the dialect to be the basis of the vulgare illustre on the basic of abstract and disinterested principles, when the result tends instead to constitute his own experience as universal, and universalizable.

Romance-speaking world but also more broadly across Europe and South Asia (the region whose vernacularization bears the strongest resemblance to that of Europe, though of course predating any conceivable European influence by a millennium).

As we shall see in detail in the rest of this chapter, the Romance, Germanic, and Slavic languages of Europe, along with the Indic and Dravidian languages of South Asia, are best understood as extensive dialect continua, over which are overlain written literary languages, many of which began as vernaculars and most of which have long since made the transition to "national" status. Yet there are very real distinctions between vernacular and national languages, even when the former are the direct ancestors of (or even indistinguishable from) the latter. As Sheldon Pollock observes, and as many of his South Asianist colleagues affirm in detail in a volume edited by him,[26] while literary vernaculars frequently emerged in the contexts of specific courts and were thus from the beginning implicated in networks of political relationships, those relationships rarely, if ever, resembled the homology of people language-nation-state that is the desired object of nationalist production.

The production and circulation of literary texts in Telugu, one of the literarized vernaculars of the Dravidian family in south India, form a case in point. Today, Telugu is probably best known as the official language of the states of Andhra Pradesh and Telangana, located on the Deccan plain and the adjacent Bay of Bengal coast in south-central India. Since independence, the political geography of India has been repeatedly reconfigured in an attempt to perfect the mapping of literary languages onto state boundaries in a process I examine in more detail in my chapter on global literary ecologies. But the literary geography of Telugu in pre-modern times in no way maps onto the area of modern Andhra Pradesh, nor does it even map onto some other different but still discrete region. In the sixteenth century, for example, the city of Hampi in Karnataka was the leading center of Telugu literary activity, even though it was under the rule of King Kṛṣṇadēvarāya, who styled himself a Kannada king. Under the Nayakas, who were Telugu-speaking but whose rule stretched far to the south of modern Andhra Pradesh, the center of Telugu literary activity was in the south in places such as Madurai, where Telugu literature remained active after the Nayaka fell. Areas within the territory of Andhra were often

---

26   Sheldon Pollock, *Literary Cultures in History: Reconstructions from South Asia*, Berkeley: University of California Press, 2003.

multilingual, such that the sultans of Golconda used Persian for administrative purposes but eagerly cultivated poetry in Telugu. In the northwestern Andhra town of Srisailam in the thirteenth century, Telugu, Kannada, Tamil, and Marathi (the latter an Indic language, not a Dravidian one, and thus not sharing a family resemblance to the other three) were all major literary languages, and Tirupati, in the southeast, was a center for both Tamil and Telugu in the fifteenth and sixteenth centuries. Conversely, many of the Telugu-speaking rulers in Andhra promoted Sanskrit, rather than Telugu, poetry, while many of the greatest Telugu poets gained official recognition in Tamil or Kannada-speaking areas.[27]

Pollock explicitly contrasts cases like Telugu (and examples could be multiplied across all of South Asia), to the European case, where he sees Dante's discussion of "Italian" in the *De vulgari eloquentia* as much more explicitly proto-national than anything found in contemporary South Asia.[28] There is some truth to this case, and Pollock also makes clear that his own claims here are a rhetorical strategy designed as a corrective to the too-easy contemporary reappropriation of older Orientalist paradigms, in which European models of vernacularization would necessarily be more progressive than those found elsewhere.

A closer examination of both the text of the *De vulgari eloquentia* and of medieval European literary practice, however, suggests not only that the situation in Europe resembled that in South Asia much more closely than Pollock imagines, but also hints thereby at possibilities for escaping outmoded Orientalist paradigms without simply falling into the reverse error of insisting on the failures of European models compared with non-European ones. Dante's own text, as I have already suggested, claims that each of the three vernaculars—those of *oc*, *oïl*, and *si*—has its own advantages from a literary perspective: the language of *oc* has the advantage, Dante says, of having the longest history of poetic production; that of *oïl*, is ideally suited to the romance and to other prose forms, while the language of *si*, more recently developed for poetic purposes, is sweeter even than the language of *oc* for those purposes and additionally, as we saw earlier, is the closest in form to *gramatica* (I.X). While this series of distinctions preserves, at least implicitly, an advantage for Dante's own

---

27   The above discussion is derived from, Velcheru Narayana Rao, "Multiple Literary Cultures in Telugu: Court, Temple, and Public," in *Literary Cultures in History*, edited by Sheldon I. Pollock, 2003, 383–436.

28   Pollock, *The Language of the Gods*, 456.

language of *si*, that advantage is clearly relative rather than absolute, and the choice of vernacular in which to write is framed rather more in terms of genre and of the history of literary custom than in either the inherent superiority of one vernacular over another or even in the native speech of the author. Both the general tenor of this discussion, as well as most of its specific details, owe much to Raimon Vidal's own defense of the vernacular from a century before Dante, which I discuss below. Of course, we should not assume that Vidal's claims here are in any way original or provocative; they likely reflect, rather, something of the received wisdom of the period. Moreover, we have considerable evidence that the actual literary practice of the Romance world in medieval times was quite as Dante and Ramon Vidal describe it, with genre and function shaping the linguistic choices of an author far more than mother tongue, that of the audience, or that of the sovereign, beginning with Dante's own acknowledgement of the superiority of each of the vernaculars for different literary purposes. As such, they bear more than a passing resemblance to the phenomena observed by Pollock and other South Asianists, as described earlier.

All of this is quite confusing, of course, especially if understood (as it usually is) through a framework that takes the modern national languages of Europe as a given and understands the literary production of medieval and early modern Europe as teleologically directed towards those national languages, when it cannot be directly subsumed under them. How can we understand, in that context, a manuscript of the *Chanson de Roland*, composed in Treviso in a "French" overlain with elements from northern Italian languages[29] or a work of troubadour poetry written as an exchange between a male poet and his female lover in which the man speaks in Occitan and the woman in Genoese dialect?[30] Such works either belong to multiple national histories or, more often, to none at all and frequently find themselves consigned to oblivion when vernaculars give way to national literatures.

If, however, we understand vernacular languages as nodes of literization and literarization along a dialect continuum changing constantly with time, it begins to seem easier to understand how slightly different nodes can

---

29   Stephen Patrick McCormick, "Remapping the Story: Franco-Italian Epic and Lombardia as a Narrative Community (1250–1441)," Ph.D. dissertation, Oregon: University of Oregon, 2011.

30   Gaunt, "Sexual Difference and the Metaphor of Language."

assume greater or lesser significance in different times, places, genres, or registers. Since all are somewhat stylized and somewhat removed from the daily speech of any individual (and all owe much of their more sophisticated vocabulary to cosmopolitan languages, whether Latin and Greek in Europe or Sanskrit and Persian in South Asia), all are potentially open to speakers living at any point along the continuum. As they evolve over time, it can be argued that the standardized forms of French, Spanish, and Italian share a greater family resemblance, both in terms of diction and of syntax, than each does with many of the spoken dialects subsumed under them. As a result, and especially since in a vernacular era literacy implies literacy in the cosmopolitan language as well (or at least a strong awareness of that language and its legacy), it is almost as easy for a poet to assume one vernacular as another, to occupy one node rather than another, as the case requires.

Dante's major predecessor as an expositor of vernacular poetics, Ramon Vidal, provides confirmation of this pattern. Himself a native of Besalú, in what is now the northeast corner of Catalonia in Spain, Vidal would have been a native speaker of a dialect that would today be considered a part of the Catalan language, and yet the language of Vidal's poetry, the language he seeks to define and affirm in his *Razos de trobar* (c. 1200), is what is now known as Provençal or Occitan—Dante's language of *oc*. Vidal's treatise circulated widely in Catalonia, in Italy, and eventually in what is now southern France, the homeland of Occitan; a grammatical account of the language was of particular interest at early stages, in other words, to poets who used the language but whose native language was relatively distant from it. Vidal's discussion of the relationship between French and Occitan (for which he prefers the name "Lemosin") is an obvious source for Dante's later discussion:

> Every man who wants to produce or understand troubadour verse must first know that no other speech (*parladura*) in our language is more natural or more correct than that of Provence or Limousin or Saintonge or Auvergne or Quercy. This is why, I tell you, that when I speak of Lemosin, that I mean all of these lands, and all their neighbors, and all the lands which are between them. And all men born and raised in these lands have a natural and right speech . . .
>
> French speech is best and most suited for composing [the genres of] romances and *pastourelles*; but that of Limousin is best for [the genres of] *vers, canzones* and for *sirventes*, and through all the lands of our language the singers of the Limousin tounge have a greater authority than those of any other speech, which is why I will speak of it first.

That is why I tell you that all men who wish to learn to produce or understand troubadour verse must first study well the speech of Limousin. And after that, they must know something of the nature of gramatica, if he truly wants to produce or understand troubadour verse, since the entire speech of Limousin is spoken naturally through case and gender and tense and person and through nouns, as you can hear well if you listen.[31]

As is well known to specialists, Dante thus borrows much of his rhetoric in the *De vulgari eloquentia* fairly directly from Ramon Vidal—the division of "our language" into a variety of spoken idioms, of which some are especially well suited to certain literary genres, while one form of the language (for Vidal, Lemosin; for Dante; a vulgare illustre derived from the language of *si*) is especially privileged by its closeness to gramatica, which for both authors (as for many others of their period), is virtually a synonym for Latin. Vidal's case is in some ways stronger than Dante's, in that he can make the claim, as Dante cannot, that his preferred dialect retains something of the case-endings of Latin, distinguishing at least nominative and oblique cases where Italian dialects do not.

Dante's emulation of Ramon Vidal substantially complicates a key argument made by Pascale Casanova in her *République mondiale des lettres*, namely that Joachim du Bellay, and not Dante, is the first to found a national literature, in that the French literature constructed by du Bellay's *Defense et illustration de la langue française* (1549) "se fonde dans la relation complexe

---

31   Totz hom qe vol trobar ni entendre deu primierament saber qe neguna parladura no es tant naturals ni tant drecha del nostre lingage con aqella de Proenza o de Lemosi o de saintonge o d'Alvergna o de Caerci. Per qe ieu vos dic qe qant ieu parlarai de Lemosis, qe totas estas terras entendas, et totas lor vezinas, et totas cellas qe son entre ellas. Et tot l'ome qe en aqellas sont nat ni norit an la parladura natural et drecha . . .
La parladura Francesa val mais et plus avinenz a far *romanz* et *pasturellas* ; mas cella de Lemosin val mais per far *vers* et *cansons* et *serventes* ; et per totas las terras de nostre lengage so de maior autoritat li cantar de la lenga Lemosina que de negun' autra parladura, per q'ieu vos en parlarai primeramen . . .
Per q'ieu vos dic qe totz hom qe vuella trobar ni entendre deu aver fort privada la parladura de Lemosin. Et apres deu saber alques de la natura de la gramatica, si fort primamenz vol trobar ni entendre car tota la parladura de Lemosin se parla naturalmenz et per cas et per generes et per temps et per personas et per motz, aisi com poretz auzir si ben o escoutas. Translation adapted from Juliet Lucy Anne O'Brien, "Trobar Cor(s)| Erotics and poetics in Flamenca," Ph.D. dissertation, Princeton, NJ: Princeton University, 2006, 103.

à une autre nation, et, à travers elle, à une autre langue, dominante et en apparence indépassable, le latin" ("is founded in a complex relationship with another nation, and through it, with another language, dominant and apparently unbeatable, Latin").[32] As we can see from the well-established relationship between Vidal's treatise and Dante's, Dante, in seeking to found a literature in a *volgare illustre*, is in fact doing so not in relationship to another nation but to other languages (Occitan and French), whose significance in the Italy of Dante's time cannot be overstated. Even Brunetto Latini (1220–94), the famous teacher of Dante, encountered in the *Inferno*, wrote his major work, the encyclopedic *Li Livres dou Trésor*, in French.

We will explore the complexities of the situation in which du Bellay is working further in the next chapter, where my emphasis will be on the changing relationship between vernacular and Latin as French literature moves towards a specifically "national" focus. For the moment, I wish to underline the weakly territorialized and nationalized nature of the use of the vernacular in the age of Dante. While *De vulgari eloquentia* seeks to establish a transregional vernacular identifiable with a particular territory, the text also betrays the reality of its own time, in which a variety of vernaculars coexisted, each potentially available to a variety of authors who might or might not have had a territorial or mother-tongue relationship to any one of them and who might instead choose to write in Latin or any of the vernaculars for reasons of genre or audience. Vidal is the first European we know of (after King Alfred, whom I discuss later) to issue a vernacular manifesto, and he does so for a language that is not his own by birth or "nation." In imitating Vidal, Dante may have been seeking to territorialize the vernacular, and the received history of Italian literature, from Dante to Petrarch and Boccacio, may suggest that he was successful. At roughly the time that Dante was writing *De vulgari eloquentia*, however, other residents of Dante's *Ytalia* were retelling the story of Roland in an art-language containing elements of both Old French and Italian, the Venetian Marco Polo was dictating his adventures to Rustichiello da Pisa, who circulated them in an amalgam of French and Pisan, while others were writing in rather purer French, in Occitan, and in other regional Italian vernaculars. The territorialization of language would have to wait.

As I have already suggested, Raimon Vidal was not the first European to compose any sort of vernacular manifesto. Alfred, King of Wessex (849–99 AD; r. 871–99), known to generations as Alfred the Great, was

---

32   Casanova, *La republique mondiale des lettres* 1999, 71.

not only the first Anglo-Saxon king to successfully resist the Danish incursions into Great Britain and to claim some sort of leadership over the other Anglo-Saxon states, he was also the leader of a significant intellectual and cultural program, which had as its explicit aim the restoration and propagation of Latin and Christian learning under his aegis. In so doing, Alfred was likely inspired to some extent by his continental predecessor Charlemagne (742–814), whose own "Carolingian Renaissance" was crucially indebted to the work of the British scholar and ecclesiastic, Alcuin. The crucial difference between the educational and cultural programs of Charlemagne and of Alfred, of course, is that while Charlemagne's was built around a revitalization of both knowledge and production of texts in classical Latin (indeed, the Carolingian Renaissance is often pointed to as evidence that the spoken standard had deviated far enough from the classical language to make such reforms necessary),[33] Alfred's was built around the first major project of translation into a vernacular language in the territory of modern Europe. Among the works he translated was Gregory I's *Cura Pastoralis*, (c. 590). The preface to this translation, also said to be composed by Alfred himself, is written in Anglo-Saxon, and describes Alfred's linguistic choice:

> When I remembered all this, then I wondered greatly why those good wise men who formerly existed throughout England, and had fully studied all those books, did not wish to translate any part of them into their own language. But I immediately answered myself, and said: "They did not imagine that men would ever become so careless and learning so decayed; they refrained from it by intention and hoped that there would be the greater knowledge in this land the more languages we knew." Then I remembered how the law was first found in the Hebrew language, and afterwards, when the Greeks learned it, they translated it all into their own language; and all the other books as well. And afterwards in the same way the Romans, when they had learned them, they translated them all into their own language through learned interpreters. And all other Christian nations also translated some part of them into their own language.[34]

---

33   For a critical discussion of this view, see Paul M. Lloyd, "On the Names of Languages (and Other Things)," in *Latin and the Romance Languages in the Early Middle Ages*, edited by Roger Wright, New York: Routledge, 1991, 9–18.

34   Elaine Treharne, *Old and Middle English, c.890–c.1450: An Anthology*, John Wiley and Sons, 2009, 15–16.

The historical significance of Alfred's preface is clear and noted by Pollock, among others.[35] For the first time in the history of Western Europe (that we are aware of, anyway; see the discussion below of other possible early vernaculars under and after Roman rule), a writer not only translated major works of the classical or Christian past into a local language but offered an explicit justification for why he was doing so. Alfred's justification is simple—there are, he says, too few people in his kingdom who know Latin, and for Gregory's work to have the impact he needs it to have (the work is a guide to the proper role of bishops within the church), it must be accessible in Anglo-Saxon as well as in Latin. Such a claim, similar as it is to the justifications for most translations made today, may seem insignificant to a modern reader. In the context of its time, however, and given in particular the role that Anglo-Saxon and Irish monasticism had played in the prior century or two in preserving ancient and Christian learning, Alfred's claim that Anglo-Saxon translations were necessary even for the elites of his kingdom marks either a stunning admission of cultural failure or a radically new way of thinking about culture and power, couched in euphemistic terms.

That the latter might in fact be the truer motivation behind Alfred's translation project is suggested by the continuation of the passage cited above, where the king recounts his train of thought, and suggests that, just as the Greeks needed to translate the law of the Hebrew Bible into their language, and the Romans, that of both the Hebrew Bible and the Greek New Testament, so, too, must he, Alfred, preside over a third round of translation, into what we call Anglo-Saxon (Alfred himself does not give a name to the language in which he is writing, describing it only as *hiora āgen geðīode*, "[their] own language," as he wonders why his predecessors had not employed it for translations). That Alfred cites, in effect, the Septuagint and the Latin Vulgate as precedents, necessarily places his own project in rather more illustrious company than his modest and deploring tone would otherwise suggest. There is also at least some evidence to suggest that the decline in Latin learning was less precipitous than suggested by Alfred's preface; certainly, there were ecclesiastics at court who had good knowledge of Latin (as well, presumably, as Alfred himself), who could, in principle, have led a revival of the learning that had undoubtedly been hurt by the Danish invasions. The claim that other Christian nations translate these works as well is a more problematic claim; it is unclear which nations

---

35   Pollock, *The Language of the Gods*, 2009, 444–5.

Alfred could possibly have in mind here, though it is also quite possible that the king is simply appealing to spurious precedent to lend authority to what is otherwise a rather audacious enterprise.

The idea that one should "write the way one speaks," adopted by linguistic reformers as diverse as Vuk Karadžić (1787–1864) for Serbian and Hu Shi (1891–1962) for Chinese, has been so deeply ingrained in modern ways of thinking that the radicalism of such an idea is easy to understate. In addition to his translation projects, Alfred also promulgated a legal code (which, like the preface to Gregory's *Pastoral Care*, explicitly linked the Anglo-Saxon legal tradition to the Hebrew Bible). Further, he is believed to have commissioned the writing of a history in the vernacular, which now, with later additions, goes under the name of the *Anglo-Saxon Chronicle*;[36] copies of this chronicle were then distributed to monastic centers across the kingdom, providing at once a royally sanctioned historical narrative and a significant school text and prose model in the emergent vernacular prose tradition. The literary production of Alfred's era, then, can be (and usually is) seen as a coherent program, situating Alfred's kingdom as a new center for learning but for a learning in the vernacular. Alfred and his court did not initiate the writing of Anglo-Saxon, but through their efforts they achieved something of a monopoly on its early expression, producing not only a series of texts centered around the authority of the king but also a model for prose and poetic style regulated by the king himself. Language and literature, for the first time in Europe, was representable as the monopoly of a particular polity, where the polity in question was also understood as defined at least partly by the language. To be sure, other Anglo-Saxon kingdoms remained, and thus other potential centers of cultural authority, but the efforts of Alfred guaranteed that the language he had done so much to render usable for sophisticated literary purposes would remain permanently identified with him and with his kingdom.

Similar efforts to establish the vernacular as a legitimate vehicle for literature, likewise integrated into political claims, were found in the wenyan cosmopolis of East Asia. This chapter opened with a consideration of a vernacular manifesto of sorts for Korean, but in Japan such statements were both earlier and more emphatic. Traditional literature in Japanese can be said to begin with a series of poetic anthologies, in particular with the

---

36 Thomas A. Bredehoft, *Textual Histories: Readings in the Anglo-Saxon Chronicle*, Toronto: University of Toronto Press, 2001, 39.

Man'yoshu 萬葉集 (or "Collection of Ten Thousand Leaves," compiled after AD 759) and the *Kokinshu* 古今集 (or "Collection of Poems Old and New," originally circulated c. AD 905). This gesture of anthologizing is itself a clear imitation of the Chinese literary tradition, in which poetry symbolically begins with two anthologies, the *Canon of Songs* 詩經 and the *Songs of Chu* 楚辭. Both of the Japanese anthologies collect poetry written in Japanese (the former, transcribed in a complicated system using Chinese characters and resembling thus the hyangchal system in Korea mentioned earlier; the latter, using the *kana* syllabic script still used in Japan today), as opposed to the also sizeable body of *kanshi* 漢詩, or poetry in wenyan, which had itself first been anthologized in the *Kaifusō* 懷風藻, in 751. Cosmopolitan and vernacular traditions thus coexisted from the very beginnings of Japanese literature as we know it through written sources. The *Kokinshu* is noteworthy in particular for having both a preface in Japanese, which articulates an indigenous Japanese poetics, and a preface in wenyan, which seeks to legitimate that poetics in terms of traditional Chinese poetic concepts:

> Now Japanese poetry (*waka*) takes root in the heart's soil, and flowers in the forest of words. Since men dwell in the world, it is impossible for them to be inactive. Their thoughts are constantly shifting; joy and sorrow changing into each other. Emotions are born of intent; song takes form in words. That's why the voice of a person at leisure is happy; the cries of a resentful person are sad. This can be used to convey emotions; it can be used to express indignation. To move heaven and earth, to compel ghosts and spirits, to transform human relations, to harmonize man and wife – nothing is as suitable as Japanese poetry (*waka*) . . . [37]

> From the time when Prince Ōtsu began to write (Chinese) *shi* poetry and *fu* rhyme-prose, poets and capable men admired this fashion and carried on this practice. They imported Chinese writing, and transformed our Japanese customs. The people's customs changed at once, and Japanese poetry (*waka*) began to decline. [38]

---

37   夫和歌者，託其根於心地，發其華於詞林者也。人之在世，不能無為，思慮易遷，哀樂相變。感生於志，詠形於言。是以逸者其聲樂，怨者其吟悲。可以述懷，可以發憤。動天地，感鬼神，化人倫，和夫婦，莫宜於和歌。

38   自大津皇子之初作詩賦，詞人才子慕風繼塵，移彼漢家之字，化我日域之俗。民業一改，和歌漸衰。   Translation adapted from Laurel Rasplica Rodd, Mary Catherine Henkenius, and Tsurayuki Ki, *Kokinshū: A Collection of Poems Ancient and Modern*, Cheng & T∘sui, 1996, 379–85.

The debt that the first paragraph cited here owes to a particular Chinese precedent, the Mao preface to the *Canon of Songs*, is striking, particularly the language concerning the emergence of song as an external manifestation of internal intent, and the transformative capacities of song, many of which are taken directly from the Mao preface.[39] At the same time (and alongside the Japanese-language preface), the subtle differences between the Chinese preface to the *Kokinshu* and the Mao preface seem designed to underline the autonomy of the Japanese tradition in some sense. Obviously, the language of the poetry is marked as Japanese, both establishing an autonomous tradition and serving as a reminder that that tradition needs to be marked as something other than the default category of cultural production, which would be in Chinese. Also significantly, the *Kokinshu* preface in a sense "depoliticizes" the Mao preface; where the latter explicitly links internal emotional states, poetic form, and the quality of governance, the former makes poetry an index of inner emotion alone and not of governance. Finally, the introduction of vegetal imagery—"the heart's soil," "flowering in the forest of words"—seems also to ground Japanese-language poetry as poetry of place in some sense, where the Mao preface refers not to place but to government and human communities. Through all of these devices, then, the *Kokinshu* preface in Chinese simultaneously marks Japanese-langauge poetry as a distinct cultural formation and subordinates that formation to the cosmopolitan tradition.

The vernacular literatures of South Asia offer examples of both vernacular manifestocs and of translations and emulations of cosmopolitan literature. I discuss these phenomena briefly here, and especially the latter, drawing on the work of Pollock and others, before returning to this question of translation from the cosmopolitan in the Latin context a little later in this chapter. The first surviving text in Kannada, the South Indian Dravidian language that Pollock identifies as the first to create a vernacular literature, is the *Kavirājamārga*, (or "Way of the King of Poets") attributed to Śrīvijaya and composed at the court of the Rāṣṭrakūṭa Dynasty, centered in the northern part of what is now the state of Karnataka in southern India, during the reign of Nṛpatuṅga Amoghavarṣa, around 875 AD.[40] This text, a treatise on poetics

39   For a further discussion of the Mao Preface, see the first chapter of Beecroft, *Authorship and Cultural Identity*, 2010.

40   Pollock, *The Language of the Gods*, 352–6; D. R. Nagaraj, "Critical Tensions in the History of Kannada Literary Culture," in *Literary Cultures in History*, edited by Sheldon Pollock, 2003, 323–82.

written in a heavily Sanskritized style, and borrowing from Sanskrit poetic theory, explicitly seeks to justify the use of the vernacular for refined literary purposes, much as (in different ways) Alfred the Great had very recently done in England and as Raimon Vidal and Dante would later do in continental Europe. Other texts of grammar and poetics, such as Nannaya's Telugu grammar of the eleventh century,[41] the fourteenth-century *Līlātilakam*, written for a literary language antecedent to modern Malayalam,[42] and the ninth-century Sinhalese *Siyabaslakara*,[43] play a manifesto role as well. Translations from the cosmopolitan tradition are obviously extremely important to South Asian vernacular traditions, frequently playing a significant role in the early history of those vernacular literatures and/or marking a significant transition from a phase in which limited literary materials were composed in a vernacular to one in which the vernacular was used extensively in a wide range of genres. Examples here would include the eleventh-century Telugu *Mahābhārata* by the same Nannaya who composed the foundational grammar for that language;[44] the thirteenth–fourteenth century *Rāmacaritam*, ancestral to Malayalam;[45] the fourteenth-century Assamese and fifteenth-century Bengali and Oriya *Rāmāyaṇas*[46]; Vi udās's 1442 *Rāmāyaṇa* in Brajbhasha, a North Indian literary language related to modern Hindi;[47] and, most famously of all, Tulsidas's *Rāmcaritmānas*, composed in Avadhi (another literary standard related to modern Hindi) in 1574, today central to the canon of Hindi literature.[48] Versions of the *Ramayana* exist even in Tibetan[49] and in Persian, in translations supervised by the Mughal emperor Akbar (1542–1605),[50] a language whose own cosmopolitan status rivaled that of Sanskrit in early modern South Asia.

41   Rao, "Multiple Literary Cultures in Telugu," 2003, 390.
42   Freeman, "Genre and Society," 2003, 442.
43   Charles Hallisey, "Works and Persons in Sinhala Literary Culture," in *Literary Cultures in History*, edited by Sheldon Pollock, 2003, 690.
44   Velcheru Narayana Rao, "Multiple Literary Cultures in Telugu," 2003, 390.
45   Freeman, "Genre and Society," 2003, 457.
46   Pollock, *The Language of the Gods*, 2009, 449n18.
47   Stuart McGregor, "The Progress of Hindi, Part I: The Development of a Transregional Idiom," in *Literary Cultures in History*, edited by Sheldon Pollock, 2003, 917.
48   Ibid., 937.
49   Matthew T. Kapstein, "The Indian Literary Identity in Tibet," in *Literary Cultures in History*, edited by Sheldon Pollock, 2003, 759, 783.
50   Muzaffar Alam, "The Culture and Politics of Persian in Precolonial Hindustan," in *Literary Cultures in History*, edited by Sheldon Pollock, 2003, 170.

The vernacular literatures of southeast Asia, which likewise emerged in interaction with the Sanskrit cosmopolis, are not very well known in Europe or North America,[51] though their histories stretch over and beyond the past millennium (making their emergence roughly contemporary with European vernaculars), and many of them are spoken today by tens of millions of people. In most cases, Buddhist scriptures in Pali and the Sanskrit epics, particularly the *Rāmāyaṇa*, form a crucial component of the vernacular tradition, though in many cases the translations of the *Rāmāyaṇa* known today are relatively recent innovations. Thus the earliest inscriptions in Burmese, for example, date from the early twelfth century AD, and already betray a knowledge of the *Rāmāyaṇa* narrative. The earliest Burmese poetry transmitted in the manuscript tradition dates from the mid-fifteenth century and is on a mix of Buddhist and indigenous political and cultural themes. Only in the late eighteenth century, and then under Thai influence, did the Burmese *Rāmāyaṇa* translation known today take shape.[52] The Thai *Rāmāyaṇa* itself, the *Ramakian*, was redacted by King Rama I in 1797, drawing on earlier materials, while the Thai alphabet is said to date to the late thirteenth century, and the poetic tradition is continuous and abundant from the mid-fifteenth century onwards.[53] Inscriptions in Khmer are even older, with the earliest dating to the seventh century AD; again, knowledge of Sanskrit epic is a component of both the inscriptional and manuscript based literary texts known to us, the latter beginning in the fifteenth century. The two great epics of the Khmer language, both initially composed in the seventeenth century, are the *Ramakerti*, a *Rāmāyaṇa* translation, and the *Lpoek Angar Vatt*, an epic commemorating the construction of the famous temple complex of Angkor Wat.[54] Javanese represents something of an exception to this pattern found in mainland Southeast Asian languages—early inscriptional history, followed a few centuries later by a manuscript-based literary culture, with *Rāmāyaṇa* translations consolidating

---

51   For a general introduction, with bibliography, see Patricia M. Herbert, and Anthony Crothers Milner, eds., *South-East Asia: Languages and Literatures: A Select Guide*, Honolulu: University of Hawaii Press, 1989, from which the following discussion is taken.

52   Anna Allott, Patricia Herbert, and John Okell, "Burma," in *South-East Asia : Languages and Literatures*, 1989, 1–22.

53   P. J. Bee, I. Brown, Patricia Herbert, and Manas Chitakasem, "Thailand," in *South-East Asia: Languages and Literatures*, 1989, 23–48.

54   Hoc Dy King, Mak Phoeun, and P.-B. Lafont, "Cambodia," in *South-East Asia: Languages and Literatures*, 1989, 49–66.

only in the very years in which the European presence was beginning to assert itself in the region. Inscriptions in Old Javanese begin in the early ninth century, after five centuries of inscriptions in highly sophisticated Sanskrit; by the mid-ninth century, a highly sophisticated translation of the *Rāmāyaṇa*, drawing on a complex range of Sanskrit source texts, had emerged.[55] The Sanskrit-influenced literature in Old Javanese continued to develop over the ensuing six hundred years until the arrival of Islam on Java around 1500 led to a shift in literary production. Even after the arrival of Islam, however, production of Sanskrit-inspired literature continued on Java, with, for example, the production of a sequel to the *Rāmāyaṇa* in the Sundanese language, whose text implies the existence also of a *Rāmāyaṇa* in that language, in the sixteenth century.[56]

WHEN DO VERNACULARS BEGIN?

One of the questions that remain to be addressed, as we enumerate vernaculars and observe their characteristics, is that of identifying the historical origins of vernacular languages. Although Pollock identifies this development very strongly with Kannada and Anglo-Saxon in the eighth century AD, cosmopolitan languages themselves long predate this era, and so we should look to still earlier times for the first vernacular emergence. Strong candidates would have to be Ugaritic and Hittite. Ugaritic, a Semitic language spoken in the Syrian coastal city of Ugarit, was first committed to writing in the fourteenth century BC. The archaeological work done on the site of Ugarit since 1928 has uncovered considerable libraries of texts in Akkadian and Sumerian (the cosmopolitan languages of the era, as we have seen), as well as in Hittite, but also in the local Ugaritic, including not only a number of administrative, financial, and legal texts (indicating status as a "chancery language") but also imaginative literature.[57] This imaginative literature, in a striking contrast with many later vernacular literatures, seems derived from local sources, rather than from the rich cosmopolitan tradition, and includes a series of poems on mythological themes, involving

55   Vinod Khanna, and Malini Saran, "The Rāmāyana Kakawin: A Product of Sanskrit Scholarship and Independent Literary Genius," *Bijdragen tot de Taal-, Land- en Volkenkunde* 149 (2), 1993: 226–49; Pollock, *The Language of the Gods*, 389.

56   J. Noorduyn, "Traces of an Old Sundanese Ramayana Tradition," *Indonesia* (12), 1971: 151–7.

57   For a discussion of the history of the Ugaritic language and its rediscovery, see Daniel Sivan, *A Grammar of the Ugaritic Language,* Leiden: Brill, 1997, 1–2.

the worlds of both gods and men.[58] Hittite, spoken by the rulers of a large state centered in Asia Minor, presents a more complex case; originally literized in the sixteenth century BC, largely as a chancery language, Hittite was later used more extensively for literary purposes, down to the thirteenth century BC; especially after the crisis of the late twelfth century BC, when new polities emerged, the closely related Luwian language replaced Hittite.[59] Much of the literature in Hittite follows later patterns of vernacular literarization, with a preponderance of translated texts from Akkadian (including a translation of the Gilgamesh epic), although some measure of indigenous material seems also to have played a role in Hittite literature.[60]

These early cases aside (and the Hebrew tradition, likely a few centuries younger, could be added to their number), I turn to what is for me a more familiar case, that of the earliest stages of Latin. The earliest known inscriptions in Latin date from the middle of the sixth century BC (although there is more problematic evidence suggesting that the language was literized to some extent in the previous century). These early inscriptions are mostly legal, votive, or funerary in nature, and while they attest to a culture already highly developed in many respects, they do not constitute a literary tradition as such, and thus do not become a full vernacular until the third century BC.

Notionally, and in later Roman retellings, Latin literature began with Livius Andronicus in the third century BC. Cicero tells us he first presented a play in 240 BC, the year after the end of the first Punic war. (Cicero, *Brutus* 72–3); the emergence of a vernacular literary tradition in Rome was thus understood as coincident with the emergence of Rome as a major political power in the larger Mediterranean world. Livius Andronicus's name suggests the possibility that his original Greek name was Andronicus and that Livius was the gentilic name of his patron/master; Cicero further reports that he was captured from Tarentum, although modern historians have cast doubt on this. The historian Suetonius (c. 69–c. 122 AD) describes

---

58   Mark S. Smith and Simon B. Parker, *Ugaritic Narrative Poetry*, Atlanta, GA: Society of Biblical Literature, 1997.

59   Annick Payne, *Hieroglyphic Luwian: An Introduction with Original Texts*, Waisbade, Germany: Otto Harrassowitz Verlag, 2010, 1–3.

60   Hans G. Güterbock, "A View of Hittite Literature," *Journal of the American Oriental Society* 84 (2), 1964: 107–15; Itamar Singer, "Some thoughts on translated and original Hittite literature," *Israel Oriental Studies* XV, 1995: 123–8 offers a slightly revisionist view, which allows for more indigenous content to Hittite literary texts.

him as *semigraecus*, an ambivalent term in that it could indicate either half-Greek ethnic origin (viewed pejoratively) or quasi-Greek literary proclivities (viewed positively) (*De grammaticis* I). One way or another, the suggestion is that Livius Andronicus had his origins in the south of the Italian peninsula and was not a native speaker of Latin. The Romans, then, represented the origins of their own literary tradition as not only indebted to Greek source texts but also to individuals whose own identities were in some sense intermediate between the two cultures. In addition to his now-lost tragedies and comedies, all of which seem to have been based on Greek originals or derived from Greek mythological themes, Livius Andronicus is best known for his *Odusia*, the translation of the *Odyssey* into Latin, which marks for later Latin writers the beginnings of Latin literature. While Livius's dramatic works are in meters adapted from Greek poetry; his epic is composed in the Saturnian meter, found also in others of the Italic languages of Iron Age Italy and likely reflecting prosodic features characteristic of those languages.[61]

Despite its considerable importance to the history of Latin literature, very little of Livius Andronicus's *Odusia* survives; there are a total of about thirty-five fragments, not all of which are certain to be from the *Odusia*, and none of which are longer than a single line. It is therefore difficult to assess the work's qualities in any very meaningful way, although an examination of the most famous of these fragments, the first line of the poem, is revealing:

> Virum mihi, Camena, insece versutum
> Tell me, Muse, of the clever man

The line thus translates quite carefully the opening line of the Homeric epic: ἄνδρα μοι ἔννεπε, μοῦσα, πολύτροπον ("Tell me, Muse, of the man of many ways"). How to understand Livius's diction here is, however, a somewhat complex question, the answer to which may ultimately depend on how one wishes to read Livius, and early Latin literature more generally. The choice of "Camena," the name of a local Italian water goddess, identified with a spring on the outskirts of Rome, to translate the Greek Muse, was not followed by later Roman authors and, since the time of Ennius (in the

---

61   Jed Parsons, "A New Approach to the Saturnian Verse and Its Relation to Latin Prosody," *Transactions of the American Philological Association* (1974–) 129, 1999: 117–37.

generation after Livius Andronicus), has conventionally been understood as an index of Livius's clumsy grafting of Greek literary culture onto rustic and unrelated Italic material, though recently scholars such as Stephen Hinds have suggested that the choice might instead reflect a literary program of Livius's own, one arguably at least as sophisticated as the later Roman choice to gloss the Greek *mousa* more straightforwardly as Musa.[62] Similarly, recent scholars have explored the use of *versutum* as a translation for the Greek *polutropos*, or "having many ways or turns." Not only does *versutus*, derived from the verb *verto, vertere*, "to turn," trope on the *tropos* of the Greek original, but, as Hinds reminds us, vertere is the standard Latin verb for the act of translation.[63] Livius's Odysseus, then, may not merely be a "man of many turns" but also a "translated man," carried over from Greek literature into Latin and reminding us in the process of Odysseus's own role as an allegory for the westward colonization by the Greeks in the Dark Ages and beyond.[64]

It is the rare word *insece*, translating the Greek *ennepe* as a verb for the act of narration, that attracts the most divergent and interesting readings. Ancient readers of Livius seem to have seen insece quite uncomplicatedly as an ungainly and archaic usage; Horace, for example, (at *Ep.* 2.1.69) protests that he enjoys the archaism of Livius Andronicus, in a manner that suggests that few share Horace's taste here. As such, Livius's use of insece is read against the backdrop of an idea, common since Ennius, that Livius represents a halting and inept beginning to a Latin poetic tradition that gains full refinement (usually) only in the author's own generation. Recent readers, perhaps predictably, have seen in Livius's insece traces of something more interesting. Gerald Browne has suggested that Livius's insece might derive from a native Latin epic tradition. The word derives from the same Indo-European root as the Homeric ἔννεπε, opening, for Browne, the possibility that Livius used a verb of programmatic significance within an indigenous tradition as a (perhaps inadvertent) exact equivalent to the term from the cosmopolitan language.[65] George Sheets has suggested, alternatively, that Livius borrows insece from the related Umbrian language,

---

62   Stephen Hinds, *Allusion and Intertext*, Cambridge: Cambridge University Press, 1998, 58.

63   Ibid., 61–2.

64   Irad Malkin, *The Returns of Odysseus: Colonization and Ethnicity*, Berkeley: University of California Press, 1998.

65   Gerald M. Browne, "Two Notes on Pre-Homeric Epic," *Mnemosyne* 53 (6), Fourth Series, 2000: 712.

thus imitating the Homeric use of the Aeolic dialect form ἔννεπε, not necessarily to be expected in this context.[66] On this reading, Livius Andronicus, far from being rustic and inelegant in his choice of words, is in fact a sophisticated and playful poet, matching on a highly sophisticated level the specific dynamics of Homeric diction and displaying his own multilingual erudition in the process. In so doing, he would also be acting in accord with the poetics of the Hellenistic Greek poets of his own era, notorious themselves for similar etymological and philological play in their work. It has been objected that, according to Suetonius, Hellenistic-style learning only arrived in Rome with Crates of Mallos, approximately seventy years after the composition of the *Odusia*,[67] although this may be simply another case of the later Roman construction of Livius as a "primitive."

Despite, then, the fact that only the tiniest fragments of Livius Andronicus's *Odusia* survive, we are confronted with several possible readings of this text. Ancient readers constructed Livius (reasonably or otherwise) as a rustic and primitive author, interpreting his diction as driven largely by an unpolished style and an imperfect understanding of his source text, in no small part because those readers were eager to see later generations (often, indeed, themselves, in a pattern repeated from Ennius to Virgil) as the key innovators in forging Latin as a rich and sophisticated literary language. One modern reading hints at an (admittedly unattested) prior indigenous epic tradition in Latin, a move that might make Latin epic cognate and synchronous with Homer, destabilizing to some degree the hierarchical relationship between the two. Another modern reading situates Livius in the context of the Greek poetry of his own era, making him at once an innovator (in creating literature in Latin) and a product of his era (in using philological thinking as an engine of his creative process) and refusing to see these two roles as incompatible.

It is of course unknowable which (if any) of these readings would have made sense to Livius himself, or to anyone in his original audience, not only because of the usual problems of the intentional fallacy but also because of the scarcity of evidence. The reading of Livius as a Hellenistic poet, founding a new literary tradition in his target language while following the latest literary trends in his source language, does, however, offer

---

66   George A. Sheets, "The Dialect Gloss, Hellenistic Poetics and Livius Andronicus," *The American Journal of Philology* 102 (1), 1981: 58–78

67   Sander M. Goldberg, *Epic in Republican Rome*, New York: Oxford University Press, 1995, 48.

interesting lessons for this project, whether or not this reading would survive an engagement with the whole text of the *Odusia*. From the retrospective view of the vernacular tradition, founding authors frequently seem primitive and inept, stumbling blindly toward the more refined use of their language that will characterize their successors. Indeed, from the perspective of those successors, whose own literary tastes have changed, the style and diction of founding authors may, almost inevitably, seem dated. Viewed synchronically, however, as part of an established cosmopolitan literary ecology, founding authors in the vernacular may in fact possess an exceptionally sophisticated understanding, both of that cosmopolitan literature and of the challenges of constructing something to rival it in a newly literized vernacular. As such, these vernacular founders are likely to be situated within the cosmopolitan ecology, if frequently on its periphery.

There are comparative analogues for this phenomenon. Sheldon Pollock discusses, as I mentioned earlier, the first work in the Old Kannada literary tradition (which he identifies as the first South Asian vernacular), the *Kavirājamargam* (or "Way of the King of Poets"), attributed to Śrīvijaya and composed at the court of the Rāṣṭrakūṭa Dynasty, centered in the northern part of what is now the state of Karnataka in southern India, during the reign of Nṛpatuṅga Amoghavarṣa, around 875 AD. This text, a treatise on poetics, is, like much early vernacular literature in South Asia, heavily derived from Sanskrit models and indeed employs a highly Sanskritic diction. It is therefore situated much more securely than Livius's *Odusia* in two literary ecologies, the well-established cosmopolitan and the emergent vernacular. In the following chapter, we will see that similar phenomena can operate in emergent national literatures as well: Philippe Aubert de Gaspé *fils*' 1837 novel *L'influence d'un livre*, the first novel written in French in Canada, has most frequently been studied for its use of folkloric material, which aligns nicely with the expectations later readers have for a primitive origin for their literature; the frequent citation by Aubert de Gaspé *fils* of recently published French poetry of Romantic and Radical persuasions went largely unexamined until quite recently.

If Anglo-Saxon cannot lay claim to status as the first European vernacular, neither can it be described as the first vernacular of the Greco-Roman and Christian cosmopolis, since Armenian, Coptic, and Syriac are all earlier. Syriac (as opposed to earlier dialects of Aramaic, long a lingua franca in the region) began use in inscriptions in the first century AD; legal use began in the third century, as did the earliest literary texts. In the third and fourth centuries, a lively tradition including not only biblical translations but also hymns, homilies, and philosophical texts betraying a clear Greek influence, began to take root. A significant part of the literature takes the form of translation, but other works, like the apocryphal *Acts of Thomas*, describing the apostle's journey to India, are likely Syriac originals, as may well be the *Apology* of the philosopher Meliton. Smaller bodies of literary work may well have been produced by Manichaeans, and even by pagans, though much less of this survives.[68] At about the same time, a quite distinct literature in Coptic, derived from ancient Egyptian but now written in a Greek-inspired alphabetic script, emerged, with magical texts in the first century AD and Christian, Gnostic, and Manichaean literature emerging from the third century AD onward; in most cases Coptic literary texts were translations from Greek or other languages, though after the schism between the Egyptian and Greek churches cemented by the Council of Chalcedon in 451, the quantity of original work produced in Coptic increased considerably.[69] Something similar can be seen with Armenian literature. The Armenians, on the fringes of both the Roman and the Sassanid worlds, saw the establishment of Christianity as a state religion as an important tool in the establishment of their autonomy. The Armenian alphabet was developed in 405 AD, and over the next century vast projects of translation were undertaken, including the Bible and a large quantity of religious and philosophical work; other writers began to produce indigenous texts, especially historical and religious works, all quite distinct from prior pagan and oral traditions.[70] This literary tradition grew over time and remains a vital literary tradition to this day, though in a modernized linguistic form, which first developed, in part, through the work of the Armenian diaspora in Venice, Constantinople, and elsewhere in the seventeenth and eighteenth centuries.[71]

While Syriac, Coptic, and Armenian all developed extensive literary traditions, other regional languages were also committed to writing under

---

68   Sebastian P. Brock, "The Earliest Syriac Literature," in *The Cambridge History of Early Christian Literature*, edited by Frances Margaret Young, Lewis Ayres, and Andrew Louth, Cambridge: Cambridge University Press, 2004, 161–71.

69   Mark Smith, "Coptic Literature, 337–425," in *The Late Empire, A.D. 337–425*, edited by Averil Cameron and Peter Garnsey, Cambridge: Cambridge University Press, 2001, 720–35.

70   Nourhan Ouzounian, *The Heritage of Armenian Literature: From the Oral Tradition to the Golden Age*, Detroit: Wayne State University Press, 2000.

71   Kamusella, *The Politics of Language and Nationalism* 2009, 320ff.

Roman rule, with less lasting consequences. Numerous inscriptions exist in Punic, the language of Carthage, and there is also some evidence for a translation of the Bible, though whatever opportunities writing may have afforded Punic, by the fourth and fifth centuries the language seems to have been in decline.[72] Epigraphical evidence also exists for the use of indigenous Libyan (i.e., an early Berber dialect) alongside Punic.[73] Occasional inscriptions are found in the Celtic language of Roman Gaul—mostly dedications and transcriptions of magical incantations, from the second through fifth centuries—though since the religion and culture of the Gauls placed a high priority on orality, no consistent habit of conveying the language in writing ever emerged.

That these tentative essays written in Punic, Libyco-Berber, or Gaulish did not lead to the establishment of a vernacular literature is not simply a result of the cosmopolitan power of Latin, acting as an agent of Roman imperial power. First of all, it was under Roman rule that the writing of these languages both began and accelerated. Second, the position of Latin vis-à-vis Greek remained somewhat complex, though less so in the Western world of Punic, Libyco-Berber, and Gaulish than in the Eastern world of Coptic and Syriac (where, indeed, Greek rather than Latin was the main cosmopolitan language against which the vernacular operated). Third, it seems clear that all of these possible vernaculars were in the end thwarted not by the charismatic power of cosmopolitan Latin but by the invasions of Vandals and Franks and, later, Arabs. Arabic, as much as Latin, was the cosmopolitan language that blocked the development of Punic or Libyco-Berber literature and that slowed the use of Coptic and Syriac; if Gaulish failed to become the basis of a vernacular literature, the language of the Franks surely did—in a context in which the cosmopolitan power of Latin was all the stronger for no longer being associated with a single, increasingly fragile polity but rather with a great and universal religion.

If Celts on the continent failed to develop a consistent tradition of writing, the situation was of course different on the British Isles. Old Irish, we know, was written at an earlier date, with inscriptions, from Great Britain as much as from Ireland, very possibly dating from the fourth century AD—in which case, the use of Old Irish as an inscriptional language may well

---

72   R. MacMullen, "Provincial Languages in the Roman Empire," *American Journal of Philology* 87 (1), 1966.

73   Fergus Millar, "Local Cultures in the Roman Empire: Libyan, Punic and Latin in Roman Africa," *The Journal of Roman Studies* 58, 1968: 126–34.

predate the departure of the Romans;[74] whether or not this is true, the writing of Irish clearly began as a vernacular formation in reaction to Latin. The earliest surviving manuscripts in Old Irish, glosses found in Latin manuscripts preserved on the European continent and dating perhaps to the early eighth century, likewise predate Alfred's reign, but their function clearly suggests a subordinate and pedagogical role for the use of the Irish language and not on the whole the use of the written Irish language as a literary vehicle, evidence for which exists elsewhere.[75] The earliest surviving manuscripts containing literary texts date from the early twelfth century, although on linguistic grounds it seems likely that some of the texts thus preserved must have been written down by the seventh century.[76] There is thus considerable, if somewhat complex, evidence to suggest that Irish functioned as a full vernacular language, used for purposes ranging from the translation of Latin texts to the transcription of oral poetry, to the writing of history, and that it did so as early as the 600s, after several centuries in which the language was written on at least limited occasions. Old Irish thus clearly predates Old English as a vernacular language, under the definitions used by Pollock and by myself.

Between the thriving vernacular literatures in Syriac, Coptic, Armenian, and Old Irish (each of which seems to have begun to be written under Roman rule) and the abortive attempts to write in Gaulish, Punic, and Libyco-Berber, we can see that, *pace* Pollock, the Roman empire, and its attachment to Latin, did not prevent the emergence of vernacular literatures at a very early state. To be sure, these efforts made the most progress in regions on the peripheries of the empire or experiencing greater contact with Greek than with Latin or in regions where written literary traditions long predated not only Greco-Roman control but indeed literacy in Greece and Rome itself. The situation was very different, obviously, in Gaul and in Africa (i.e., modern Tunisia), where Greek would have been less powerful and where there was no ancient literary tradition. The situation was also different for the Italic vernaculars, such as Oscan and Umbrian, and for Etruscan, which had formed at the same time as Latin and in which writing

---

74   Michael Fulford, Mark Handley, and Amanda Clarke, "An Early Date For Ogham: The Silchester Ogham Stone Rehabilitated," *Medieval Archaeology* 44 (1), 2000: 10.

75   Jacopo Bisagni and Immo Warntjes, "Latin and Old Irish in the Munich Computus: A Reassessment and Further Evidence," *ÉRIU* 57, 2007: 1–33.

76   See, e.g., Nicholas Evans, *The Present and the Past in Medieval Irish Chronicles*, Woodbridge: Boydell & Brewer, 2010, 3–4.

was extensively used in the first millennium BC and which continued to be spoken into imperial times. We know that theater in Oscan (and maybe even in Etruscan) was performed at Rome in the age of Augustus,[77] despite two centuries or more of Roman rule over most of Italy, but within a century or two more, these languages were extinct. The picture of vernacular literatures under the Romans is thus complex, supporting neither Pollock's claim that Latin extinguished all other languages in its path nor yet quite the opposite claim that Rome caused vernaculars to flourish. Some vernaculars, though, clearly did flourish under Roman rule, a phenomenon that makes more sense if we think of Latin itself as still a vernacular language during the reign of Augustus, and even, to some extent, afterwards.

COSMOPOLITANS WITHOUT VERNACULARS? CHINESE AND ARABIC

As we have seen, while vernacular literatures first emerged in the ancient Near East, Latin represents another early literature on the vernacular model. More complex vernacular ecologies emerged later, in the late first millennium AD, in both Europe and South Asia and in the East Asian periphery, giving rise in each case to major literary languages still in wide use today, built initially around, and in symbiosis with, the cosmopolitan literary languages Latin, Sanskrit, and classical Chinese. Yet this process of vernacularization did not proceed everywhere or uniformly. Neither Arabic nor classical Chinese participated in a full-fledged vernacularization at this time, for distinct reasons and with distinct results.

In the case of China, it would be a mistake to say that vernacularization did not happen at all. From the earliest stages of the transmission of Buddhism to China, beginning in the second century AD, we find vernacular expressions used in scriptural translation, albeit in a largely wenyan syntactic environment; a "second vernacular revolution" in the eighth century leads to a more thorough vernacularization of Buddhist scripture in Chinese.[78] Vernacular writing grew in volume from this point forward, especially in the early second millennium AD, with the emergence of

---

77   Nicholas Horsfall, "The Cultural Horizons of the 'Plebs Romana,'" *Memoirs of the American Academy in Rome* 41, 1996: 105.

78   For a useful, if polemical, summary, see Victor H. Mair, "Buddhism and the Rise of the Written Vernacular in East Asia: The Making of National Languages," *The Journal of Asian Studies* 53 (3), 1994. Note, however, the discussion of the Mozi jiluo lun in the previous chapter—an early Buddhist text written in highly classical style.

popular literary forms, such as drama and prose fiction, both frequently employing the vernacular in whole or in part. In the following chapter, we will see how early twentieth-century reformers, such as Hu Shi, retrospectively reconstructed Chinese literary history as a movement toward the vernacular, gaining momentum through the Yuan Dynasty (1179–1368), though with a retrograde return to the classical idiom thereafter, a construction that had the effect of marginalizing the very considerable body of classical-language literature that dominated elite cultural production in the Ming (1368–1644) and Qing (1644–1911) Dynasties until at least the late nineteenth century. In the process, they also for the first time identified the distinction between the vernacular (which they now characterized as a distinct language, *baihua*) and the classical language (known as wenyan) and invested that distinction with ideological significance.[79]

The reality is, in fact, that it would be impossible to imagine Chinese literature in the late imperial period as *either* purely vernacular *or* purely classical. Both idioms exist in a state of diglossia, with certain genres favoring one over the other. Moreover, this diglossia is found within individual texts, at very deep levels, as Zhang Zhongxing has shown.[80] Genres, such as drama and prose fiction, which are predominantly in baihua, frequently include poetry and aphorisms in wenyan, while dialogue in baihua can find its way into documents otherwise written in wenyan. Even more problematically, while there are some lexical and syntactical forms that unambiguously belong to one or the other of the two registers, there are others that are ambiguous between the two. In the case of many texts, it would be difficult to classify them as either baihua or wenyan on the basis of objective criteria, and in fact that classification is frequently based as much on the genre in which the work appears or on the general predilections of its author, as on anything else.[81]

In a sense, then, classical Chinese, or wenyan, did not vernacularize prior to the twentieth century because it was able to vernacularize internally, to develop linguistic resources and registers that imitated spoken language and were more accessible to readers with lower levels of education but that did not represent a clean break with the past. Several other factors

---

79   Zhang, Zhongxing, *Wen yan he bai hua*, Di 1 ban. Ha'erbin: Heilongjiang ren min chu ban she, 1988, 202.

80   Ibid., 192 characterizes the relationship between the two registers as 一種語言走向兩歧的路, "'a sort of linguistic two-way street.'"

81   Ibid., 196–7.

likely contributed here. One is the nature of the Chinese writing system, ideally suited, as Victor Mair has observed, to use as a transregional and transhistorical medium for elite expression but poorly adapted for use in the transcriptions of regional vernaculars.[82] To this day, the repertoire of Chinese characters does not encompass even the full phonetic range of the so-called Chinese dialects, let alone allow for the full representation of the lexica of those regional languages, significantly more distinct in diction and syntax than the Indic or Romance languages. To write regional vernaculars, then, would have required a completely new writing system, education in which would have cut off access to the cosmopolitan past (in a way that, say, education in French and Italian did not preclude the learning of Latin, written in the same script). Moreover, the fact that the region speaking Sinitic languages was generally (not always) more-or-less under the rule of one empire, and thus potentially a single market for books from the (very early) emergence of printing in China, would have had the tendency to promote the study of the cosmopolitan language, and to act as a disincentive for the development of multiple vernaculars A single vernacular language covering the whole of the Sinosphere was, perhaps, a possibility—except that the huge differences among the regional vernaculars would have made the task of learning any one vernacular not necessarily any easier than the learning of the classical language for many individuals and regions. To the extent that vernacular language is used in pre-twentieth century Chinese texts, it does tend to be a transregional vernacular, easier for many readers than the unadulterated classical language but necessarily not the everyday speech of the majority. In general, then, ecological factors in the Sinosphere tended to hinder the development of vernacular literatures.

The same seems to have been the case in the Arabophone world, although for somewhat different reasons. Sheldon Pollock has drawn attention to the near-simultaneous emergence, in and around the eighth century AD, of vernacular literatures in both Europe and South Asia (Japan should be added to this list). Although I am by nature reluctant to grant much weight to such coincidences, unless backed by compelling evidence, it is striking that the two regions of the world that were the slowest to develop vernaculars (China and the Arab world) are also the two regions that enjoyed the greatest peace and prosperity and were each comprised within a single world-empire (the Abbasid Caliphate and the Tang, respectively), during this era. By contrast, both Europe and South Asia in the latter part of the

---

82   Mair, "Buddhism and the Rise of the Written Vernacular," 1994, 730.

first millennium AD were largely divided into much smaller polities, after previous centuries of unified rule under the Roman and Gupta empires respectively and in spite of periodic attempts in both regions to reestablish some form of universal rule.

In the case of China, the Tang represented in many respects a return to a formation seen earlier under the Han, in terms of the linguistic usage of the ruling classes, the texture of the religious terrain, and the system of government. The Arab world (newly emergent as such, thanks to the conquests of Mohammed and his successors) was instead experiencing something rather new in the Caliphate, which may have drawn on preexisting Persian and Roman structures in some cases but which presented to the world both an entirely new religion, Islam, and a new cosmopolitan literary language, Arabic. If the late first millennium was an era of radical change in literary and linguistic ecologies in much of the world, in the Middle East and North Africa that change took the form not of vernacularization, but of a new cosmopolitan language. The very newness of this formation (which, as we have seen, damaged in its wake several emergent vernaculars, from Syriac to Libyco-Berber) would have militated against the emergence of new vernaculars. The evidence for the emergence of regional vernaculars in the Arabic world is scattered and incomplete, but it seems clear that the Arabic spread through conquest was itself a panchoric hybrid, mixing dialectal forms from the linguistic heartland, forms that would then evolve differently in different regions.[83] To the extent that pre-Islamic Arabic was indeed a panchoric language, as I suggested in Chapter 2, the value of maintaining a literary standard across a suddenly dispersed population will have seemed high, and the rewards of literizing, let alone literarizing, regional vernaculars will have seemed low. Moreover, as we shall see in the following chapter, the Islamic world over time became a region with three overlain cosmopolitan languages—first Arabic, then Persian, and finally Ottoman Turkish (used, to be sure, more for administrative purposes by non-native speakers, but an important part of the literary ecology nonetheless); for much of the early modern period, Persian was in fact the prestige language for literary composition in much of the Arabophone world. All of these factors, together of course with attitudes towards Arabic as the language of the Qur'ān, seem to have combined to reduce the potential advantages to the

---

83   For a discussion of the issues pertaining to the history of the Arabic dialects, see Jonathan Owens, "Arabic Dialect History and Historical Linguistic Mythology," *Journal of the American Oriental Society* 123 (4), 2003: 715–40.

adoption of literary vernaculars, although there was certainly a great deal of literature, including poetry, produced in various registers of dialect throughout the so-called "post-classical" era.[84]

Conclusion

The evidence we have seen, then, permits some generalizations on the contexts in which cosmopolitan literary ecologies successfully generate vernacular literatures. Least promising is an environment like that in the Chinese and Arab worlds of the pre-modern era, in which large-scale polities remain in place for long periods of time over territories in which are spoken a range of dialects that are interrelated but extend well beyond the boundaries of mutual intelligibility. In such circumstances, the resources required to develop a vernacular language capable of covering the political territory that would demand it simply outweigh the disadvantages of the cosmopolitan idiom, namely its own remoteness, for reasons of geography, chronology, and register, from the spoken language of anyone. Most promising are regions on the peripheries of a cosmopolis, outside the political reach of any centralizing imperial state but within the sway of cosmopolitan literary culture. Such regions are especially likely to develop vernacular literatures when their own spoken languages (as is true in contexts from Japanese to Irish, from Tamil to Javanese) are unrelated to the cosmopolitan language, making the resources and energy required to learn that language greater, in the long run, than those required to literize and literarize a vernacular. They are also likely to develop a vernacular during eras when regional polities emerge on a scale proportionate to that of the mutually intelligible range of a dialect continuum. Religious developments, from the spread of Christianity, Islam, or Buddhism to the rise of *bhakti* devotionalism in India, can add a further incentive to vernacularization, though attempts by missionaries to impose a literary vernacular from without are generally less successful than those that come from within and are bolstered by political and cultural agendas. Regions that have never had their own indigenous written literary tradition frequently pass through a cosmopolitan phase as a necessary part of the literarization of their language; in those regions where long literary traditions predated cosmopolitan influence, such as Syria and Egypt, the emergence of a new

---

84   See e.g. Thomas Bauer, "Mamluk Literature: Misunderstandings and New Approaches," *Mamluk Studies Review* 9 (2), 2005.

vernacular (Coptic, Syriac), more frequently turned out to be an intermediate stage on the way to the adoption of a new cosmopolitan language.

Vernaculars and cosmopolitans can coexist for long periods of time; indeed, in some respects they can be said to need each other. The vernacular gains literary resources from the cosmopolitan language, while the cosmopolitan language is in some ways better able to create a viable niche for itself if vernaculars exist for more purely local cultural functions. Thus, Latin remained a major European literary language till the seventeenth century (and indispensable for even longer to intellectual life); Sanskrit, through the eighteenth century;[85] classical Chinese, through much of the nineteenth and into the twentieth century; Arabic, to this day. Readers and writers in each of those contexts could value the translocal possibilities offered by the cosmopolitan literary language, even as they may also have appreciated the charms of the vernacular.

Over time, however, several forces tended to gather strength. The literary resources gathered under vernacular languages grew stronger and stronger, as longer traditions existed in those languages, and the literary traditions they embodied came to seem more useful than those from the cosmopolitan tradition, increasingly localized for readers in the past, in old genres and old styles. Just as Roman poets of the first century AD increasingly saw Virgil and his contemporaries, and not Greek literature, as the works they wished to emulate or to surpass, so too did writers in modern European languages, using forms like the sonnet and the emergent prose fiction tradition, increasingly find their models in other modern and vernacular writers, whether in their own languages or not. Similar phenomena emerged in the East Asian periphery and, especially, in South Asia. The costs of learning the cosmopolitan language grew as it became ever more distant from the spoken language; conversely, the emergence of broader-based systems of education, as well as of the production and circulation of texts, increased the potential audience for written verbal art to new sectors of society, particularly to women and to the middle classes, groups less interested in the cosmopolitan language for its own sake.

These forces, and others, pushed all regions toward the notion of a literary ecology dominated by the vernacular, in which the cosmopolitan no longer played anything but an antiquarian role. The gradual diminution in

---

85   Sheldon Pollock, ed., *Forms of Knowledge in Early Modern Asia: Explorations in the Intellectual History of India and Tibet, 1500–1800*, Durham, NC: Duke University Press, 2011.

the role of cosmopolitan literary languages would, no doubt, have led to a new literary-ecological formation, one in which vernacular literatures coexisted with each other in the absence of their cosmopolitan rivals. By the time this phenomenon reached full strength in most parts of the world, however, it found itself integrated with a different, and much more powerful, set of changes—those associated with the emergence of European modernity, and with its often forcible spread to other regions. As a result, when the era of the coexistence of cosmopolitan and vernacular came to an end, it was a specifically European ecology that was to take its place, even in regions such as South Asia, where vernaculars were already highly advanced at the moment of the establishment of European dominance. That new, European-derived ecology is that of the national literature, and it forms the subject of the next chapter.

CHAPTER 5

National Literature

In one of the first letters in Frances Brooke's 1769 epistolary novel *The History of Emily Montague*, the first novel written in English in what is now Canada, the protagonist, Captain Rivers, describes his first sighting of the shores of the St. Lawrence River:

> On approaching the coast of America, I felt a kind of religious veneration, on seeing rocks which almost touch'd the clouds, cover'd with tall groves of pines that seemed coeval with the world itself: to which veneration the solemn silence not a little contributed; from Cape Rosieres, up the river St. Lawrence, during a course of more than two hundred miles, there is not the least appearance of a human footstep; no objects meet the eye but mountains, woods, and numerous rivers, which seem to roll their waters in vain.[1]

Beyond those two hundred miles, but still far short of Captain Rivers's destination of Québec, his ship will have passed by the town of St.-Jean-Port-Joli, later the setting for the opening of Philippe Aubert de Gaspé *fils*'s 1837 novel *L'influence d'un livre*, itself the first novel written in French in Canada:

> On the south shore of the St. Lawrence River, on a plain which stretches towards a chain of mountains, whose name we don't know, there is a small cottage, unremarkable in every respect. Located at the foot of a hill, it is hidden from view for travelers by a pine grove which protects it from the north wind, which is so common in this part of the land.[2]

---

1   Frances Brooke, *The History of Emily Montague*, Book Jungle (2008), 1769, 11.

2   Sur la rive sud du fleuve Saint-Laurent, dans une plaine qui s'étend jusqu'à une chaîne de montagnes, dont nous ignorons le nom, se trouve une petite chaumière, qui n'a rien de remarquable par elle-même ; située au bas d'une colline, sa vue est dérobée aux voyageurs par un bosquet de pins qui la défend contre le vent du nord, si fréquent dans cette partie de la contrée. (Philippe Aubert de Gaspé, *L'influence d'un livre: Roman Historique*, BiblioBazaar, 2007, 13.)

The juxtaposition of these scenes—the English ship gliding past the French village; the former seemingly unaware of the existence of the latter, which in turn has screened itself from the view of outside visitors—seems to enact all too well the "two solitudes" made famous by Hugh MacLennan's 1945 novel of that name, or the "two nations warring within the bosom of a single state" of Lord Durham's 1838 report into the constitutional position of Britain's Canadian colonies. Even more evocatively, perhaps, this silent and mutually unrecognized passage might recall the image suggested by the Québec politician and man of letters Pierre Joseph Olivier Chauveau (1820–90):

> On another occasion, and at the risk of being accused of eccentricity, we were permitted to compare our social situation to that famous staircase of the *château* at Chambord which, through an architectural fantasy, was built such that two people could climb it at the same time without meeting each other, and without seeing each other except at intervals. English and French, we ascend as if by these double stairs towards the destinies chosen for us on this continent, without know-ing each other, meeting each other, nor even seeing each other except on the landing of politics. Socially and literarily speaking, we are more foreign to each other by far than are the English and the French of Europe.[3]

Certainly, the very mutual invisibility of English-Canadian and Québécois cultures in these, notionally the foundational novels of each literature, illus-trates something of the challenges of forming two or more national literatures (or a major national literature and minority literatures) within a single nation-state. Even more striking, however, is the profound ambiva-lence towards *both* of these novels within their own traditions, a point I have discussed in detail elsewhere.[4] In the context of literatures always

---

3   Dans une autre occasion, au risque d'être accusé de bizarrerie, nous nous sommes permis de comparer notre état social à ce fameux escalier du château de Chambord qui, par une fantaisie de l'architecte, a été construit de manière que deux personnes puissent monter en même temps sans se rencontrer, et en ne s'apercevant que par intervalles. Anglais et français, nous montons comme par une double rampe vers les destinées qui nous sont réservées sur ce continent, sans nous connaî-tre, nous rencontrer, ni même nous voir ailleurs que sur le palier de la politique. Socialement et littérairement parlant, nous sommes plus étrangers les uns aux autres de beaucoup que ne le sont les Anglais et les Français d'Europe. (Pierre Joseph Olivier Chauveau, *L'Instruction publique au Canada*, Précis historique et statistique. Cote, 1876, 335.)

4   Alexander Beecroft, "The Bird of Passage and the Petit Panthéon: Frances

painfully aware of their belatedness in comparison with the literatures of Europe, the fairly consistent disavowal of Brooke and de Gaspé as foundational figures suggests much about the challenges inherent in creating and defending the claims of national literary history, not only in a New World settler society but even in the heart of Europe itself.

The reasons for rejecting these two novelists are different. Brooke was the wife of a British chaplain stationed briefly in Québec in the aftermath of the Seven Years' War, with a prolific literary career of her own in London prior to the publication of this novel (as a novelist, translator from French, playwright, and editor of a periodical for women titled *The Old Maid*). In the words of one Anglo-Canadian literary historian, she was thus a "bird of passage," too temporary a visitor to constitute a foundational figure for a settler literature. The problems with Gaspé are more complicated: though a native of Québec, his bilingual education and upbringing (and penchant for quoting British literature and for defending the English language as *sublime et énergique*) make him anathema to many Québécois nationalist critics, while his anti-clericalism and identification with the Romanticism of Hugo and others likewise worried more conservative and Catholic critics, who ignored all dimensions of his work except for the picturesque and folkloric. Both Brooke and Gaspé, in other words, are too committed to literary projects centered in Europe, and both too fascinated with the charms of each other's languages, to act as literary founders. Together they demonstrate some of the ecological challenges inherent in constructing national literatures and in reading texts as "national." Most immediately, of course, each acts as a reminder of the challenges inherent to an ecology that presumes a one-to-one correspondence between languages, literatures, and political units; as we shall see below, implicit in the reception of these two quasi-Canadian authors are the devices of literary history and of Quarrels between Ancients and Moderns, devices central to the evolution and success of the national literary ecology in Europe and beyond.

What Is the National Literary Ecology?

Since my understanding of the concept of a literature is formed chiefly through practices of reading and interpretation, a national literature is one that reads and interprets texts through the lens of the nation-state, whether as

Brooke, Philippe Aubert de Gaspé fils, and Where to Begin a National Literature," *Studies in Canadian Literature-Études en littérature canadienne* 38 (1) 2013, 31–49.

that state's embodiment, as the dissent tolerated within its public sphere, as its legitimating precursors, or as its future aspirations. Issues of the constitution of the literary language of course provide a crucial nexus between literary and political debates and will receive due attention in what follows. More salient still, however, are the questions of how national literatures differentiate themselves from both cosmopolitan and other national rivals, matters, I argue, chiefly negotiated through the mechanism of the Quarrel and through charter-myths (such as the "shibboleth text" and the narrative of progressive vernacularization) contained within the work of literary history. This technique of literary history, uniquely emergent in the national literary ecology, is a crucial device that at once legitimates a literature and the nation it embodies, integrates it into an existing system of national literatures, and reduces the quantity of information within the literary system.

The different ecological constraints operative in the era and context of the nation-state, in other words, configure a national literature as something distinct from the other five literary ecologies discussed in this book. One of the chief tasks for each ecology as it emerges is to reduce the quantity of information within the system; some existing texts cannot survive in the new environment, others survive in a marginal or altered role, while others still flourish in unexpected ways in their new surroundings. As a result of these shifts, previously unmanageable quantities of information (that is, literature) are rendered manageable by a new structure; the local particularities of epichoric texts are smoothed out by panchoric readers, while cosmopolitan readers simplify panchoric texts by stripping them of their cultural specificity. Vernacular literatures in a sense increase the complexity of the system (by adding new languages to it), but in another sense this very act of creation reduces information locally by creating, with a new literature, a small subsystem. As national literatures emerge from vernaculars, I will argue, two kinds of information are lost: first, the cosmopolitan source literature (and most particularly its continuations into the present) are obscured, and second, those texts in the vernacular/national language that cannot be assimilated to the narrative of national literary history are marginalized.

I will postpone a fuller discussion of the relationship between national and global literatures (the latter, in my view, still an incipient or prospective ecology rather than one fully operative) for the following chapter but will here confine myself to the observation that, in constructing themselves as global, literatures must perform a forgetting of their national origins. Global English, in other words, must not only forget the literature of Britain (and still more the literature of England) but must also forget the history of how English became global. This is why global literature represents a rupture not only with the identification of the literature with its nation of origin but also with postcolonial literatures *as such*. By this argument, a "postcolonial literature" such as Indian literature in English represents an attempt to create a narrative for a national literature in English out of the colonial experience, where a Global English literature (if such a thing yet exists) instead constructs a community of English speakers (or English readers) through a myth of origin that foregrounds interconnection rather than subjugation.

To return to those ecologies already present at the emergence of national literature, we can first say that a national literature is not an epichoric literature; that is, a literature imagined as circulating exclusively within a restricted local region, such as a small-scale tribal community or a Greek polis. Both systems share a strong connection between the boundaries of the literature and those of the political unit, but the unavoidably translocal nature of the nation-state requires a different myth of origin, one that, as we shall see, emphasizes evolution over autochthony. Moreover, where epichoric literatures, as the hypothetical zero-grade of literary circulation, do not circulate beyond their own borders, national literatures are from the beginning constructed as elements of an *inter-national* system of literatures; English literature, in other words, can only exist *as such* if it can be set against French literature, German literature, and so on.

National literatures are also distinct from panchoric literatures, literatures circulating across political units but within a single language community, as in Archaic Greece or Warring States China. Where a panchoric literature claims to speak for the entire community of language speakers (and, as I have shown elsewhere, are one of the principal means by which such communities are created)[5] even though that community does not correspond to a political entity, a national literature performs the converse task, claiming to speak for a state notionally comprised of speakers of a particular language, whether that language in fact stops at the state's borders or whether that state includes substantial minority populations speaking other languages. In the words of Jonathan Hall, panchoric literatures such as that of classical Greece construct first an "aggregative," rather than an "oppositional" notion of identity.[6] As a result, the charter myths of

5   Alexander Beecroft, *Authorship and Cultural Identity in Early Greece and China: Patterns of Literary Circulation*, Cambridge: Cambridge University Press, 2010.

6   Jonathan M. Hall, *Hellenicity: Between Ethnicity and Culture*, Chicago: University of Chicago Press, 2002.

panchoric literatures tend to represent the assemblage of the literature out of epichoric elements, where national literatures, as we shall see, need to see their environment as perennially whole, even if forgotten or misunderstood, as evolving out of vernacular or other origins, even as those origins are reimagined as national.

The contrast between national and cosmopolitan literatures is more straightforward, in that cosmopolitan literatures (such as Classical Chinese in East Asia, Greek under Roman rule, or Latin in medieval and early modern Europe) seek to represent the world as a whole, unified under a single political, cultural, or religious vision, and to articulate a community of literate elites across a substratum of other spoken languages through a shared hyper-literary medium. Where national literatures assume by their nature that Babel has already fallen and that words can (or should) speak only to a more circumscribed audience. That said, the status of French literature is ambiguous, especially in the seventeenth through nineteenth centuries, possessing elements of both the cosmopolitan and the national. Inasmuch as French became, for a time, the language in which the idea of Europe was spoken in a variety of political and social contexts and by residents of many nations, the French language certainly filled a cosmopolitan role, first supplementing, then gradually replacing, Latin in that role. At the same time, through the status of French as the native language of France, the nation-state par excellence, French literature serves, along with British, as the paradigm of the national literature, and as we shall see below, the very emergence of French as a cosmopolitan rival to Latin can be seen as the product of a specifically national political agenda.

If, as we have seen in the previous chapter, vernacular literatures emerge in reaction to an existing cosmopolitan literature (as Latin emerges against Greek; English, French, and Italian against Latin; Japanese against Classical Chinese; Tamil and the various North Indian vernaculars against Sanskrit) and coexist with them in some form of symbiotic relationship, national literatures are marked by a rupture with the cosmopolitan past, by the assertion of the national literary language as superior to its cosmopolitan antecedents, better suited to contemporary circumstances, or more accessible to a larger public. Pressures to reorganize the political realm into nation-states (whether driven by internal political dynamics or by colonialism and its resistance) tend to pull the understanding of literature toward a national model, where each nation is understood as possessing its own unique literary language with an extensive history.

Within the literary system itself, these external pressures acted in different ways, depending in large part on the existing tensions between cosmopolitan and vernacular literatures; where vernaculars were stronger and more readily mapped onto the nation-state, there tended to be a forgetting of the cosmopolitan tradition; where vernaculars were weaker or nonexistent (or were distributed in a way incompatible with the goals of nation-building), cosmopolitan literatures took on the role of national literary language or vernaculars retained stronger links to their cosmopolitan antecedents. In almost every case, emergent notions of literary history (related to the increasing tendency to view the literary canon as a guide to reading rather than a model for literary production) tended to emphasize the gap between the cosmopolitan past and the national present, to assimilate the vernacular heritage into a progressive national history—and to ignore those texts that could not be assimilated to this narrative.

My understanding of the distinction between vernacular and national literatures borrows from debates among historians on the origins of the nation-state. Aside from a long-discredited "primordialist" notion, that tribal or national identity is inherent to human nature, historians of the nation-state tend to divide into camps of "modernists" and "perennialists." Modernists hold that the nation is a modern construction, a product of ideologies operative in the wake of the French Revolution and of modernity generally.[7] Perennialists argue instead that, while the nation is indeed a product of history (and not, as the primordialists claim, an innate feature of human consciousness), its origins can be located earlier in time, whether specifically in the Judaeo-Christian tradition and the development of vernacular languages[8] or more generally in the ethno-symbolic heritage of a community,[9] and that nineteenth-century nationalism is a force that

---

7   See E. J. Hobsbawm, *Nations and Nationalism since 1780: Programme, Myth, Reality*, 2nd ed., Cambridge University Press, 1992; Liah Greenfeld, *Nationalism: Five Roads to Modernity*, Cambridge, MA: Harvard University Press, 1993; Ernest Gellner, *Nations and Nationalism*, 2nd ed., Ithaca, NY: Cornell University Press, 2009, and especially Benedict Anderson, *Imagined Communities: Reflections on the Origin and Spread of Nationalism*, revised, London: Verso, 1991.

8   Adrian Hastings, *The Construction of Nationhood: Ethnicity, Religion and Nationalism*, Cambridge: Cambridge University Press, 1997. On this point, it should be remembered that the circulation of Buddhism in East Asia likewise drove the development of vernacular literary languages, in a context that it would be difficult to connect with the nation-state. See Victor H. Mair, "Buddhism and the Rise of the Written Vernacular in East Asia: The Making of National Languages," *The Journal of Asian Studies* 53 (3), 1994.

9   Anthony D. Smith, *The Antiquity of Nations*, Cambridge: Polity, 2004.

gave form to preexisting national sentiments[10] rather than their creator. The distinction between the two positions, in essence, reduces to the question of whether the French Revolution and its era merely gave new form and urgency to existing communal sentiments or whether a decisively new political and social formation emerges at that time.

My model of literary ecologies, I would argue, can contribute to thinking on this question by recontextualizing the differences between early modern and modern "nationalisms" around their respective relationships to existing cosmopolitan languages (in the case of Europe, Latin). It will be my contention that the critical index of the transformation to a national ecology and ideology lies in the supplanting of the cosmopolitan past. Where early modern cultures (and here I would include not only Europe into the eighteenth century but also most of the non-European world into the nineteenth and even early twentieth centuries) employ varying kinds of vernacular literatures in some kind of complementary distribution with a cosmopolitan literature or literatures, the entry into modernity (and thus into "national literatures") is marked by a decisive transformation in the relationship with cosmopolitan literature, frequently taking the form of a "Quarrel of the Ancients and the Moderns," in which cosmopolitan literary languages are associated with the Ancients, usually to their detriment. In the national literary ecology's original home, Western Europe, this new ecology takes the form of a notional ontological equivalence between national literatures, which does little to hide the structuring inequalities of the system, just as the post-Westphalian system of international law creates a fiction of the equality of nations while simultaneously enabling the inequalities of power inherent to the European order. As this political order spreads through the rest of the world, through conquest, colonization, and resistance, we enter the first era in which the entire habitable territory of the planet is subsumed under a single model of territorial sovereignty, that of the nation-state, which projects globally the inequities subsumed under the claim of ontological equivalence that began in Europe. While notions of communal identity and fellow-feeling among members of a shared linguistic, religious or cultural community are nothing new, the framework of the nation-state represents a qualitatively different version of these sentiments, shaping them into a uniform and universalizing system of notionally discrete identities, an experience very much at odds with the complex and overlapping categories of identity common to the pre-modern world.[11]

---

10   Ibid., 165.

11   On this subject, see especially Pamela Kyle Crossley, *A Translucent Mirror:*

This peculiar status of the national literary ecology as the only such ecology to have evolved in a single region of the world and then to have been exported universally makes especially urgent the use of the comparative methodology at work throughout this book. As I have argued at length elsewhere, cross-cultural comparisons (especially those undertaken across broad chronological or geographic reaches) tend to fall into the trap of reifying the cultures in question rather than viewing culture (as I believe we must) as the space within which debates occur.[12] This understanding is of course easier to maintain when scholarship is bound within a single cultural space; in performing typological comparisons (as the earlier chapters of this book have done) or in documenting episodes of cultural contact (as this chapter must do) there is a much greater danger that the debates and tensions that define each culture will be reduced to a monologic and hegemonic narrative, whose interactions with the monologic narratives of other cultures can in turn be reduced either to exoticism or to universalism.

A particularly telling case in point is the concept of "literature" itself, or rather on its Chinese analogue, wenxue 文學, which I have alluded to briefly in the introduction. Used in a (probably late) section of the Confucian *Analects* to refer to the learning and knowledge associated with canonical written texts,[13] the term has a long history in the classical language, gradually coming to be used as a term for cultured textuality generally, including not only poetry and imaginative prose but also historical, philosophical, and exegetical writings, among others. By at least 1831, the term wenxue begins to be used as an equivalent for the English and generally European word "literature," at first by European missionaries in China, in a move that was then borrowed in Japan before being borrowed back to become the dominant meaning of the term by the late 1890s in China itself.[14] Read on one level, this is a simple and familiar story of the erosion of indigenous

---

History and Identity in Qing Imperial Ideology, Berkeley: University of California Press, 2002, 32.

12   Alexander Beecroft, "Review Ming Xie Conditions of Comparison: Reflections on Comparative Intercultural Inquiry," *Comparative Literature Studies* 49 (4), 2012: 622–6.

13   Martin Kern, "Ritual, Text, and the Formation of the Canon: Historical Transitions of 'Wen' in Early China," *T'oung Pao* 87 (1/3), Second Series, 2001: 48.

14   Lydia He Liu, *Translingual Practice: Literature, National Culture, and Translated Modernity—China, 1900–1937*, Stanford, CA: Stanford University Press, 1995, 35; Theodore Huters, "A New Way of Writing: The Possibilities for Literature in Late Qing China, 1895–1908," *Modern China* 14 (3), 1988: 243–76, 243.

concepts in subaltern cultures replaced by terms borrowed from hegemonic European cultures.

And yet, the question is not so simple, as the European term "literature" was itself subject to shifting meanings. As Raymond Williams, among others, has observed, "literature" in English had the sense of being well-read, or of the sorts of texts the well-read had read, through the end of the eighteenth century; in a telling example, he notes that Hazlitt describes the two greatest figures of English literature as Newton and Locke.[15] Only in the nineteenth century does "literature" come to be fully restricted to its modern sense of imaginative textuality, including poetry, drama, and prose fiction but excluding philosophy, history, and science.[16] Furthermore, ample evidence also exists for the complexity of the associations wenxue and its allied terms had in pre-modern times in China; the enormously influential *Wen Xuan* 文選 anthology compiled by Xiao Tong (501–31), for example, includes a variety of official and inscriptional prose genres but not philosophical or historical texts. There is also considerable evidence for nineteenth-century debates in China about whether philosophy and history should be considered literary; a notable case in point is the scholar Ruan Yuan 阮元 (1764–1849), editor of a significant edition of the Confucian classics with their traditional commentaries.[17]

In other words, if we examine the concept of "literature" from within a strictly European context, it is clear that the term evolved from one meaning to another over the course of the late eighteenth and early nineteenth centuries and that, in the interim, (at least) the meaning of the term was contested. Examining wenxue as a concept within the Chinese tradition allows us to uncover a traditional definition, always including "literature" in the modern European sense but often including many other things as well (many of them in fact things that would have been included under earlier European definitions). This definition of wenxue was challenged in pre-modern times around its limits, especially with philosophical and historical texts, before giving way to use as a calque for the European term "literature" by the late nineteenth century. A perspective internal to either

---

15   Raymond Williams, *Keywords: A Vocabulary of Culture and Society*, Rev. Sub. ed., Oxford: Oxford University Press, 1985, 183–88.

16   See also Trevor Ross, *The Making of the English Literary Canon from the Middle Ages to the Late Eighteenth Century*, Montreal: McGill-Queen's University Press, 1998, 293–301.

17   Theodore Huters, "From Writing to Literature: The Development of Late Qing Theories of Prose," *Harvard Journal of Asiatic Studies* 47 (1), 1987: 86.

culture, then, necessarily emphasizes the complexity of the debate surrounding either of these words, but when the discussion becomes comparative, there is a tendency to imagine both Europe and China as static and monologic cultural entities, with the latter, in the late nineteenth century, rejecting its own formations in favor of those of the former. Sinologists writing on the question tend to acknowledge the dialogic complexities of terms like "literature" and "culture" when discussing the calquing of these terms into Chinese,[18] but in so doing the assumption seems to be that the dialogism of each internal cultural debate is put aside during moments of translation.

Only through the use of a model of cultural contact that insists on preserving the internal complexities and debates of the cultures in question can we see that, in fact, both China and Europe experience broadly similar debates about their respective categories of wenxue and "literature," with in both cases a more traditionalist definition referring to texts usable as models for good writing in any genre doing battle with a more restricted definition analogous to *belles-lettres* or "imaginative literature." Over time, the debates in each region were won by the latter definition, and in the case of China it is certainly clear that the influence of the European debate was felt very palpably. Nonetheless, it would be a mistake to believe that China, in the late nineteenth century, under the pressure of European colonialism and modernity, merely abandoned its own (monologic) understanding of wenxue, redeploying the now evacuated term as a calque for the English "literature." Instead, the contested English term "literature" intervened decisively in an existing Chinese debate. The end results of both processes are the same—wenxue and "literature" now cover roughly analogous ranges of genre in both languages—but only by recognizing the dialogy in both cultures as crucial to the story of their interaction can we recuperate this exercise in cultural translation as something other than a simple act of cultural imperialism and/or appropriation, and only in this way do we uncover the typological similarities between both cultures in pre-modern times, which opens up a richer field for comparative analysis.

These cautions in mind, I now turn to an examination of several of the strategies used to found national literatures and to consolidate their ecological positions, both against prior systems, and with respect to other national

---

18   On "literature" in particular, see Huters, "A New Way of Writing," 1988, 272n1; Liu, *Translingual Practice* 1995, 429n1 does similar work on the term "culture."

literatures. My work here is necessarily suggestive rather than comprehensive; I offer not an exhaustive account of how national literatures work but rather sketches of several strategies that seem to have enjoyed considerable currency, the comparative study of which would seem likely to prove fruitful. Since the national-literature ecology emerges in Europe and only gradually permeates elsewhere, European examples feature prominently in the discussion of each strategy; I also devote some attention to the reception of each strategy in China, along with much more rudimentary sketches of the situations in other parts of the world. I examine three interlinked themes, each of which seems to assume considerable importance in the emergence and consolidation of national literatures and the national literary ecology: the construction of national literary languages, Quarrels of Ancients and Moderns, and the writing of literary history.

NATIONAL LANGUAGES, NATIONAL LITERATURES

The emergence of the nation-state, with its assumption of a congruence between territorial units of political and cultural authority, brought with it a particular challenge to the question of the language(s) to be used for the composition of literary texts. As early modernity gave way to modernity proper across Eurasia, the linguistic terrain of many regions contained a typological similarity familiar from earlier times: a continuum of spoken dialects, varying in their degrees of mutual intelligibility, acting as a substratum over which there circulated a variety of literary languages, both vernacular and cosmopolitan, in overlapping and non-contiguous circuits, themselves only loosely tied to the similarly complex and variegated political order. In Europe, the widespread use of Latin as a medium for literary and intellectual life coexisted with a variety of literary vernaculars, with Italian, and, gradually, with French, taking on supra-regional roles even as literary production in other languages, from English to Portuguese, flourished.

In East Asia, literary Chinese provided a common medium for certain elevated literary forms, contrasting with vernacular literatures in Japanese, Korean, and Vietnamese and the use of vernacular registers of Chinese in certain literary genres. In South Asia, Sanskrit's traditional cosmopolitan role was now shared by Persian, with various vernacular registers of what would later be called Hindustani borrowing from both, while elsewhere in the subcontinent other vernaculars, both Indo-Aryan and Dravidian, continued to thrive and develop. In the Arabic-speaking world, the Arabic literary language (itself a highly cosmopolitan register by this point) , while still dominant in religious contexts, was competing for prestige (though not necessarily for volume) in secular literature with the Persian and Turkic vernaculars. Southeast Asia presented a particularly complex situation, with cosmopolitan uses of Sanskrit and Arabic coinciding with vernacular literatures in Malay, Javanese, Thai, and other languages.[19]

In each of these regions, then, the original cosmopolitan language (Latin, literary Chinese, Sanskrit, and Arabic) persisted in some form as a significant literary language alongside literary vernaculars, both derived from the cosmopolitan language (French, Italian, Hindi, Bengali, vernacular registers in literary Chinese) and from elsewhere (the Germanic languages, Japanese, Turkish, Tamil). In some places, other cosmopolitan languages, such as Persian, entered the system. In general, Europe and South Asia moved the farthest towards vernacularization (along with the East Asian periphery), and China and, especially, the Arab world the least. Moreover, the four original cosmopolitan languages had generated, in addition to a series of vernacular literary languages, a continuum of spoken dialects, bearing a complex relationship to the literary languages imposed on top of them.

Spoken and literary languages were thus relatively far apart almost everywhere; as many have noted, a minority of the population of France on the eve of the Revolution were native speakers of the literary standard language, with smaller percentages still in Spain and Italy.[20] Spoken versions of Chinese, at least as distinct from each other as the spoken vernaculars of Lisbon and Naples, coexisted both with vernacular registers of the written language (which only vaguely reflected dialectal differences) and a quasi-standardized spoken language, guanhua, used for communication among government officials. The literary vernaculars of

---

19   Ronit Ricci, *Islam Translated: Literature, Conversion, and the Arabic Cosmopolis of South and Southeast Asia*, Chicago: University Of Chicago Press, 2011.

20   For France, the famous report of the Abbé Grégoire, commissioned in 1794, established that roughly one in five citizens of France spoke and understood the standard French language. Augustin Gazier and Henri Grégoire, *Lettres à Grégoire sur les patois de France, 1790-1794: documents inédit sur la langue, les moeurs et l'état des esprits dans les diverses régions de la France, au début de la Révolution, suivis du rapport de Grégoire à la Convention*, Geneva: Slatkine Reprints, 1969. For Italy, it has been estimated that, at unification in 1870, perhaps 2.5 percent of the population spoke Standard Italian as a native language, with another 10 percent or so more-or-less fluent second-language speakers. Arturo Tosi, "The Language Situation in Italy," *Current Issues in Language Planning* 5 (3), 2004: 277.

North India—Urdu and the various varieties of Hindi—likewise coexisted with a multiplicity of spoken dialects, while the classical Arabic of the Qur'ān and of poetry served speakers of local dialects from Morocco to Oman, alongside emergent literary forms using vernacular registers. Even more divergently, Sanskrit performed a meaningful role for speakers of Tamil and Javanese, classical Chinese for speakers of the mutually unrelated languages of Japanese, Korean, Vietnamese, and Manchu, while Arabic circulated as a sacred and secular language from Java to West Africa.

As the various regions of Eurasia moved from their divergent political formations (ranging from tiny German principalities and maritime trading entrepôts to the Qing and Mughal empires) towards the European model of the nation-state, these differences in existing ecological conditions played a significant role in shaping the choices made. In Western Europe, the home of the nation-state, the boundaries between existing literary vernaculars and emergent nation-states aligned comparatively well, and the choice of literary language provided comparatively few challenges, as was also the case in the Americas, where most nation-states emerged from settler colonies where the consensus concerning the literary and spoken vernacular was relatively strong.[21] The chief exception in the Americas is of course Canada, where the historical contingency of the British conquest of Québec in 1759, closely preceding the emergence of unrest in the Thirteen Colonies to the south, led inadvertently to the emergence of a bilingual nation. As the prologue to this chapter suggests, despite occasional attempts at synthesis between the two major literary traditions in Canada, including those of the first novelists in each, English and French literature in Canada have remained much more engaged with the metropolitan literature of their own languages (and, in due course, with other literatures in that language) than with each other. Similar problems have

---

21   Québec provides a useful case in point here: the original migration of the French to North America came to a close with the British conquest of 1759, in an era when, as we have seen, only a minority of the French population would have understood standard French, yet the evidence suggests that, since most of the colonists were town-dwellers from northern and western France, the popular version of standard French used in Paris and major provincial cities became the language of *la Nouvelle France*. Henri Witmann, "Le français de Paris dans le français des Amériques," *Proceedings of the International Congress of Linguists* 16, 1997. For an alternative view, see Philippe Barbaud, *Le choc des patois en Nouvelle-France: Essai sur l'histoire de la francisation au Canada*, Québec: University Québec Les Presses, 1984.

plagued all multilingual nation-states (which is to say, of course, most nation-states), with additional complications in those regions, ranging from Central Europe to sub-Saharan Africa, where the emergence of literary standard languages out of dialect continua was either late to emerge or mapped poorly onto political boundaries.

Here the case (admittedly extreme) of South Asia may serve as a further example. On the verge of modernity in the eighteenth century, Sanskrit maintained its cosmopolitan status and, under the Mughals Persian, also found use as a rival cosmopolitan idiom.[22] Moreover, by this time, a millennium's worth of vernacular literature in various languages, some derived from Sanskrit, some from the distinct Dravidian family of South India, had been thriving to varying degrees in competition with these cosmopolitan languages. In particular, literature in a variety of registers of the dialects of the Indo-Gangetic plain were highly active, most notably including those registers known as Urdu (subject to comparatively greater Perso-Arabic influence) and those that could be called Hindi (less Perso-Arabized and in earlier periods more provincial), which operated to some extent as cosmopolitan languages in their own right in a manner partly analogous to the role of French in the Europe of the time.[23] To an extent that remains controversial, Hindi and Urdu might be regarded as different registers of a single vernacular, Hindustani.

European imperialism in South Asia, distinct of course from that experienced by either East Asia or the Arab world, exerted its own effect on this already complex literary ecology. In contrast to the other two regions, South Asia came under almost complete colonial control, whether under direct rule or through the medium of British protectorates; in further contrast, since non-British colonial presence was confined to small trading communities such as Goa and Pondicherry, English was to exert a profound influence on the development of South Asia's literary terrain, greater by far

---

22 For the status of Persian in Mughal India see Muzaffar Alam, "The Pursuit of Persian: Language in Mughal Politics," *Modern Asian Studies* 32 (2), 1998: 317–49. Alam argues that the somewhat de-Arabized register of Persian used by the Mughals was an effective linguistic choice because it was non-local and non-sectarian, and (thanks in part to the persistence of pre-Islamic traditions), associated with liberal or universalist values. See Chapter 3 above for a discussion of these characteristic qualities of cosmopolitan literary languages.

23 For a discussion of these issues, see the essays in Sheldon Pollock, *Literary Cultures in History: Reconstructions from South Asia*, Berkeley: University of California Press, 2003.

than that of French on the Arab world as a whole. South India, where the majority of the population speaks Dravidian languages, is a particularly complex region; certainly South Indian resistance to Hindi has helped to maintain the status of English in politics and culture across India. Here as elsewhere, the interests of colonial administrators and Christian missionaries play a significant role; Rama Mantena has shown, for example, that colonial administrators in the nineteenth century played a significant role in the revival and development of literary Telugu.[24]

Many important leaders of the movement for independence, notably both Gandhi and Nehru, as well as the Progressive Writers Movement, fought initially for the recognition of Hindustani as the national language—that is, for a register of Hindi-Urdu stripped as completely as possible of both Perso-Arabic and Sanskritic influences and written equally in both the Perso-Arabic script of Urdu and the indigenous Devanagari script of Hindi. The elevation of Hindustani, rather than either Hindi or Urdu (or both as separate languages) was motivated not only by the perceived efficiency gains of a single national language but also to some extent by religious dimensions: Urdu was more closely aligned with Islam and Hindi with Hinduism, although in this period issues of class and urban status were important as well—as a small but telling example, Nehru, a Hindu, spoke Urdu as his mother tongue.[25] The promotion of Hindustani was controversial (as was even the claim that it existed as a real rather than a hypothetical linguistic register), and in the event political and religious constraints doomed the project to failure.

The emergence of (and British support for) a distinctive Muslim nationalist movement led to the creation of Pakistan, which chose Urdu (as recently as 2001 the native language of just 8 percent of Pakistan's population) as its national language; in communal reaction, the choice of national language for the reconstituted and more heavily Hindu India was almost inevitably drawn toward Hindi (itself the mother tongue of 43 percent of India's population, using the census of India's classification of the dialects of North India). From an ecological perspective, a nationalism based in religion encouraged the coalescence of two literary languages out of the continuum of "Hindustani" spoken and written languages, rather than the single such

---

24   Rama Sundari Mantena, "Vernacular Futures: Colonial Philology and the Idea of History in Nineteenth-Century South India," *Indian Economic Social History Review* 42 (4), 2005: 513–34.

25   Talat Ahmed, *Literature and Politics in the Age of Nationalism: The Progressive Episode in South Asia, 1932–56*, New Delhi: Routledge India, 2008, 120–1.

language that might have emerged out of a secular pan-South Asian nationalism. To this day, debate persists about the extent to which Hindustani was ever a viable linguistic model,[26] although it can be argued that the language of Bollywood cinema, designed to reach the largest audience, is a plausible claimant for the mantle of non-communal Hindustani as a language of culture. Market forces have succeeded where nonsectarian nationalist idealism failed in creating a unified literary language. The diversity and complexity of the linguistic situation in India (and, to a lesser extent, in Pakistan) leaves South Asia as perhaps the only major region of the world in which multiple literary registers (Hindi/Urdu, English, and regional languages) continue to coexist in some kind of complementary distribution.

The Arab world represents a very different response to a somewhat similar ecological terrain. By the eighteenth century, the linguistic ecology of the region was complexly cosmopolitan; while Arabic retained its religious role, and classical Arabic literature retained a prestige value, this ecological space was shared with Persian as an alternative cosmopolitan literary idiom, along with both Persian and Ottoman Turkish as languages of administration.[27] As political resistance both to Ottoman rule and to European imperial activity increased during the nineteenth century, Arabic experienced a literary revival, known as *Al-Nahda*, or the Awakening.[28] While the differential experience of Ottoman and European pressures in different parts of the Arab world led to a variety of regionally based national resistance movements and, in due course, to a variety of nation-states, and while the issue of the use of regional vernaculars was raised at times, the general verdict is that the advantages of the cosmopolitan idiom (wider accessibility, continuity with the past, and strength in numbers against the pressures of Westernization) outweighed the possible particularist advantages of developing national vernaculars as literary languages (ease of learning and the development of national solidarity). Tellingly, the strongest early voices in favor of the development of literary vernaculars in Arabic were Christian missionaries, eager here as elsewhere to proselytize in a language as close to

---

26   Alok Rai, "The Persistence of Hindustani," *The Annual of Urdu Studies* 20, 2005: 135–44; S. Imtiaz Hasnain and K. S. Rajyashree, "Hindustani as an Anxiety Between Hindi-Urdu Commitment," *The Yearbook of South Asian Literatures and Linguistics*, 2004: 247–66.

27   C. H. M. Versteegh, *The Arabic Language*, New York: Columbia University Press, 1997, 71–2.

28   Muhammad Mustaf Badaw‾i, ed., *The Cambridge History of Modern Arabic Literature*, Cambridge: Cambridge University Press, 1992.

their target population as possible and, as always, seeking to supplant the local cosmopolitan tradition with European Christian civilization.²⁹ To this day, Modern Standard Arabic (a range of forms closely connected to Classical Arabic) remains the literary and intellectual language of the Arabic world, with the exception of growing bodies of dialect poetry, and of the tendency for dramatic works to be performed in the vernacular, especially in Egypt, although the written script will be in Modern Standard Arabic.³⁰ In the Maghreb in particular, the presence of French as a rival cosmopolitan standard (and in many cases, as the effective first language of the intellectual classes), offers access to a different audience and acts as a further constraint on the evolution of the literary system.

While to the casual outside observer China may seem to represent the largest region of linguistic homogeneity in the world, the reality is far more complex. Even leaving aside the fifty-five recognized minority language groups within China today (collectively comprising nearly one-tenth of the population), the Han Chinese population speaks a bewildering number of mutually unintelligible languages; even the roughly 70 percent of Han Chinese who speak so-called Mandarin dialects average only 72 percent mutual intelligibility on the lexical level,³¹ or roughly the same percentage as between French and Spanish; other "dialects" are much more divergent. The choice of a common spoken idiom for the Chinese nation-state, then, was far from a simple one, and the choice of a literary idiom presented further challenges. First of all, the difference between literary and vernacular Chinese (known, post–May Fourth, as wenyan 文言 and baihua 白話, respectively), is a question of register and of degree, as opposed to the qualitative distinctions between, for example, Latin and the Romance vernaculars in the eras of Dante and du Bellay. Further, the new literary standard for baihua could not simply imitate the spoken language, since the "dialects" of China represent a linguistic continuum with far greater phonetic, lexical, and semantic range than the Romance languages. If the written language was to be modernized, it could not *simply* become the language of speech, since that language was

---

29   Percy Smith, "Another Plea for Literature in Vernacular Arabic," *The Muslim World* 9 (4), 1919: 351–62. Proselytizing religions are frequently catalysts for vernacularization. For the experience with Buddhism in East Asia, see Mair, "Buddhism and the Rise of the Written Vernacular," 1994.

30   Marilyn Booth, "Poetry in the Vernacular," in *The Cambridge History of Modern Arabic Literature*, edited by Muhammad Mustaf Badawīi, 1992, 480.

31   Chaoju Tang, *Mutual Intelligibility of Chinese Dialects: An Experimental Approach*, Utrecht: LOT, 2009, 182.

itself far from simple. The guanhua spoken by officials could (and did) form the basis for the spoken linguistic standard that emerged in this period, labeled at first *guoyu* 國語,[32] or "national language", and then, on the Chinese mainland, *putonghua* 普通話, or "common speech," and later *Hanyu* 漢語, or "language of the Han," a terminological transition that encapsulates the shift from a nationalism that equated ethnic Chineseness with the nation-state, to a Marxist claim to be the language of the masses, to a more contemporary sense of ethnic identity as one (albeit valorized) component of a pluralistic state. Interestingly, this spoken standard was not seen as a sound basis for the written language.

The question of what form the new literary medium of baihua should take is perhaps deliberately left unclear. At times, we read impassioned calls for the "merging of speech and writing," but at other times the great novels of the Ming, especially *The Water Margin* (traditionally attributed to Shi Nai'an [c. 1296–1372]), seem to be held up not only as literary precursors of the vernacular but as embodiments of that vernacular in a more contemporary sense; in the passage from Hu Shi discussed below, the parallel structure reinforces an equivalence between the spoken language of the twentieth century and the dialogue of the fourteenth-century novel. The literary idiom developed during this period does indeed bear a stronger resemblance to the style of Ming (and Qing) fiction than to the spoken language of the streets of early twentieth-century Beijing, a choice ostensibly made to ensure a literary language both elegant and universal; that said, the insistence on the merging of speech and writing and on "living language" is thus slightly at odds with the specific recommendations made.

Hu's views also contrast strikingly with the superficially similar sentiments of Alessandro Manzoni, who, in revising his *I promessi sposi* to standardize the language, famously sought to "wash his sheets in the Arno," that is, to refine his prose style in accordance with Tuscan standards, originally established as the literary norm for vernacular writing in Italy thanks to the works of Dante, Petrarch, and Boccaccio, and later regularized through the activities of the Accademia della Crusca, established in Florence in 1582. Manzoni's determination to conform his own use of the vernacular

---

32   As Fu Liu notes, this term has a complex prehistory, having been used originally as a general term for the langauges of non-Chinese tribes located to the north. See Fu Liu, *Les Mouvements De La Langue Nationale En Chine*, Paris: Pékin, 1925, 2. The term is still in regular use in Taiwan.

language to the Tuscan standard, established in the fourteenth century, seems thus to recall Hu's similar determination.

A closer examination of Manzoni's remarks reveals, however, a crucial difference. The actual phrase is found in a letter to Tommaso Grossi dated October 7, 1827, which remarks on the differences between the spoken idiom of Florence at the time and the dictionaries of correct usage based on the literary tradition and then observes: "You know how I am occupied. I have seventy-one sheets to rinse, and water such as the Arno, and laundresses such as Cioni and Niccolini, whom I could not find in any other place."[33] In context, Manzoni is consulting with leading Florentine intellectuals of his day not simply to replicate the language of Dante and Petrarch but to emulate actual (elite) contemporary Florentine usage. The national language Manzoni seeks to create, in other words, is intended to reflect both the great classics of the vernacular tradition *and* contemporary spoken language in a privileged region. Hu Shi, by contrast, rejects the use of the actual spoken vernacular of Beijing in 1917 in favor of much older prose literature, while establishing a strange and improbable congruency between the two:

> Using language of the Qin, Han and Six Dynasties, which can be neither widespread nor universal, is not as good as using the language of *The Water Margin* and *The Journey to the West*, which is "understood in every home, known at every door".[34]

There is thus tension inherent in the construction of a national literary language out of existing cosmopolitan and vernacular literary traditions. On the one hand, there is the temptation to develop a language close to everyday speech, a temptation that brings with it the double risk of unduly privileging inhabitants of one city or region over others and of alienating future readers from elite traditions of the past. Alternatively, a new literary language may be modeled on earlier stages of the vernacular, as was the case in varying degrees with Italian and with Chinese, but this in turn risks making the language difficult enough to learn to defeat some of the purpose

---

33   Tu sai come io sono occupato. Ho settantun lenzuola da risciacquare e un'acqua come l'Arno e lavandaie come Cioni e Niccolini fuori di qui non le trovo in alcun luogo. Alessandro Manzoni, Cesare Arieti, and Dante Isella, *Tutte le lettere: Tomo primo*, Milan: Adelphi Edizioni, 1986, I 483.

34   與其作不能行遠、不能普及之秦、漢、六朝文字，不如作家喻戶曉之"水滸"、"西遊"文字也。

of avoiding the cosmopolitan idiom, while still being far enough removed from that idiom to make learning it difficult for newly minted speakers of the national language. Arabic (and, for a time, Greek) resisted the impulse to leave the cosmopolitan language altogether behind, which enhanced continuity with the past and across national boundaries, with possible costs in ease of learning. Certainly, wherever national languages emerged as distinct from cosmopolitan languages of the past, continuity with the literature of that past was in some measure lost—though for many, this was seen as a positive gain.

Quarrels

The question of the relationship to the cosmopolitan past is clearly of significance to any emergent national literature; it is also, I would further argue, constitutive of that system, through the structure of the Quarrel of the Ancient and the Modern, a structure first observed in seventeenth- and eighteenth-century Italy and France but evident in many other places as well. The language debates we examined briefly earlier can certainly participate in such Quarrels, but the substance of the Quarrel goes much deeper, including not only the use of the cosmopolitan language but also access to the textual tradition encoded in it and to the values and practices associated with it.

As suggested earlier, the national-literature ecology emerges out of a vernacular ecology, specifically out of that found in Europe in the early modern era, and marks itself as distinct chiefly through its relationship to the cosmopolitan background of Latin, still very much an active literary language (if not *the* literary and intellectual language) in Europe in the seventeenth century. Nowhere is this change of relationship seen more clearly than in the manifestoes that accompany the emergence of these literary practices. Joachim du Bellay's *Défense et illustration de la langue françoyse* of 1549, specifically the chapter entitled "Pourquoi la langue française n'est si riche que la grecque et latine," a crucial text in the emergence of French as a viable vernacular literature, represents an early stage of this development:

> And if our language is neither as copious nor as rich as Greek or Latin, that should not be attributed to its own weaknesses, as if of itself it could never be anything but impoverished and sterile, but rather to the ignorance of our elders, who (as it has been said of the ancient Romans), holding correct action in much greater

esteem than correct speech, and much preferring to leave to their posterity examples of virtue rather than precepts, deprived themselves of the glory of their deeds, and us of the fruit of our imitation of them, and by the same means we have let our language remain so impoverished and naked that it needs ornaments and (if we must speak thus) of the feathers of another.[35]

Du Bellay's treatise thus performs the same work as Dante's *De vulgari eloquentia*, acting as an apologetic for the vernacular, which assumes as a central premise the inherent superiority of Latin and Greek to French for literary purposes. One obvious difference between Dante's treatise and that of du Bellay is, of course, that where Dante could only defend the vernacular by writing in Latin, du Bellay defends the vernacular in the vernacular itself. This shift in the choice of language for the vernacular manifesto is an index of the changing significance of the cosmopolitan-vernacular relationship, and in particular of the adoption of French as the language of administration in the then-recent *Ordonnance de Villers-Cotterêts* of 1539. If du Bellay's text thus reflects a greater practical significance for the French language with respect to Latin, his rhetoric nonetheless continues to assert the comparative inadequacy of the former as a literary language when compared to the latter.

Especially significant here is the comparison to early Roman culture; as I showed in the previous chapter, Latin in the last two centuries BC stood as one of the earliest vernacular literatures, asserting its right of access to the literary system while conceding its impoverishment with respect to then-cosmopolitan Greek literature. Du Bellay, like Dante before him, acted as an advocate for a literary language of the future, stressing the contemporary inadequacy of the French language for literary purposes. As we shall see as this chapter unfolds, this apology for the vernacular (in terms of the cosmopolitan) will find its analogues in laments for literary underdevelopment, common everywhere from England to Argentina, from Canada to China.

---

35   Et si notre langue n'est si copieuse et riche que la grecque ou latine, cela ne doit être imputé au défaut d'icelle, comme si d'elle-même elle ne pouvait jamais être sinon pauvre et stérile: mais bien on le doit attribuer à l'ignorance de nos majeurs, qui, ayant (comme dit quelqu'un, parlant des anciens Romains) en plus grande recommandation le bien faire, que le bien dire, et mieux aimant laisser à leur postérité les exemples de vertu que des préceptes, se sont privés de la gloire de leurs bienfaits, et nous du fruit de l'imitation d'iceux: et par même moyen nous ont laissé notre langue si pauvre et nue qu'elle a besoin des ornements, et (s'il faut ainsi parler) des plumes d'autrui.

Contrast this with the following passage, taken from the epistolary introduction to Jean Desmarets de Saint-Sorlin's *La Comparaison de la langue, et de la poésie française, Avec la Grecque et la Latine, et des Poètes Grecs, Latins et Français* (1670). Desmarets, a protégé of Cardinal Richelieu and the first chancellor of the *Académie française*, was the author of *Clovis, ou la France chrétienne*, one of the many French national epics of his era, and a key defender of the Moderns against the Ancients. His *Comparaison* places Latin poetry in French translation beside poetry originally written in French, ostensibly to give neutral observers (for Desmarets, those who do not read Greek or Latin) the opportunity to judge the relative merits of each:

> [Nature], having given birth to geniuses in this age, makes sure that it is know that each of them surpasses by far the Ancients in their genre, and that they are good witnesses that the poet's reign was not limited to Greece and Italy. It would be a strange shame for the French Empire, which is now the first and most noble empire of the universe, and which cannot finish but with the ages, that it had a language and spirits less noble and less elevated, than the language and spirits of the Greeks and Latins.[36]

It is worth noting here that Desmarets's assertion of the superiority of the French language for literary purposes, while ostensibly directed against the Greco-Roman cosmopolitan past, manages also, through the easy metonymy of Italy and Latin, implicitly to suggest the superiority of French over Italian as well. Also telling is the general relationship to the Greco-Roman tradition asserted by Desmarets, beginning with his insistence on equating Greek and Latin, a gesture that firmly situates both languages as part of the shared European past, in which a greater emphasis on Latin alone would have reminded the reader of the continued rivalry with contemporary Latin literary and intellectual production.

Even more tellingly, of course, Desmarets insists on a necessary

---

36   Elle le fait bien connaître, ayant fait naître en ce siècle de génies, qui chacun en leur genre surpassent de beaucoup les Anciens, et qui sont de bons témoins que la poète n'a pas borné son règne dans la Grèce et dans l'Italie. Ce serait une honte étrange à l'Empire de France, qui est maintenant le premier et le plus noble de l'Univers, et qui ne doit finir qu'avec les siècles ; qu'il eût un langage et des esprits moins nobles et moins élevés, que le langage et les esprits des Grecs et des Latins. (Jean Desmarets de Saint-Sorlin, *La comparaison de la langue et de la poësie françoise, avec la grecque et la latine . . . ; Et Les amours de Protée et de Physis . . .* [Reprod.] / par le sieur Desmarests, 1670, v–vi.)

connection between the imperial power wielded by Louis XIV and the greatness of the literature produced in his orbit. This theme, of the mutual relationship between political and cultural hegemony, is not altogether absent from du Bellay (for whom, however, past and current French military triumphs are figured as harbingers of future literary prowess) but attains a special urgency in Desmarets's assertion of the superiority of his era in all respects over that of the ancients. This link between the triumph of the vernacular and political renewal finds its reflexes elsewhere in the world, as in Hu Shi's 胡適 (1891–1962) famous essay "A Tentative Discussion of Literary Reform," 文學改良芻議, published in January 1917 in the journal *New Youth* 新青年, a crucial document of the so-called May Fourth Movement:

> I take only Shi Nai'an, Cao Xueqin and Wu Woyao to be the main literary lineage, which is why I say "don't avoid common characters and common language." . . . Actually, spoken and written language have been running apart from each other for a long time. Since Buddhist scriptures were imported into China, and translators found the literary language (wenyan) insufficient to convey their ideas; accordingly, for ease of translation, they used a form approaching the vernacular (baihua). Later, a great many Buddhist conversations and explications used baihua as well. This was the origin of the "conversational" style. Song dynasty intellectuals used baihua for their *Conversations*, and this became the standard style for intellectual discussion. (Ming scholars followed them in this). By this time, baihua had already entered rhymed prose genres, as can be seen from an examination of Tang and Song *shi* and *ci* poetry in baihua. By the time of the Yuan dynasty, the northern part of China had already been ruled by alien nations under the Liao, Jin and Yuan. During these three hundred years, China developed a sort of popular literature: in prose, there were works like *The Water Margin*, *The Journey to the West* and *The Romance of the Three Kingdoms*; in drama, an incalculable number of works . . . From the perspective of modern times, Chinese literature should consider the Yuan to be its acme; the number of works that will last was without a doubt greatest in the Yuan. At this time, Chinese literature was closest to the spoken language, which almost became the literary language. Had this tendency not been checked, a living literature might have developed in China, and the achievements of a Dante or Luther would have taken place in our land. (In the European Middle Ages, each nation had its own vulgar tongue (*liyu* 俚語), and Latin was the wenyan, and all authors wrote their works in Latin, just as in our country they all wrote in wenyan. Later, the Italian literary giant Dante began to write in his own liyu, and national languages (guoyu) began to replace Latin. The

religious reformer Luther began to use German to translate the Old and New Testaments, and thereby began German literature. English and French followed a similar pattern; the normal Bible translation in English today was written in 1611, only three hundred years ago. Accordingly, the literatures of all of the European nations use their own liyu. Literary giants began to emerge, living literatures began to replace a dead literature in Latin, and with a living literature came a guoyu which merged speech and writing). This tendency, then, was unexpectedly checked in the Ming, when the "eight-legged" essay style was used to select civil servants, and when contemporary literati like the Seven Ming Masters such as He Jingming 何景明 (1483–1521) and Li Mengyang 李夢陽 (1473–1530) contentiously elevated "returning to antiquity"; the once-in-a-millennium opportunity to merge writing and speech was prematurely killed off half-way there. However, from the perspective of recent historical evolution, it can be asserted that baihua literature is the main lineage of Chinese literature, and that future literature must use this medium (this assertion is the author's own; those today who support his position may not be numerous). For these reasons, I believe that today's writers of poetry and prose should use common characters and words. Using dead words from three thousand years ago is not as good as using living words of the twentieth century, and using language of the Qin, Han and Six Dynasties, which can be neither widespread nor universal, is not as good as using the language of *The Water Margin* and *The Journey to the West*.[37]

37　吾惟以施耐庵、曹雪芹、吳趼人為文學正宗，故有”不避俗字俗語”之論也。...蓋吾國言文之背馳久矣。自佛書之輸入，譯者以文言不足以達意，故以淺近之文譯之，其體已近白話。其後佛氏講義語錄尤多用白話為之者，是為語錄體之原始。及宋人講學以白話為語錄，此體遂成講學正宗。(明人因之。)　當是時，白話已久人韻文，觀唐、宋人白話之詩詞可見也。及至元時，中國北部已在異族之下三百餘年矣　（遼、金、元）。此三百年中，中國乃發生一種通俗行遠之文學。文則有”水滸”、”西遊”、”三國”......之類，戲曲則尤不可勝計。...今世眼光觀之，則中國文學當以元代為最盛；可傳世不朽之作，當以元代為最多。此可無疑也。當是時，中國之文學最 近言交合一，白話幾成文學的語言矣。使此趨勢不受阻遏，則中國幾有一”活文學”出現，而但丁、路得之偉業，(歐洲中古時，各國皆有俚語，而以拉丁文為文言，凡著作書籍皆用之，如吾國之以文言著書也。其後義大利有但丁〔Dante〕　諸文豪，始以其國俚語著作，諸國踵興，國語亦代起。路得〔Luther〕創新教，始以德文譯”舊約”、”新約”，遂開德文學之先。英、法諸國亦復如是。今世通用之英文”新舊約”乃一六一一年譯本，距今才三百年耳。故今日歐洲諸國　之文學，在當日皆為俚語。迨諸文豪興，始以”活文學”代拉丁之死文學；有活文學而後有言文合一之國語也。)　幾發生於神州。不意此趨勢驟為明代所阻，政府既以八股取士，而當時文人如何、李七子之徒，又爭以復古為高，於是此千年難遇言文合一之機會，遂中道天折矣。然以今世歷史進化的眼光觀之，則白話文學之為中國文學之正宗，又為將來文學必用之利器，可斷言也。(此”斷言”乃自作者言之，贊成此說者今日未必甚多也。)　以此之故，吾主張今日作文作詩，宜採用俗語俗　字。與其用三千年前之死字(如”于鑠國會，遵晦時休”之類)，不如用二十

This passage is worth exploring on a number of levels; here I wish to draw attention to the author's explicit self-identification with Dante and Luther as literary apologists for the vernacular. This identification, I argue, is misleading; Hu Shi is arguing not for the viability of a literature in the vernacular (something that the very content of this extract reminds us had already nearly a two thousand year history by Hu's era) but rather for the complete obsolescence of literature in the earlier cosmopolitan idiom (i.e., wenyan), and in particular for the uselessness of that literature in the political and social climate of the time (six years after the overthrow of the last emperor and in the midst of the First World War). Where Desmarets is able to argue for an expected consonance between military and literary greatness, Hu Shi argues instead for the underdevelopment of Chinese as a national literary language in comparison to the national languages of Europe. The gesture resembles that of du Bellay in structure, but the difference in content is telling: Hu Shi does not apologize for the vernacular's literary poverty in comparison to its classical antecedent but rather for the backwardness of Chinese as a national language (guoyu) when compared to better-established national languages in Europe.

Moderns as we necessarily are, it is easy for us to side with the Modern, to see the defeat of the Ancient as a victory for a liberal, individualist, secularist public sphere against obscurantism and antiquarianism. Such was obviously the narrative of the Moderns themselves, and versions of their rhetoric have been the common property of all aesthetic and intellectual innovators since, including first of all the Romantics whose own manifestoes tended to attack, in the name of innovation, precisely the values that the Moderns of a previous century had embodied. The preface to Aubert de Gaspé's *L'influence d'un livre* of 1837, discussed earlier, thus proclaims, in a manner indebted to Victor Hugo's preface to *Cromwell*, that "Les romanciers du dix-neuvième siècle ne font plus consister le mérite d'un roman en belles phrases fleuries ou en incidents multipliés ; c'est la nature humaine qu'il faut exploiter pour ce siècle positif"[38] ("Novelists of the nineteenth century no longer situate the merits of a novel in flowery fine phrases or in the proliferation of incidents; human nature is what this evidentiary century must explore").

世紀之活字；與其作不能行遠、不能普及之秦、漢、六朝文字，不如作家喻戶曉之"水滸"、"西遊"文字也。

38   Aubert de Gaspé , *L'influence d'un livre: Roman Historique*, prologue.

Scholars and intellectuals from Habermas to Casanova have recognized the "public sphere" of the Moderns as the decisive break with the illiberal past. And yet we should be careful not to support the Moderns uncritically in their efforts. As Marc Fumaroli has shown, the party of the Ancients offered a sort of public sphere of their own in the form of the "republic of letters" in its original sense of the European community of scholars engaged in the recovery of the classical past—and in the use of their engagement with that past as a vehicle for their critique of contemporary political conditions. Many of the earliest defendants of the Ancients against the Moderns were Italians, such as Alessandro Tassoni (1565–1635), who, in addition to his *Filippiche* against Spanish rule, published a collected *Pensieri* of 1620, a section of which engages in specific comparison between the Ancients and Moderns, to the advantage of the former. Another leading figure among the Ancients of this period was Trajano Boccalini (1556–1616), author of the *Ragguagli di Parnasso*, or "News from Parnassus" (1612), a series of parodic journalistic sketches from a Parnassian Republic of Letters ruled by Apollo. Significantly, one of these sketches imagines the arrest of the Roman historian Tacitus, whose writings are imagined as a pair of glasses that allow their readers to see the behavior of princes as they are within and not as they are forced to appear on the outside through the devices necessary for rule (*quali essi erano di dentro, non quali con gli artificii necessarii per regnare si sforzavano di far parer di fuori*).

If the shared pursuit of the Classics thus provided for many of these men (and for the women among their number) a space within which literary and intellectual life could exceed the petty and often repressive confines of their immediate political surroundings, those who supported the Modern against the Ancient tended, at least in seventeenth-century Italy, to speak explicitly for the state and for the established political order. In particular, Fumaroli argues, the earliest explicit claim for the Modern as opposed to the Ancient came in 1623, with the publication of *L'oggidì, ovvero il Mondo non peggiore né più calamitoso del passato* ("Today: or, the World Neither Worse nor More Calamitous than the Past") by Secondo Lancellotti. Fulsomely dedicated to Urban VIII, this work took specific aim at the partisans of the Ancients and made clear that its purpose in so doing was to glorify its patron by suggesting that, as the present era was the most glorious in history, the study of the Ancients should be curtailed in preference to the study of modern times. As Fumaroli points out, the reception of Lancellotti's work in France (Cardinal Richelieu commissioned a reworking of its contents in French by Daniel de Rampalle, *L'Erreur combattue, discours académique, où il est curieusement prouvé que le monde ne va point de mal en pis*, which appeared in 1641) did much to determine the shape of the Quarrel of the Ancients and the Moderns in France during the reigns of Louis XIII and XIV.[39] In place of the Italian Quarrel, under whose guise debates concerning the autonomy of the literary and intellectual sphere took place, the French Quarrel of this period featured contestants from both sides competing in panegyric to the monarch, with Moderns exalting their king's greatness at the expense of rulers of the Greco-Roman past, and Ancients pleading the inadequacy of the literature of their own time to the task of praising that greatness (in the words of Boileau's *Discours au roi*, "Pour chanter un Auguste, il faut être un Virgile," "One must be a Virgil to praise an Augustus in song").[40] A further consequence of these shifts (of the epicenter of the Quarrel to Paris and of its focus to *raisons d'état*) was to elevate the status of French with respect both to Latin and to Italian, a move of obvious political significance for the French court. Henceforth, and as documented by, among others, Pascale Casanova in *La république mondiale des lettres*, the French language and French literature would assume something of the cosmopolitan role previously enjoyed by Latin, a sort of vernacular cosmopolitanism. This cosmopolitanism certainly had a very real force in the eighteenth, nineteenth, and early twentieth centuries but was always in a dynamic tension with the status of French as the national language of the nation-state par excellence. As we saw in the chapter on cosmopolitanism, it is often the *lack* of a clear mapping of language onto polity that makes a cosmopolitan language flourish as such, and while French certainly provided many writers with a medium through which to escape domestic political entanglements, it was hardly innocent of such entanglements of its own, as our discussion of the discovery of the *Chanson de Roland* will suggest. Moreover, the very status of French as a cosmopolitan language was, to some extent, the result of official French policy, under Richelieu and later, a very self-conscious attempt to seize this prerogative from Latin (and Italian), thus enhancing the glory of the French nation.

In the previous chapter, we saw the relatively muted form that advocacy for the vernacular took in early modern China. The Quarrel, when it arrived, would be expressed in explicitly national terms by the debates surrounding the so-called May Fourth Movement, named after student

---

39   Marc Fumaroli, "Les abeilles et les araignées," in *La Querelle des Anciens et des Modernes*, edited by Anne-Marie Lecoq, Paris: Éditions Gallimard, 2001, 101.

40   Ibid., 144–5.

protests held in Beijing on May 4, 1919, to protest the nascent Republican government's ineffectual stance in the negotiations for the Treaty of Versailles with respect to the status of the former German concessions in Shandong province. In this movement (also known as the "New Culture Movement" 新文化運動) the Moderns were forcefully represented by Hu Shi 胡適 (1891–1962), whose essay on the subject we have already examined briefly, and by Chen Duxiu 陳獨秀 (1879–1942), among others, while the Ancients, as it were, enjoyed strong support from figures such as Yan Fu 嚴復 (1854–1921) and Lin Shu 林紓 (1852–1924), both prominent translators of European fiction into literary Chinese.[41]

In returning to Hu Shi here, I wish to emphasize in particular the relationship he posits between the vernacular and inputs from outside China. At each stage, the vernacularization he lauds is specifically linked to an outside influence, whether with the translation of Buddhist texts or with rule by Northern "barbarian" dynasties under the Liao, Jin, and Yuan. The reassertion of authority by the Ming, usually seen as something of a triumph of "Chinese" culture over its regional rivals, Hu instead represents as the return of the deadening hand of the cosmopolitan language. Hu is silent on the most recent dynasty, the Qing; also foreign (in this case Manchu), the Qing cannot of course represent a resurgence of the vernacular for Hu, despite the considerable bulk of vernacular literature published during the era, since to do so would make it impossible for Hu's own Republican era to right the wrongs of the past. The Qing, like the Ming, becomes in this history an era in which official literature became ever more backward-looking, while vital popular literature bubbled with increasing vigor beneath the surface. That Hu should link openness to the outside world to vernacularization and national literature may seem odd at first, but the implicit argument here is reinforced by the references to Dante and Luther; just as China profited from outside influences in assimilating Buddhism and in democratizing its culture in the Yuan, so, too, can it profit now (and become more truly its own national self) by again accepting outside influence, this time from Europe. More specifically, the sort of influence to be taken is

41   The leading sources for the canonical history of the May Fourth Movement in European languages are Cezong Zhou, *The May Fourth Movement: Intellectual Revolution in Modern China*, Harvard East Asian Studies 6, Cambridge, MA: Harvard University Press, 1960; Liu, *Les Mouvements De La Langue Nationale En Chine*. For a variety of revisionist accounts, see Milena Dolezelova-Velingerova and Oldrich Kral, eds., *The Appropriation of Cultural Capital: China's May Fourth Project*, Cambridge, MA: Harvard University Asia Center, 2002.

explicitly national in scope; although Hu places great importance on the emergence of spontaneous vernacular in China (and implicitly reminds his audience of the comparative length of that history, longer than that in Europe), the revolution cannot be complete for him without an explicit and conscious manifesto of the vernacular. The content of nationalist sentiment in China (as elsewhere in Asia) may have emphasized resistance to European influence; in form, as Hu understands things, the only way to fight European nationalism is with a European-style nationalism (and with it, national literature and literary history) of one's own.

If Hu represents the Modern position in this Quarrel and explicitly links linguistic and literary nationalism to the acceptance of Western influence, then Lin Shu, one of the leading Ancients, offers a much more complex picture of this relationship. Himself a prolific and successful translator of Western fiction,[42] although without knowledge of Western languages, Lin does not reject all outside influence, nor does he necessarily reject vernacularization *tout court*. Instead, Lin's position, much like that of the European Ancients, argues both for the advantages of continuity with the cosmopolitan tradition and for the ethical values that tradition taught, claiming them as more useful than ever in the contemporary era of crisis.

One of the most interesting interventions in the Chinese Quarrel is found in Lin Shu's satirical essay "Nightmare" (妖夢), originally published in the March 19–21, 1919, edition of the *New Shanghai News* 新申報. The conceit of the essay is that a student of Lin's, Zheng Sikang, recounts a nightmare in which he journeys through a version of the Buddhist Hell, encountering therein a city containing a "Baihua (Vernacular) Academy" 白化學堂. The intellectual leaders of this academy (thinly disguised representations of Hu Shi, Chen Duxiu, and Cai Yuanpei 蔡元培 (1868–1940), the then-chancellor of Peking University) unite in their scorn for both the classical literary tradition and the Confucian values it is said to embody, until they are eaten by the *asura* demon Rahu, whose consequent defecation obliterates the academy. Of particular interest here are the temple inscriptions Zheng Sikang describes. On the outer door of the Baihua Academy is the couplet:

---

42   For a much fuller account of the career of Lin Shu, see Michael Hill, *Lin Shu, Inc.: The Making of an Icon in Modern China*, Oxford: Oxford University Press, 2012.

> Baihua can do anything! *The Dream of the Red Chamber* and *Water Margin*
>   hint at enlightenment,[43]
> *Guwen* is gross! And what are Ouyang Xiu and Han Yu, anyway?[44]

Moving inwards, and using a topos whereby the successive gates of a Buddhist temple allegorize increasingly esoteric levels of teaching, Zheng encounters the "Shoot Confucius Hall," 斃孔堂, whose inscription reads:

> Birds and beasts are truly free, so what's the point of "constancy in human
>   relationships"?
> "Humaneness" and "righteousness" are really bad things, so we must tear
>   them up by the roots.[45]

As my translation hopefully makes clear, the language of these couplets is in a highly vernacular register, much more vernacularized in fact than the language used by Hu Shi. In particular, the line "What are Ouyang Xiu and Han Yu, anyway?" (歐陽修、韓愈，是什麼東西) dismisses in a highly colloquial style the great figures of the so-called Guwen, or "Ancient Prose," movement of the Tang and Song Dynasties, figures in other words who were known in their time (a thousand years prior to Lin Shu's) as archaizers, employing a deliberately old-fashioned prose style as part of an attempt to recover the ethical virtues they associated with it. In a gesture clearly legible to anyone fluent in the classical language (and designed to be opaque to those hypothetical future readers familiar only with the vernacular), the passage argues for what Boccalini might have called *occhiali di Confucio*, lenses of Confucian skepticism, themselves borrowed from Ancients of Quarrels past, through which to examine the present's frenzied rejection of both Confucian language and Confucian virtues (i.e., "Humaneness and righteousness," and, later in the passage, "Constancy in human relationships"). There is, moreover, a causal link between language and virtue here; pursuing the topos of the successive gates of the temple, vernacularization is the exoteric teaching for which the abandonment of Confucian ethics is the esoteric.

---

43   This last phrase, 真不可思議, could simply mean "is incredible." In the context, however, of the Buddhist imagery of the essay as a whole, I am inclined to the translation above, based on Buddhist usage.

44   白話通神，紅樓夢、水滸，真不可思議。/ 古文討厭，歐陽修、韓愈，是什麼東西。

45   禽獸真自由，要這倫常何用；/ 仁義太壞事，須從根本打消。

Throughout the piece, Lin is careful to avoid the suggestion that Western influence be rejected completely. He cites both Dickens and Francis Bacon in the moralizing epilogue to the essay in order to underscore his claim that the Moderns lack familiarity both with Western learning and with the Chinese tradition. More significantly, perhaps, he makes the claim that knowledge of the two need not prove incompatible:

> They take both constancy in human relationships and the classical language (*wenzi*) to be enough to crush men, and to harm the new learning; it is necessary to keep in mind that classical language (*guwen*) does not harm science, and that science in turn is useless to classical language. The two are unrelated, and every-one knows this.[46]

In the radically compressed timeframe of this Chinese Quarrel, then, we find the earliest partisans of the Ancients taking a position only gradually adopted by their continental European comrades-in-arms, conceding the merits of Modern science while arguing for the autonomy of the cosmopolitan tradition as a space within which to debate political and ethical issues. As in Europe, then, Chinese Ancients do not reject modernity as such, but rather argue for the usefulness of a sort of "public sphere" built out of shared reading of the classical past. I do not wish to suggest that Ancients such as Lin (or their European counterparts) were without their flaws; certainly, "Nightmare" is marked by moments of misogyny and xenophobia (the Hu Shi figure, for example, is described contemptuously as looking European), which can remind the contemporary reader of the real gains associated with modernity. Nonetheless, there is reason enough, I would suggest, to note at least in passing that, in distancing themselves from their classical and cosmopolitan pasts, both China and Europe also eliminated a particular possibility of intellectual autonomy, separated from the political realm by the use of the cosmopolitan language.

One of the consequences of the gradual defeat of the Ancients, in Europe and elsewhere, was a shift of emphasis away from this cosmopolitan ideal of the republic of letters towards a historicizing understanding of cosmopolitan literature as a part of the past.[47] In Europe, this meant a greater emphasis on Homeric epic as opposed to on ancient historians and to a model of Homer

---

46   以為倫常，文字均足陷人，且害新學。　須知古文無害於科學。科學亦不用於古文。兩不相涉。盡人知之。

47   Marc Fumaroli, "The Republic of Letters," *Diogenes* 36, 1988: 203.

understood in terms of folk tradition and orality, thanks to Jean-Baptiste de Villoison's 1788 edition of the *Iliad*, based on his discovery of the Venetus A manuscript of that poem,[48] and to Friedrich August Wolf's *Prolegomena to Homer* (1795).[49] The work of men like Wolf and Villoison was crucial, in the long run, for the emergence of Classics as an autonomous field of academic study, one that viewed its object of study as external to its own culture. With this turn to epic, then, Greek and Roman literature begin to be represented as important, but external, contributors to the literary ecology of modern Europe, now understood as including vernacular literature only.

This development has a close parallel in early modern Japan, where the assertion of the canonical superiority of indigenous Japanese literature over Chinese literature can be seen to have begun as early as the late fifteenth century.[50] As Japan began to emulate European models of the nation-state, particularly after the Meiji Restoration of 1867, this tended to lead to a devalorization of both the Chinese literary tradition and of the kanbun 漢 文, or Sino-Japanese literature (that is, texts written by Japanese authors in a hybrid of Chinese and Japanese, where the lexicon and word order are taken from Chinese but a variety of diacritical marks guide the reader to the correct Japanese word order, inflection, and syntax).[51] That Chinese and kanbun literature did not disappear utterly from the Japanese canon (in the way, say, that Neo-Latin literature, by and large, has from the European canon) is perhaps a consequence of the countervailing desire by some Japanese intellectuals of the era to situate Japan's national greatness within the context of a larger East Asian regionalist pride—a function of Japan's status at the time as the only Asian nation to modernize successfully. This led, by the early twentieth century, to a movement to "think for the Chinese in place of the Chinese"; that is, for Japan to promote a Sinocentric world view to compete with the prevailing Eurocentrism of the era—but to see Japan as the truer representative of "Chineseness." Simultaneously with this

---

48   See the discussion in Gregory Nagy, *Homer's Text and Language*, Champaign: University of Illinois Press, 2004, 7–15.

49   F. A. Wolf, *Prolegomena to Homer* (1795), Princeton, NJ: Princeton University Press, 1985.

50   Haruo Shirane, "Curriculum and Competing Canons," in *Inventing the Classics: Modernity, National Identity, and Japanese Literature*, edited by Haruo Shirane and Tomi Suzuki, Stanford, CA: Stanford University Press, 2002, 226.

51   Haruo Shirane and Tomi Suzuki, eds., *Inventing the Classics* 14; John Timothy Wixted, "Kanbun, Histories of Japanese Literature, and Japanologists," *Sino-Japanese Studies* 10 (2), 1998.

development, the academic study of Sinology (*shinagaku* 支那學) began to represent classical Chinese culture as an autonomous field of academic study, detachable from its contemporary Japanese context in much the way that classical scholarship in Europe from the eighteenth century began to see Greece and Rome as external to the literary ecology, rather than integral to it.[52] Contemporary debates in India and in the Indological community about the status of Sanskrit in twenty-first century India suggest a similar dynamic operative there.[53]

Shibboleth Texts and Literary History

The identification of Homer with popular oral tradition in turn shaped early nationalists (heirs to the Moderns) as they began to uncover early European vernacular epics, such as *Beowulf* and the *Chanson de Roland*, in the early nineteenth century, propelling the reading of those texts as oral and traditional as well, although with a difference: where the representation of Homer as oral served to distance Homeric epic from the present, the representation of early vernacular texts as oral, traditional, or folkloric was frequently deployed to emphasize historical continuity between primordial expressions of the nation and contemporary national literature. Traces of this move can be seen in eighteenth-century representations of Chaucer's role in English literature; in part, the reappraisal of Chaucer at this time can be seen as an English embrace of "variety" and the "rough but natural British voice"[54] as its governing virtue, as a strategy of differentiation against the French, who, Ancients or Moderns, valued purity of form above all else. Beyond this, Trevor Ross understands this development of eighteenth-century thinking about English literature in terms of a reassessment of works of literature no longer seen as rhetorical models but instead as creations of autonomous value; no longer as objects produced but as objects consumed.[55]

---

52   Kurozumi Makoto, "Kangaku: Writing and Institutional Authority," in *Inventing the Classics*, edited by Haruo Shirane and Tomi Suzuki, translated by David Lurie, 2002, 217–19. The quotation is from Naitō Konan, writing in 1914.

53   For the more pessimistic view, see Sheldon Pollock, "The Death of Sanskrit," *Comparative Studies in Society and History* 43, 2001: 392–426; Jurgen Hanneder, "On 'The Death of Sanskrit,'" *Indo-Iranian Journal* 45 (4), 2002: 293–310 offers a critical reassessment of Pollock's views.

54   Howard D. Weinbrot, *Britannia's Issue*, Cambridge: Cambridge University Press, 2007, 115.

55   Ross, *The Making of the English Literary Canon* 1998, 5.

Whatever the origins of this move, the consequences—moving the beginning of canonical British literature backwards from the 1580s[56] to the late fourteenth century—were considerable, making much easier the process of rendering earlier British authors "ancient" enough to effectively compete with the Greco-Roman tradition as objects of imitation and of consumption.[57] This device of chronological depth, of reading the national literature as a worthy competitor to cosmopolitan rivals through its own duration, is another one widely imitated in other contexts, most particularly in the form of the "shibboleth text."

I borrow the term "shibboleth text" from the work of Marita Mathijsen, who uses the term to refer to those medieval literary texts recovered in the early nineteenth century as a part of the project of constructing a sense of national history—most famously, *Beowulf* and the *Chanson de Roland*.[58] Derived in part obviously from the work of the Brothers Grimm and others (not least of them James Macpherson, whose publication of the supposed works of Ossian in 1762 provided a controversial but influential precedent), these texts were clearly the fulfillment of any national literature's dream of chronological depth. Here is seen one of the clearest differences between vernacular and national literatures, as well as one of the most powerful reasons to understand *any* variety of literature as a practice of reading. In their original compositional contexts, *Beowulf* and the *Chanson de Roland* functioned as vernacular texts, fulfilling literary functions in a restricted local context (possibly orally, though the matter is controversial for both texts), as an alternative to the cosmopolitan tradition in Latin. Rediscovered in the nineteenth century, both texts became instead works of national literature, read now both as providing chronological depth to modern literatures and, frequently, as embodiments of national characteristics.[59] The Ancients, in other words, no longer have even their own Ancientness as a defense.

---

56   Jonathan Kramnick points out that Johnson announced that he will would cite in his dictionary only texts written between 1580 and the Restoration. Kramnick, *Making the English Canon: Print-Capitalism and the Cultural Past, 1700–1770*, Cambridge: Cambridge University Press, 2008, 200.

57   Ibid., 4; Weinbrot, *Britannia's Issue* 2007, 140.

58   Marita Mathijsen, "The Editing of National Shibboleth Texts: An Historical Account," *Text* 17, 2005: 223–35.

59   For *Beowulf*, the crucial text in this regard is J. R. R. Tolkien, "Beowulf: The Monsters and the Critics," *Proceedings of the British Academy* 22, 1936: 245–95. On the *Chanson de Roland*, see Isabel N. DiVanna, "Politicizing National Literature: The Scholarly Debate around La chanson de Roland in the Nineteenth Century," *Historical Research*, 2010.

For all that texts such as *Beowulf* and the *Chanson de Roland* may well have *served* explicitly nationalistic purposes when added to the canons of national literatures, the actual history of the discovery of both texts reflects rather more the concerted efforts of an international scholarly republic of letters. Though it is known that the manuscript of *Beowulf* was in the possession of Sir Robert Cotton (1570–1631), tutor to the Earl of Oxford and one of the first English scholars to study Anglo-Saxon texts, the actual poem remained unstudied until the Danish philologist Grímur Thorkelin (1752–1829) travelled to England to read the manuscript in 1785. Thorkelin's attempts to edit and read the manuscript continued for many years and suffered many delays, including the destruction of the manuscript of his edition in the British siege of Copenhagen in 1807, before receiving final publication in 1815.[60] Even this laborious history of publication is not the end of things, since Thorkelin mistakenly believed the poem to be in an ancient dialect of Danish and to have been written in the fourth century AD; only with the work of Nikolai Grundtvig (1783–1872) was the poem's dialect correctly understood and, for the first time, translated into a modern European language—Danish—in 1820.[61] Only in 1826, with the publication of John Conybeare's translation of the poem into English (and, significantly, Latin) in 1826 did the poem begin to assume its status as a foundational work of "English" literature and of "English" identity.[62]

As if in recompense, the key manuscript of the *Chanson de Roland* was discovered by a Frenchman—but in the Bodleian Library at Oxford, not in France. Although John Conybeare had announced in 1817 his intention to publish *Illustrations of the Early History of English and French Poetry*, including an epic he knew as the *Roncesvalles*, his failure to publish this text, combined, perhaps, with a French lack of enthusiasm for discussing the matter of Roncesvalles in the immediate aftermath of the matter of Waterloo, delayed further discovery for another eighteen years.[63] Finally, in 1833, Francisque Michel, a young medievalist, eager to acquire for France the glories of medieval literature that the Germans had been exploiting since the Grimms and Herder (and that the English had just, almost in spite of themselves, acquired with the reception of *Beowulf* in

---

60   Franklin Cooley, "Early Danish Criticism of Beowulf," *ELH* 7 (1), 1940: 45.
61   Ibid., 52–55.
62   R. M. Liuzza, "Lost in Translation: Some Versions of Beowulf in the Nineteenth Century," *English Studies* 83 (4), 2002: 285.
63   DiVanna, "Politicizing National Literature," 2010, 7.

England), petitioned the Minister of Public Instruction, François Guizot, for funds to go to Oxford to study the Anglo-Norman manuscripts there, a petition that led, in due course, to the publication of Michel's edition of the *Chanson de Roland* (a title chosen by him) in 1837, an edition that framed the text as a model of appropriate monarchical and patriotic citizenship.[64]

Drawing for intellectual inspiration on the fascination with medieval and folk literature in Germany of the era (a phenomenon arguably anticipated in Britain, both with Ossian and with the canonization of Chaucer), French literary scholarship of the nineteenth century was thus able to provide their literary tradition with much-desired chronological depth, albeit in a way that depended on a text found in a British library and possibly composed for an Anglo-Norman audience.[65] As with *Beowulf*, a vernacular text with a cosmopolitan setting (it should be remembered that *Beowulf*'s action occurs in Scandinavia, the *Chanson de Roland*'s in Spain) is recovered by the citizens of a cosmopolitan republic of letters, put to work in the service of national interests, and read as a model of national literary and moral values.

In the process in both cases, sentimental eagerness to project the text as far as possible into the past may have overridden philological rigor. Certainly, Thorkelin's initial dating of *Beowulf* to the fourth century was unduly optimistic, and it was seen as such by his contemporaries; recent research, however, has suggested that the traditional date of the seventh/eighth century for the composition of the poem may be equally unsound and that the poem may date in its current form to the era of its manuscript, that is, to the tenth/eleventh centuries, and roughly to the era of King Canute (r. 1016–35).[66] Similarly, recent attention to the manuscript of the *Chanson de Roland* (which notes, among other things, that the Bodleian manuscript seems to have been from an early stage attached to a Latin translation of Plato's *Timaeus*), suggests that that poem may likewise have

---

64   Ibid., 9–10. As DiVanna demonstrates, the very remoteness of the *Chanson de Roland* from contemporary political concerns in nineteenth-century France rendered it all the more available to a variety of political readings: monarchist and republican, Catholic and anti-clerical.

65   Andrew Taylor, "Was There a Song of Roland?," *Speculum* 76 (1), 2001: 28–65.

66   Kevin S. Kiernan, "The Eleventh-Century Origin of Beowulf and the Beowulf Manuscript," in *Anglo-Saxon Manuscripts: Basic Readings*, New York and London: Routledge, 2001, 277–99.

assumed its present form only in the twelfth-century manuscript that has been transmitted to us *via* the Bodleian.[67]

Examples of such optimistic and chauvinistic projections of the national literary tradition into the past can easily be multiplied. Tomasz Kamusella points, for instance, to the appropriation of ninth-century liturgical texts in what is called by scholars "Old Church Slavonic" as, variously, "Old Bulgarian," "Old Macedonian," and "Old Croatian."[68] The discoveries of *Beowulf* and of the *Chanson de Roland* find a close parallel in the discovery of the *Charyapada*, a collection of poems thought to date from the eighth–twelfth centuries AD and found in the royal library in Nepal by Haraprasad Shastri, a scholar from the Sanskrit College of Calcutta, whose visit to Nepal in 1907 was motivated specifically by the desire to uncover early vernacular and folkloric texts; the poems thus uncovered are variously considered foundational works of vernacular literature in the regional Indian languages of Bengali, Assamese, Oriya, and Maithili;[69] in the aftermath of the creation of the tribally oriented state of Jharkhand in 2000, the *Charyapada* has also been interpreted as reflecting the early stages of the local Kurmali language.[70]

Modern readers of shibboleth texts, in other words, find it difficult not to impose on those texts the structures of the modern national-literature ecology, in which literature is composed in one of a discrete series of regionally distinct languages extending backward in time, a model that rarely holds much explanatory value for such early vernacular texts. At times, this nationalist appropriation of the vernacular past can take the form of temporal distortion, of insisting on the earliest plausible (or implausible) date for such texts in order to magnify the chronological depth of the national literature. More seriously and systemically, however, these appropriations assume that early vernacular literature functions within a national literary system and corresponds to national "languages," which emerge as literary standards only much later (often, indeed, simultaneously with the act of appropriation).

If the shibboleth text provides a national literature with chronological depth by projecting the origins of that literature far into the past, possibly

---

67   Taylor, "Was There a Song of Roland?," 2001, 53.

68   Tomasz Kamusella, *The Politics of Language and Nationalism in Modern Central Europe*, Basingstoke: Palgrave Macmillan, 2009, 28.

69   Amaresh Datta, *The Encyclopaedia of Indian Literature Volume One (A to Devo)*, Sahitya Akademi, 2006, 646–48.

70   Govinda Chandra Rath, *Tribal Development in India: The Contemporary Debate*, New Delhi: SAGE, 2006, 146.

creating a substantial gap between that text and the later, more continuous tradition, the device of literary history seeks to strengthen that claim to depth by constructing a continuous narrative of literary production. René Wellek, among others, has noticed the connection between the writing of literary history and the emergence of the notion of the national literature and in particular the contemporaneous development of the idea of progress and the recovery of medieval literature.[71] This recovery, as I have suggested, continued in many respects the work of the Moderns. Renaissance humanists (and the party of the Ancients descended from them) sought to elevate the present through the recovery of the Greco-Roman past and the emulation of its values (and in the process sought to bracket the Middle Ages as a time best forgotten). In contrast, Moderns and nationalists alike found in the medieval period an "Ancient" of their own, one linked to their own world through the metonymies of temporal narrative, geographic contiguity, and cultural identity. It is worth remembering in this context Jean Desmarets, defender of French literature against the Classical past, was also the author of the *Clovis* (1657), an epic poem on the fifth-century king, the first Catholic to rule France. Where the Ancients had understood European literary ecology in terms of a cosmopolitan past and engaged in the shared labor of the recovery of (and vernacular rivalry with) Greek and Latin antiquity, Moderns increasingly thought in terms of the simultaneous evolution of national literatures in competition and in complementary distribution across the political landscape, with the classical past a marginal background presence. Literary history, like other forms of narrative, then, has a beginning, a middle, and an end: a beginning in early vernacular literature written against a cosmopolitan background, a middle consisting of all the rises and falls, complications and reversals found in any plot, and, if not an end, at least a *telos* in the triumph of the national literature, both against its cosmopolitan past and as an embodiment of national virtues in competition with its rivals.

Both Wellek and Claudio Guillén find the origins of literary history in the Italy of the late seventeenth and eighteenth centuries in works such as Gian Mario Crescimbeni's *Istoria della vulgar poesia* (1698), Giacinto Gimma's *Idea della storia dell'Italia letterata* (1723), and Marco Foscarini's *Storia della letteratura veneziana* (1752).[72] The positions taken by these

---

71   René Wellek, *A History of Modern Criticism: 1750–1950*, New Haven, CT: Yale University Press, 1955, I.27–28.

72   Wellek, *A History of Modern Criticism* 1955, I.29; Claudio Guillén, *The*

works suggest that later narratives had not yet crystallized; Crescimbeni, for example, was one of the founders of the *Accademia degli Arcadi*, dedicated to refounding Italian literature on decidedly Ancient principles, in 1690, yet his history is a study of vernacular poetry only. Foscarini, elected Doge in 1762 in the declining years of the Venetian Republic, serves as a reminder that, while literary history and "national literature" imply a certain typology of the relationship between literature and the political order, the precise contours of that order were still evolving even as the ecology was emerging.

It is in the early nineteenth century that the discipline of literary history emerged in a more recognizable form; Wellek identifies in particular the *Geschichte der neuern Poesie und Beredsamkeit* (1801–19) of Friedrich Bouterwek, Friedrich Schlegel's *Geschichte der alten und neuen Literatur* (1815), Abel François Villemain's *Tableau de la littérature au moyen âge en France, en Italie, en Espagne et en Angleterre* (1830), Jean-Charles-Léonard Sismondi's *De la littérature du Midi de l'Europe* (1813), and Paolo Emiliani Giudici's *Storia delle belle lettere in Italia* (1845).[73] Wellek claims that the earliest works of literary history were specifically national in character, motivated above all by patriotism. Certainly, there is much of the patriotic in these writers. Schlegel praises "die Kraft, der Reichtum und die Biegsamkeit" ("the strength, the richness, and the flexibility") of the German language and regrets that national traditions have been preserved only in scattered, fragmentary form among the people.[74] For his part, Sismondi, at the close of his study, accounts for his decision not to discuss French literature in terms that emphasize both that literature's dominant position and its uniquely successful appropriation of the stylistic merits of the Greek and Latin traditions.[75]

Such examples could, of course, be multiplied indefinitely. It is thus all the more interesting that, of all the works cited by Wellek, only that of Giudici is not in fact international in scope (and Giudici's history, the latest

---

Challenge of Comparative Literature, trans. Cola Franzen, Vol. 42, Cambridge, MA: Harvard University Press, 1993, 27.

73   Wellek, *A History of Modern Criticism* 1955, I.29.

74   Friedrich von Schlegel, *Geschichte der alten und neuen Literatur: Vorlesungen, gehalten zu Wien im Jahre 1812*, New York: Atheneum, 1841, 4. Note that Schlegel's terms of praise for the German language echo at a distance Philippe Aubert de Gaspé's characterization of English as "sublime et énergique."

75   J. C. L. Simonde de Sismondi, *De La Littérature Du Midi De l'Europe*, Paris: Treuttel et Würtz, 1813, II, 683.

of the group, is also the most explicitly nationalistic, motivated by a liberal nationalism in the mode of Mazzini).[76] At a minimum, each of these works deals with multiple modern European literatures; in addition to those works whose titles announce their international scope, Sismondi includes literatures in Portuguese, Spanish, Provencal, and Italian, while Bouterwek's twelve volumes covers the *Nationalliteraturen* (a term for which Bouterwek is an early source) in Italian, Spanish, Portuguese, French, English, and German, and Schlegel promises his reader *"ein Bild im Ganzen von der Entwicklung und dem Geiste der Literatur bei den vornehmsten Nationem des Alterthums und der neueren Zeit"* ("an overall picture of the development and spirit of literature in the principal nations of antiquity and modern times").[77] Far from simply recounting the glories of the national patrimony, then, these literary histories construct European literary space as a series of national literatures, each possessing a parallel history of development from the middle ages to the present; Schlegel goes so far as to add Greece and Rome to the list of "nations" whose literary history he will relate, subsuming even the classical past under the national-literature ecology. Indeed, these texts even reach beyond Europe to account for the literary system they describe: Schlegel includes a lecture on Indian literature, and a discussion of Arabic and Persian literature in his discussion of medieval poetry, while Sismondi, in an admittedly Orientalist gesture, claims that Spanish literature reveals *les parfums de l'Orient et l'encens de l'Arabie* ("oriental perfumes and Arabian incense") in a language accessible to European readers.[78]

If European literary histories seem to leave room for non-European literatures as external influences on the European system, then literary history, as it is exported to the rest of the world, seeks from the beginning to emulate European models and structures. Here, again, my discussion will revolve around the emergence of literary history in and around the May Fourth Movement in China. As Milena Dolezelova-Velingerova has pointed out, the revolutionary era of the early twentieth century brought with it the first works of synthetic literary history in the Chinese tradition, notably Lin Chuanjia's 林傳甲 (1877–1921) *History of Chinese Literature* (中國文學史) of 1904 and Huang Ren's 黃人 (1866–1913) 1905

---

76   Wellek, *A History of Modern Criticism*, 1955, III.83.
77   Schlegel, *Geschichte der alten und neuen Literatur*, 1841, 3.
78   Sismondi, *De La Littérature Du Midi De l'Europe*, 1813, II.493.

work of the same title.[79] As I have suggested, literary history in the European context is very much a product of the emergence of nationalism in the early nineteenth century; as such, this May Fourth interest in literary history can be read as another dimension of that movement's nationalism. Certainly, we can already see a strong interest in literary history as an instrument of nationalism, as demonstrated by the very use of the term "Chinese Literature," (*Zhongguo* wenxue 中國文學), a strikingly national label for a literature that had previously represented itself as universal and cosmopolitan, and by the repeated use of the term "national language" (guoyu 國語) to refer both to baihua in China and to national literary languages in Europe.

Even more strikingly, the passage from Hu Shi cited earlier constructs a miniature literary history of "Chinese Literature," complete with the desired beginning, middle, and end, structured according to a narrative in which progress equals vernacularization. As represented by Hu Shi, Chinese Literature begins with texts in wenyan style: terse, allusive, and artificial (and, although he does not press this point, generally allied with orthodox state Confucianism). The narrative arc of Chinese literary history for Hu is the story of the gradual vernacularization of the literary language; in this passage, this story is embodied in the sequence of translations of Buddhist scriptures, informal philosophical texts of the Song Dynasty, vernacular elements in Tang (618–907) and Song (960–1279) poetry, and then the great flowering of vernacular fiction and drama beginning during the foreign Liao (907–1125) and Jin (1115–1234) Dynasties in Northern China and reaching its peak under the Mongol Yuan Dynasty (1271–1368; an era that conveniently coincides with Dante's lifespan). The plot thereafter becomes somewhat confused; Hu wants to see the Ming as an era of decline (since official and canonical literature returned to a more classicizing register of the language); yet his greatest models for baihua prose, including Shi Nai'an, are actually active under the Ming, not the Yuan. This seeming inconsistency is less problematic for Hu in that his entire literary history is implicitly hostile to the orthodox political and intellectual culture, preferring throughout the essay Daoist or Buddhist texts to orthodox Confucian ones. Hu is thus able in effect to argue that, as official political culture moves farther and farther

---

79   Milena Dolezelova-Velingerova, "Literary Historiography in Early Twentieth-Century China (1904–28): Constructions of Cultural Memory," in *The Appropriation of Cultural Capital*, edited by Milena Dolezelova-Velingerova and Oldrich Kral, 2002, 123.

from the vernacular ideal he finds in the Yuan, popular literature continues to grope towards that ideal—needing of course his manifesto and the histories that surround and endorse it to legitimate and guide that movement. The literary history Hu sketches has a narrative of progress towards the future, as the literary language ever more closely approximates the spoken language and moves ever farther away from the classical past (even if, as we have already seen, Hu has trouble distinguishing between the contemporary vernacular and the representation of vernacular language in fourteenth-century fiction). Just as (in a parallel explicitly drawn by Hu) the European Moderns of the seventeenth and eighteenth centuries were able to kill off the "dead" Latin literature of the republic of letters, so Hu hoped to erase the classicizing literary tradition of China, concealing it under the sign of progress. The very success of the May Fourth Movement (and the gradual reemergence of China on the world stage as the twentieth century continued) consolidated this narrative, by now orthodox, rendering much of the literary tradition, particularly that of the Song Dynasty and after, invisible by reason of its insufficient vernacularity.

Conclusion: Underdevelopment and Other Embarrassments

So powerful are these literary historical narratives of progressive vernacularization and of the emergence of national literature out of vernacular shibboleth-texts that even their absences or failures structure the literary histories of nations. Those nations who find their own vernacular traditions too brief or too insubstantial (a category to which all nations at some time belong) replace the narration of chronological depth by apologias for literary underdevelopment. These can follow in the paths of a Dante, a du Bellay, or a Hu Shi, concentrating on the perceived inadequacy of the vernacular language as a literary medium. Frequently, however, and especially where the language in question is already well-established in literary use elsewhere, we find instead protestations of backwardness, together with promises for the future. These apologies frequently connect literary to economic development, sometimes suggesting that the latter needs to be tempered by the former, as with Edward Hartley Dewart in the introduction to his 1864 anthology of (English-) Canadian poetry:

> There is probably no country in the world, making equal pretensions to intelligence and progress, where the claims of native literature are so little felt, and

where every effort in poetry has been met with so much coldness and indifference, as in Canada.[80]

At the opposite end of the Americas, Bartolomé Mitre, in lamenting the poverty of the Latin American novelistic tradition, wrote in the prologue to his *Soledad* (1847), the first complete novel published in Argentina:

> South America is the poorest region of the world in original novelists. If we tried to investigate the causes of this poverty, we would say that it seems that the novel is the highest expression of the civilization of a people, like those fruits which blossom only when the tree is in the full plenitude of its development.[81]

As a Unitarian advocating a strong central state as part of the political debates of the era, Mitre characteristically ignores the lively regional lyric tradition of his era (much admired by Federalist public figures and rooted in local popular traditions[82]) and, later in the prologue, draws an explicit parallel between stages of economic development and the evolution from epic to lyric to novel. The narrative of literary history is meant to be a progressive one, with progress (in Argentina and elsewhere) represented in terms of this same evolution of genres as well as in the sloughing off of the cosmopolitan past (as we saw in particular with Hu Shi). Left out of these highly legible narratives are extant cosmopolitan traditions (and cosmopolitan registers in vernacular texts), as well as texts whose ambitions are ill-suited to their position within the narrative, whether because they aim at a level of literary sophistication thought inappropriate to their place in the historical narrative or because their commitment to the nation is too ambivalent or framed too much in terms of international or metropolitan trends (some texts, such as Gaspé's *L'influence d'un livre*, manage both). Omitted also, one might add, are texts written in regional dialects or failed

---

80   Edward Hartley Dewart, *Selections from Canadian Poets*, s.n., 1864, ix–x.

81   La América del Sur es la parte del mundo más pobre de novelistas originales. Si tratásemos de investigar las causas de esta pobreza, diríamos que parece que la novela es la más alta expresión de la civilización de un pueblo, a semejanza de aquellos frutos que sólo brotan cuando el árbol está en toda la plenitud de su desarrollo.

82   See Beatriz Bragoni, "Lenguaje, formatos literarios y relatos historiográficos. La creación de culturas nacionales en los márgenes australes del antiguo imperio español," in *Relatos de Nacion. La construccin de las identidades nacionales en el mundo hispnico* (2 vols.), edited by Francisco Colom Gonzlez, Madrid: Iberoamericana Vervuert, 2005, 561–96.

versions of national vernaculars. All such texts encounter difficulty in adapting to the national literary environment and tend to struggle to be heard in the venues in which that environment is organized—literary histories, as we have seen, most of all, but also school curricula in this era of mass education and the emergence of university programs in national literatures and of course through such publishing venues as anthologies and collections of "great books."

What survives, indeed thrives, in these eras, are of course those texts that fit the narrative of literary history especially well, and it is worth remembering that the success of these texts in a national-literature ecology is often in direct contrast to their fate in earlier eras; *Beowulf,* the *Chanson de Roland*, and the *Charyapada* languished on library shelves for so many centuries because what they had to offer—a pre-history of literature in the vernacular—was not especially compelling to eras prior to the great Quarrels, when scholars combed many of the same shelves but in search of texts from the cosmopolitan tradition. Similarly, the canon of pre-modern Chinese literature was upended by the advent of Western-style literary history, and Hu Shi and others placed extreme value on forms (Buddhist literature, early vernacular short stories, and the great novels and dramas of the Yuan) treated with little respect in their eras of composition. Manzoni's sheets became the more valuable for his washing them in the Arno, and Chaucer's rough British naturalness gained favor in an England searching for distinctive literary virtues against the hegemony of the French.

To a great extent, of course, it is within the national literary ecology that we still find ourselves today; certainly, the institutional structures around which literature operates—school curricula, literary histories, anthologies, and reference works, publishing houses, and prize committees—still generally operate on national assumptions. The political legacy of state formation in early modern Europe, and of European colonialism and its resistance, of course, have much to do with this. As we have seen throughout this book, however, one of the imperatives of *any* literary system is to reduce information, to reduce canons to manageable proportions by identifying entire categories of literature that can be ignored and by establishing criteria for evaluating what remains. The means by which this reduction of information takes place have never been politically neutral, and the criteria for reduction always have political causes, but the need for this reduction to take place is, in the end, an inevitable consequence of the sheer volume of literary production. No literary ecology, therefore, should be disparaged simply because some form of literary production fails to be viable within it; that much is unavoidable.

Finally, while any nation-state can constitute itself as a national literary space, it is clear that the overall system of national literatures cannot accommodate an unlimited number of nations. Again, this question is never politically neutral; a rough estimate would suggest that the national-literary world-system accommodates, first of all, "major" European literatures (especially relatively early entrants, such as France, Britain, Italy, Spain, and Germany), then the literatures of European settler-colonies (especially when they are large enough to overshadow their metropolitan antecedents, as in English, Spanish, and Portuguese), followed by postcolonial literatures in major European languages (frequently considered *en masse* rather than as individual national traditions). Next we find a handful of literatures in non-European languages (notably Chinese, Japanese, and Arabic), traditions large and enduring enough to remain visible in spite of their distance from the core of the system; finally, the various literatures of minor European nations, minority literatures within nations otherwise represented, and, most remote of all, literatures in smaller or less commonly studied non-European languages, which the national-literature system is barely able to notice at all.

Even in the case of settler and postcolonial literatures in European languages, the academy (and, a fortiori, the larger reading public) has a tendency to envision New World and postcolonial literatures in terms of regions rather than nations. For example, a recent handbook conjoins the literatures of Papua New Guinea and the various Pacific Islands (written in English, French, and Spanish) with literature by Māori authors and that by New Zealand settlers into an "Oceanian" literature.[83] Tellingly, the *Oxford Studies in Postcolonial Literature*, to which the volume belongs, contains in addition volumes on Australian literature, the Indian English novel, and West African literature, as well as a general volume on postcolonial poetry in English. Within a national or regional context, it might be desirable to speak of the literature of Papua New Guinea or of Ghana, and certainly

---

83   Michelle Keown, *Pacific Islands Writing: The Postcolonial Literatures of Aotearoa/New Zealand and Oceania*, New York: Oxford University Press, 2007. Notably, Australian literatures (whether Aboriginal or settler) are excluded from Keown's book, both because the indigenous cultures of Australia are not related to those of the broader Pacific—and because Australia is large enough and visible enough to the core regions of the world-system to merit its own volume within the *Oxford Studies in Postcolonial Literature*. (Ibid., 17.)

writers from these nations frequently write from a position critically concerned with their own nation-state; within the broader Anglosphere, these national literatures get subsumed under larger regional categories, if not under a general "Postcolonial Literature," a national literature for a lost empire, as do their equivalents in the *Francophonie*; even the literatures of Latin America, which certainly represent themselves as specifically national in scope, tend to be thought of as a unit by Anglophone readers. As we shall see in the next chapter, the reception of two of the major world novels of the past half-century, Gabriel García Márquez's *Cien años de soledad* and Salman Rushdie's *Midnight's Children*, at least in Europe and North America, has tended to see the former as a work of "Latin American" fiction and the latter as a novel of the "Postcolonial" world, downplaying the very unambiguous status of both works as novels of explicitly national history, very much in the mode, say, of Manzoni's *I promessi sposi*.

As this last paragraph suggests, there is reason to suppose that the national-literature system may be reaching the limits of its capacity to effectively reduce information at precisely the moment when globalization and the gradual weakening of Euro-American economic hegemony are beginning to suggest the need to incorporate non-European literatures more fully into the system. Quite simply, there are too many nations for the system to accommodate a literature for each while still maintaining the privileges of early entrants to the system. The tendency (in the core of the system, at least) to think of non-European national literatures in groups, such as "Latin American literature," "Arabic literature," "South Asian literature in English," "Francophone literature," and so on, is an index of the system's strain. There are early signs that a handful of literary languages, mostly of European origin, may be moving towards post-national configurations in which language, rather than nation, is the primary criterion for classification and in which literatures begin to become truly global. How far this tendency has progressed, what its limitations might be, and what niches might be available for non-globalizing literatures will be the subject of the next chapter.

CHAPTER 6

Global Literature

This chapter, which unlike those that precede it discusses a hypothetical future ecology, rather than one that has existed in the past or exists today, requires a conceptual and methodological shift. Where in previous chapters my focus has been on an empirical examination of evidence for the structure and function of actually existing literary ecologies (present or past), particularly through the reading of texts that reflect in some way on ecological conditions, this chapter lacks a readily identifiable body of texts available for examination. Therefore, while I do turn in a later portion of the chapter to examine a particular narrative structure that I identify as representative of an emergent global literary ecology (a structure that I term the "plot of globalization"), the major focus of this chapter is instead on ecological conditions operative in the present, with a view towards an understanding of how those conditions might change in the future. What is the literary environment of the world like today, and how might currently existing trends, or unpredictable future ones, transform that environment?

In conducting this examination, I find it helpful to borrow certain notions from the discipline of ecology, and in particular thinking on the question of the minimum viable population (MVP) for a given species; that is, the minimum population of that species needed in the present to ensure its long-term viability. The need for such a concept is apparent in, for example, balancing the establishment of parks and wildlife reserves against the claims of human economic development; if the goal of such reserves is to maintain the viability of one or several species, then it would be useful to know just how many of that species we need to preserve now in order to ensure the species' future and, consequently perhaps, just how much (and which) land must be set aside to do so. That said, the variables involved are complex and interact with each other in complex ways, and all predictions about the future are inherently uncertain, with the result that this vitally important calculation is difficult to resolve with any reasonable degree of certainty.

At the same time, the urgency of the issues involved makes it necessary at least to attempt to produce a number. In an influential and often-cited

1992 article, ecologist Mark Boyce identifies the key issues faced in making calculations about minimum viable populations.[1] According to Boyce, and the work that has followed his, with small populations, *stochastic* factors are often as significant (or more so) than *deterministic* ones; in other words, factors that have an element of randomness to their effects can have particularly catastrophic effects when populations are small, where a larger population would survive such a fluctuation virtually unaffected. Boyce identifies three kinds of stochastic factors at work in population viability analysis: genetic, demographic, and ecological. In genetic terms, a small population is comparatively likely to experience *genetic drift* (the presence of a particular genetic variation more frequently than would be expected in a random sample because small groups are inherently less random than large ones) and *inbreeding depression* (the greater likelihood that harmful but recessive genes will thrive in a smaller population with greater inbreeding). Demographically speaking, small deviations from expected outcomes in birth rate, life expectancy, age distribution, and the percentage of offspring surviving can have massive impacts on small populations, when with larger populations the same deviation would have a minimal impact. Finally, ecological changes (like a loss of habitat or climate change) are likely to have a more catastrophic impact on a smaller population, which may, for example, be very highly adapted to the very specialized environment in which it finds itself, where a larger population, with greater internal variation in genetics and adaptation, is more likely to contain elements within itself that are able to adapt to a new environment. The result of all of this is that it is not enough simply to calculate a threshold number above which a species is likely to be safe and below which it is likely to become extinct; population diversity and other factors are likely to prove critical as well, especially with populations that are small to begin with. All of these factors tend to support the increased likelihood of survival for larger and more diverse populations occupying a wider range of territory, but the results are not likely to be uniform across species; many plants, for example, are hermaphroditic and thus more prone to genetic drift, while some species are particularly resistant to it (to say nothing, for example, of the

---

1   Mark S. Boyce, "Population Viability Analysis," *Annual Review of Ecology and Systematics* 23, 1992: 481–506; Lochran W. Traill, Corey J. A. Bradshaw, and Barry W. Brook, "Minimum viable population size: A meta-analysis of 30 years of published estimates," *Biological Conservation* 139 (1–2), 2007: 159–66 offers a more recent survey of the state of the field.

low genetic diversity of commercially harvested varieties, which in this argument may be particularly vulnerable to change). Further, while attempts to increase the diversity of a population through mixing with a related but physically separated population may introduce new genetic material into that population, they may reduce diversity overall and may in particular eliminate locally advantageous adaptations. Predictions about the future viability of genetic populations are thus inherently complex and uncertain for multiple reasons.

In this, they resemble, I would argue, any attempt to predict the linguistic and/or literary future of the world. The analogy here is strongest of course with the question of the survival of human languages. Early work on this subject was focused on the question of a minimum viable population, making the tacit assumption that there would be a roughly uniform number across all languages; an early estimate of a minimum viable population of 100,000 led to the oft-quoted suggestion that 90 percent of all languages alive today would become extinct by 2100.[2] Subsequent work has paid more attention to additional factors beyond population size, and it has been shown compellingly that questions such as whether or not children are taught a language, the range of domains within which a language is spoken, and attitudes towards the language will be of at least equal significance. Terry Crowley, for example, argued for the medium term viability of Sye, a language spoken on the island of Erromango in the South Pacific nation of Vanuatu.[3] Although spoken by fewer than two thousand individuals, it remains (or remained, in the 1990s) the dominant language for communication in its local context on Erromango, especially after the extinction of two of the other languages of the island and the near-extinction of the third. The population is mostly fluent in both English (the language of primary education) and Bislama, an English-based pidgin language common across Vanuatu, yet according to Crowe, even those with post-secondary education feel more comfortable in Bislama than in English, the use of English in daily life is greeted with ridicule, and children continue to speak in Sye as their first language. Thus, a language spoken by one or two thousand people, adults and children, across their daily life, is far more likely to survive to the

---

2   Ken Hale, Michael Krauss, Lucille J. Watahomigie, Akira Y. Yamamoto, Colette Craig, LaVerne Masayesva Jeanne, and Nora C. England, "Endangered Languages," *Language* 68 (1), 1992: 1–42.

3   Terry Crowley, "Melanesian Languages: Do They Have a Future?" *Oceanic Linguistics* 34 (2), 1995: 327–44; Crowley, "How Many Languages Will Survive in the Pacific?" *Te Reo* 41, 1998: 116–25.

twenty-second century than, perhaps, the Italian "dialects" (more properly, languages distinct in historical evolution from the standard national language). The largest of these dialects, like Lombard, Venetian, and Neapolitan, are still spoken by millions and were the first languages of most Italians as recently as 1945, but their usage is declining drastically: between 1988 and 2006, for example, the percentage of families speaking exclusively dialect in the home fell from 32 percent to 16 percent, while the percentage of Italians communicating with strangers exclusively in dialect fell from 13.9 percent to 5.4 percent.[4]

If numbers alone are inadequate to predict the viability of a language, then the same is even truer of a literature. All other things being equal, a larger language is more likely to sustain a vital literary tradition than a smaller language, but there are real disparities between the strengths of particular languages and those of the literatures in those languages. As I will show in more detail below, a critical difference comes in terms of access to the global literary system; statistics on translation make clear that texts in even minor European languages are more likely to be translated than texts in major non-European languages. Sheer quantity of production (another "demographic" factor, if you will), matters as well, though unfortunately we lack good statistics on global book production by language. Other differences, of course, matter even more obviously, such as income levels and literacy rates among speakers of a language, the strength of the publishing and book distribution systems in that language, the presence or absence of significant levels of censorship, and the prevalence of competing literary languages within the same population. Moreover, each of these ecological factors is subject to considerable, even rapid change, and, as in the biological case, smaller literary languages are likely more vulnerable to these kinds of environmental shocks than are larger languages.

Worth considering as well, are analogues to the genetic stochastic factors taken from population ecology. At a given population level, some languages are spoken across a larger and more diverse territory than others, a phenomenon that brings with it advantages and disadvantages. Obviously, small and dispersed literary languages (the paradigm case here might be Yiddish) are always in a precarious position, as they are vulnerable to competition in every niche they occupy, while small but regionally concentrated literary

---

4   "La lingua italiana, i dialetti e le lingue straniere," http://www3.istat.it/ salastampa/comunicati/non_calendario/20070420_00/, accessed February 23, 2012.

languages (such as the smaller national languages in Europe) may have the evolutionary advantage of being well adapted to their local environments. So long as readers want to read stories about people like them and near them, such literary languages will continue to have a market.

At the same time, there are arguable dangers for a literary language in being small and concentrated (or even large and concentrated), dangers related to a lack of diversity. Consider the case of a hypothetical small national literature in a relatively prosperous nation, where institutions for producing, publishing, and interpreting literature are well established. However well established, these institutions will nonetheless be few in number and thus at risk, I would suggest, for the intellectual equivalent of genetic drift or inbreeding depression. Given a small number of publishers, a small number of periodicals reviewing literature, a small number of universities where literature is studied, it is statistically likely that a non-random collection of literary features—genres, styles, forms, tropes, themes, settings, and so forth—(to say nothing of such matters as popular reading tastes or schools of literary theory or criticism) will be privileged at the expense of others. Writers who write in particular ways will find it easier to get published and to gain recognition than do other writers. Moreover, since literary influence functions on something of an analogy to genetics, those kinds of writing that are rewarded in one generation are more likely to pass their features on to subsequent generations, with writers who choose divergent styles reduced to nonviable status, or inclined to seek audiences elsewhere in other languages. A literature that evolves in this manner may be viable for a considerable period of time (the more so since it is well adapted to its local environment) but may prove more vulnerable to the sorts of ecological shocks likely to affect all literatures in the future—notably, technological developments, changes in the economics of book publishing, changes (liberalizing or otherwise) in censorship regimes or in literary tastes, and changing competition with larger literatures, such as English, to name but a few. Larger literary languages, or those used in more diverse environments, may conversely confer recognition on a wider variety of texts, and thus prove more resilient in the face of external challenges.

All of the above may suggest guidelines by which the long-term viability of a literary tradition might be assessed, in ways that extend far beyond sheer demographic mass. In particular, it should be noted that there are alternative pathways to continued viability; size and diversity is the combination most likely to endure and adapt over the longer term, but for smaller languages, the most viable strategy might well be to conform as closely as possible to local conditions, forsaking diversity for adaptation and incurring the risk of "genetic drift" in the process. Beyond sheer size (demographics) and ecological factors, such as the strength of literary institutions or the wealth and literacy of native speakers, I would suggest that there are factors of diversity that are likely to matter. Even among relatively large literary languages, those used in many regions or nations are more likely to thrive than those used in just one nation, and those used in a polycentric nation are more likely to thrive than those whose nation is monocentric. A larger number of cities in which literature is produced, circulated, consumed, and interpreted creates the opportunity for more diverse criteria for recognition and thus more pathways to success for individual authors. Likewise, the more diverse the range of experience among authors and readers in a language (whether based on gender, socioeconomic status, immigration, first language, nation, region, or any other factor), the more likely that language should be to sustain literary innovation. Finally, the more access that literature has to the global literary ecology (through translations both into and out of the language), the more likely a literature is to evolve continuously over time and to adapt gradually to changing circumstances, rather than to remain static for long periods, only to succumb in the face of sudden change.

The phenomena I have described in earlier chapters in terms of necessary reductions in the level of information in a literary system can, I would suggest, have implications in terms of the population genetics concepts I outlined above. A panchoric system, especially one organized along the "Olympic" lines I suggested in Chapter 2, reduces considerably the quantity of literary "information" circulating, by presenting a seemingly uniform system of myth and/or poetry into which generic versions of localism can be inserted rather than allowing theoretically unlimited epichoric variations to circulate unchecked. In population genetics terms, the panchoric system integrates local populations, homogenizing those local populations to some extent but also linking those populations together to create a sum containing more diversity than each of its parts. The standardizations and universalizations that reduce the level of information within a cosmopolitan system likewise link larger and larger groups, increasing overall levels of diversity. Vernacular reformations reduce information by restricting its circulation to a subsystem, partly (but not exclusively) regionally determined; in this case, there is a certain potential for "genetic drift" within the (necessarily smaller) new vernacular;

that is, a danger that the small number of participants within that literature will express a more restricted and somewhat arbitrary subset of the
literary possibilities inherent in the cosmopolitan language. Nonetheless,
as we saw in Chapter 4, the interactions between cosmopolitan and
vernacular literatures do provide opportunities to expand the horizons of
possibilities for each; again, a development whose function is to remove
significant amounts of information from the system nonetheless leads to
a net increase in the system's overall diversity. As we saw in the previous
chapter, the national literary ecology removes a considerable quantity of
information from the system (principally, texts in the cosmopolitan
language as well as those in the vernacular not suited to the national
narrative); as this was replicated across the initial national-literature ecology (in Europe), which had already been well integrated in its earlier
vernacular guise, this led, arguably, to a reduction in information overall,
at least until the post-1945 era, in which non-European national literatures began to enter the ecology.

At each shift between one ecology and another, then, there has been a
tension between the development of literatures that reduced their internal
levels of information (or "genetic diversity") and a gradual increase in genetic
diversity at the system level, through the new ecology's capacity to absorb new
entrants. How will this tension work itself out in relation to an emergent global
ecology? Arguments can be made on both sides: the increasing dominance of
a handful of languages, especially English, the increasing concentration of the
publishing industry, and the increasing need for sales in translation to sustain
a literary career, are all factors pushing towards an increasingly homogeneous
literary world, one in which universality is achieved through the creation of a
monoculture. By this argument, which I discuss in more detail below, a global
literary ecology will result either in the hegemonic domination of literature in
English at the expense of all other literatures (and perhaps many languages),
or in the emergence of a sort of standardized "world-novel," designed for easy
translation and consumption abroad. At the same time, there are other trends
operative that might point in a different direction, technological changes that
(at least in principle) should reduce barriers to entry to the literary system for
authors and languages alike, the emergence of greater governmental support
for regional and minority languages across much of the world, and, on the
level of literary form, an increasing use of stylistic and formal devices to mirror
the complexities of our global system within the novel itself. These trends,
which point in the general direction of a more integrated, but not homogeneous, global literary system, may well have weaker forces at work behind them

than the forces of homogeneity I described earlier, though they may possess other advantages. In what follows, I sketch the literary and linguistic ecology of our time and speculate (based on the criteria above) on what the ecology of the future might look like, in addition to offering some suggestions for ways in which these trends might be reflected on the level of literary form; I further suggest possible steps to be taken to encourage a non-homogeneous global literary ecology.

THE LINGUISTIC AND LITERARY ECOLOGY OF THE WORLD

In thinking about literary ecology in our time, it may be helpful to turn to linguistic ecology, and particularly to the work of the Dutch sociologist Abram de Swaan.[5] De Swaan understands the languages of the world as linked by bilingual speakers, and his object of study consists of the network of such speakers connecting all languages into a global system. He identifies the vast majority of the world's languages—perhaps 98 percent of the estimated 7,000 languages in the world, but spoken by well under 10 percent of the world's population—as *peripheral* languages, languages known as mother tongues by their communities, but rarely if ever learned by others. De Swaan identifies as *central* languages the hundred and fifty or so languages that link peripheral languages through communities of bilingual speakers; the category includes most of the languages recognized as "national," as well as a number of regional lingua francas, and collectively they are spoken by more than 90 percent of the world's population. Included within this set are the *super-central* languages, twelve in number (Arabic, Chinese, English, French, German, Hindi, Japanese, Malay, Portuguese, Russian, Spanish, and Swahili), spoken by particularly large numbers of second-language speakers and providing thereby connections between speakers of the other central languages; in turn, knowledge of English as the *hyper-central* language links the other twelve super-central languages and thus the entire global linguistic system. Of course, any language that occupies a more central position within this system will occupy all the other roles for its own native speakers; as a native speaker of English, that language performs the mother-tongue roles of a peripheral language for me and is also the medium through which the overwhelming majority of my communication

---

5   For what follows, see Abram De Swaan, "Language Systems," in *The Hand-book of Language and Globalization*, Hoboken, NJ: Wiley-Blackwell, 2010, 56–76.

with speakers of other languages takes place, even if I know those other languages myself. The asymmetry of the system, in other words, provides enormous incentives for speakers of more peripheral languages to learn languages more central to the system but virtually no incentive for language learning that moves from center to periphery. Although de Swaan does not speak in these terms, clearly a greater degree of centrality is also a factor in the viability of a language; a more-central language with a smaller native-speaker population may be more viable than a less-central language with a larger native-speaker population, as in the case of the less-central language, native speakers may need to use a more-central language in significant domains of their life (including, possibly, literature) and may over time cease to use their native but less central language altogether.

There are challenges in applying this model from linguistic ecology to literary ecology. First of all, while verbal art is produced in languages at every point along the scale, from the peripheral to the hyper-central, written and commercially circulated literature is concentrated in the central languages, with super-central languages performing a disproportionate role. Here it is important to recall my paraphrase of Max Weinreich's famous expression that "a language is a dialect with a literature," discussed at further length in the introduction; not everything counted as a language in most contemporary listings of languages would qualify as a language under my paraphrased definition. As a result, de Swaan's category of central languages maps only imperfectly on to the list of languages central to the global literary system. De Swaan does not enumerate the languages he identifies as central but rather suggests that they are approximately 150 in number. Using the statistics of the SIL Ethnologue, the 150 largest languages in the world (not necessarily the most central, of course), would include all those languages spoken by more than 3–4 million people. Certainly, languages much smaller than this will only rarely form a significant part of the global literary system, but even many languages much larger than this number are all but entirely excluded from the literary system in the twenty-first century because of their non-correspondence to existing political structures. Many nations, from Germany and Italy to Indonesia, the Philippines, and Thailand, have seen the use of a single national language (derived often from a vernacular language with a strong literary heritage) as an important dimension of nation-building and have therefore (at least until recently) tended to discourage literary production in "languages" such as Bavarian (13 million speakers) and Lombard (9 million); Sunda (34 million), Cebuano (16 million) and North-East Thai (15 million). Even in India, where many regional languages enjoy the protections afforded by the support of a state government as well as institutional support at the national level, there exist comparatively large languages, in the sense understood by the Ethnologue database, that are not recognized at the state level, notably including Bhojpuri and Awadhi, both spoken by around 38 million people, nearly as many as Polish or Ukrainian (in certain contexts, both Bhojpuri and Awadhi are considered dialects of Hindi). As I will show below, there is an increasing tendency around the world towards the recognition of more languages on an official level, but when, as with the examples listed above, those languages represent regions of a dialect continuum without a long history of standardization and literary production ("dialects without a written literature"), contemporary attempts to create newly standardized forms risk creating a *mise en abyme*, where the very process of standardization creates demands for the recognition of ever more localized regional variants, which are in turn standardized, and so on. The attempt to generate a new written standard for regional languages in dialect continua may not only fail to secure the viability of the regional language vis-à-vis the preexisting national language (which, by virtue of its centrality, is more viable) but must also compete with still more local dialectal varieties, whose viability may in some ways be greater (since they can fulfill strictly local functions in communication with family, friends, and neighbors, for whom a newly standardized regional language is no more accessible than the national language already imposed from without). Literary languages have long acted as central languages (in de Swaan's sense) for a dialect continuum, whether through a cosmopolitan standard like literary Chinese or classical Arabic, or through a regional vernacular standard like the Tuscan promoted by Dante and sustained by his successors, but the communities they link are not always the same as those linked by spoken vernaculars.

Even to identify a list of the world's most-spoken languages is of course a task filled with controversy; boundaries between languages are fuzzy, and two of the very largest "languages" in the world, Chinese and Arabic, are in fact families of distinct spoken languages with an overarching written language, and the number of native speakers of different languages is often a matter of intense controversy. For the purposes of argument, I here draw on the work of the Summer Institute of Linguistics, a Christian missionary organization; problematic in the above respects and others but nonetheless one of the few standard references on the subject.[6] According to their statistics, and counting Chinese and Arabic as single languages, the twenty-five largest languages in the world are as follows:

Rank	Language	Total speakers[7]
1	Chinese [zho]	1,213
2	Spanish [spa]	329
3	English [eng]	328
4	Arabic [ara]	221
5	Hindi [hin]	182
6	Bengali [ben]	181
7	Portuguese [por]	178
8	Russian [rus]	144
9	Japanese [jpn]	122
10	German, Standard [deu]	90.3
11	Javanese [jav]	84.6
12	Lahnda [lah][8]	78.3
13	Telugu [tel]	69.8
14	Vietnamese [vie]	68.6
15	Marathi [mar]	68.1
16	French [fra]	67.8
17	Korean [kor]	66.3
18	Tamil [tam]	65.7
19	Italian [ita]	61.7
20	Urdu [urd]	60.6
21	Turkish [tur]	50.8
22	Gujarati [guj]	46.5
23	Polish [pol]	40
24	Malay [msa]	39.1
25	Bhojpuri [bho]	38.5

Eight of the largest languages are native to Europe, of which five (English, Spanish, Portuguese, Russian, and French) circulate across large former

---

6 Ethnologue: Statistical Summaries at http://www.ethnologue.com/ethno_docs/distribution.asp?by=sizehttp:// www.ethnologue.com/ethno_docs/distribution.asp?by=size, accessed January 14, 2012.

7 In millions.

8 That is the western dialects, mostly, of what is better known as Punjabi.

empires, and three (German, Italian, and Polish) are the national languages of large European nation-states, spoken also by significant diasporic populations. Nine (Hindi, Bengali, what the SIL calls "Lahnda," Telugu, Marathi, Tamil, Urdu, Gujarati, and Bhojpuri) are native to South Asia; many of these also have large diasporas, but are primarily regional languages within South Asia. Chinese, really as noted a language family, has more native speakers than the next five languages put together; 70 percent of this total speak Mandarin dialects, while five of the remaining dialect groups, Wu (including Shanghainese, total 77 million speakers), Yue (including Cantonese, 55 million speakers), Min Nan (spoken in Fujian province and on Taiwan by 47 million), Jinyu (spoken mostly in Shanxi province by 45 million), and Xiang (spoken in Hunan by 36 million), would be on or near the top twenty-five list in their own right. Arabic is likewise a family of spoken dialects, though as subdivided by the SIL only Egyptian Arabic (55 million) would make this list in its own right. The remaining six languages (Japanese, Javanese, Vietnamese, Korean, Turkish, and Malay) are the major or official languages of large Asian nation-states. No language native to Africa scores higher than thirty-eighth (Hausa, native to Nigeria, spoken by 25 million); none native to the Americas is higher than Quechua (seventy-ninth; 10 million). Eleven out of the twelve super-central languages identified by de Swaan are included here, the exception being Swahili, which the Ethnologue credits with an unexpectedly precise and low number of 787,630 native speakers; estimates of second-language speakers reach as high as one hundred million.[9]

FROM LINGUISTIC TO LITERARY ECOLOGY

An examination of the book trade in light of these statistics is illuminating. Unfortunately, no good statistics exist on book publishing by language; statistics are available from UNESCO by nation, but given that, as I noted earlier, nine of the twenty-five largest languages in the world are found in India alone (not counting English), these numbers shed little light on the prevalence of book publishing in different languages. More information is available for translations, also from UNESCO, covering the years 1979–2011; we are thus better informed about patterns of circulation than about literary activity per

---

9   Felicitas Becker, "Swahili Thought," in *The Oxford Encyclopedia of African Thought: Two-Volume Set*, edited by F. Abiola Irele and Biodun Jeyifo, New York: Oxford University Press, 2010, 362. No source is given for this estimate.

se and must exercise caution in making assumptions about the relationships between the two. Here, for what it is worth, are the top twenty-five source and target languages for translations, according to UNESCO:

Rank	Source Language	Number of Titles		Target Language	Number of Titles
1	English	1,168,470	1	German	290,386
2	French	210,159	2	French	237,646
3	German	193,219	3	Spanish	227,939
4	Russian	99,341	4	English	142,467
5	Italian	64,662	5	Japanese	124,213
6	Spanish	51,465	6	Dutch	111,203
7	Swedish	35,007	7	Russian	83,073
8	Japanese	24,618	8	Polish	76,510
9	Latin	18,742	9	Portuguese	73,266
10	Danish	18,633	10	Danish	64,729
11	Dutch	18,190	11	Italian	59,673
12	Greek, Ancient	16,751	12	Czech	59,453
13	Czech	15,659	13	Hungarian	51,403
14	Polish	13,759	14	Chinese	48,649
15	Norwegian	11,846	15	Finnish	45,760
16	Chinese	11,615	16	Norwegian	35,085
17	Arabic	11,556	17	Swedish	31,144
18	Portuguese	10,921	18	Greek, Modern	27,387
19	Hungarian	10,894	19	Bulgarian	25,787
20	Hebrew	9,563	20	Korean	21,722
21	Multiple languages	8,643	21	Estonian	20,482
22	Catalan	7,897	22	Slovak	19,567
23	Finnish	7,719	23	Serbian	18,733
24	Estonian	5,429	24	Romanian	18,474
25	Romanian	5,318	25	Catalan	17,966

While much discussion has focused on the position of English as a distant fourth target language (a discussion that usually omits mention of the fact English is itself the source language for more than half the translations done in the world, which serves as a real limit on the number of possible translations into English), another fact should be at least as striking here, especially in conjunction with the list of the top twenty-five languages above. Twenty-one of the top twenty-five source languages (all but Japanese, Chinese, Arabic, and Hebrew) are European in origin, as are twenty-two of the top twenty-five target languages (all but Japanese, Chinese, and Korean). Swedish, the eighty-eighth most commonly spoken language in the world is a more common source language than Japanese; Norwegian (ranked 132nd as a spoken language) is more frequently translated than Chinese or Arabic. Among the next twenty-five source languages, non-European languages fare somewhat better, with seven (Sanskrit, Korean, Farsi, Turkish, Bengali, Tibetan, and Hindi), but even so, this leaves Hindi, one of the five most spoken languages in the world, approximately as common a source language as such peripheral European languages as Macedonian and Albanian, Galician and Georgian.

The three dominant facts of the literary world in our time, then, are the general preponderance of English, the presence of a comparatively lively circulation of translated texts among European languages, and the general isolation of even very populous non-European languages from any kind of global literary system. These phenomena structure the global literary system, with English, thanks to both the British Empire and American capitalism, at the heart. Five other European languages—French, Spanish, Russian, German, and Italian—occupy positions close to the center, the first three partly because of their imperial circulations,[10] the last two in part because of the relative weight of their literary traditions within the European canon. Three non-European literary languages—Chinese, Japanese, and Arabic—maintain a significant, though disproportionately small, presence within the system, thanks to the chronological depth of their respective traditions and their sheer size and scope. The smaller national languages of Europe (and Portuguese, which despite its large native-speaker population and global spread remains peripheral) maintain a relatively sturdy presence within the system, reinforced by comparatively frequent translations into the larger European languages and into each other. The national languages of the non-Western world (aside from Chinese, Japanese, and Arabic) may feature substantial internal markets and lively literary activity, as well as rich literary traditions going back centuries, but they barely participate in the global literary system; when

---

10   For more on Soviet-era global literary circulations, see the 2011 dissertation by Rossen Djagalov, Yale University: *Literary Imaginings of Socialist Internationalism in the Age of the Three Worlds.* See also Djagalov, "'I Don't Boast About It, but I'm the Most Widely Read Author of This Century': Howard Fast and International Leftist Literary Culture, ca. Mid-Twentieth Century," *Anthropology of East Europe Review* 27 (2), 2009: 40–55.

they do, it is with the frequency of the smaller national languages and regional languages of Europe. As for the vast majority of languages, not made official at the national level and not originating in Europe, they remain almost completely invisible to the world system, their very names all but unknown.

As with translation, so with the formal study of the languages: while Chinese, Japanese, and Arabic are relatively well-established parts of the curriculum at many American and European universities, other non-European languages are generally only studied for antiquarian purposes or where there are large populations of heritage speakers. The Nobel Prize for Literature likewise sketches a similar pattern for a global literary system; of the 110 men and women awarded a Nobel Prize in Literature between 1900 and 2013, eight (Rabindranath Tagore in Bengali; Shmuel Yoseph Agnon in Hebrew; Kawabata Yasunari and Oe Kenzabuo in Japanese; Naguib Mahfouz in Arabic; Gao Xingjian and Mo Yan in Chinese; Orhan Pamuk in Turkish) wrote in non-European languages, of whom all except Mo Yan and the two Japanese writers wrote in Europe itself, on Europe's periphery, or while under European rule. By contrast, six Nobel Prize winners wrote in Swedish, three each in Danish and Norwegian, and one each in Icelandic and Finnish, for a total of fourteen in the languages of Nordic Europe. Other peripheral European languages likewise fared comparatively well (Polish: four laureates; Hungarian and Greek, two each; Czech, Occitan, Portuguese, Serbo-Croat, and Yiddish, one each; note again the perhaps surprisingly peripheral status of Portuguese), for a total of thirteen. Despite the sometimes paranoid concerns of Anglophone writers, English is in fact by far the most common language of Nobel laureate's work, with twenty-eight writers working in English, followed by French, German, and Spanish (fourteen, thirteen, and eleven), then Italian and Russian (six and five).[11]

That the systems of Nobel Prize laureates and of translations should mirror each other so closely is hardly a surprise; judges, after all, can only evaluate works they can read in the original language or that have been translated, and thus inequities in the translation system are almost bound to be reflected in the prize system. That the largest difference between the

---

11   Note that the statistics for languages add up to 112; two writers were awarded the prize for work in more than one language: Samuel Beckett (English and French) and Joseph Brodsky (English and Russian).

two systems is the relative prominence of the European periphery in the Nobel system is hardly surprising, given that the prize is in the gift of the Swedish Academy. Indeed, one useful way of thinking about the Nobel Prize might be to imagine it not so much as a device for establishing a canon of world literature but rather as a means of establishing a European canon, to which occasional non-European works can be admitted, with the specific task of augmenting the role of the European periphery within the European literary system.

That the inequities in the awarding of the Nobel are largely related to language, and not simply to nation, race, or ethnicity, is borne out by the nine Anglophone nations represented (the UK, the United States, Canada, Ireland, Australia, Nigeria, St. Lucia, Trinidad, and South Africa). Writers working in French have come from Ireland, Belgium, Guadeloupe, and Mauritius, in addition to metropolitan France, and writers in Spanish from six nations (Spain, Chile, Guatemala, Colombia, Mexico, and Peru). We see similar phenomena in the leading multinational prizes based in a single language: the Prix Goncourt has been awarded to writers from Reunion, French Guyana, Belgium, Algeria, Switzerland, Canada, Martinique, Morocco, Lebanon, the United States, and Afghanistan, as well as to French writers of ethnic origins ranging from Armenian to Senegalese. The Premio Miguel de Cervantes (first awarded in 1976) has been awarded to citizens of nine Spanish-speaking nations; the Man Booker Prize, to writers representing ten Anglophone nations (with several winners with dual allegiances). Winners of the Camões Prize (first awarded in 1989) have come from five out of the eight sovereign nations where Portuguese is an official language.

In what follows, I examine the status and prospects of a number of languages and groups of languages, divided according to criteria resembling, but distinct from, De Swaan's, using a perspective derived from the population genetics models I discussed earlier. For my purposes, I will treat English and French as *sui generis* languages in the global ecology, English for all the reasons De Swaan mentions, and French because, although it is no longer in such direct competition with English for global status, it is nonetheless the language most like English in terms of its global reach. I then consider a group of languages (a subset of De Swaan's central languages) that might lay claim to global status, as what I will call "regional world-languages": Spanish, Arabic, Portuguese, Russian, Chinese, Hindi, and Malay. Each of these is spoken by an extremely large number of people, either in many nations or in one large nation, usually over a broad but largely contiguous geographic area. I group the three remaining of De Swaan's central languages (German,

Japanese, and Swahili) together with languages such as Bengali, Italian, Turkish, and Korean, as "major national languages," languages mostly confined to one nation or to a small number of closely linked nations, with a rich national tradition, and (especially for the European major national languages) some significant capacity to enter the global literary ecology but comparatively few second-language speakers beyond their own region. I then consider smaller national languages as a group, followed by minority languages and then endangered languages; each of these categories participates (and will participate) in global literary and linguistic systems in limited ways, if at all. Each of these categories of languages has complex and distinct prospects and challenges within an emergent global literary ecology, determined not only by population size but also by number of second-language speakers, by the geographical situation of the language, its competitive position vis-à-vis more central languages, and the socioeconomic situation of its speakers, among many other factors. Note, in particular, that I have mostly ignored the latter criterion in my classifications of languages, preferring here to explore the potential each language might have given the sufficient economic development of its speakers.

English

The status of English as the world's preeminent vehicular language is almost too obvious to bear repeating, but a few statistics are in order. English is the native language of some three- to four-hundred million people worldwide, a second language known to some degree by unknown hundreds of millions more, and almost everywhere the most widely taught foreign language where it is not native. It is an official language of some fifty-nine of the world's nations, including four of the ten most populous (India, the United States, Pakistan, and Nigeria; it is also in widespread use in another of the top ten, Bangladesh) as well as increasingly enjoying official status in nations where it was never a language of colonization, such as Madagascar, Rwanda, and Eritrea.[12] A significant majority of all translated texts in the

---

12   For a discussion of the persistence of English in Bangladesh, in spite of decades of official efforts to make Bengali the sole language of government, see Rahela Banu and Roland Sussex, "English in Bangladesh after Independence: Dynamics of Policy and Practice," in *Who's Centric Now? The Present State of Post-Colonial Englishes*, edited by B. Moore, Melbourne: Oxford University Press, 2001, 122–47. It should be noted that of the decolonized Anglophone nations, Bangladesh has certain advantages that should make the replacement of English more

world have English as their source language, reminding us of the preponderant role the language plays as a vehicle for international cultural, commercial, scientific, and diplomatic transactions.

Given all of these very familiar facts, the dominant position of English within a global literary ecology for the foreseeable future seems assured. Indeed, the interesting questions to ask about the role of English are quite different: Will English literature remain under the control of its historical native-speaker communities, or will a kind of Global English take its place as a rootless lingua franca? And what role will other languages find for themselves within the ecology? The latter issue forms the subject of much of the rest of this chapter; a sizable literature now exists on the former.[13] Some linguists have argued that English should now be understood as a lingua franca, with efforts made to produce a descriptive account of that form of the language as distinct from the various native-speaker Englishes and calls for the teaching of English as a lingua franca (ELF) in classrooms across the non-English-speaking world.[14] Others have argued that the ELF model is itself too monocentric, seeking to replace the notion of a single, native-speaker authorized version of English (or a small number of such versions) with a polycentric model in which the vernacular Englishes of various nations (notably India, Singapore, and the Philippines) are recognized as coequal with native-speaker variants.[15] This model of World Englishes, in turn, has been subjected to still further critiques of its own, arguing that the assumption of national standards for World Englishes themselves suppress substantial variations of class, register, context, and so on, reifying on a new level the outmoded and problematic categories of language and nation-state.[16]

---

viable there than elsewhere: The overwhelming majority of the population are native speakers of one language, Bengali, widely spoken also in India, and enjoying a long and rich literary history of its own.

13   For a brief survey, see Alastair Pennycook, "English and Globalization," in *The Routledge Companion to English Language Studies*, edited by Janet Maybin and Joan Swann, New York: Routledge, 2009, 113–21.

14   See, e.g., Barbara Seidlhofer, "Closing a Conceptual Gap: The Case for a Description of English as a Lingua Franca," *International Journal of Applied Linguistics* 11 (2), 2001: 133–58.

15   Yamuna Kachru and Cecil L. Nelson, *World Englishes in Asian Contexts*, Hong Kong: Hong Kong University Press, 2006.

16   Paul Bruthiaux, "Squaring the Circles: Issues in Modeling English Worldwide," *International Journal of Applied Linguistics* 13 (2), 2003: 159–78; Suresh Canagarajah, "Lingua Franca English, Multilingual Communities, and Language Acquisition," *The Modern Language Journal* 91, 2007: 923–39.

These various options, obviously, offer recognition to an increasingly broad range of Englishes, certainly enhancing the diversity of inputs into the literary language and from that perspective enhancing its survival and health in population-genetics terms. Much of this argumentation is, of course, likely to prove somewhat upsetting and destabilizing to a native speaker of English, especially one from what Yamuna Kachru describes as the "Inner Circle" of nations where English is both official and the majority language.[17] In an often-cited quotation, David Graddol has claimed that "in [the] future [English] will be a language used mainly in multilingual contexts as a second language and for communication between non-native speakers."[18] In spite of the presence of hundreds of millions of wealthy, highly literate native speakers, is native-speaker English somehow endangered as a medium of expression? Where in particular does this leave literature in English? Will the English literature of the future be written in a variety of Global Englishes, or in English as a lingua franca, or will native-speaker varieties continue to predominate?

Clearly, the sheer numbers of fluent native speakers of English should ensure the viability of literature in native-speaker forms of English for some time. At the same time, I would argue that there are aspects of contemporary literature that may reflect an anxiety on the part of native English speakers over our control over our language, an issue I discuss at more length below but anticipate here. Horace Engdahl's comments on American literature as not participating "in the big dialogue of literature," Tim Parks's contrast between the pared-down style of contemporary writers in European languages and the exuberant diction and local color of American writers such as Jonathan Franzen, Vittorio Coletti's observation that American literature (like, for him, Israeli and Italian literature) remains more resolutely national than most other literatures today, even the linguistic subtleties of that ambivalent ESL teacher, James Joyce[19]—could these observations

---

17   Braj B. Kachru, *The Other Tongue: English across Cultures*, Champaign: University of Illinois Press, 1992. For Kachru, this "Inner Circle" of nations (including the United States, UK, Australia, (English) Canada, etc.) is contrasted with an "Outer Circle" of nations where English has official status but is not the mother tongue of the majority (e.g., India, Pakistan, Nigeria, the Philippines), and an "Expanding Circle" of nations where English is widely known but not official.

18   David Graddol, "The decline of the native speaker," *AILA Review* 13, 1993: 57–68.

19   Mario Nordio, "My First English Teacher," *James Joyce Quarterly* 9 (3), 1972: 323–5.

perhaps be understood in terms not of a hegemonic Anglophone culture indifferent to whether its products are accessible to foreigners but rather of a somewhat fragile and threatened culture, using its capacity to generate slang and pop-culture mythologies as an adaptation to ensure its continued viability in the world of Global Englishes? Many will disagree with this assessment, but it might be useful to remember here the discussion of Greek literary diction in the Hellenistic era from the chapter on cosmopolitan ecologies—even as the varieties of Greek used for political and commercial purposes converged on a lingua franca standard, koinê Greek, which stripped away the complexities of dialect and morphology found in local Greeks of the Archaic and Classical period, the linguistic resources of those same local Greeks became central to poetic language, which, in the Hellenistic era, became ever more recondite, erecting higher barriers against understanding by non-native speaker and by poorly educated native speaker alike, counterbalancing the tendency towards a linguistic monoculture represented by the koinê. Certainly, even if the linguistic exuberance of contemporary American writers has more to do with the traditional celebration of such exuberance in "nationalist" accounts of English literatures than with any anxiety about competition with Global English, it is possible to imagine such a one taking root in the future. A novel such as Paul Kingsnorth's *The Wake* (Unbound, 2014), written in what its author describes as a "shadow language" derived from Anglo-Saxon, might be understood as another working-through of the same anxiety.

And what of these future Englishes and the literatures (or literature) they may spawn? Will a literature in ELF take shape that uses some standardized and simplified form of lexicon and grammar to create a more universally accessible literature, avoiding the undeniable difficulties of native-speaker Englishes at the expense, perhaps, of variety and interest? Will English triumph as the world's literary language only to lose its distinctiveness in the process and, in losing that distinctiveness, sow the seeds for its own replacement by something richer and more attuned to local circumstances? Or will literatures emerge (or continue to emerge) in Global Englishes, exploiting the globalization and indeed creolization of the language as yet another resource to add to the richness of the literary language? The early evidence certainly seems to point towards the latter outcome, though it is worth noting here that there is a potential for tension between the creative impulses of Global English authors, on the one hand, and the desires of non-native readers and of publishers eager for global markets, on the other.

As even a casual study of postcolonial and world literature in English demonstrates the commitment that the writers of that emergent tradition share to enriching, rather than impoverishing, the English language; while it is possible to imagine a global literature in ELF that would feel impoverished to native speakers, the actually existing literatures in Global Englishes are, and will surely continue to be, vital and enriching dimensions of the English language. Whether through the use of Indian English in the narrative voice of *Midnight's Children* by Salman Rushdie or by the embrace of multiple registers of Global English (the pidgin-English of Canton, the learned English of the Bengali Brahman Neel, the mangled Franglais of Paulette, or the complex patois of Laskari sailors in the Indian Ocean), with narration in Standard English, in Amitav Ghosh's *Sea of Poppies* and *River of Smoke*, contemporary writing in English as a world-language remains as committed to the notion of English as an exuberant and varied language open to outside influence as were the eighteenth-century national accounts of English literary history we considered in the previous chapter. The continued vitality of literatures in English seems secured not only on the level of sheer size but also in terms of the range of participants within the tradition.

This, of course, raises another question, that of what sorts of relationships there may be among the various literatures in English in the future. As already suggested in the previous chapter, there exists a current tendency to think not of fifty-nine or more "national" literatures in English but rather in terms of a series of partially overlapping categories. British and American literature stand as distinct traditions, as do (at least within their own borders) the national literatures in English of Canada, Australia, New Zealand, South Africa, and Ireland. Literatures in English from Africa, the Caribbean, South Asia, and Southeast Asia and the South Pacific tend, for many readers in the developed world, to be understood either in regional terms (as above) or under the rubric of a generic "Postcolonial literature," with the status of postcoloniality occupying the ontological position of the nation. There is, further, a sort of "Booker Prize literature," consisting of the literatures eligible for that prize (the Commonwealth, plus Ireland and Zimbabwe; effectively, everything except the United States); now perhaps, with the new eligibility of American authors for the Booker, on the verge of merging into a single global English literature.

How will this complex system evolve over time? Will the national literatures in English of the various nations decolonized after the Second World War gain increasingly distinct positions within a global meta-literature in English? Will national-literature categories disappear altogether, merging into a single seamless global literature in English? For that matter, will literatures in English from outside the (currently) developed world begin to reach larger audiences in their home countries, or will those audiences continue to look towards national language literature for their reading? Any answers must remain speculative, although one clue, I think, lies in the complex citizenships and identities of many contemporary American and "Booker Prize" writers; the categories by which we organize English literatures are likely to remain, although with varying relevance in varying contexts. The distinction between Indian literature in English and Pakistani literature in English, for example, may be, and may remain, crucial for some readers and writers in both nations while a barrier to be overcome for others and an all-but-invisible distinction for readers beyond the subcontinent, especially when so many writers in either category make their homes, at least part-time, in New York, London, or Toronto. I suspect (and indeed hope) that writers of the future Anglosphere, whether natives of Chicago or of Chittagong, will carry dual passports: as writers in a national English-language literary tradition and as writers of Global English. The other question here, of course, is whether American writers in particular will choose to take on such an identity or whether they will remain in splendid, and lucrative, isolation

French

If there is a language that can in any way compete with English in terms of global reach, it is French, despite the comparatively small number of first-language speakers (estimates range from 70–120 million: at the lower end, comparable to Marathi or Korean; at the higher, to Japanese). One of the features making French a genuinely global language is the large number of second-language speakers (perhaps 200 million, depending on how broadly "second-language speaker" is defined); certainly, one of the largest such populations in the world. Further, it is an official language in twenty-nine nations (and fourteen territories) on every continent except Asia, and additionally serves important political and cultural functions in several other nations (such as Morocco, Tunisia, Algeria, and Lebanon), although it has official status in only two of the twenty-five most populous nations in the world: the Democratic Republic of the Congo and France itself (Vietnam, more populous than either, is a more distant member of the *Francophonie*). It is one of the six official languages of the United Nations, one of the three working languages of the European Union, and (along with

English) a working language of nearly every international organization in the world. The vast colonial empires built by France in the seventeenth and again in the nineteenth centuries are responsible, in large measure, for this spread. The strongly centralized nature of the French state has long been mirrored on the cultural level, with the result that French as a language and a literature is much more heavily focused on its center than is the case for English. Nonetheless, writers from the periphery have long achieved recognition, beginning with the awarding of the *Prix Goncourt* to René Maran of French Guiana in 1921, admittedly a gesture famously dismissed by Jean-Paul Sartre in his preface to Frantz Fanon's 1961 *Les damnés de la terre*.

It was as recently as 2006, however, that the truly global nature of literature in French became an active subject for discussion, beginning with the fact that five of the seven major literary prizes awarded in France that year were awarded to writers who were not ethnically French. The American Jonathan Littell, resident in Paris, won the *Prix Goncourt* and the *Grand prix du roman de l'Académie française* for his novel *Les Bienveillantes*; Alain Mabanckou, born in Congo, won the *Prix Renaudot* for his novel *Memoires de porc-épic*; the Anglo-Canadian Nancy Huston, resident in Paris, won the *Prix Femina* for her *Lignes de faille*; and Léonora Miano, born in Cameroon, won the *Prix Goncourt des Lycéens* for her *Contours du jour qui vient*. That any of these prizes should have been won by a writer not of French ethnic origin would have been no surprise; that all of them should was cause for discussion and was one of the inspirations for the manifesto "Pour une littérature-monde en français,"[20] expanded into a collection of essays later that year.[21] The manifesto argues for a radical rethinking of French literature as a world-literature, or *littérature-monde*, a polycentric system encompassing all literary production in French rather than a monocentric system built on the national literature of France with its hegemonic center in Paris. The writers draw explicit parallels with the analogic transformation of English-language literature over the past forty years, discussing with approval the integration of postcolonial literature in English into the mainstream of the Anglophone literary tradition, as measured by the Booker Prize, among other things.

---

20   Muriel Barbery, Tahar Ben Jelloun, Alain Borer, et al., "Pour une 'littérature-monde' en français," *Le Monde*, LeMonde.fr, 2007.

21   Michel Le Bris, Jean Rouaud, and Collectif, *Pour une littérature-monde*, Paris: Editions Gallimard, 2007.

The *littérature-monde* manifesto has attracted a great deal of discussion in the Francophone world and outside, not all of it positive.[22] The textures of this debate need not concern us here; for my purposes, the interesting thing is that the debate is happening at all, that a case is being made in France that the future vitality of the French language (both in terms of the extent of its use and of its internal resources) depends in some measure on the global status of French. Of the four European languages spoken widely outside Europe, there are three for which the largest number of native speakers is found in a non-European nation (English, with the United States, Spanish, with Mexico, and Portuguese, with Brazil). In spite of its global reach, French is the only one of these four whose major population of native speakers continues to reside in Europe. This continued centering in Europe has its advantages, including far greater access to the European literary system than that available to either Spanish or (especially) Portuguese, but it has its risks as well. With the exception of Québec and a handful of other locations, French outside of Europe plays a role more like that of English in India than that of English in the United States: a language of cultural, economic, and political prestige, one avidly learned by the upwardly mobile (and thus well suited for use as a literary language) but not a native language for many. As a result, it is perhaps slightly vulnerable to competition from English as a central language. It is also a much more highly monocentric, and thus monocultural, literary tradition than English. Potential centers for cultural recognition in French outside France are few, and each is problematic in some way. Outside of France, the three leading developed nations in which French is spoken (Canada, Belgium, Switzerland) each have a different language as its majority language; other large nations in which French is prominent (Morocco, Algeria, Tunisia, the Congo, Senegal, Côte d'Ivoire, etc.) are generally lacking in cultural

---

22 For discussions, see Alessandra Rollo, "Quel(s) français à l'heure actuelle? La littérature monde et ses retombées sur le pacte langue nation en France," *Lingue e Linguaggi* 6, 2011; Kathryn Kleppinger, "What's Wrong with the Littérature-Monde Manifesto?" *Contemporary French and Francophone Studies* 14 (1), 2010: 77–84; Charles Forsdick, "From 'littérature voyageuse' to 'littérature-monde': The Manifesto in Context," *Contemporary French and Francophone Studies* 14 (1), 2010: 9–17; Alison Rice, "'Pour une littérature-monde au féminin': Global Women's Writing in French," *Contemporary French and Francophone Studies* 14 (1), 2010: 19–27; Jeanne Garane, "Littérature-monde and the Space of Translation, Or, Where is la littérature-monde?" In *Transnational French Studies: Postcolonialism and Littérature-Monde*, edited by Alec G Hargreaves, Charles Forsdick, and David Murphy, Liverpool University Press, 2010, 227–39.

infrastructure and/or have experienced long periods of political repression. Future generations of Francophone writers around the world may grow to view Brussels, Montréal, Kinshasa, Dakar, or Algiers as rival centers counterbalancing Paris (in the same way that New York and London, Toronto and Sydney, for example, form rival centers for Anglophone literature, or Madrid, Buenos Aires, and Mexico City for Hispanophone), but for the time being, literature in French remains unusually concentrated in one city for a language so large and broad in scope, with possible consequences, positive and negative, for its long-term viability and strength. Tighter integration between metropolitan France and the Francophone and Francophilic peripheries (and closer cultural relations among those peripheries) can do much to ensure the vitality of French as a world-language and as a vehicle for world literature.

Regional World-Languages: Spanish, Portuguese, Russian, Arabic, Chinese, Hindi/Urdu, Malay/Indonesian

I discuss these languages together because they have certain properties in common. Each is among the ten most commonly spoken languages in the world, and each has a lengthy and rich literary tradition. As already noted, Spanish and Arabic are the official languages of more than twenty nations, and Portuguese of more than ten. Chinese, Russian, and Hindi are official in far fewer nations, but this is much more a historical contingency than a genuine reflection on the scale of the regions in which each is spoken. Chinese provinces and Indian states have populations of the magnitude of large European or South American nations; that these massive regions are merely sub-national units, while Latin America and the Arab world are divided into many smaller nations, has much to do with, for example, the unfolding of the Bolivarian revolution against Spanish rule in the New World, the regulation of the Arab world under a series of protectorates effectively controlled by England and France on the one hand, and on the other hand by the fact that China never passed directly into colonial hands, that the independence of India was negotiated as two (later three) nations and that of the Dutch East Indies as one. All of these factors are of considerable historical interest, which does not change the fact that each of these languages is spoken by an extremely large population over what is (mostly) a geographically circumscribed area, where the language in question is either the first language of the majority (Spanish, Portuguese, Russian), or is the only or the principal written language and interregional vehicular language across a dialect continuum (Chinese, Arabic, Hindi/Urdu, Malay). Spanish and Portuguese are of course partial exceptions here, since each is spoken on multiple continents, but in both cases the large majority of speakers are found in the Americas, providing an extremely large "domestic" or quasi-domestic market for cultural production in those languages. These two languages have relatively well-developed infrastructure for supporting transnational cultural exchange, including cooperative work on the regulation of the language (the *Asociación de Academias de la Lengua Española* and the treaty on Portuguese spelling, the *Acordo Ortográfico da Língua Portuguesa de 1990*), shared literary prizes, (the *Premio Cervantes* and the *Premio Camões*), and a long history of the circulation and reading of work produced across the nations. Such cultural infrastructure may be somewhat weaker in the case of the other regional world-languages, but they do have compensating advantages: status as a scriptural language (Arabic); continuity with leading traditions of the cosmopolitan era (Arabic and to a lesser extent Chinese);[23] close association with some of the largest and most successful projects of nation-building of the postcolonial era (Chinese, Hindi/Urdu, Malay/Indonesian); or association with a great almost-empire (Russian). Each of these languages coexists to some extent with (and in many cases is on the point of supplanting) hundreds of regional and local languages, from the Amazonian rainforest to the Himalayas to New Guinea to Siberia.

The status of these languages as regional in scope has implications, from a population genetics perspective, for their long-term viability. On the one hand, they are less truly global in reach than English or French and thus in a sense less diverse in the resources they bring to literature. On the other hand, the sheer size of the regions in which they dominate as literary languages carries with it certain advantages as compared with French, especially with respect to polycentricity. Spanish and Portuguese have major cultural resources located on both sides of the Atlantic, and there are likewise multiple cultural centers for Arabic. Chinese, Hindi-Urdu, and Malay-Indonesian, widely used in only a small number of nations, are more monocentric than Spanish and Portuguese but benefit from the sheer size

---

23   In that a common written language (with considerable historical continuity) circulates above a continuum of spoken dialects, and that this same language circulates for religious and cultural purposes over a still larger area (from Mauretania to the Moluccas), it is in fact arguable that Arabic remains a cosmopolitan language in a global era.

of their nations and the resultant large number of at least regional cultural centers available, as well as large populations from which cultural elites can be renewed. Russian alone (which is a regional world-language in part for historical reasons) is highly monocentric. Polycentrism has proved especially useful for Spanish, Portuguese, and Arabic, since all or most of the nations using those languages have experienced significant periods of political oppression during the twentieth century. The capacity to move, for example, from Madrid to Mexico City, or from Buenos Aires to Barcelona, has allowed a great many Spanish-language writers of the twentieth century the opportunity to continue to write freely in the face of adverse political conditions at home. Even in periods or contexts of greater freedom, this polycentricity obviously makes it possible for a wider variety of writers to gain at least some level of recognition.

I identify these languages as regional world-languages (with a hyphen between world and languages), because their role is less that of languages *of* the world, in the way that English and French truly cover the planet, than languages *that constitute* worlds.[24] The populations that speak these languages are vast enough, geographically proximate enough, and interconnected enough that the Hispanosphere, Lusosphere, Sinosphere, and so forth function as worlds unto themselves. These languages are also super-regional rather than national. Strictly national languages risk a certain kind of provincialism: heavily concentrated as their literary resources are in a single city (or in a very few cities), dependent on a small number of publishers, of universities, of periodicals publishing literary reviews, they risk the development of a literary and intellectual monoculture, consistently rewarding very similar kinds of work from very similar people, a phenomenon that may draw more innovative talents towards larger languages and markets. The regional world-languages, which either exceed the span of a single nation or belong to vast nations of great internal diversity, are by their nature more polycentric and thus have a greater potential for nurturing vitality within their confines. Spanish (and to a much lesser extent Russian) may participate in the Eurocentric literary ecology of our time, but none of these languages *needs* to; the size of the internal market, together with the diverse range of human experience shared among native speakers, in each case seems more than adequate to guarantee a strong and continuing literary tradition in each case. In some ways, as I suggest, the

---

24   For more on this distinction, see Alexander Beecroft, "World Literature Without a Hyphen: Towards a Typology of Literary Systems," *New Left Review* (54), 2008.

polycentricity of these languages may serve as an advantage when compared to French, more widely spread around the world but with its cultural institutions still more narrowly concentrated in one nation and indeed in one city. Others of my regional world-languages face different challenges: Hindi-Urdu and, to a lesser extent, Malay-Indonesian experience significant competition as central languages from English, while Russian's position as a central language for the former East Bloc may itself cede place to English. The non-European languages generally possess less well-developed cultural infrastructure than would a comparably sized European language, weakening their position in the present, although of course it is possible that this situation might change over time. National barriers are fairly effectively transcended for publishing in Spanish and Portuguese, less so for Arabic. Nonetheless, each of these languages possesses many of the resources needed to thrive as a vital and enduring global literary tradition.

"Major National Languages"

Under this heading, I consider languages that are either the official and national language of medium-sized nation-states or of the sub-national language-based Indian states. These languages do not have the global reach of English and French, nor do they create regional "worlds" in the manner of Spanish or Arabic, but they do possess at the very least significant internal markets for cultural production. Among European languages, German, Italian, Polish, Ukrainian, Romanian, and perhaps Dutch would qualify on the basis of numbers, though of course these languages vary considerably in their range of infrastructural development and of competition with more central languages. Of non-European national languages, obvious candidates here are Japanese, Korean, Vietnamese, Filipino/Tagalog, Burmese, Thai, Turkish, and Persian; the major regional languages of India, such as Bengali, Marathi, Tamil, and Telugu, could also qualify. Swahili, as a widely spoken language with official status in several East African nations (but, as yet, still subordinate to English in all but Tanzania), is another potential candidate, as are a handful of national languages in Africa, like Amharic in Ethiopia or Hausa, Yoruba, and Ibo in Nigeria. Considerable variation exists, of course, among these languages. Some, like Bengali, Japanese, and German, are quite large, have very long and complex literary histories, and thus share properties with the regional world-languages; others are much smaller. Some (German, Italian, Polish, Japanese, Korean) belong to large, stable nation-states with a long history of promoting the national language and with a wide range of cultural institutions. Others, particularly among the national languages of poorer African or Asian nations, lack many of these resources, and the effective reading populations can be smaller than their overall numbers would suggest, due to poverty and lower levels of literacy. Moreover, as we have seen, the European languages, regardless of their size or strength, tend to have greater access to the European-centered literary system of the present.

What unites all of these languages, however, is the presence, at least hypothetically for the future, of a sizeable domestic market. Enough people speak these languages natively, or use them as central languages, that their viability for literary purposes should not come under threat for the foreseeable future. The European languages on the list, along with Japanese, are especially strong in the present, though unlikely to grow much in the future; some of the Asian languages are much weaker in the present but have the potential for considerable future growth. German, Italian, and Japanese are, in particular, virtually the only languages other than English, French, and the regional world-languages to be learned as second languages outside their immediate regions. In each case this probably makes a negligible difference to the size of the reading population in the original, though it may well increase the market for literature in translation

Most, though not all, of these languages are relatively monocentric, and many are additionally comparatively culturally homogeneous, at least in terms of literary culture. This is relative, rather than absolute, homogeneity, of course; many of the non-European national languages circulate above a series of less central regional languages; the vitality of literature in German from recent immigrant communities is well known, and even in Italian there are signs of an emergent immigrant literary tradition.[25] Regional Indian languages circulate across divisions of religion and caste, and among regional dialects and minority language communities. Nonetheless, these national languages face greater challenges on the level of diversity than do English, French, or the world-languages. With literary and cultural resources concentrated in one city, or in a handful of cities, with comparatively homogeneous populations and with little to no use as vehicular languages outside their own nation, they lack many of the inputs that make the languages discussed earlier better able to remain vital and adaptive. The association with a nation-state, of course brings other, compensating

---

25   Vittorio Coletti, *Romanzo mondo. La letteratura nel villaggio globale*, Bologna: Il Mulino, 2011, 95–106.

advantages—the existence or potential for government support for cultural enterprises, the presence of or potential for a national curriculum generating awareness of and pride in the national literary tradition (and of a university system that can place emphasis on that tradition), the strength that private cultural institutions, such as prizes, publishers, and literary reviewers, can draw from alignment with the nation-state. Even more importantly, of course, the sense of identification with the nation-state on the part of readers helps to secure domestic audiences.

All that notwithstanding, all of these literatures depend relatively heavily on access to the world literary ecology, both for markets and for new and diverse inputs. Such access occurs through the media of translation (both as source and as target language), and through second-language learning. As already noted several times, it is here that the European literatures seem to enjoy particular advantages; their work is more likely to be translated into more central languages (opening up wider audiences, albeit with the risks associated with writing for the "world novel" market rather than for local circumstances). They are likely, also, to benefit from a wider range of world literature translated into their own language, providing a wider range of models to engage with. Deprived of access to the system of translation, authors in non-European national languages need to rely more on their own knowledge of English, French, or other world-languages for access to works written in other languages. German, Italian, and Japanese all benefit to some extent from populations of language learners in other developed countries. The varied degrees of access to the world system provide opportunities for some languages and challenges for others, but all of these languages share large domestic audiences, current or potential, making literary success a viable possibility for individual writers and the new or continued viability of the literary language a possibility for the nation.

"Minor National Languages"

The challenges faced by the major national languages I identify above are all the more acute with the minor national languages. There are dozens of languages in this category, ranging from the Scandinavian and smaller Slavic languages and well-established regional languages, such as Catalan in Europe, to the official languages of smaller non-European states, like Mongolian, Cambodian, and the smaller state languages of India, such as Kashmiri or Assamese. I include here also, at least prospectively, the fifty or so vehicular languages of Africa, either widely spoken within one nation or by communities spanning several nations.[26] It is difficult to construct a minimum population required for a literary language to be viable, for all the reasons discussed already. Evidence from Europe shows that a nation as small as, say, Norway, can, under the right circumstances, have a vital and stable literary culture. Norway is, of course, a wealthy, highly literate nation with well-established cultural institutions and a continuous literary tradition (even if there are two written standards for the language and even if Norway's modern political independence dates only to 1905). Issues of poverty and literacy will likely threaten the development of many Asian and African languages in this category for some time, as will the lack of cultural infrastructure to support literature. Further complications arise in some cases: the absence of a literary standard form of the language or of a clear sense of how much of the dialect continuum a written language might cover; competition with more central languages (English and French in much of Africa; Hindi and to some extent English for some of the smaller regional languages of India); with the exception of European languages, the lack of access to the global literary system. The chief advantage that minor national languages have for literary purposes is that they can be ideally adapted to a local environment, telling local stories in a local style in regions beyond the reach of larger languages and literatures; if this adaptation responds to genuinely felt needs, literature in these languages has the capacity to thrive. This advantage carries with it, of course, the parallel dangers of genetic drift and of potentially poor adaptation to change, but the existence of a clear ecological niche speaks to the capacity for these languages to endure and even to thrive, even if for many domains speakers need to turn to more central languages.

Minority Languages

One of the more striking trends of the years since roughly the fall of the Berlin Wall has been the worldwide trend towards greater recognition for minority languages, even as (or perhaps because) those languages are increasingly under threat. The phenomenon is particularly familiar within

---

26 The current policy of the African Union (AU) is to recognize all languages spoken in Africa as official, and to promote the use of all of the languages of European colonization, plus Arabic and Swahili, as working languages. Beyond this, the AU, through the African Academy of Languages, hopes to promote the use of trans-border vehicular languages, many of which are spoken by millions, in a wider range of domains. For more on their work, see acalan.org.

Europe, where the Council of Europe promulgated the European Charter for Regional or Minority Languages in 1993; this charter currently provides some form of recognition for no fewer than 154 linguistic minorities across Europe (counting each language once for each country in which it is recognized and with the caveat that some minority languages recognized, such as German, Italian, and Russian, are highly successful national languages elsewhere in Europe; German, for example, has minority recognition in eight different nations). Even France, whose constitution guarantees the status of French as the official language of the nation and which thus did not ratify the Charter, has, in the constitutional reforms of July 23, 2008, recognized that "Les langues régionales appartiennent au patrimoine de la France" (regional languages belong to the heritage of France), albeit in a manner that confers no special rights or protections on them.

This move towards the recognition of minority languages was not confined to Europe. Across Latin America, several nations have written the recognition of indigenous languages into their constitutions since 1990, granting these languages official status where they predominate in countries such as Colombia (1991), Peru and Chile (1993), Venezuela (1999), Mexico and Guatemala (2003), and Bolivia (2009); the latter nation in fact requires all municipalities and provinces to adopt at least two official languages. In the meantime, Paraguay, which had long recognized Guaraní as a national language, in 1992 made it official and equal in status with Spanish. Brazil and Argentina have not adopted such policies at the national level, but at a more local level, indigenous languages and immigrant languages have been given recognition: In Argentina's Corrientes Province, for example, Guaraní was made an alternative official language in 2005, and in the Brazilian states of Rio Grande do Sul and Espírito Santo, respectively, the immigrant languages of Talian (a Venetian dialect with Portuguese loanwords) and both Pomeranian and Standard German have recently (2007 and 2009) been recognized. Several Brazilian municipalities also now confer official recognition on local indigenous languages.

Across Asia and the Pacific, centripetal pressures to conform to standard national languages mostly continue to outweigh the centrifugal influence of minority or regional languages. There are, however, noteworthy exceptions. The new constitutions of Iraq (2004) and Nepal (2007) were established after radically different transformative events: the former in the aftermath of the United States–led invasion of 2003, the latter as Nepal became a republic in the aftermath of the Maoist uprising of 1996–2006. Both new constitutions, however, add recognitions for minority languages; in Iraq,

Kurdish is now a joint official language with Arabic, while in Nepal, local governments are declared free to employ "the mother language" of the region. Similarly, where earlier constitutions had proclaimed Pilipino (to all intents and purposes, Tagalog, "developed and enriched on the basis of existing Philippine and other languages") to be the official language of the Philippines, the 1987 constitution, implemented after the overthrow of Ferdinand Marcos, adds the proviso that "The regional languages are the auxiliary official languages in the regions and shall serve as auxiliary media of instruction therein (Art. 7)," retaining also earlier provisions governing the roles of English, Spanish, and Arabic. Taiwan, where the once-hegemonic Kuomintang endorses reunion with mainland China, and the opposition instead seeks to establish and consolidate a distinctive Taiwanese identity, introduced in 2001 a curricular requirement that students study a "Taiwanese Native Language" for at least an hour a week; the list of approved languages include Hoklo (otherwise known as Minnan, or the Taiwanese "dialect" of Chinese), Hakka (another Chinese "dialect," spoken widely in the diaspora), or one of the dozen or so languages of the Taiwanese Aboriginal population. The People's Republic of China grants official recognition to a single standardized version of Mandarin Chinese (roughly the same standard as in effect in Taiwan), and legislation in 2001 further enhanced the position of standard Chinese as the official language of the media; nonetheless, television and radio programming in regional "dialects" has continued to flourish.[27] India has long been a multilingual nation, with two official languages (Hindi and English) and numerous other languages given official recognition, many also with their own state governments. If the global axiom is that "a language is a dialect with an army," in India one might well say that "a language is a dialect with a state assembly"; and the number of states has continued to grow, with the addition of the new states of Jharkhand, Uttarakhand, and Chhattisgarh in 2000, and Telangana in 2014 (although not all of these latest states are linguistically based). Meanwhile, the number of scheduled languages has also grown; beginning at fourteen (an already prodigious number), they increased to eighteen by 1992 with the addition of Sindhi, Konkani, Meithei, and Nepali, and to twenty-two in 2002 with the further addition of Bodo, Maithili, Dogri, and Santali (languages spoken at the time by a combined total of about 22 million people, or about 2 percent of the 2001 census population of India).

27　Jin Liu, *Signifying the Local: Media Productions Rendered in Local Languages in Mainland China Since 2000*, Ithaca, NY: Cornell University, 2008.

New Zealand, which has a well-established tradition of recognition of the special rights of the Māori people, has more extended recognition to the Māori language as one of the three official languages of the nation (alongside English and New Zealand Sign Language) with the Māori Language Act of 1987.

The recognition of regional and minority languages has also been a feature of almost every constitutional or structural transition in Africa during this period. I offer here a few representative examples. South Africa's post-Apartheid constitution of 1996 recognizes eleven official languages. The post–civil war constitution of 2005 in the Democratic Republic of the Congo recognizes as "national languages" (below the official language, French) the regional vehicular languages of Kikongo, Lingala, Swahili, and Tshiluba. Eritrea's post-independence constitution of 1997 (never implemented) recognizes the equality of all Eritrean languages. The 1997 Ghanaian constitution makes knowledge of a native language a prerequisite of citizenship. Where as recently as in the Fifth Republic constitution of 1999 Niger had recognized no language other than French, the Seventh Republic constitution of 2010 also recognizes as national languages those spoken by each of the communities making up Niger. Finally, a constitutional amendment promulgated in 2011, in the midst of the Arab Spring, makes the Berber language Tamazight co-official with Arabic in Morocco, and the provisional constitution of Libya, proclaimed on August 13, 2011, declares Arabic official, but all the other languages of Libya national.

This trend towards the official recognition of minority languages, while far from universal, is nonetheless extraordinarily widespread and has taken place at the behest of a wide range of political actors, ranging from regional conservatives to left-wing populists to foreign invasions to domestic *coups d'état*. In many cases, this official recognition may well be little more than token; in some cases, official recognition at this stage may represent more a memorial for a language past than a genuine or viable attempt to revive or strengthen an existing language. In still other cases, this recognition is a kind of pious window-dressing designed to conceal the violent and repressive designs of an authoritarian regime. The promotion of dialects to the status of "regional languages," moreover, may, if successful, bring with it the standardization of written forms and (through the public school system) even spoken forms, obliterating in the process still more local varieties of the language. In any event, few of these languages possess the basic linguistic resources necessary to a viable literary language—an agreed-upon orthography, dictionaries, and an existing canon of written texts from which to draw inspiration (though oral traditions may be quite active and significant). Moreover, cultural institutions—presses, journals, universities—are likely to be almost entirely lacking, making it difficult for these languages to build up critical reserves of cultural capital.

Furthermore, literatures in these minority or regional languages represent an extreme case of the trade-off between adaptation to local environments and susceptibility to genetic drift. Literatures in these languages are likely to interact little with the larger literary system through translation, and few speakers of more central languages will ever read the texts of these literatures in the original language. Mediation between the regional literature and the outside world will be largely, if not exclusively, through bilingual authors and readers for whom the regional language is native, and because bilingualism will always be high among literate populations in such communities, the challenge will be to encourage production and consumption of literature in the regional language when readers have access to larger and more vital traditions. Local cultural institutions will be few in number and highly susceptible to personal influence. At the same time, the capacity to reach a small but clearly focused audience is valuable in its own right, if institutions can be created to foster it. Almost none of these languages possess a viable written literary tradition today; some may in the future, where linguistic resources and cultural institutions can be established and where the language fills a genuine niche, relatively free of direct competition from more central languages. In most cases, however, authors—and readers—are more likely to choose a more central language for literary purposes, as for many other domains.

Endangered Languages

I have already spoken above about the question of endangered languages, and about the fact that size of speaking population is at best a poor indicator of endangerment. The question of which languages are endangered also depends crucially on just what counts as a language; the more languages a dialect continuum is divided up into, the more likely it is that some of those languages will disappear, harmonized into newly standardized forms (though possibly with some local variations preserved in the daily speech of regions where the extinct language was once spoken, just as some expressions from the regional languages of China or of Italy persist in regional dialects of standard Mandarin or standard Italian). As one index of the difficulties involved, noted earlier, Ken Hale estimated in 1992 that some 90 percent of the 6,000 languages then alive might become extinct by 2100.[28] Many languages have become extinct in the intervening twenty years, yet the total number of languages in the world is now estimated at 6,909 by the SIL Ethnologue. Clearly, nine hundred new languages have not emerged in the last twenty years; rather, a few have been discovered and many more have been retrospectively identified as distinct languages, as opposed to dialects.

Preserving these languages, and the cultural richness they embody, is an important priority. That said, doing so is challenging and often imposes particular burdens on groups already highly vulnerable. For a language to survive and thrive, it must be spoken by young people, and ideally in many domains of their lives. Use in primary education is highly useful, yet speakers of endangered languages generally need to learn some more central language(s) as well and probably currently speak such a language at home; to require such populations to learn additional languages beyond those expected of other citizens may enhance regional pride but may also represent one more burden on communities already disadvantaged in other ways. Moreover, adults only continue to speak the language of their childhood if that language is usable in a wide range of domains, notably work and economic life generally. Verbal art, especially if it is compelling, can certainly be one of the vital domains here, as Terry Crowley has observed,[29] though it is unlikely to be enough on its own if work requires the use of another language. In general, language choice is motivated less by sentiment than by necessity; if a community can live a good life in a small local language, it will continue to do so, but if economic survival depends on the use of another language, then that will in time become the spoken language of the community (usually the next most-central language in that region; English is a threat to language survival for the indigenous languages of Australia and North America, but Indonesian and Tok Pisin are the bigger threats in Indonesia and Papua New Guinea). Languages cannot, therefore, be preserved solely by external fiat; they need strong local commitment. Where that commitment exists, external assistance with matters of standardization and transcription, as well as financial support for publishing works beyond the Bible in translation, may be appropriate; where it does not, external support might perhaps be directed at efforts to document the verbal art tradition of the language rather than at extending that tradition.

Each of these categories of language, then, faces its own set of challenges

28   Hale et al., "Endangered Languages," 1992.
29   Crowley, "How Many Languages will Survive in the Pacific?," 1998.

in the (as yet hypothetical) global literary ecology. Small literatures face challenges of survival, of adaptation and of integration into a global system or risk becoming less relevant to the lived experience of their native speakers if they do not handle these challenges well. Larger and more central languages have a more assured position within the system, but those not based in Europe face disproportionate difficulties in gaining access to the system. The most central languages of all—English, French, and the regional world-languages—are mostly already well represented in the emergent system (with the exception of the Asian world-languages) and have large and diverse enough internal audiences to thrive as complex literatures, but they do face competition with each other as well as the challenges and opportunities of thinking themselves beyond national borders.

Toward a Literary Ecology of the Future

The linguistic and literary ecology of the present and foreseeable future, then, presents opportunities and challenges for all languages but particularly severe challenges for those languages spoken or written by few or circulating narrowly. If, in an avowedly speculative vein, we try to imagine the future evolution of this system, what possibilities exist? Many possible futures can, of course, be imagined, but I will cluster my observations under two possible paths: a move towards homogenization of some kind and an alternative (perhaps less likely) path in which greater interconnection is achieved without greater homogeneity. The above discussion of questions of structure and circulation within the literary ecology has already pointed at both of these possibilities—at a world where an increasingly large number of people rely on an increasingly small number of languages for imaginative self-representation, and at another possible future in which the number of viable literary languages remains stable, or even increases. In what follows, I examine both of these paths with respect to questions of literary form.

While an extreme position would argue for the eventual disappearance of all languages (or at least all literary languages) other than English, this seems an implausible outcome for the immediate future. More plausibly, and more intriguingly, Tim Parks has argued in a series of essays that literature written in other (European) languages is increasingly written in a style in which the influence of English is readily detectable. Using the research of his colleagues in Milan, for example, Parks argues that contemporary Italian prose increasingly places adjectives before nouns, uses possessives rather than reflexives to indicate body parts, and expresses subject pronouns, all as a result of contact, through translation, with English.[30] Parks identifies similar phenomena on the level of literary style and plot construction, arguing that many contemporary European authors have abandoned modernist linguistic experimentation, and write in a simplified style devoid of local cultural references, all in the hope of increasing their chances of being translated; Parks contrasts this development with the literary style of an American writer such as Jonathan Franzen, whose exuberant diction and incessant reference to American mass culture is enabled, according to Parks, by the massiveness of the domestic American market, rendering American (and, generally, Anglophone) writers less dependent on translation and the accommodations it demands.[31] If Parks is right (and of course it would be easy enough to identify exceptions to his pattern), it is certainly possible to imagine a future literary ecology in which a relatively large number of literary languages persist but the literature consumed in each of them is extremely similar in terms of diction, style, and theme.

Parks's argument is reminiscent of an argument made a number of years ago by the American Sinologist Stephen Owen with respect to contemporary poetry in Chinese.[32] Writing on a recent translation of the dissident poet Bei Dao, Owen controversially argued that contemporary poets writing in non-European languages such as Chinese not only write in a style influenced by (inadequate translations of) European romantic and modernist poetry but also direct their poetry at Western, especially American, publics through the strategic combination of spare, easily translated diction, universal themes, and a judicious dose of local color; as with Parks, Owen draws an explicit contrast to American poets, who are freer to use contemporary slang, however ephemeral, in their poetry.[33] Owen's argument attracted the ire of many critics, notably Rey Chow, who argued that Owen's critique of contemporary poetry in non-Western languages reflected a sort of Orientalist melancholia, a helpless anger on the part of Western Sinologists and other Orientalists that their disciplinary knowledge no longer gives them a privileged status as mediators between East and West.[34]

---

30   Tim Parks, "Your English Is Showing," *NYRblog*, 2011, at nybooks.com.
31   Tim Parks, "Franzen's Ugly Americans Abroad," *NYRblog*, 2011, at nybooks.com.
32   Stephen Owen, "What is World Poetry?" *The New Republic* 203 (21), 1990: 28. I am grateful to my colleague, Michael Gibbs Hill, for the comparison.
33   Ibid.
34   See especially Rey Chow, *Writing Diaspora: Tactics of Intervention in Contemporary Cultural Studies*, Bloomington: Indiana University Press, 1993, 1–4.

Others have offered nuanced and intermediate positions on the question,[35] and Owen himself has revisited his earlier essay, still stating his position on "World Poetry" in polemical terms (using, for example, the analogy of the food court) but drawing his readers' attention as well to lesser-known circulations of poetry in China, such as popular journals of contemporary classical poetry and the diffusion of all forms of poetry on the internet.[36]

Orientalist melancholia aside, the juxtaposition of Parks and Owen allows us to identify a shared set of anxieties about the adaptation of literature in national languages to a global marketplace. Both scholars suggest that writers working outside the English language are designing their work for ease of translation, excising local content that exceeds the interest level of an audience in translation. Most notably, perhaps, this can include reference to the literary and political environment in which the writer works; audiences in translation being arguably more interested in descriptions of exotic foods and colorful festivals than they are in references to tenth-century poets or contemporary debates on education policy. What emerges, then (and what one can imagine emerging further in the future) is a global literature designed to narrate shared global experiences in a linguistic register freed from slang and ambiguity in order to be translated as seamlessly as possible from one language to another. Only those literatures large enough to generate sufficient economies of scale to generate profits in the original language (and only English, perhaps, can be entirely certain of this status) will be able to maintain literary ecologies that nurture rich, complex works, deeply engaged with local circumstances and/or with local literary pasts, as well as with the contemporary and the universal. Then again, and as I have already suggested, the increasing globalization of English itself (as well, perhaps, as French), may exert increasing pressures in the future even on English-language writers in Karachi or Kansas City to purify their language, washing their sheets (to borrow a phrase from Manzoni) in the transatlantic.

Parks, as much as Owen, approaches the prospect of such a global literature with a kind of melancholy, and there is indeed cause for trepidation. To return to the cybernetic metaphor I have used elsewhere in the book, shifts in literary ecology tend to be the result of a desire for a reduction in

---

35   David Damrosch, *What Is World Literature?*, illustrated edition, Princeton, NJ: Princeton University Press, 2003, 20–3.

36   Stephen Owen, "Stepping Forward and Back: Issues and Possibilities for 'World' Poetry," *Modern Philology* 100 (4), 2003: 532–48.

information. Panchoric and cosmopolitan literatures simplified linguistic standards and literary conventions across larger areas, vernaculars restricted the scope of literary circulation by inventing a newer, less universal literary language, the national literary ecology streamlined vernacular literary history and made it possible, for the first time, to imagine a worldwide literary system, understanding it as the sum of a finite number of national literatures, with only a limited number of pathways of circulation deemed meaningful (periphery to center and those between a handful of literatures at the center). As we move, perhaps, to a new literary ecology, one that encompasses the planet, the kind of global literature envisioned by Parks and Owen would achieve its own reduction in information by drastically narrowing the norms of style and plot and perhaps by gradually excluding from the global canon those texts, older or more recalcitrant, that do not conform to those norms. We would gain a global literature but at the cost, perhaps, of a critical loss of diversity; in ecological terms, such a monocultural dependency on a certain strain of literature could pose genuine dangers for the continued vitality of literature as a medium of creative expression, no matter the massive scale on which such a literature would operate.

Working in a similar vein, Vittorio Coletti argues that the *romanzo mondo* ("world novel") of our time approaches the representation of place very differently from earlier novels, focused on the nation-state. He argues that, while place was generally central to the great novels of the nineteenth and early twentieth centuries (as he argues, to remove Emma Bovary from Normandy and make her a member of the *petit bourgeoisie* of Rome in the nineteenth century would render Flaubert's novel unintelligible), contemporary fiction aimed at a global audience, whether in mass-market genres, such as fantasy or crime fiction, or in literary fiction, uses local color as a purely decorative element, while constructing plots that could readily be transferred anywhere in the world, or at least the developed world.[37] Coletti persuasively argues, for example, that while the contemporary crime novel is a genre that thrives in translation (even into English, as witness the extraordinary success of *The Girl With the Dragon Tattoo*), successful international crime novels use their cities (whether New York or Stockholm), merely as noir-ish backdrops, rarely engaging with their immediate political or cultural contexts in the ways that national-era detective fiction, from Agatha Christie to Georges Simenon to Dashiell Hammet, manage to do.

---

37   Coletti, *Romanzo mondo*, 2011.

The contemporary crime novel (and, Coletti and Parks would argue, even "serious" fiction) is a commodity packaged for export, nearly mass-produced and indistinguishable from its counterparts produced in other nations. It is difficult to feel much excitement for a literary future that develops along these lines.

Building on the insights of Parks and Coletti, I would like to discuss what I see as another formal feature distinctive in contemporary fiction and film, one that I believe offers more hope for a richer literary future, even as it remains fully available to the kind of export-driven literary production both decry. This device I will call the "plot of globalization." Many contemporary works employ the narrative device of *entrelacement*, or multi-strand narration, as a means of narrating the experience of globalization, usually, though not always, with negative consequences for many involved (the double meaning of "plot" being therefore generally activated in these texts). There is of course nothing new about the narrative technique itself; the term entrelacement was in fact first employed almost a century ago in discussion of medieval French romance,[38] and the strategy of moving back and forth between a variety of different narratives, the interconnections between which drive the narrative of the larger work, is one already familiar to readers and film audiences from numerous works.

What is new, I argue, is the use of this device as a way to project onto the level of form the paranoiac interconnectedness of life in a globalized era and the expansion of the scale on which these narratives are interwoven to the level of the planet itself. The form has been quite common in early twenty-first century film and fiction; examples include the films *Traffic*, directed by Steven Soderbergh in 2000 and based on a television series by the British network Channel 4, and *Babel*, directed by Alejandro González Iñárritu in 2006. In fiction, the form is found in novels as diverse as Roberto Bolaño's *2666* (2004) and Amitav Ghosh's *Ibis* trilogy, the first two works of which are *A Sea of Poppies* (2008) and *River of Smoke* (2011). All of these works, in varying ways and for varying purposes, employ entrelacement as a means of representing a contemporary world (in Ghosh's case, a past world, of the 1840s, that bears marked similarities to our own time), in which earlier core-periphery models no longer offer completely satisfying explanations for the economic and political exploitation that nonetheless remains in place. Multi-strand narration allows these works instead to offer

---

38   James Douglas Bruce, *Rezension: Ferdinand Lot: Etude sur le Lancelot en prose*, New York: Columbia University Press, 1919.

a networked model of social and economic interaction, one in which globalization, for good and for ill, is no longer simply equivalent to Americanization (or even Westernization), in which the links between former peripheries are as significant, and potentially as disruptive, as more familiar patterns of North–South relations.

In these two films, these questions of circulation are thought through the prism of the United States–Mexico border; produced with the American market in mind, both condense global networks to that particular border as an index. One of the starkest contrasts in per capita income across a national border, the line between the United States and Mexico is a readily available device for representing global inequalities. These two movies each use that device, however, to represent something more, if in the case of *Traffic* largely through negation of its Channel 4 precursor.

Certainly the Soderbergh version of *Traffic* seems to represent the drug trade (always a highly visible index of the exploitation of the Third World by the First) in highly United States–centric terms. There are three strands to the plot of the Soderbergh *Traffic*: first, a plot in Mexico, where an honest policeman is seconded by his superiors to capture a hit man working for a drug gang, and the superiors, as it happens, are in the pay of a rival gang; second, a plot in which a conservative Ohio judge is appointed as a drug czar (played by Michael Douglas) by the American government, while, unknown to the administration, his daughter is a cocaine addict; third, a plot involving a DEA sting operation (ordered by the Michael Douglas character) in San Diego goes awry, as the wife of the target of the operation tries unsuccessfully to assassinate the key witness. What is absent, of course, in the network of circulation represented here is the actual production of cocaine, in South America, and for that matter anything actually taking place south of the immediate border region. In the Soderbergh *Traffic*, the technique of multi-strand narration is used to reflect on consumers of drugs, on traffickers, and on those who seek to enforce the law but not on the other participants in the process; an omission all the more striking because in the British *Traffik* of 1999, a significant part of the plot involved opium growers in Pakistan. In Soderbergh's version, the complex global networks of the drug trade are suggested but are reduced in narrative terms to the United States–Mexico border, on its own a relatively simplistic device for understanding the systems at work.

Alejandro González Iñárritu's 2006 film *Babel* offers a more complex cinematic version of the plot of globalization, one that makes use of the United States–Mexico border without relying on it to carry the entire weight of North–South relations. Three narrative strands are here interwoven. The first involves two Moroccan boys playing with a gun they've acquired; they accidently shoot an American woman tourist travelling on a bus with her husband. Various difficulties delay the arrival of medical help; in the process, the boys and their father attempt to flee but are cornered by the police, and one of the boys is shot. The second strand is set in California and in Mexico and involves the children and nanny (an undocumented immigrant) of the American couple travelling in Morocco; the nanny wants to return to Mexico for a family wedding, and can neither contact the parents (since the mother is, of course, suffering from the shooting injury she has received) nor arrange alternative care for the children. The nanny takes the American children (illegally) to Mexico; on her return, her drunken cousin attracts the attention of the border authorities, and she and the children flee across the desert. They are eventually rescued, but the nanny is deported. In the third strand of the narrative, a troubled deaf teenaged girl in Japan struggles to cope with her mother's suicide. A policeman arrives at her apartment and, thinking he is there to interrogate her about her mother's death, she flirts with him provocatively. In fact, the policeman has come to inquire about her father's gun, which he had taken with him on a hunting trip to Morocco after his wife's suicide, where he had given it as a present to two young boys who had acted as his guides while there.

The interconnectedness of everyone in today's globalized world is thus made somewhat painfully literal and explicit, where the weapon with which the subaltern Moroccans injure the American woman is itself a product of an unequal exchange between North and South (albeit one for which the North is represented by Japan, not by Europe or the United States). It seems significant here that the weapon is supplied from Japan and that the victims of the "attack" (which is viewed as a potential terrorist incident within the movie) are American, rather than the other way around. A film in which an American-sourced weapon was used by Moroccans to injure a Japanese national would be read as an allegory of American imperialism and as a commentary on domestic debates within the United States about gun control; the (less probable) arrangement of the plot in *Babel* allows the movie instead to act as a commentary on the unintended consequences of highly networked globalization. Rather than simply creating a film about illegal immigration in the United States or about the Global War on Terror of the first decade of the twenty-first century, González Iñárritu's juxtaposition of both themes using my plot of globalization allows him to comment on both phenomena at once and thus implicitly on homologies between the two as structures imposing brutal consequences on the random connections fostered through global contact.

The opening scene of *Babel*, featuring an American couple travelling around Morocco on a local bus, deliberately recalls another film that opens in that same way, Alfred Hitchcock's 1956 remake of his 1934 *The Man Who Knew Too Much*, with Brad Pitt and Cate Blanchett acting in place of Jimmy Stewart and Doris Day. The comparison invited by this citation is illuminating. Very much a product of its time, Hitchcock's film involves a Cold War–era European diplomatic intrigue (culminating in an assassination attempt in the Royal Albert Hall in London); despite being released in the year of Moroccan independence from France (an event ignored by the film), there are few speaking characters who are natively Moroccan, and the espionage plot around which the movie revolves has no implications for Moroccan affairs. Hitchcock thus uses Morocco as an exotic flourish precisely in the way that James Bond films will feature several international settings, only one or two of which are essential to the plot (and, indeed, in precisely the way that Vittorio Coletti criticizes Steig Larsson and his peers for the representation of their own nations). González Iñárritu's film, by contrast, provides its viewers with access to the conversations taking place within the Moroccan family implicated in its narrative (even as it also reprises the "innocents abroad" theme of *The Man Who Knew Too Much*), giving at least limited agency to its Moroccan characters and demonstrating that the film's plot has domestic implications within Morocco as well. Overall, *Babel*'s agenda is ambiguous; the film may be read at least as easily as a cautionary tale against foreign adventurism by Americans as a parable for the unintended and tragic consequences of globalization, but measured against its Hitchcockian intertext we can see that the prominence of the latter theme does at least something to mitigate the former, and the use of my plot of globalization allows for a more nuanced representation of the global dimensions of what remains, in some respects, a narcissistically American story (even if created by a Mexican director).

Recent fiction offers more nuanced versions of the plot of globalization. Both Roberto Bolaño's highly acclaimed (and posthumous) novel *2666* and Amitav Ghosh's *Ibis* trilogy make use of complex forms of multi-strand narration to tell global stories, each with a localized focus but larger implications. As such, I suggest, they offer much more interesting and hopeful possibilities for the "world novel" of the future than those supplied by critics such as Tim Parks and Vittorio Coletti, among others, while each enjoying considerable critical and commercial success. While their stories are global in reach, both Bolaño and Ghosh are also strongly committed to notions of place, and, in their respective works, the (fictional) United States–Mexico border town of Santa Teresa and the opium-producing towns of the lower Ganges, as well as colonial Canton, are central to the stories they tell, not mere ornamental local color. Furthermore, the attention paid by each author to the status of Spanish and English, respectively, as world-languages, rich in regional variation and (especially with Ghosh's English) highly permeable to outside influences, offer writers, at least in major global languages, a third way, besides the linguistic minimalism of English as a lingua franca and Tim Parks's assessment of the diction of contemporary European fiction, on the one hand, and the intensely parochial interests Parks, Engdahl, and others see in contemporary American fiction, on the other.

The use of the technique of entrelacement in these recent works is especially striking when one compares them with their antecedents in popular culture interest, Gabriel García Márquez's *One Hundred Years of Solitude* (1967) and Salman Rushdie's *Midnight's Children* (1981), the respective poster-children for the Latin American "Boom" and for post-colonial fiction in English.[39] These two books do something of the work that Franco Moretti identifies with his theory of the novel, combining local content with the European narrative form to narrate a fiction of the nation-state.[40] Both are also clearly written with at least one eye on the export market and represent attempts not to found a national literature as such (since obviously Colombia and India already had those, if complicatedly in the case of India), but rather to install some version of that national literature within the pantheon of national literatures within the Eurocentric canon, even at the price of becoming what Timothy Brennan has called the "politico-exotic," a commodified "Third World literature" robbed, by its commodification, of the capacity significantly to alter its readers' thinking.[41] Significantly, both

---

39 For evidence of the hegemonic position of Salman Rushdie within the post-colonial canon, at least as measured in entries in the MLA Bibliography, see David Damrosch, "World Literature in a Postcanonical, Hypercanonical Age," in *Comparative Literature in an Age of Globalization*, edited by Haun Saussy, Baltimore: Johns Hopkins University Press, 2006, 49.

40 Franco Moretti, "Conjectures on World Literature," *New Left Review* 1, 2000.

41 Timothy Brennan, *At Home in the World: Cosmopolitanism Now*, Cambridge, MA: Harvard University Press, 1997; Timothy Brennan, "The Cuts of Language: The East/West of North/South," *Public Culture* 13 (1), 2001: 39–64.

Márquez's novel and Rushdie's are strongly oriented towards the conceit that their story is a microcosm of national history; *One Hundred Years of Solitude* recounts the history of Colombia through the history of a family, and *Midnight's Children* takes its title from the group of a thousand and one children born within an hour of midnight, August 15, 1947—the hour of independence for India and Pakistan. Few novels anywhere in the European tradition are as overtly and explicitly (even if, on some level, parodically) narratives of the nation, and yet each is received into that canon in a post-national form; *One Hundred Years of Solitude* as "Latin American Literature,"[42] *Midnight's Children* as "Postcolonial Literature in English."[43]

Strikingly, despite the identification of both *Midnight's Children* and *One Hundred Years of Solitude* as "magic realist" novels, both texts maintain a fairly consistent narrative focus on either a single character (Saleem Sinai) or at least on a family line (the Buendías), and, despite (or because of) episodes of flashback and their occasionally "magical" narrative content, both are also fairly conventional European novels in the grand tradition in terms of narrative form. Both novels are actively engaged with the colonial experience, with struggles for independence and their aftermaths, but in each case the outside world is seen through its impact on the world of the novel. Programmatically, both novels represent a bid for equal status as national literatures, conforming largely to the narrative conventions of the novel and using their magic realist content to differentiate themselves from their Euro-American novel cousins; European form plus local content, as Franco Moretti would say. This is not to claim that the larger oeuvres of Rushdie and García Márquez are lacking formal experimentation, still less that their literatures are; moving through the canon of the Latin American "boom", we need turn no further than Cortázar's *Rayuela* to find as

---

42   The most famous critique of "magic realist" fiction along these lines is that found in Fuguet and Gómez 1996. Alberto Fuguet and Sergio Gómez, "Presentación del país McOndo," In *McOndo*, Barcelona: Grijalbo Mondadori, 1996. For a survey in English of the "McOndo" movement and its critique of what it saw as the export-oriented commodified "Latin American literature" of García Márquez and others, see Emilse Beatriz Hidalgo, "National/transnational negotiations: the renewal of the cultural languages in Latin America and Rodrigo Fresan's "Argentine History, the Speed of Things and Kensington Gardens," *LLJournal* 2 (1), 2007.

43   For discussions of this aspect of the reception of *Midnight's Children*, see G. Huggan, "Consuming India," *Ariel* 29 (1), 1998; N. Kortenaar, "'Midnight's Children' and the Allegory of History," *Ariel* 26 (2), 1995.

fragmentary and experimental a narrative form as one could wish for (since the reader is invited to reread the novel when finished, "hopscotching" through the chapters in a different order). The privileging of works like *One Hundred Years of Solitude* and *Midnight's Children* within the canon of (Third) World Literature may thus represent, as many critics have suggested, the desires of a Euro-American reading public to combine exotic content with conventional form.

Quite different is Roberto Bolaño's five-part novel *2666*, released posthumously to great acclaim in 2004 and first translated into English in 2008. Bolaño's novel is certainly not immune to market forces—as a note in the English translation makes clear, Bolaño had originally intended the five parts of the novel to be published as separate works in the belief that this arrangement would offer his widow and children greater financial security, a decision countermanded by his literary executor and his publisher. Bolaño is also known for having claimed that his move from writing poetry to writing fiction was determined solely by financial motivation. Where *One Hundred Years of Solitude*, as we have seen, explicitly thematizes the nation-state, even as its reception is governed by its Latin American "regional" status, *2666* (like the rest of Bolaño's work) eschews the paradigm of the nation-state altogether to tell a story that cannot be contained within national borders. Bolaño himself lived a transnational existence: born in Chile, he moved to Mexico as a teenager, then returned to Chile briefly, was arrested by the emergent Pinochet regime, and spent much of the remainder of his life in Spain. He never considered himself a part of a Chilean national literature; he was famous in fact for dismissing the eminent Chilean novelist Isabel Allende as "not a novelist (*escritora*), but a scriptwriter (*escribidora*),"[44] and was also known for having claimed (like many authors in exile before him) that his homeland was his language.

The plot of *2666*, broken as it is into five loosely related parts, is similarly rootless, although the United States–Mexico border is crucial to each section; each section furthermore deals with some form of cultural or

---

44 Cited at Patricia Poblete Alday, "El balido de la oveja negra la obra de Roberto Bolaño en el marco de la Nueva Narrativa Chilena," Ph.D. dissertation, Universidad Complutense de Madrid, 2007, 20. Bolaño's pun here seems to derive in part from the title of Mario Vargas Llosa's novel *La Tía Julia y el escribidor*, where in which *escribidor(a)* has connotations of commercially motivated writing for profit, as opposed to literature. I borrow my translation of Bolaño's critique of Allende from the translation of Vargas Llosa's title, and am grateful to Moira Fradinger for a discussion of the implications of the term.

economic circulation. The whole that the five parts constitute is only tenu-ously strung together—minor characters move from one part to another, and all five parts are concerned in some (usually limited) way with a series of murders of young women, mostly in the 1990s, described as having taken place in the (fictional) border town of Santa Teresa, which Bolaño locates between Sonora and Arizona; these murders are based on a real series of unsolved murders that took place over the same time period in the real border town of Ciudad Juárez. The first part "The Part about the Critics," models a European intellectual system, with four scholars from the UK, France, Italy, and Spain who meet at conferences, gossip, and fall in love, all around the study of an obscure and reclusive German novelist, Benno von Archimboldi, whom they pursue to Santa Teresa. The second part, "The Part about Amalfitano," describes the life of a Chilean intellec-tual, Oscar Amalfitano, who lives for a time in Spain, before moving to Santa Teresa to teach at the university there. The third part, "The Part about Fate," concerns Oscar Fate, the pseudonym of a political reporter for a struggling black magazine in the United States, assigned to cover a boxing match in Santa Teresa. Part four, "The Part about the Crimes," is the longest and most challenging section of the novel; it describes dozens of the murders in graphic but deliberately clinical detail, along with the inefficient and venally corrupt process of criminal investigation. The final part, "The Part about Archimboldi," is something of a literary *Bildungsroman* of the German novelist whose presence has haunted the earlier parts of the novel, from his birth in Prussia through his military service in the invasion of the Soviet Union during the Second World War, through his career as a writer and his journey to Santa Teresa in search of his son, who may be a suspect in the murders.

This novel represents a kind of entrelacement on a very large scale: "The Part about the Crimes" alone is almost 300 pages long, and the novel as a whole, over nine hundred. To read this massive and complex novel strictly in terms of its interlacings of these systems of circulation is to do violence, obviously, to the text, but in those terms we see a pretty coherent vision: economics as a sphere of American (and perhaps, more distantly, European—Archimboldi's son runs a camera store in Santa Teresa) exploitation of the periphery; culture as a sphere of still unequal exchange but one for which the United States, far from the center of the flows, is almost completely cut off from them. The European scholars who open the novel visit each other's nations incessantly; when they hear of a large German Studies conference to be held at the University of Minnesota, they are incredulous. Oscar Fate is the sole representative of American culture in the novel and the only context in which we learn of his cultural engagements is when he attends a church service at which a former Black Panther delivers a rambling sermon in which reminiscences and recipes are interspersed. This Eurocentric model of global cultural circulation, which seeks to balance American economic and military hegemony with a more benign European sphere of influence in the cultural and social-policy realms marks a difference between this novel and the films we discussed earlier. As with *Traffic* and *Babel*, the economic inequities of our time are understood metonymically through the image of the United States–Mexico border. Unlike those films, Bolaño's *2666* offers an alternative, and somewhat more benign and egalitarian, vision of global cultural circulation, though it is a vision that constitutively requires the almost complete exclusion of the United States, which may simply replace American cultural hegemony with European cultural hegemony and which in fact has little to say about the world outside of a European-Latin American axis.

If the works I have discussed so far focus on United States–Mexico and European-Latin American relations and circulations as metonyms for broader patterns of economic and cultural circulation and exploitation, Amitav Ghosh's *Sea of Poppies* and *River of Smoke*, the first two books in a projected trilogy, constitute an interesting exception, set respectively and for the most part in Bengal and in Canton in the 1840s. This is a pivotal era in the history of European intervention in Asia, at the cusp of the Opium wars and immediately before the Indian Rebellion of 1857, which will of course have the consequence of placing most of India under British rule; the period in which, in other words, these two great world-regions definitively fall behind Europe in economic and political terms, not to recover until our own time. The period also attracts considerable interest from revisionist economic historians, who have recently argued that traditional Eurocentric narratives representing the West as a hegemonic global region from as early as the sixteenth century need revision in light of new understandings of the economic and institutional strengths of China and India, particularly in the early modern period.[45] According to this recent

---

45   See, e.g., Kenneth Pomeranz, *The Great Divergence: China, Europe, and the Making of the Modern World Economy*, revised, Princeton, NJ: Princeton University Press, 2001; Jean-Laurent Rosenthal and R. Bin Wong, *Before and Beyond Divergence: The Politics of Economic Change in China and Europe*, Cambridge, MA: Harvard University Press, 2011.

scholarship, the years 1750–1840 represent not only a great acceleration in European colonial power in Asia but also, and not coincidentally, the first era in which Europe (or at least its leading northwestern fringe nations, such as Britain, France, and the Netherlands) enjoyed a competitive economic advantage against both India and China. Ghosh's trilogy thus represents something like a narrativized version of this revisionist economic history, sharing with the other works I have discussed an interest in the trade in illicit drugs as a figure for the inherently exploitative nature of the global economic order and for the powerlessness of the nation-state to combat global forces of supply and demand. Ghosh's *Ibis* trilogy shifts the interest to a different time and to a distinctive geographic network, though his novels clearly have implications for an understanding of our own histor-ical moment, particularly as one during which the relative weights of India and China within that global economic order have increased without necessarily reducing the exploitative force of that order. In what follows, I briefly discuss the plot of globalization manifested in *Sea of Poppies*; *River of Smoke* offers a similar structure, but I omit further discussion of it here for reasons of space. The novel consists of four interwoven narratives. The first involves Deeti, a Bhojpuri peasant woman married to a crippled man who works in the opium factory in Ghaziabad; when he dies, she is expected to commit *sati*, but at the last minute escapes with the help of Kalua, the ox man from a neighboring village; they elope and eventually end up on the *Ibis*, a former slave ship from Baltimore. Its second-in-command is Zachary Reid, a mulatto from Baltimore, who rises to this rank after the death of his (white) predecessor, in part because he is able to "pass" as white himself and with the help of the leader of the multiethnic Laskar sailors onboard, Serang Ali. The ship is supposed to be carrying opium to China but instead ends up transporting prisoners to Mauritius. The *Ibis* is in turn owned by British opium magnate Benjamin Burnham, on whose Bengali estate lives his ward, Paulette, daughter of a French botanist. Paulette, leery of Burnham's advances on her and of his marriage plans for her, disguises herself as an Indian woman (she speaks fluent Bengali as a result of being raised by a Bengali foster-mother) and escapes onto the *Ibis* accompanied by her friend and foster-brother, the boatman Jodu. Meanwhile, Rajah Neel Rattan Halder, a Bengali landowner, becomes indebted to Burnham and is thrown in debtor's prison, awaiting transport to Mauritius; there he meets Ah Fatt (half-Cantonese, half-Parsi, and an opium addict), a fellow-prisoner. These four narratives, built around Deeti, Zachary, Paulette, and Neil, evolve separately (though with occasional links) throughout the novel before these characters are brought together aboard the *Ibis* near the end of the novel; their adventures there, and beyond, constitute the climax of *Sea of Poppies* and point towards the future directions the trilogy will take.

Immediately striking, of course, is how complex the identities of each of these four characters is. Several of the characters are multiracial; others inhabit more than one linguistic world, often in unexpected combinations; all inhabit to some extent more than one culture. Each of these characters, in other words, have identities that could be characterized as "hybrid." Arguably, however, the notion of hybridity is itself inadequate for them, assuming as it does the reification of the mutually exclusive ethnic and national or proto-national categories, which makes hybridity the only possible rubric through which such individuals can be understood. As the historian of late imperial China Pamela Crossley has argued, the construction of such ethnic and national identities is in many ways a product of the empires of the early modern era, and we are as yet lacking a conceptual vocabulary to understand the forms of identity operative in prior eras; individuals whose identities seem complex and hybrid to us may therefore have understood themselves as belonging to different, and perhaps simpler, categories than those we tend to construct for them. According to Crossley, prior to the era of the great pre-modern land-based empires, such as the Qing and the Ottomans, "economic livelihoods, religions, languages and in many cases gene pools were distributed according to the common routes of commerce, war and pilgrimage and mixed as the flow of goods and people determined,"[46] creating patterns of circulation and constructions of identity not reducible to proto-national forms. Where *Midnight's Children* narrates a national history through metonymy, even as it (and its author) posits the inadequacy of the national model and propose forms of hybrid identity, *Sea of Poppies*, I would argue, goes one step further and attempts to imagine identities prior to, and other than, the national.

A passage in *River of Smoke* thematizes this issue. Neel Rattan, now a fugitive from the law and living in disguise as the secretary to a Parsi merchant in Canton (Guangzhou), comes to be aware that the fellow residents of his trading-house, or *hong*, are seen by their Chinese interlocutors as belonging to a single community; the *hong* is known as the "Achha Hong," after the Hindustani word meaning "good," or "all right":

---

46   Pamela Kyle Crossley, *A Translucent Mirror: History and Identity in Qing Imperial Ideology*, Berkeley: University of California Press, 2002, 31.

The urchins cared nothing for whether you were a Kachhi Muslim or a Brahmin Catholic or a Parsi from Bombay. Was it possibly a matter of appearance? Or was it your clothes? Or the sound of your languages (but how, when they were all so different)? Or was it perhaps just a smell of spices that clung indifferently to all of you? Whatever it was, after a point you came to accept that there was something that tied you to the other Achhas: it was just a fact, inescapable, and you could not leave it behind any more than you could slough off your own skin and put on another. And strangely, once you had accepted this, it became real, this mysterious commonality that existed only in the eyes of the jinns and jai-boys of the Maidan, and you came to recognize that all of you had a stake in how the others were perceived and treated.[47]

For Neel, then, a sense of "Indian," or "South Asian," identity emerges only in exile, in the context of the global marketplace, where contact with the outside world forces a simplified construction of identity on the complex and intersecting categories of language, religion, and caste through which the residents of "Achha-sthan" understood themselves. Just as the complex internal networks of consumption and trade in a wide variety of goods becomes simplified in a global economy (so that "India" sells opium to China in exchange for silver), so cultural identity becomes simplified and commodified for export purposes. Revealingly, Ghosh anachronistically has Neel's interior monologue here refer to the "Indian subcontinent" as the geographic expression of Achha-sthan, not to indigenous cosmopolitan geographic notions such as *Jambūdvīpa* or *Bhāratavarṣa*;[48] the identity Neel is uncovering for himself here is proto-national, not a nostalgic return to the cosmopolitan order, a by-product of the global economy, not of an ancient imperial or cosmological imaginary. At the same time, the characters of the *Ibis* trilogy, with their multiple origins and their imagined community constructed entirely through the happenstance of their shared experience on board the *Ibis*, not only serve as a figure for the artificial construction of a national identity in the wake of British imperialism but also point towards something else, some kind of non-national or post-national, heterogeneous, contingent imagined community of the willing, one

---

47   Amitav Ghosh, *River of Smoke: A Novel*, New York: Farrar Straus & Giroux, 2011, 181.

48   Sheldon Pollock, *The Language of the Gods in the World of Men: Sanskrit, Culture, and Power in Premodern India*, Berkeley: University of California Press, 2009, 191.

that the early chapters of *River of Smoke*, proleptically set on Mauritius several decades after the rest of the novel, suggest will enjoy a surprising level of permanence. The community formed by the *Ibis*, in other words, serves as a convenient emblem for the more optimistic of the two visions of global literature and culture, where cultural difference is not simply erased in the name of commodification but becomes the premise for broader, more complex, and more flexible, forms of identity, even in the face of ruthless political and economic exploitation.

These concerns are reflected on the level of language as well. As noted, the novel makes extensive and programmatic use of various proto-Global Englishes, of the language used by Lascars, multiethnic sailors of the period, drawing heavily but not exclusively on Hindi, Persian, and Arabic, mixed with Portuguese and English; of the Hindustani- and jargon-peppered English of British colonizers, the Chinese relexicalized with English vocabulary of the *pidgin* of Canton, of Paulette's Francophile malapropisms. *Sea of Poppies* in fact concludes with a *Chrestomathy* of words incorporated into these Englishes, ostensibly compiled by Neel Rattan himself beginning during the action of *River of Smoke*. Offering the modern Anglophone reader a tongue-in-cheek, and sometimes deliberately misleading, guide to the vast vocabulary of non-indigenous English words used in the novel, the *Chrestomathy* is deliberately juxtaposed by Ghosh against the *Oxford English Dictionary*, or "Oracle," consulted by Neel as it emerged and published in 1928, the year when one of Neel's granddaughters is said to have unearthed his lexicographical work. The *Chrestomathy*, then, is also a counter-history of the English language, one that reminds us that English has always been Global English, that the decades of the 1580s and 1590s when modern English literature emerges as a continuous tradition very nearly overlap with the settling of Jamestown and the founding of the British East India Company. Through the *Chrestomathy* and through his diction, Ghosh shows us a future for literature in English, a future grounded in a past we have always known but rarely remembered, and a future strikingly different from that imagined by prophets of English as a lingua franca.

Conclusion

On the levels of linguistic ecology and of literary form, then, it is possible to imagine at least two very different futures. In the first, the growing dominance and centrality of English, combined with the extinction of smaller languages, the leveling of dialect continua, and the inexorable march of global market forces, lead towards a global literary ecology in which fewer and fewer literary languages thrive, and where those that do preside over larger and larger regions of linguistic homogeneity. In formal terms, this future would likely favor the sort of "world novel" sketched out by Coletti and Parks, with simplified diction (English as a lingua franca, or versions of other languages easily translated into it) and telling predictable, market-tested stories easily transplanted from one global city to another to suit the needs of publishing houses chasing after dwindling markets.

The alternative model, one for which evidence can also be found, is one in which the number of literary languages actually increases, thanks to the development of new transnational literary languages in Africa, and to the promotion of regional languages for literary purposes around the world. In this model, existing major literary languages (mostly originating in Europe) are reinforced, while the widely spoken national languages of the non-Eurosphere take their rightful places in the global literary ecology. Translation increases as the number of bilinguals increases and new technologies of distribution make literary production and circulation viable on smaller scales than before. In formal terms, this increasingly open ecology permits a wide range of forms to thrive, and the desire to reach global audiences is satisfied through increasingly rich and complex versions of my "plot of globalization" and related strategies, through texts with a cosmopolitan yet richly detailed sense of place.

It should not be difficult to determine from the above descriptions which of these outcomes I view as more desirable, and more exciting. At the same time, the economic realities pushing towards the former outcome, the homogenized globality, are undeniable. How, then, to work towards the more heterogeneous version of a global literary ecology? I believe there are a number of strategies for doing so, many of which build on the strategies that have built the comparatively integrated European literary ecology of our time and that are documented in Pascale Casanova's *La république mondiale des lettres*. As noted earlier, translation is critical, and the lack of translations out of non-European languages represents the single greatest barrier to the free flow of literature and ideas around the world. The lack of translation, as I have suggested, leads to the inability of writers in non-European languages to win major prizes such as the Nobel, which in turn makes it harder for literatures in those languages to build up the kinds of resources that permit full entry to the global literary ecology. Potential solutions are easy enough to see here, if challenging to implement in practice. The increasing numbers of individuals who are bilingual in European and non-European languages (from North Americans learning Chinese to South Asians fluent in English as well as their native languages) should ensure the greater availability of skilled literary translators in the future; what is needed beyond that are incentives for publishers to support translations from non-European languages. Subsidies might of course help here, but so might a commitment from those of us who teach comparative or world literatures to assign more texts translated from non-European languages in our undergraduate courses, thus enlarging the potential market for such translations.

The failure of the Nobel Prize for literature (at least to date) to adequately reflect the literatures of the whole world is, as Tim Parks has noted, partly a consequence of the lack of available translations.[49] There is, however, nothing wrong per se with the idea that the Nobel exists primarily to recognize literature in European languages (and particularly from the European periphery), so long as we do not continue to make the historic error of making universal whatever happens in European languages. Prizes certainly play a role in structuring global literatures; the Man Booker Prize has been enormously successful, for example, in promoting awareness of literatures in English from outside the United States and United Kingdom, while the recent flurry of winners of major French prizes who are not French by descent, and the comparatively recent establishment of the Cervantes Prize (1976) in Spanish and the Camões Prize (1989) in Portuguese have likewise promoted awareness of those literatures as global in scope. The Nobel, likewise, arguably serves to recognize work in European languages and might function best if it were allowed to perform that role more explicitly. International prizes to recognize literature produced in non-European languages would allow those literatures to accumulate greater cultural capital in the larger world and might facilitate the emergence of a genuinely global literary ecology, in much the way that, through the twentieth century, the Nobel Prize helped confer recognition on writers in the various European languages and thereby helped to create a shared European literary space, to the extent that that exists today. That space is an important element of the overall literary ecology and needs to be protected and promoted, even if we seek to expand the horizons of literature.

Further emphasis on the learning of non-European languages will help. In North America at least, undergraduate enrollments in Chinese and

---

49   Tim Parks, "What's Wrong With the Nobel Prize in Literature," *NYRblog*, 2011, at nybooks.com.

Arabic have grown enormously over the past decade, although Japanese has not enjoyed the same success, and few other non-European languages are taught at all. The increased economic prominence of Asian nations in particular should continue to generate greater interest in languages and cultures outside Europe; again, skillful teaching at the high-school and undergraduate levels can generate lifetime interest, which can generate further demand for literary texts to read. The internet can play a part as well; although literary reputations are still not made through internet publishing, the medium could be used effectively to generate greater interest in and awareness of writers active in other languages.

The internet can be of value as well for a different kind of writer, noted in passing by Stephen Owen,[50] the kind who is not in fact interested in a worldwide audience or recognition in Paris but cares deeply about reaching a more local and rooted audience. For Pascale Casanova, such authors (and such literatures) are inherently conservative, nationalistic, lacking in innovative or creative energies, but as Barry McCrea has observed in the case of Irish and Friulian, modern writers' motivations for choosing minor languages can be much more complex and personal, and such languages can as easily be the site of modernist experimentation as of reactionary provincialism.[51] Further, as we have seen throughout this book, two tendencies coexist in writers, texts, and literatures: the desire to speak as widely as possible, over time and space, and the desire to reach a carefully targeted and constructed audience. Thus, epichoric texts and readings did not disappear with the advent of the panchoric, nor the panchoric with the advent of the cosmopolitan. Authors versed in cosmopolitan literatures have often chosen to found new vernacular literatures, and the movement towards national literatures is as often atomistic as it is syncretic.

Of these various manifestations of the same polarity, the tension between cosmopolitan and vernacular literatures might be the most relevant to our times. Cosmopolitan literatures bear certain obvious similarities to the global literatures of our time in their reach and their ambition to become a universal medium of communication. Certainly, to be an intellectual leader in medieval Europe or pre-modern Japan meant writing well in Latin and classical Chinese, respectively, and literary success that counted for the

---

50   Owen, "Stepping Forward and Back: Issues and Possibilities for 'World' Poetry," 2003.

51   Barry McCrea, *Languages of the Night: In Search of Minor Language Utopia*, 2015.

men or women of those times and places was that in the cosmopolitan literatures. And yet, it is the emergence of the vernacular literatures, whether with Dante or with *The Tale of Genji*, that seem in retrospect the most innovative and significant, indeed the most revolutionary, developments of those eras. Dante may have chosen to speak to a geographically restricted audience by writing in his native Tuscan rather than in Latin (although that audience would clearly have extended beyond Italy), but he was also choosing to speak to a deeper and broader cross-section of his linguistic community than would have been possible in Latin.

The same remains true today, and for the foreseeable future. English as a second language may be sweeping the world, but as the sheer volume of mass-market literature translated out of English every year attests, few of those second-language learners choose to read in English for pleasure. Cosmopolitan literatures throve best in contexts in which they had no vernacular rivals, at least at first, and in which to be literate meant being literate in the cosmopolitan language. Likewise in our times, English (and the other world-languages) have spread through many domains and will spread through more, but literature in world-languages will spread fastest where it has no written rivals—and will likely, as Akkadian, Latin, Sanskrit, and classical Chinese did before it, inspire the emergence of written verbal art in local vernaculars. The world may be shrinking and flattening in many respects, but until we all speak English (or Esperanto), our bedside reading will remain, often, in our own native languages. Will the texts that we read speak to us as citizens of the world or as residents of a specific place? In translation or indigenously in our language? Using the resources of that language richly and inventively or in a manner stripped of particularlity? All these are questions whose answers will be shaped by the choices we make as readers and as writers, teachers, and scholars.

Index